Phenomenology: Dialogues and Bridges

SELECTED STUDIES IN PHENOMENOLOGY
AND EXISTENTIAL PHILOSOPHY

8

GENERAL EDITOR

RICHARD M. ZANER (VANDERBILT UNIVERSITY)

BOARD OF EDITORS:

^{TM}

Phenomenology,
dialogues and bridges

edited by
RONALD BRUZINA
and BRUCE WILSHIRE

State University of New York Press

ALBANY

Published by State University of New York Press, Albany

©1982 State University of New York

Printed in the United States of America

For information, address State University of New York Press, State University Plaza, Albany, N.Y., 12246

Library of Congress Cataloging in Publication Data
Main entry under title:

Phenomenology: dialogues and bridges.

1. Phenomenology — Addresses, essays, lectures. 2. Heidegger, Martin, 1889-1976 — Addresses, essays, lectures. I. Bruzina, Ronald. II. Wilshire, Bruce W.
B829.5.P46 1983   142′.7   82-10593
ISBN 0-87395-690-7
ISBN 0-87395-691-5 (pbk.)

TABLE OF CONTENTS

SECTION I

MARTIN HEIDEGGER: IN MEMORIAM (1889-1976)

SECTION II

PHENOMENOLOGY AND THE THOUGHT OF HEIDEGGER

INTRODUCTION

Since philosophers are concerned with the broadest questions and with the most inclusive views, and since they deal with notoriously difficult problems, it is reasonable to expect that they will communicate broadly with other philosophers. This expectation is strengthened when we consider that we exist today in a 'global village,' the beneficiaries of a remarkable communications technology.

The expectation is regularly disappointed. Students of philosophy in England and America who receive PhD degrees often know little or nothing of the metaphysical and phenomenological thought which has appeared on the Continent in the nineteenth and twentieth centuries. Martin Heidegger's epochal *Being and Time* remained untranslated into English for thirty six years. Karl Jaspers' *Von der Wahrheit* remains untranslated. Less and less is mastery of foreign languages expected of graduate students in philosophy. We could go on with examples.

Ironically, it is as if the technological gains in communications capabilities had so flooded us with possibilities of exchange, that philosophers had been overwhelmed, and had retired into domains which are narrow but manageable. These domains tend to become ever narrower, for as learned communications increase in one's philosophical specialty, one must narrow what can count as an acceptable problem or topic if one is to keep up with what is written or spoken about it. Instead of expanding the horizons of our concerns, our communications technology has typically tended to constrict them. This fact is evidence for Heidegger's contention that Being reveals itself predominantly to our age through technology, but since we exist in forgetfulness of Being, we must exist in forgetfulness of the limitations and paradoxes of technology.

It was with the purpose of countering the parochialness of recent American philosophy that the Society for Phenomenology and Existential Philosophy was founded in 1961; the proceedings of its meetings are published in this series. While there is some evidence of success, progress is slow. The obstacles are cultural 'forms of life' so engulfing of us that we are typically unaware of them. For example, though it is now widely known that William James' thought emerged from a New York and trans-atlantic background which featured Continental thinking and training prominantly, and though it has been shown that James' insights feed the phenomenological movement directly, many writers in America persist in dividing our James scholars into 'nativists' and 'foreigners,' i.e., those who discuss James within an exclusively American context, and those who make reference to Continental thought.

As another example, notice the work of noted American 'analytical' thinkers such as Max Black and Nelson Goodman, which now verges at certain points on Continental concerns. But one looks in vain in their work for any body of references to phenomenological thinkers, or for any body of students generated by these philosophers who are similarly catholic in their approach. We see here the initiative, creativity and vision of individuals, but they appear neither willing nor able to draw the rest of the scholarly culture along with them. Again, we encounter the obduracy and opacity of social movements, of social and economic classes now outfitted technologically, 'forms of life,' which should be subjected to the phenomenological analysis of the *Lebenswelt*.

We begin our volume with presentations given in commemoration of the death of Martin Heidegger by two philosophers who have done much to transmit his thought to the English speaking world, Joan Stambaugh and William Barrett. In these short pieces they supply bridges of a very special sort.

The remainder of the articles on Heidegger initiate dialogues of a more typical scholarly character, many of which, nevertheless, are novel and provocative. Reiner Schürmann, Charles Sherover and William Barrett all agree that ethics has a problematical status in Heidegger's thought. After this initial agreement they diverge radically. Schürmann argues that once we are aware of the implications of Heidegger's destruction of metaphysics we will see that ethics is deprived of its legitimating ground. Sherover argues, on the contrary, that Heidegger's notions of authentic solicitude, resoluteness and capacity for conscience contain the half-hidden seeds of an existential ethic which Heidegger himself never developed. Barrett argues that we must achieve an ethics, and that to do so we must incorporate elements foreign to Heidegger's thought.

Similarly, diverse notes are struck from Heidegger by Marjorie Grene and David Levin on the subject of the body. Grene focusses on the early Heidegger and the paucity of treatment of human bodily being and of the surrounding landscape. Levin focusses on the later Heidegger and develops what he takes to be the crucial significance of Heidegger's notion of the body for the philosopher's companion notion of a thinking that does not merely calculate and entertain propositions, but which stands open to the intelligibility of the sensuous.

In a far-reaching paper, Otto Pöggeler contends that Heidegger's attempt in *Being and Time* to found a new ontology, with the distinctive reality of human existence as primordial, is still attached to Aristotle's concept of the analogy of Being: The notion of a basic sense of Being is retained; it is merely a new occupant that is inserted in the old slot. Pöggeler then documents the difficulties Heidegger experienced in thinking ontologically about time as humans live it, and examines his treatment of Being as an 'abyss,' a 'groundless ground,' in his later work.

Karl-Otto Apel argues in his response that while Pöggeler asserts that Heidegger's work is epoch making, he gives us an incomplete idea of why this is so. After freeing the term 'transcendental' from many distracting associations, Apel argues, in effect, that Heidegger's thought is epoch-making because it radicalizes the transcendental investigation (initiated by Kant) of the conditions of the experienceability of the world. So deep does it go that the notion of the 'abyss' — far from being a dead-end — allows us to understand how phenomenology and pragmatism arose at about the same time in the western world, and how they point to a new horizon of development.

With this the Continental thinker Apel joins hands with American thinkers who have been endeavoring to interrelate phenomenology and pragmatism, and to heal the artificially induced rift between American and Continental thought. Richard Cobb-Stevens contributes a highly creative interpretation of William James' idea of 'pure experience' as a 'transcendental zone of absolute givenness.' Sandra Rosenthal, on the other hand, retrieves C.I. Lewis from the custodianship of 'analytical' thinkers. She argues that his functionalist account of meaning is more phenomenological than phenomenolist, and that his pragmatic *apriori* must be re-studied. Indeed, it seems to us that there is a connection to be worked out between it and the 'abyss' in Heidegger's thought: Though the conceptual network of a given epoch may dictate that particular beliefs are necessary truths, and may require that we expect them ever to obtain, nevertheless with the passing of time and the modification of conceptual connections, they may be found at some time in future not to obtain, or to obtain to only a restricted realm. In addition, Victor Kestenbaum deals with the thought of Dewey as an attempt to elucidate the pre-theoretical context of all theory — 'the beginning which is embodied in implicit habit is not a first thought which can be undone and then reconstituted as an explicit origen.' This resonates deeply with Heidegger's notion of the abyss as the incalculable source of all calculation and thematization.

Kestenbaum's overt comparisons link Dewey and Merleau-Ponty. The latter's views on the implicit, pre-theoretical background of all theory are importantly similar to Heidegger's, and yet they exhibit differences, both stylistic and substantive, which exert different attractions on commentators. Thus Robert Romanyshyn, whose interest in his article centers around psychoanalysis and the unconscious, fixes his attention on Merleau-Ponty's explicit psychological theories and his references to the work of psychologists such as Freud — neither of which sorts of purchase are often obtainable in the work of Heidegger. Romanyshyn uses Merleau-Ponty to criticise and refine the idea of the unconscious mind. (Note also the possible connection between Merleau-Ponty's discussion of the mirroring of things in each other, as this is grasped by artists, and Richard Cobb-Stevens' view of such a relationship between pure experiences, as understood by James.) Miguel Iturrate's response to Romanyshyn expands on Merleau-Ponty's intriguing statement that phenomenology and psychoanalysis are 'both aiming at the same latency.'

Wesley Morriston offers a paper in which he argues closely that Merleau-Ponty's theory of experience cannot properly accomodate the idea of causation. John Flynn assembles a counter argument, and maintains that Morriston has projected into Merleau-Ponty's thought a notion of the self's being over against the world — and a companion idea of causation — which is foreign to that thought. Finally, Clyde Pax contributes analysis of Merleau-Ponty's cryptic observation that the nearest approximation we have to the understanding of death lies in our meeting with another person.

The next three papers concern the work of Alexius Meinong, and raise again the question of just how it pertains to phenomenology. Janet Farrell Smith suggests that Meinong's idea of the connection between objects and assumptions (and objects and psychical contents) can illuminate the connection between intentional objects and intentional acts. She suggests further that the complex assumptions we make when witnessing a drama in the theatre may throw light on the complex assumptions we make in everyday life. Marie-Luise Schubert-Kalsi presents a translation of Meinong's hitherto unpublished remarks on Husserl's *Idea-I*: Meinong objects that Husserl is too concerned to constitute reality with his 'idealism,' and that he is not sufficiently 'empirical,' not sufficiently observant of what actually goes on in consciousness. To be properly observant, it is suggested, we must first take a 'let be' attitude toward the many sorts of objects, actual, possible, and impossible. In the highly original paper which concludes this section, Richard Dyche maintains that if we take a 'let be' attitude toward Meinong's texts, let them speak for themselves, we will see that the entrenched interpretation of Meinong's 'possible and impossible objects' as individuals — although strange ones — is mistaken.

The techniques of phenomenology give us fresh access to our experience. This occurs in a post-Kantian framework. That is, insights concerning the structure of experiencing must generate insights concerning the structure of what is experienced. These insights cut across scientific and academic disciplines. Don Ihde, in his 'On Hearing Shapes, Surfaces and Interiors,' discloses that spatial features of the world — not just temporal ones — can be heard. This is revealed when we are restored to hearing itself; when we cease to pre-judge hearing on the model of the auditory organs of the objectified body; when, that is, we cease to assume a disembodied point of view on the body itself. In his 'Distortion in Human Embodiment: A Study of Surgically Treated Obesity,' Donald McKenna Moss employs phenomenology to cut beneath the artificial boundaries that divide psychology from physiology. He discloses how our owning — and attempted disowning of the body — is fundamental to who we are as selves. He regards cases of surgically treated obesity as variations on normality which reveal its taken for granted 'shape.' Finally, Francis Zucker applies phenomenological techniques to concepts of physics which have usually been considered too technical to profit from the application. In being restored to our experiencing, we re-cast what can count as evidence, so ultimately re-cast our concepts of objective reality itself. Specifically, Zucker employs the experiencing/experienced correlation in the form of the measuring/individuating correlation and maintains that phenomenology can sometimes generate stricter criteria of evidence than can traditional, analytical philosophy of science with its conventionalist orientation. We also include David Hemmendinger's commentary on Zucker's paper.

The penultimate section of this book is constituted in large part by a discussion between Paul Ricoeur and Hans Georg Gadamer on the conflict of interpretations. It is difficult to imagine a dialogue on hermeneutics which ranges further afield. The historical roots of theory of interpretation are connected conceptually with contemporary problems of interpretation in action theory, history, structuralism, and psychoanalysis. These problems are seen to spring from current versions of the comprehension-explanation controversy first outlined by Dilthey. Ricoeur and Gadamer attempt to turn unmediated conflicts into mediated ones, and they reinterpret textual interpretation so that moments both of comprehension and explanation can take place. Contemporary disciplines are regarded as interpretations of quasi-texts by an historical community of interpreters. We conclude this section with a paper formulated independently by Eugene Gendlin, 'Two Phenomenologists Do Not Disagree.' It explores in inventive ways the manners in which conflicts can be mediated.

The final section of the book concerns hermeneutical considerations with respect to theatre. In a comprehensive paper James Edie applies the categories both of hermeneutical philosophy and classical phenomenology to the complex human activity we call theatre. What is the role of text in theatre? What is the relation between the act of imagination onstage and off? How can theatre – an idealization – be true of actuality? In the final paper, Bruce Wilshire treats theatre as a *de facto* phenomenology: Incarnated fictive variations on human imitative involvements – a detachment from them – which reveals their meaning. A number of examples are employed.

Ronald Bruzina
Bruce Wilshire

SECTION I

MARTIN HEIDEGGER

IN MEMORIAM (1889-1976)

HEIDEGGER: ANDENKEN

WILLIAM BARRETT

Martin Heidegger died in May 1976. It is fitting that this society should take notice, and that we now hold part of these meetings in commemoration. No one interested in phenomenology, or in the phenomenological way of thinking, can remain altogether untouched by Heidegger's achievement. Even those who wish to continue in a line different from his, or on subjects which he has not touched, can hardly fail to be aware of the powerful impulse he gave to this mode of thought.

It will take time before the body of his work and its full meaning are assimilated. And that, of course, will be a kind of commemoration more important than the ritual of any meeting. Time too will be required to set in perspective that part of his life which made him a controversial figure. It is with his thought, however, that this society has principally to do, and particularly with that part of it that is likely to prove enduring.

What Heidegger's ultimate stature will be, is also a matter that must be left to time to determine. But I do not think it is rushing to judgment to say now that he is one of the few really significant thinkers of the century. And that in itself should be sufficient to have earned him this commemorative meeting.

There is, nevertheless, a special contingency that confronts us in the question of Heidegger's enduring reputation, as he himself must have been thoroughly aware. It is the question whether this culture, in the direction it is now going, may eventually become blind to the themes that engaged him — that it may become incapable, may make itself incapable, of his kind of thinking. A considerable part of the philosophical Establishment in this country seems presently engaged in the project of making itself unable even to entertain the thought of Being. Most ordinary people do have from time to time, however fitfully, the experience of Being, of its overwhelming mystery, though the experience is usually left unpondered. They could once leave it to philosophers to do that pondering for them. But nowadays philosophers seem intent on training themselves never even to have the experience. And in this, of course, they are no more than the compliant victims of a technical culture.

All of which may mean that phenomenologists may have to take upon themselves the deliberate role of a *Resistance* in order to keep certain *themes* alive. The emphasis here is upon themes, however desirable in itself or incidentally helpful a close attention to Heidegger's text may be. In short, while calling for a certain sense of dedication on your part, I am also warning against succumbing to the spirit of a coterie — that petrefaction of the mind to which philosophers seem especially prey.

One of Heidegger's great gifts is that he subordinates himself to his themes — to the matter (*Sache*) that has to be thought. If we speak of them as *his* themes, it is equally true to say that he is *theirs* — they claim and possess him; he belongs to them as much, nay more, as they to him. To remember his thought properly is to try to carry it forward in that spirit.

He also said that the great thinkers had only one thought to communicate, which nevertheless remains unsaid through all that they have written. Unsaid — because the saying of it can never reach the fullness of what is to be said. Of no other subject for thinking is this more true than of Being. In giving ourselves to it, I should expect that somewhere along the line we should be led to quarrel with Heidegger himself. But that could be a commemoration of him more essential and honoring than a certain over-pious scholasticism, which I seem to discern arising in some quarters.

In a late poem, Robert Frost looking back over his life says of himself that he 'carried on a lover's quarrel with the world'. The poet means this to be an affirmation; and it is; indeed I can scarcely think of any tribute to life and the world at once so wry, homsely, and yet exalted. For myself — to speak personally for a moment — it will serve for the present occasion: I expect my commemoration of Heidegger will be a life-long lover's quarrel with his text.

Since I've introduced one personal note, let me conclude these remarks with another. I've been jotting these notes under a severe distraction of the spirit — the enchantment of a perfect Indian summers day out of doors that will not let me stay at my desk. Outside the window, the maple tree in the yard is aflame with autumn. Through its almost translucent leaves the sunlight kindles rubies against the dark background of the pine beyond. The radiance of Being! It is out there, under this cloudless October sky, that I can more properly carry out these thoughts in remembrance. Autumn is the season of harvest and thanksgiving, and treading the furrows of drifted leaves, I become more mindful of the pilosopher who patiently traced some furrows of his thought for us in language. To think in this open air, in the clear light, outside the Cartesian mind and within Being — my heart stirs in gratitude for the gift of his thought this thinker brought us. To think, thank, remember (*andenken*), he reminded us, were cognate words. And he was right to perceive that the three come together in the one act of hommage that really matters.

HEIDEGGER

JOAN STAMBAUGH

I speak of Heidegger as a person whom I knew and had the privilege of working with for a period of 10 years. Perhaps some of his method of working or at least of his way of living will creep through these remarks.

During the 9 years I lived in Freiburg, I was introduced to Heidegger once on the street by my Doktorvater. But there was such an enormous cult of piously admiring students (mostly *Ausländer*, foreigners) around him making constant reverential pilgrimages with ontologically folded hands to his house that I had no desire to be part of that cult. So I *read* him, but I did not go to see him.

After I had returned to this country, one summer I suddenly thought: Why not? Why not go see the thinker whom I had been studying all these years? And so I wrote him a note asking for permission to visit him. I already knew that you could not just 'drop by'. There was a sign on his door which read: 'Please do not ring bell before 5 o'clock', and his wife functioned admirably as his Cerberus, keeping the many unwanted visitors at bay who often came by just to have a look at the famed philosopher much the same way that one goes to gape at some exotic animal in the zoo.

Heidegger answered promptly and gave me a date at 5 o'clock on what turned out to be a hot day in August, 1966. Anyone who has ever visited Heidegger will recall that the first visit can be a bit awesome. I showed up at 5 o'clock on the nose, and rang the bell. He himself opened the door — said nothing — and stared with a somewhat astonished expression on his countenance. I might note here that he was not at all an 'homme du monde', temperamentwise he remained a *Bauer*, a peasant, quite shy and in unaccustomed social situations rather awkward, even mistrustful. So you can imagine what he was thinking when he saw a completely strange American girl standing at his door without saying a word. But the American girl got a hold of herself and started to chatter voluminously in German about the weather and other harmless trivialities in order to reassure him that she at least could speak a little of his language. Then he finally asked me to come in. We then went to his study, where I spent 2 highly interesting hours talking with him. As I left, he lent me an autobiographical sketch of the young Nietzsche with which I was unfamiliar.

About two weeks later I sent back the sketch together with a short essay of mine on Nietzsche. The next day — after *weeks* of constant downpour — the way it can rain perhaps only in Freiburg — came an absolutely perfect, *strahlen-*

der Sonnenschein. I happen to like being outdoors, and had really had enough of stomping around in pouring rain under an umbrella with wet feet. So I took the cable car to the *Schauinsland* (mountain), returning home only towards evening. As I came into the house where I was staying with two friends, one of them said: There is mail for you upstairs. I said I didn't want to see any mail, mostly it was bills or else bad news or at any rate something unpleasant, and I was far too happy with this beautiful day to take on anything like that. But my friend insisted and so I hesitantly went upstairs. There, like a hallowed shrine, was a vase with a rose on the table, a glowing candle and a letter from Heidegger. He wrote that he had read my essay with great interest, my essay which I had sent him just the day before. Your essay takes up an important question, he wrote, I should like to ask for your address in the States.

That was the beginning of a ten year relationship which led to Heidegger's asking me a year later to become a translator. From then on I went over to see him every summer, often staying for supper, and gradually got to know him well. During these visits which usually lasted about two hours, I would ask him questions about translation problems, not, of course, about the actual English words – although after some years he was beginning to read some English – but about the *meaning*. The answers which he gave were astonishing. He would look out the window – first of his study in the house, later, after he moved, of his apartment study – and after a short pause slowly answer with an unparalleled concentration. Often he said things which to my knowledge he had never written or thought of before. I put some of those questions in my introduction to *The End of Philosophy*, questions concerning Temporality, Ontological Difference and Being. He must have been an admirable teacher, and he remained so to the end of his life.

I recall one question about the German word '*Mystik.*' Heidegger had written: '*Mystik – blosses Gegenbild der Metaphysik.*' Knowing his appreciation of Meister Eckhart I asked him if he really meant that statement. He answered: 'put *Mystik* in quotation marks', to show that he meant a sort of pseudomysticism. His attitude toward mysticism in general was rather ambivalent; he was drawn to it, but would not relinquish the *Logos*.

I apologize for the sketchy and cryptic nature of these notes. They are from a journal I kept in German, and when I start translating myself into English things are beginning to border on the ridiculous. When Sartre visited Heidegger, he said he was no longer interested in philosophy. Heidegger said that Sartre had barred the way to understanding with his concept of existence. Hence he, Heidegger, no longer used the word '*Dasein*' which was, after all, close to him. I said that the encounter of Japan and Germany could really be fruitful, whereas that of India and England was not so fruitful. Yes, he said, absolutely right, the latter is terrible with all its empiricism. He brought out nearly 50 books to show me.

Lichtung – not really brightness, but lightening (as in lightening the load of a boat). It gets lightened. In this context he mentioned freedom. *Lichtung* is the presupposition for brightness *and* darkness. A *Lichtung* (clearing) in the forest could also be quite 'dark'. It gets clear. That is between, between *Lichtung* and brightness, French *claireissement.*

Überkommnis, Ereignis, Lichtung.

I said: 'different aspects, no causal or foundational connection.' He said: '*Lichtung* is the presupposition for unconcealing and concealing.'

Überkommnis, surprise (the sudden). Grounding seeks the ground of Being as Being. Grounding concerns Being, the ontological; accounting for concerns beings, the ontic. I said: You *made* a distinction there. Yes, he admitted, it is very sparsely developed.

Wesen, Never 'nature', if nature means the universal, the *koinon.*

Ereignis, Not Being — *Er-eignen, Er-augnen (Augen-blick).*

Austrag, Stand-in for nothingness. To endure, but without exertion, under-going — A never letting up. (The *temporal* element in perdurance, the *un-ablässige*, unceasing).

In Master Eckhart there is no separation between essence (*Wesen*) and existence (*Dasein*). Essence is how whatness is as such.

Essence — whatness, inner possibility, ground of possibility.

Ereignis — to bring something to itself as itself. To catch sight of something as itself, to see it (*erblicken*). Lightning makes things visible. The epochal element. Any movement (events in the usual sense) must be defined in terms of the *Ereignis*.

Gestell — Metaphysics cannot think the *Gestell* as *Gestell*. Manipulation-*physis* and *poesis* disappear.

1971   — He said he had never read Sartre's *Being and Nothingness.*

In 1932 he wrote a self-criticism of *Being and Time*, but right then did not know where it was in the study.

He showed me the manuscript of his Schelling book, to come out in a few months. I said that Schelling was the first to say that one could not explain everything with reason, that he was thus at the borderline of German Idealism. He agreed. This book (*Of Human Freedom*) is Schelling's answer (i.e. refutation) to Hegel's *Phenomenology*, especially the introduction.

After Heidegger's stroke, I was requested to send my questions in writing in advance to give him more time. One time he answered them in writing and gave them to Hannah Arendt who then gave them to me over coffee in a Freiburg café. To the last set of questions I brought him, the ones in *The End of Philosophy*, he simply said: 'You have answered your own questions.' In other words I had gotten to the point where no further substantive questions were answerable. He remarked that few people understood that there was a point where one could no longer ask questions.

To conclude these remarks, what can I say about Heidegger's manner of working? To begin with, he was an incredibly organized and disciplined man.

In addition to the sign on his door, one could telephone him only either at noon or at 5 o'clock, and his wife always answered the phone as she usually did the door. She protected him.

As far as I know, he always worked at his desk, mornings and afternoons. At 5 o'clock he received visitors, usually over a glass of incomparably fine Badish wine. He reread and studied his own books, making notes in the margin. During our conversations he loved to bring out books to discuss, and he knew exactly where everything was.

Finally, I should like to relate something which points up his sense of humor, conspicuously lacking in his writings. In his later years Heidegger had a calling card printed up to send to new people who wanted to come and see him which read: *In Anbetracht meines hohen Alters bitte ich von Besuchen abzusehen.* He showed it to me with a mischievous grin, his eyes twinkling. He really thought it was very funny.

SECTION II

PHENOMENOLOGY AND THE THOUGHT OF HEIDEGGER

QUESTIONING THE FOUNDATION OF PRACTICAL PHILOSOPHY

REINER SCHÜRMANN

Ever since Socrates, reflections on human action have occupied a central place in philosophy. In what follows, I should like to point to some consequences of Heidegger's destruction of metaphysics for practical philosophy. These consequences affect the domains of *poiesis* and *praxis* alike inasmuch as — I shall claim — Heidegger deprives both 'making' and 'doing' of their legitimating ground. Overcoming metaphysics thus is not an innocent undertaking. However, the extent to which it is perilous becomes patent only in the domain of politics.

PRACTICAL PHILOSOPHY AND FIRST PHILOSOPHY

Traditional philosophies of action have consistently been supported by some philosophy of Being. It is this support that Heidegger questions. I see a direct, purposeful, coherent attempt, in him, from the first to the latest writings, to show that ontology, in the widest sense, does not found human conduct — 'found' in the sense of a *fundamentum* 'on which everything rests.'[1] This elimination of a grounding ground is expressed in many ways in Heidegger. In the vocabulary of *The Principle of Ground*, for instance, his project is to think, not a ground, *Grund*, but an abyss, *Abgrund*; not to *begründen*, found, but to *ergründen*, to fathom. There are many more phrases in his texts that point to the destruction of a legitimating ground. And since we are told that 'thinking changes the world,' it should be clear also that Heidegger's destruction of the legitimating ground affects what used to be called 'theory' and 'practice' alike. The sustained offensive aimed at foundational thinking cannot be larger in scale.

1. The most appropriate way of characterizing this attempt at a non-foundational thinking — which is also an attempt on, or against, foundational thinking — is to start with a brief reminder of the understanding of the ontological difference that is operative in an ontology that aims at legitimizing human practice, and in an ontology that pulls the rug, so to speak, from underneath practical philosophy.

See notes at the end of this chapter.

An ontology that aims at securing a ground for theory as well as practice will articulate one figure of the ontological difference; an ontology that aims at deconstructing such ground, will articulate another such figure. The first notion of the ontological difference can be called metaphysical, the second phenomenological. The metaphysical difference, whether purposefully or as a matter of consequence, anchors phenomena on a grounding ground, on some indubitable First in relation to which science obtains, be this First called *ousia, ipsum esse, noumenon,* or whatever. The phenomenological difference, on the other hand, uproots such grounding. To inquire into it is not to raise the question of some ultimate reality, the inquiry is not a first philosophy.

Let me jump to what I consider the key text on this double notion of the ontological difference, although this text is difficult. It distinguishes between that which is present, *das Anwesende,* its presence, *das Anwesen,* and *Anwesen lassen,* letting presence. Of the first difference, between what is present and its presence, Heidegger says: 'Here we have to do with an interpretation of being in the way metaphysics gives it.'[2] Of the second difference, between presence and 'letting presence,' Heidegger says that it 'enjoins the ontological difference on thought'[3] — that is, the ontological difference properly speaking or phenomenologically speaking, since the first difference is assuredly ontological, too, but precisely in the sense of the difference between *to on* and *ousia,* between *ens* and *entitas,* or between *das Seiende* and *die Seiendheit.* It is clear that the step from the metaphysical difference to the phenomenological difference, the step in which the Difference (capitalized) consists, is heterogeneous — somehow analogous to the opposition that Kant would call not contradictory but disparate. It should also be clear that this step does not imply 'a gradation in the sense of an ever greater originality within the concepts named there.'[4] The text is difficult because the verbal understanding of Being is introduced here in the way Heidegger characterizes the metaphysical difference (with the verb '*Anwesen*', used as a noun), whereas the distinction between verbal and nominal understanding is introduced frequently as another way of distinguishing between the metaphysical and the phenomenological differences.

Nevertheless, the following starting point is taken from the very core of Heidegger's program of destruction: the metaphysical difference, described as that between what is present and its presence, is such that it allows the securing of foundations for beings, reasons for propositions, a 'why' for action. The phenomenological difference, on the other hand, described as that between 'presence' and 'letting-presence,' is one that founds nothing; instead of a ground it leads to an abyss, instead of pointing to the 'why' (*warum*) of phenomena, it points to their 'since' (*weil*) ('since' and *weil* are originally temporal adverbs and only derivatively causal conjunctions). 'Because' there are things, they can be explained by means of the metaphysical difference; 'since' there are things, they can be understood or thought through the phenomenological difference. The step from the metaphysical difference to the phenomenological difference is that from 'explaining' to 'thinking'; it is the step into 'the other thinking.'

It can be easily shown now that by its very nature this other thinking is unable to trace phenomena, whether theoretical or practical, to their explanatory or legitimizing ground — that the phenomenological destruction, in other words, is one of 'Being as the grounding ground.'[5] This deliberate and enduring project of destroying the representation of a grounding ground has consequences, among other things, for practical philosophy. Once these consequences are seen more clearly we shall be entitled to some doubts about statements such as the following from Heidegger: 'For me the decisive question today is how a political system, and of what kind, can at all be coordinated with the technological age. I do not know any answer to this question.'[6] It is not established that we should believe him on this point.

2. Within the problematic of founding practical philosophy, the 'other thinking' consists in showing that such grounding is always located epochally; that an ultimate foundation has its age, during which its function of grounding goes unquestioned, but that with the epochal reversals in history what is held to be ultimate in a first philosophy appears to be so only for a while. The destruction traces the successive fields, opened for thinking and living, throughout Western history. It can claim to be phenomenological insofar as these fields are the 'matter itself' that this thinking brings before our gaze. The destruction shows how, at each epoch, that which is present enters a constellation of showing and hiding. 'Whence and how is it determined what must be experienced as 'the things themselves' in accordance with the principle of phenomenology? Is it consciousness and its objectivity or is it the Being of beings in its unconcealedness and concealment?'[7] The 'thing itself' of the phenomenological destruction is the epochal unconcealedness as it arises, ever new, out of concealment.

What is permanent, what belongs to all epochs, is this interplay of *phuein*, showing forth, and *kryptein*, hiding, — hardly a ground to legitimize action from. Heidegger says clearly that this duplicity of unconcealedness and concealment is what is 'all-pervading,' *etwas Durchgängiges*, 'which pervades Being's destiny from its beginning to its completion.'[8] Thus with the phenomenological difference, as opposed to the metaphysical difference, Being — or, preferably, 'presence' — acquires a thoroughly historic character: '*Physis, Logos, Hen, Idea, Energeia*, Substantiality, Objectivity, Subjectivity, the Will, the Will to Power, the Will to Will'[9] and Technology are all names for one mode of grounding things present: modes, each of which has had its time. This de-construction of historical figures of foundation radically and irretrievably divorces the 'other thinking' from a first philosophy which would be the science of the most universal ground.

To state this attempt *on* ontology as legitimizing science otherwise: the grounding ground now becomes manifold. Likewise the practice, considered epochally, which such a manifold ground authorizes, will be irreducibly polymorphous. This multifarious character of Being is already implied in the fact that the ontological Difference requires *three* terms, in order to be thought of phenomenologically: the things present, their presence, and presencing. These three terms express Heidegger's *pollachôs legetai*, multifariousness of Being, in the latest period of his writings. In the middle period, that of so-called 'history of Being,' this multifariousness is stated in the vocabulary of the epochal reduction to fields and folds — fields of intelligibility and life, at each period, and folds from one such period to the next. Still another way, the most cryptic, to express this multifariousness is to speak of the 'fourfold,' *das Geviert* (quite appropriately translated by Richardson as 'four-fold polyvalence').

But it is clear that the phenomenological difference does not allow us to think Being as *one* if it is not the oneness of the constellation of unconcealedness and concealment — the constellation that is precisely always *other*. The question that I am raising is: how is human practice in general, and political action in particular, to be thought of if the ground from which it cannot but expect its legitimation is 'always other'? Nietzsche has thought of these practical consequences of the destruction of a self-same ground, under the title of the Eternal Recurrence. And the French poet René Char seems to think what he calls 'pulverization' to be a very practical affair, too: 'Cette part jamais fixée, en nous sommeillante, d'où jaillira DEMAIN LE MULTIPLE.'[10]

In Heidegger's understanding of the ontological Difference, the metaphysical difference is preserved together with the phenomenological difference. Indeed the three terms, 'beings', 'beingness', 'Being itself' point to a resolution (*Verwindung*) of metaphysics by which the relation between ground and grounded is preserved — but epochally so. The destruction thus assigns to metaphysical grounding its site of competence: always within one field or epoch. Thus ontology ceases to deal with a subsisting One. And legitimation of practice cannot mean, for Heidegger, referring what is done or doable to some primordial ground, some ultimate reason. The discovery of the severalness of Being reverses the essence of reason: it is not beings that call for a ground, but Being as the groundless ground calls upon existence. Stated otherwise: an epochal constellation of absence and presence calls upon man to exist in a certain way. A thing such as the Acropolis, for example, 'called upon' human practice otherwise when rhapsodes prepared for their contest at the Panathenaean festival, than when Christians transformed it into a Byzantine church; otherwise when the Turks used it as a powder magazine than when UNESCO, today, plans to spread a huge plastic cover over it for its protection. At each epoch the mode of presencing of the preceding epoch is irrevocably lost. The 'principle'[11] that a first philosophy secures is that ontic being which imposes its economy on such a finite and always provisional order of presencing. With the rise of a new constellation of truth, with a new epochal economy, the preceding constellation of unconcealedness and concealment withers away forever. But within each constellation, the mode of presencing calls upon thinking — and life altogether — to abandon itself to such a constellation, which is utterly contingent and ever new.

PRACTICE UNPRINCIPLED

I now want to show some more concrete implications of Heidegger's destruction of a grounding ground for human practice. As was suggested, these consequences hold for theory and practice alike, but they appear most strikingly in the domain of politics. I shall not undertake to distinguish political action from other types of activity, although that would be necessary. Nor do I bother now to work out an adequate notion of *praxis* and of the specific difference required to define politics. I simply want to suggest that Heidegger's texts yield – sometimes explicitly – indications regarding the question of politics that go farther indeed than his dismissal, 'I do not know any answer to this question'. These consequences result from the reciprocity, stressed in the early as well as the later writings, between what is to be thought, and an attitude in thinking (which for Heidegger always means: in living).

1. *Abolishing the Primacy of Teleology in Action*

The reciprocity between what is to be thought and an attitude in thinking, in *Being and Time*, is called 'authenticity' for *Dasein*, and 'authentic temporality' for what is to be thought. Later, among other titles, Heidegger speaks of releasement: in order to understand Being as letting beings be – in order to understand Being as releasement – we ourselves have to be perfectly released. This way of stating the reciprocity between philosophical content and a way of life is a paraphrase of Meister Eckhart: 'He who wants to understand my teaching of releasement has to be perfectly released.'[12] Heidegger also borrows from Eckhart the first consequence that I want to stress: living 'without why'.[13] Commenting on a famous verse from Angelus Silesius – who was but Meister Eckhart's versifier – Heidegger writes these astonishing lines: 'Man, in the most hidden ground of his being, truly is only when in his own way he is like the rose – without why. We cannot pursue this thought any further here, however.'[14]

It should be clear how statements like this belong to the very core of Heidegger's thinking: if the program of destroying ontological grounding is seen together with the requirement of a life attitude for thinking, this required attitude can only be one of groundless existence: life without why carries the phenomenological destruction over into the practice that is required for 'the other thinking.' The last sentence from the passage just quoted – 'We cannot pursue this thought any further here, however' – reveals a remarkable shyness, perhaps prudence, before the practical consequences of his thinking. There are nevertheless more indications for this release from purpose in action.

Heidegger borrows another phrase from Nietzsche to express the abolition of teleology in action: Nietzsche's thought of the eternal recurrence, he writes, 'eternalizes the lack of a final goal.'[15] Goalless action thus appears to be not only the condition for 'the other thinking,' but also its consequence. On this point, Heidegger comes close indeed to Pierre Klossowski's interpretation of the eternal recurrence as 'the flowering of a delirium.'[16]

The third type of texts on this destruction of teleology belongs to the metaphor of 'woodpaths.' Hannah Arendt wrote about it: 'one cannot say that the thinking so described has a goal'; it is not conducive to 'reaching a goal sighted beforehand and guided thereto ... the metaphor of 'woodpaths' hits upon something essential.'[17] To say that this metaphor is not conducive to reaching a goal suggests clearly that it is not only a metaphor for thinking, but also for practice. The declaration of faith in teleology with which Western practical philosophy began, is thus led to an end by Heidegger. Indeed, Aristotle's *Nichomachean Ethics* begins with the statement: 'Every art and every investigation, every action and pursuit, is thought to aim at some good.' Heidegger's destruction of ontology deprives the arts, investigations, actions and pursuits of their *telos*. Somehow we have to think of practice according to Heidegger otherwise than as purposive pursuit. Striving and performing seem to be basic characteristics of existence only if, prior to any practical theory, Being is understood according to causal schemes.

2. *Abolishing the Primacy of Responsibility in the Legitimation of Action*

Heidegger relies on linguistic considerations to show that our preoccupation with responsibility likewise belongs to the epoch of what he calls 'calculative thinking.' *Rechenschaft ablegen*, to account for something, *rationem reddere*: in all main Western languages accountability has to do with accounting.[18] To be responsible means to be answerable to others for one's dealings. Heidegger, however, displaces responsibility by understanding it primarily as a response. Thinking and acting are seen as a response to historical constellations of truth as *aletheia*. My acting is to be a response to the epochal order of things in which I live. In this sense any epochal truth is binding — but not in the sense of responsibility for acting. Ernst Tugenthat observes that with such a new concept of what is held to be binding, freedom gets lost.[19] What is clear, at least, is the reversal of the summons in responsibility: not I can be summoned to account for my doings, but an epochal constellation of unconcealedness and concealment always summons man to respond to the mode in which things present are present. Here is one text out of many on such summons: 'Unexpectedly it may happen that thinking finds itself called upon to ask: ... what do you make of the Difference if Being as well as beings appear by virtue of the Difference, each in its own way?'[20] The metaphysical difference leads to an understanding of responsibility as accountability; the phenomenological difference, on the other hand, leads to an understanding of responsibility as respondence.

In the way Heidegger transmutes the notion of responsibility, it no longer refers to contents and actions 'for' which one may be held accountable. The 'for' something disappears from sight altogether. Instead, we have the respondence to 'the calling of the Difference.'[21] This does not mean that no one is ever responsible for any action, decision or outcome. But it means certainly that man is placed into another position, and that the concept of responsibility is altogether taken out of the domain of moral justification. Responsibility is to the epochal field in which we always stand — I doubt that phenomenology as it is practiced by Heidegger can say more about responsibility than pointing to the reciprocity between our way of existing and the epochal way of being of the Difference.

3. Action as a Protest Against the Administered World

To deprive human doing of its *telos* and its grounds for accountability assuredly constitutes a powerful protest against the technologically organized universe. Heidegger seems to have understood the very act of sitting in his cottage in Todtnauberg and thinking as a protest against not only technology but against the question that is as old as Aristotle: 'What is the 'function' of man?' This protest by which 'the other thinking' opposes 'calculative thinking' has been suggested by Otto Pöggeler as one of the few political elements in Heidegger. According to Pöggeler, Heidegger would agree with the reform Marxists on such points as the critique of totalitarianism, the opposition between reason and nature, science as an ideology, and the claim to theory as protest.[22] On this last point, one may say that Heidegger was that contemporary philosopher who showed that asking questions is no small matter. Quite as in the life of Socrates, the questioning *is* the protest.

The existential corollary of such questioning is sometimes described by him as 'waiting,' expectancy. What is meant seems to be an attitude of readiness for a new fold in the history of epochs. The 'other thinking' indeed yields a kind of imperative, but one that says: exist in such a way that new epochs of disclosure may appropriate you. What is the condition for such readiness? Detachment from what is, says Heidegger. The *praxis* of calculative thinking thus seems to be technology, whereas the *praxis* of the other thinking would be detachment. He describes expectancy precisely in terms of detachment: 'The gathering power of detachment holds the unborn generation beyond the deceased, and saves it for the coming rebirth of mankind out of the originary.'[23] Whatever mysterious lines such as these may really be meant to say, they certainly imply a protest, a turning away from the global reach of contemporary technology. To take one's leave, *Abschied nehmen*, is what the detached always do: they are *abgeschieden*. Heidegger seems to say that detachment, not goal-directed strategies, hastens the coming rebirth, that is to say, a new epochal economy. Detachment would then be the practical protest which eventually produces a breed detached from metaphysical ontology.

After the abolition of teleology and the displacement of responsibility, detachment is the main criterion for verifying which path is aberrant and which is not. One has to be perfectly detached in order to allow for the rise of an order of things that is detached from any first principle, that is utterly contingent — in 'humanistic' terms, in order to bring about a generation no longer preoccupied with ultimate foundations. 'Protest' thus recovers its primitive meaning which is to 'testify' to epochal truth.

4. *A Certain Disinterest in the Future of Mankind, Due to a Shift in the Understanding of Destiny*

Heidegger's thinking seems to be deeply concerned with the future of man. Although technology has never been an object of condemnation for him, he wants to prepare a path that would lead beyond 'the all-out challenge to secure dominion over the earth.'[24] The completion of metaphysics in the global reach, today, points towards a new beginning. Texts about the imminence of a new era — and about Heidegger's own role in it — abound. And yet: in insisting greatly upon this concern with our future, one misses the displacement of the understanding of destiny that appears as a guiding thread throughout Heidegger's writings. From the title 'the *meaning* of Being,' to the title 'the truth, *aletheia*, of Being,' to the last writings in which he speaks of 'the *event* of Being,' Heidegger understands destiny less and less in regard to man. The very notion of history of Being is anti-humanistic: it is not man's destiny that counts, but the destiny that sends fields, epochs, 'clearings' of possible life and thought. In the third period it is even stated explicitly that '*Es gibt*' is not thought of for the sake of man at all.

The ontological Difference, when thought of phenomenologically, is seen as 'giving,' as sending the various figures of epochal economies. The matter of Heidegger's thinking remains destiny — but not man's. The Difference destines, sends, time and Being. That is, the Difference plays itself out in irreducibly manifold, finite, arrangements of phenomena. Destiny is displaced insofar as it is understood as the playing-out of the Difference in ever new topological multiplicities. One could perhaps say that the 'event' of the third period of Heidegger's writings abolishes time in the two modalities that precisely concern man: as ecstatic temporality (first period) and as cultural history (second period). The temporality of the 'event' is the playful Now[25] which seems to put an end, quite as Nietzsche's thought of the eternal recurrence does, to the struggle to decide what man's next world will be like. The next world will be the playing-out, the destiny, of the Difference. I do not see much ground there to take our destiny into our hands.

5. *Anarchy as the Essence of What is 'Doable'*

The manifold constellations of the Difference, as thought of phenomenologically, cannot be traced to an *arché*. Epochal truth, we are told, sets itself into work with a leap, that is to say, in a sudden flip of historic fields. This is the significance of Heidegger's reflections on the work of art: the artwork founds a constellation of references and thereby brings about truth as one contingent sphere of interactions. Such a rise of truth — 'origin' from *oriri*, or '*Ursprung*' from *springen* — is always other and always new. There is no place, in Heidegger's understanding of the origin, for the Aristotelian *arché*, the beginning that starts and dominates a movement. There is no place, either, for the origin as *principium*, that which is gotten hold of the first, the 'principle' that commands a doing or the *princeps*, the authority, that commands a polity. There is place only for a thought of the origin as multifarious emergence of the phenomena in a field provisionally opened by the Difference. When Heidegger asks, 'Are we in our existence historically at the origin?,'[26] what is meant seems to be a kind of existential implication: a practical *a priori* to think the origin as mere showing, mere coming forth.

Earlier it was shown of authentic temporality that its understanding requires authentic existence as its necessary condition. Likewise here: to exist an-archically is the condition, the practical *a priori*, for the understanding of the origin as an-archic. We also remember that to exist in a state of perfect releasement was the practical *a priori* for understanding presence as releasing whatever is present into an economy of interrelations.

If one keeps in mind this existential requirement for thinking one cannot stop, in tracing the practical implications of Heidegger's project of destroying metaphysics, with what might be called an ontological notion of anarchy: Being as the epochal order of presencing, and which, due to its essential contingency, can never be represented as an *arché*, as a First. Such an ontological notion of anarchy would simply be another way of expressing the 'groundless ground.' All the insistence on the 'calling upon,' *Anruf*, 'exigency,' *Anspruch*, etc. points, on the contrary, towards a practical condition for understanding the origin as an appropriating event in which finite constellations of truth assemble and disassemble themselves. The practical condition can only be to similarly assemble and disassemble beings into ever-changing arrangements of presencing. The anarchic essence of the '*Es gibt*,' it seems to me, defies fixed social constellations. Somehow we are to think of practice as espousing discontinuity. From there to a theory of the state, of law, of property, etc., more middle terms would assuredly be needed. But there cannot be much doubt that Heidegger's reformulation of the ontological Difference aims at introducing radical fluidity into social institutions as into practice in general.

The categories that I have mentioned − teleology, responsibility, protest, destiny and anarchy − all point to a reversal of the metaphysical version of the ontological Difference in Heidegger. Such a reversal is literally a subversion, an overthrow (*vertere*) from the foundations (*sub*−). In a culture where philosophy has so radically abandoned its task of criticism that it cooperates with the existing system by unending enforcements of its technological rationale, Heidegger says No to philosophy's unconditional surrender to technology. In its political dimension, his thought hails, not the chief, but radical mutability in accordance with an understanding of Being as irreducibly manifold.

20

1 Martin Heidegger, *Der Satz vom Grund*, Pfullingen, 1957, p. 207. 'The Principle of Ground,' transl. K. Hoeller, *Man and World*, VII (1974), p. 219.

2 Martin Heidegger, *Vier Seminare*, Frankfurt, 1977, p. 103.

3 Martin Heidegger, *Zur Sache des Denkens*, Tübingen, 1969, p. 40; transl. J. Stambaugh, *On Time and Being*, New York, 1972, p. 37. This translation, which I do not follow, reads: 'it becomes necessary to free thinking from the ontological difference.' *Erlassen* can indeed mean to spare, to remit, to free; in this context, however, what is at stake is the way in which presence gives, extends, sends or lets-belong the difference, not between what is present and its presence, but between the event of presencing and presence.

4 Ibid., p. 48, transl., p. 45.

5 Martin Heidegger, *Identität und Differenz*, Pfullingen, 1957, p. 55; transl. J. Stambaugh, *Identity and Difference*, New York, 1969, p. 58.

6 'Nur noch ein Gott kann uns retten,' in *Der Spiegel*, 23/1976, p. 206, transl. D. Schendler, 'Only a God Can Save Us Now,' in *Graduate Faculty Philosophy Journal*. VI, 1 (1976), p. 16. Translation modified.

7 *Zur Sache des Denkens*, op.cit., p. 86; transl., p. 79.

8 *Identität und Differenz*, op.cit., p. 66; transl., p. 67.

9 Ibid., p. 64, transl., p. 66.

10 'That part never fixed, asleep in us, from which will surge TOMORROW THE MANIFOLD,' René Char, *Commune présence*, Paris 1964, p. 255.

11 A principle 'stands on the first place, in the most advanced rank. The *principia* refer to rank and order ... We follow them without meditation,' *Der Satz vom Grund*, op.cit., pp. 40 and 42. On this notion of principle, see my 'Principles Precarious. On the Origin of the Political in Heidegger,' in *Heidegger, The Man and the Thinker*, ed. T. Sheehan, Athens, 1978; on the four concepts mentioned below – teleology, responsibility, protest, and anarchy – see my 'Political Thinking in Heidegger,' *Social Research*.

12 Meister Eckhart, *Die deutschen Werke*, vol. II, Stuttgart, 1971, p. 109.

13 Ibid., vol. I, Stuttgart, 1958, p. 90.

14 *Der Satz vom Grund*, op.cit., p. 73.

15 Martin Heidegger, *Nietzsche*, Pfullingen, 1961, vol. I, p. 437.

16 'L'épanouissement d'un delire,' Pierre Klossowski, 'Circulus vitiosus,' in *Nietzsche aujourd'hui?*, vol. I, Paris, 1973, p. 101.

17 Hannah Arendt, 'Martin Heidegger at Eighty,' *The New York Review of Books*, Oct. 21, 1971, p. 51.

18 *Der Satz vom Grund*, op.cit., pp. 167 f. and *Nietzsche*, op.cit., vol. II, p. 431.

19 Ernst Tugenthat, *Der Wahrheitsbegriff bei Husserl und Heidegger*, Berlin, 1967, p. 383.

20 *Identität und Differenz*, op.cit., p. 61, transl., pp. 63 f.

21 Martin Heidegger, *Unterwegs zur Sprache*, Pfullingen, 1959, p. 30, transl. A. Hofstadter, *Poetry, Language, Thought*, New York 1971, p. 207.

22 Otto Pöggeler, *Philosophie und Politik bei Heidegger*, Freiburg, 1972, pp. 40f.

23 *Unterwegs zur Sprache*, op.cit., p. 67; transl. P.D. Hertz, *On the Way to Language*, New York, 1971, p. 185. Translation modified.

24 Ibid., p. 212, transl., p. 105.

25 It is true that at the time of *Being and Time*, authenticity as anticipatory resolution as well as what I called utter contingency are both already understood out of the instant, e.g., Dasein 'breaks upon a perspective within beings which is always historical and, *in an ultimate sense, fortuitous*; so fortuitous that the highest form of Dasein's existence can be traced back to only very few and rare moments within Dasein's duration between birth and death, that *man exists at the peak of his own potential only in very few moments* and moves otherwise within his own entity' (emphasis added), Martin Heidegger, *Kant und das Problem der Metaphysik, fourth and expanded edition*, Frankfurt, 1973, p. 262. The appendix on

the discussion between Cassirer and Heidegger at Davos, from which these lines are taken, is not included in *Kant and the Problem of Metaphysics*, transl. J.S. Churchill, Bloomington, 1962, and the version given by N. Langiulli, ed., *The Existentialist Tradition*, New York, 1971, p. 200, not only uses an abbreviated German text but is also faulty. It is only after having lectured for five years on Nietzsche, however, that Heidegger comes to understand the 'now' as a 'punctuation' (Friedrich Nietzsche, *The Will to Power*, transl. W. Kaufmann, New York, 1968, p. 381, and the editor's footnote — *'Punktation'* is Nietzsche's literal translation of the Stoics' *epechein*) of an epochal constellation of truth, in which beings are 'appropriated' into a new order of mutual presencing.

26 Martin Heidegger, *Holzwege*, Frankfurt, 1950, p. 65, transl. A. Hofstadter, *Poetry, Language, Thought*, op.cit., p. 78.

HEIDEGGER AND PRACTICAL REASON

CHARLES M. SHEROVER

The time has perhaps come for us to evaluate the significance of the work Martin Heidegger has given us in terms of what it says to the human situation. Although he was concerned to examine different levels of human existence and experience, his work remains strangely bereft of specific suggestive guidance to the problematic nature of contemporary existence.

His major work, *Being and Time*, was concerned to elucidate the fundamental structures by which human existence manifests itself. Yet, ironically, despite using key terms that are usually taken to have a moral or religious import, his work studiously avoided the development of any moral philosophy. Just why this is so is a philosophical or historical problem to which Heidegger scholarship might well address itself. But, if one remains impressed by his analysis of the nature of human existing and of the presuppositions it reveals, and is also concerned with the continuing problematic nature of contemporary existential situations, one is bound to consider the implications, suggested or mandated, for a coherent existential ethic.

Rather than leave his work, then, as a thing to be reverentially emblamed (and subsequently forgotten), we ought to take it seriously enough to merit our constructive and critical use in developing the ethic it lacks. Emerson had urged us to 'Honor truth by its use;' if Heidegger's examination of human existence rings true, it should have something to say to the moral dilemmas of human existential situations. If Heidegger's existential analysis then, is to have any existential import, it should be made to speak to the moral problematics which constitute the existential structures in which we find ourselves. His analysis should then suggest a reconstruction of moral philosophy that is accordant with its understanding of human existence and adequate to the moral dilemmas of our time.

Heidegger did not provide a moral philosophy; but I would urge that he did lay the existential foundation for one. His categorial description of human existential structures suggests the outline for an existential ethic (and for some correctives, in this light, for the analysis itself). To make this clear, the argument proceeds in four stages: first, a brief reminder of one aspect of the philosophic legacy which founds his work; second, because this thesis may be deemed controversial, a documentation of the ground for it in *Being and Time*; third, a

See notes at the end of this chapter.

pointing out of some central themes of that work which substantiate the thesis; and, fourth, some suggestion of the kind of ethic which it seems to suggest.

I

Whatever other concerns may have animated Heidegger's early work, he explicitly stated his intention to face Kant's question, 'What is man?,' not merely 'as a natural being but as a 'citizen of the world'.'[1] Kant, in Part II of the First Critique and the entirety of the Second Critique, made clear his concern to establish the fundamental nature of human finite freedom. And this concern of Kant's transcendental philosophy was spelled out as the primacy of practical reasoning, a primacy over any specific use of the cognitive intellect. To this concern, Heidegger has brought a rich development. But this development itself raises the question of moral reasoning, which Kant had regarded as the epitome, grounding and meaning of all practical thinking.

Kant, after adumbrating the structure, the capabilities and limitations, of cognitive thought, had forcefully insisted that all human reasoning is essentially of a practical nature: 'Only if pure reason in itself can be and really is practical, as the consciousness of the moral law shows it to be, is it always one and the same reason which judges apriori by principles, be it for theoretical [cognitive] or practical purposes.'[2]

One central thrust of Heidegger's initial project was to ground and develop this Kantian thesis. In his Kant-book, using Kant's terminology, he demonstrated the common rooting of the cognitive and the practical in the activity of the transcendental imagination.[3] In *Being and Time*, working in his own terms, he demonstrated their common rooting in 'anticipatory resoluteness', the fundamental form of authentic behavior that is itself grounded in 'Care' — Heidegger's term for the encompassing form of the human outlook — in Care, 'as concernful solicitude [which] ... must already be presupposed when we distinguish between theoretical and practical behavior.'[4]

We may then see *Being and Time* as working out, among its other concerns, the practical nature of human rational behavior, exposing its apriori existential structures and unveiling its grounding presuppositions of forward-looking temporality. Doing this was termed the task of 'fundamental ontology', Heidegger's term for the being-structure of the human outlook.

And this fundamental ontology — the mode in which a human being structures his outlook and understands the world in which he finds himself — provides the foundation for the ethical. Whether an ethic concerns itself with value-actualization or with satisfaction of a previously delineated normative standard, Heidegger insisted that it necessarily presupposes its own 'ontological presuppositions:' any ethic, then, finds its ground in what Kant had already called a 'metaphysic of morals' and which Heidegger explicitly identified as an 'ontology of a person and existence.'[5] In this sense, then, I would urge that *Being and Time* may be legitimately read as effectively providing a propaedeutic to ethics, a propaedeutic necessary to the reconstruction of moral philosophy.

II

We have so frequently — and correctly — been admonished to read Heidegger's terms in a strictly ontological sense (despite the irony that they are so frequently drawn from the literature of moral experience and religious concern) that we have tended to overlook his specifically moral or ethical references. That Heidegger saw that the ontological structures of human existence are to concern themselves with ethical import becomes clear in his specific texts elucidating 'conscience', 'guilt', 'resoluteness', and 'solicitude'. This needs documentation.

The call of conscience, he tells us, radically individuates a person. The call of conscience, 'in its [ground] and its essence,' as the self of any individual, 'is in each case mine.'[6] The call of conscience points to the essence of the person. This is attested by its everyday meaning as the 'voice of conscience.'[7] It comes to one even out of inauthenticity; it is intelligible as 'an attestation of a person's ownmost potentiality for Being,' for being a whole self.[8] The call of conscience 'manifests itself as the call of care'[9] and 'relentlessly it individualizes a person down to his potentiality-for-Being-guilty.'[10] Heidegger saw this in accord with the entire tradition, for 'All experiences and interpretations of conscience are at one in that they make the 'voice' of conscience speak somehow of 'guilt'.'[11]

In its everyday meaning, he explained, this means defining 'a kind of behavior which we call *making oneself responsible*'.[12] As such, it involves 'the breach of a 'moral requirement'.[13] It is *not* to be equated with a phrase such as 'laden with guilt'. Its core-meaning emerges from being formalized and as formalized it means 'having a responsibility for.'[14] Thus, guilt or responsibility does not result *from* moral obligations; rather, moral obligation only becomes possible on the ground of a primordial capacity for taking on guilt or responsibility. Indeed, this fundamental capacity to make oneself responsible — facing Kant's question of how morality's possibility may be established — is 'the existential condition ... for morality in general and for the possible forms which this may take [in particular 'factical' situations].'[15]

In responding to the call of conscience, to the responsibility and concomitant anxiety that ensues, we enter that mode of being which Heidegger called resoluteness.[16] And here we have 'arrived at the truth of the individual person which is most primordial because it is *authentic*.'[17] It is essentially anticipatory because it 'springs from a sober understanding' of the specific possibilities before which one finds oneself.'[18] Thus, resoluteness is no abstraction. It defines the particular situations in which we find ourselves called to act. The call of conscience 'does not hold before us some empty ideal of existence.'[19] It summons me *into* the particular situation which my own judgement and decision to act define in terms of what is lacking, what is to be fulfilled. The call of conscience calls me to particular judgement, particular decision, in particular specific situations. Resoluteness consists and manifests itself as specific choosing.[20]

To comprehend what is involved in resoluteness is crucial to the project that is *Being and Time*, for at least five reasons:

- comprehending resoluteness is prerequisite, in a way akin to self-realization ethics, 'for defining the ontological meaning of ... an individual person's authentic potentiality-for-Being-a-whole:'[21]
- resoluteness brings us 'before the primordial *truth* of existence' —just because resoluteness defines the situations we delineate in terms of the imperatives we take from them in order to bring ourselves into them;[22]
- resoluteness is essentially anticipatory: as such it first reveals temporality as the structure of our being;[23]
- resoluteness historicizes us and reveals itself as 'authentic historicality;'[24]
- and, finally, in a way reminiscent of Royce's loyalty ethic, 'resoluteness constitutes the *loyalty* of existence to its own Self.'[25]

Heidegger's road to the centrality of responsibility and the resoluteness it engenders first comes to solicitous concern, a mode of responsible involvement with other persons. Building on the fundamental Kantian distinction between persons and things, Heidegger has differentiated that circumspective concern we display to the things about us from our solicitous comportment toward other persons.[26] Only through solicitous behavior do other persons enter into our experience *qua* persons (instead of things); toward them we are able to exhibit moral responsibility. Reminiscent of Kant's injunction that the prime moral responsibility is to treat them *qua* persons and to enhance *their* own free self-development, Heidegger abjured the domination of others because it infringes on their own sovereignty of care. Rather, solicitous concern for the integrity of the other is shown as that:

> kind of solicitude which does not so much leap in for the Other as *leap ahead* of him in his existentiell potentiality-for-Being, not in order to take away his 'care' but rather to give it back to him authentically as such for the first time. ... [I]t helps the Other to become transparent to himself *in* his care and to become *free* for it. ... [Authentic] solicitude is guided by *considerateness* and *forebearance*.[27]

This capacity for resolute response to the call of conscience and its demand that one make himself responsible for the free development of others as well as of one's own self 'constitutes the Being to which we give the name of 'care'.'[28] Anticipatory resoluteness, projected out of the capacity to make oneself a responsible being, provides the existential center in which an individual person finds himself.[29]

Forestalling any fall into mere abstraction, he reminded us that, in exposing the structure of 'care as the Being of the person,' he has been concerned to develop 'the right *ontological* foundation for that entity which in each case we ourselves are, and which we call 'man'.'[30] Whatever else may be said about care, it is no neutral term: for, 'Man's *perfectio* – his transformation into that which he can be in Being-free for his ownmost possibilities (projection) – is 'accomplished' by [the fundamental capability to] 'care'.'[31]

III

Because this founding of the possibility of ethics has not been noticed before, I have reviewed constituents of the structure of care whose direct relevance to moral philosophy seems clear by means of direct quotation. These expressions do not stand alone. They are sustained by some pervasive themes of *Being and Time*. A few of the more prominent should be noted.

The existential analytic, Heidegger's examination of the structure of human existence, rests on a fundamental Kantian distinction between persons and things. Only a person can be characterized by freedom, forward-looking temporality, resoluteness, and responsibility. Only a person can interpret situations in which he finds himself and retrieve himself from them in terms of possibilities he sees them as offering and which he decides to appropriate.

The focus on the individuality of the person appears throughout. We are told that 'the 'I' is an Essential characteristic' of the individual person,[32] that the 'question of the 'who' of a person has been answered with the expression 'self'.'[33] Self-hood is a recurrent theme and a continuing concern. Only through self-hood can 'an I-self relate itself to a Thou-self.'[34]

In the Kant-book, he explicated the foundational nature of self- or personhood for the authority of moral law. Working from Kant's thesis that the feeling of respect for moral law is foundational, Heidegger had urged that this respect is really 'respect for oneself' as a self. He concluded that discussion with the claim that he had succeeded in transforming this respect for the moral law, and thereby for oneself, into a 'transcendental, fundamental structure of the transcendence of the moral self.'[35] This is to say that self-respect is one with respect for moral law and an integral foundation of the person's possibility to construct a coherent experience.

As an individual person, the moral self finds itself as such in acts of freedom; these are only exercised in particular choices of specific possibilities. The person's freedom – his ability to direct thought and decision and action beyond what is immediately given is its transcendence. But the ontological understanding of this transcendental freedom, this fundamental capacity for free decision, must always 'base itself on *ontical* [specific] *possibilities*.' Unless we are able to understand the ways in which an individual exercises his 'ways of potentiality-for-Being' then any analysis of his modes of being 'will remain groundless.'[36]

Exercising freedom depends on the ability to orient oneself to the particular possibilities a given situation presents.[37] 'Freedom offers' to the person, 'the ability to be in possibilities which open up before its finite choice [and by which it chooses] his destiny.'[38]

The employment of transcendental or enabling freedom is exercised in specific particular situations; this capacity for freedom entails the constitutive structures by which each is enabled to orient himself to the future that is not yet. Presuming the priority of possibility in the human outlook, this forward-looking capacity incorporates our essential temporality as functioning out of and in terms of futurity.

Heidegger's analysis of the futural ground of experiential time, uniquely reveals and explicates the fundamental ontological grounding, the foundational possibility, for the actual exercise of human practical reason in particular situations. It thus provides the fundamental elucidation of Kant's quest for the explanatory possibility of morality in the exercise of freedom.

Because our experience is constructed in essential temporalizing terms, Heidegger pointed out, we are essentially historicizing beings in a continuity of becoming.[39] Our essential temporality enables us to choose and realize specific possibilities as the 'ought' or the 'should' which impels us to decision and to action. This temporalizing nature enables us to reach into the future as presented by possibilities discerned as present, retrieve the relevant past and thus construct the living present in which we choose, decide, and act: we are thus enabled to redirect the flow of events by integrating new possibility into the structure of the present. Experiential temporality enables practical reason to function and to be understood, in its commitments to cognitive quests, prudential activity, and moral endeavor. As the structure of care, this foundational temporality enables us to realize the possibilities of self-hood which each of us carries as the core of his being. Experiential temporality enables transcendental freedom to become existentially meaningful.

Working from Kant's insistence that freedom is fundamental, Heidegger has identified it with transcendence itself.[40] Freedom is 'the ground of grounds.'[41] It opens up the 'outlying scope of possibilities' before us; as such its *responsible* exercise is 'a transcendental obligation for the person in whose freedom it is rooted.'[42] Is this not to say that the obligation to use freedom responsibly is rooted in the nature of freedom itself, in the heart of the nature of man?

A reexamination of Heidegger's early writings, from the perspective of moral reason, shows us in all these ways, that the explication of the ontological possibility of the employment of practical reason in concretely specific situations is a running theme. Rather than leave us with the notion of moral judgement as a rootless abstraction or an empty ideal, he has sought to exhibit the categorical structure that makes moral practical reason possible. He has sought to ground the exercise of practical reasoning in the existential structure of man.

Having provided the ontological foundation of the exercise of freedom in practical reasoning, he has thus provided a propaedeutic to an authentic existential moral philosophy.

That this is consonant with his own judgement of his work, seems clear. In the 'Letter on Humanism,' he has said, 'If now ... ethics dwells in the abode of man, then that thought which thinks the truth of Being as the original element of man as existing is already in itself at the source of ethics.'[43] Rather than developing that ethic himself, he directed his own work on the project of thinking the foundation 'truth of Being;' but, he clearly declared:

> The wish for an ethics needs to be fulfilled, all the more urgently because the ... perplexity of man increases to immeasurable dimensions. Every care must be given to ethics ... in a way that corresponds to a technological age.[44]

Clearly perceiving the need for a founded ethic for the situation of our time, he provided its philosophic foundation but left the task to others. His turning away from this task which he recognized raises its own questions — questions about the unfinished state of *Being and Time*, the bearing of focused ethical considerations on some of its analyses, and possible ethical implications of concepts developed in later work. However such questions may be, it seems clear that one open problematic left by *Being and Time* as given to us is the development of an existential ethic for which it provided the foundational propaedeutic.

IV

In looking to the development of such an existential ethic, we will retrieve this open problematic. In the nature of the case, the development of such a founded ethic would flesh out, deepen, and possibly even amend the existential analysis upon which it builds. For, if the capacity for moral reasoning is rooted in the ontological nature of man, explication of moral reasons's modes of being should broaden our insight into the ways in which the structure of human nature is manifested. These ethical considerations, aside from their own intrinsic interest and import, may be expected to lead to an internal critique of the outlook from which it commences. How such an ethical inquiry which builds out of Heidegger's existential analysis may proceed can be outlined on two levels.

An individual person, we have seen, functions by evaluating the situations in which he finds himself in terms of the possibilities he sees them as offering. He defines and delimits any situation by what he sees it as offering or lacking. He reads his situation as opportunities or demands; his reading, then, expresses the judgmental criteria or principles his own perspective forces upon him and which he idiosyncratically brings into it. The imperative his conscience gives him, his acceptance of it in resolution to act, and the strength of his commitment to the resolved-upon action are grounded together on those interpretive principles which, perhaps preconceptually, he accepts as binding. These criteria of judgement delineate his own individual situation and its specifics; by them, he exercises care, acts in concernful solicitude for others, finds a self-imposed compulsion to act at all — or, as Heidegger's notion of care demonstrates, even notices a particular physical object as an instrument pointing to its environmental nexus. Any reading or deliberate action is rooted in judgmental principles one's conscience uses, valuational commitments by which one operates, the motives one accepts as binding, the actional maxims one employs. These conspire, as apriori structures, to illuminate for him the needs he perceives and feels called upon to meet.

These evaluative principles, to which one's existing gives expression, are the canons of his individual being; they delineate, define and ground the individual self he is. These principles may be prudential, economic, hedonic or esthetic; but the priorities they command are moral priorities concerning the responsible use of time. These principles and their inter-relationships comprise one's moral outlook, guide one's moral reasoning, and, indeed, all one's thinking that is concerned with actions, goals, obligations, commandments. They constitute one's principle of individuation and the peculiar existentials of the individual he makes himself to be. They are thus intrinsic to his own fundamental ontology.

To ignore these fundamental interpretive criteria in their ontologizing role, as the avoidance of moral philosophy seems to have done, is to ignore the operative keystone of the fundamental ontology of the individual person in his essentially individualizing activity of being. Decisional activity comprising the activity of existing is bound up in judgements of 'should' and 'should not'; moral imperatives are woven into our ontological structures and comprise the intrinsically individuating judgmental practical nature of human existence. They animate the particular structure of being which each one of us is.

Our fundamental capacity for the exercise of finite freedom imposes the necessity, with the ability, to choose and judge and act *and* to do so in the light of commitments and obligations which we incorporate into our activity of being. These not only define the individual self; they are integral to the exercise of that freedom which enables any individual self to be a self and to develop a coherent experience. An ethic, concerned with the structured exercise of practical reasoning in creating, defining and resolving the value-conflicts which comprise our particular situations, is intrinsic to the being-structure of an existing individual. For it is in value-creation, value-commitment, and value-resolution that individual judgmental thinking, discourse and action are constituted.

Whether we explain such activity in terms of value-loyalty or in a more Kantian vocabulary of motives, maxims, and actional principles, it would seem clear that such judgmental activity is constitutive of the self as it interprets its-world to itself in terms of lacks, possibilities, and obligations. By creating and employing evaluative standards, an individual structures his activity of being and becoming. A completed existential analysis, then, must rest on such an evaluative structure — whose functioning Heidegger has not even acknowledged. But such an evaluative structure would seem to be a necessary condition for the exercise of care and futurity in which freedom is manifested.

Such judgmental activity is primarily directed to one's relations with others. As Heidegger has shown, this being-involved with-others is fundamental. The self does not find itself alone — but always as a member of a 'we'. Alfred Schutz has observed, 'The world of the We is not private ... but [it] is our world, the one common intersubjective world which is right there in front of us' and in which we are, from the outset, involved.[45] That world is formed by one's circle of friends and associates, but also by the broad community of individuals, anonymous to us, with whom we live in a structured community of interdependence. Each of these anonymous individuals is himself a 'thou', an individual person in-the-world. 'Before the reality of the 'I' in the sense of one's own Ego and its personal private experiences, Max Scheler pointed out, this 'reality of the 'thou' and of a community is taken for granted.'[46] Indeed, as Rousseau had already argued, moral consciousness can only arise in an acknowledged community of individuals.[47] Foundational to the being of the individual self is the community in which he finds himself, a community itself structured in a complex of internal relations which spell out the finite possibilities of specific freedoms and responsibilities for each of its participants.

Heidegger has done yeoman work in pointing out the ontological primordiality of the sociality of the person. But as fundamental as the phenomenon of 'being-with', of being-with-others, is acknowledged to be, he has left it strangely bereft of any serious development. And such lack of development is seriously subversive of the project that is *Being and Time*.

Despite their differences, Aristotle, the Stoics and Rousseau, Kant, Fichte and Hegel, Emerson and Peirce, Royce and Dewey, unite in propounding one lesson we cannot ignore: man is in essence a citizen, a community-member, and one cannot legitimately separate him from the internal ramifications of his essential sociality.

True individuality, as true freedom, is inseparable from social involvement and responsibility. It is no casual accident that Kant, in his *Metaphysic of Morals*, felt it incumbent to elucidate the 'principles of political right' before proceeding to propose a 'doctrine of individual virtue'. For Kant understood well that the fundamental nature of freedom — to which Heidegger has given important ontological development — is indivisible: individual moral freedom is, in principle, inseparable from the state of freedom in one's society. Rousseau, who insisted that we are all born free, summed up well the lesson these diverse thinkers would have us learn: 'It is necessary to study society in terms of men and men in terms of society; those who would treat [either] separately will never understand the other.' It is, perhaps, because of his patent neglect of this lesson that the author of *Being and Time* was to flounder in the political morass of his own community.

One prime philosophic task, then, is the development of the phenomenon of 'being-with' into a social ontology. Such a social ontology is intrinsic to an ethic for our time. For any meaningful ethic, grounded on an existential foundation 'in this technological age' must be social; it can neither separate the individual from the context of his civic involvements and responsibilities, nor his society from its responsibilities to the freedom of its citizens. The ensuing task is to face the primordial fact of fundamental freedom seriously, seek modes of translation into specific terms, and thereby elucidate those kinds of social relations which tend to make authentic freedom meaningful to each individual person as he is afforded new opportunity for the self-development that is his history.

A founded existential ethic would ground itself in projective temporality, in the essentially ongoing historicity of all situations and decisions. It would thus take up Heidegger's preliminary analysis of 'being-with' together with his pioneer work in the elucidation of temporality and seek out the temporal modes of authentically enriching the meaning of our being-with others. Doing so would serve to secure the work already done by providing it with a firmer existential ground.

Such an ethic might well start from Heidegger's delineation of two existential phenomena — from what the English translation calls 'being guilty' and from the nature of resoluteness itself. But first we must refine their meanings.

   — Heidegger's discussions of *Schuldigsein* make it clear that what is meant is the actualized capacity 'to make oneself responsible'.[48] But this capacity for responsibility may be inauthentically manifested — by withdrawal from futurity into remorse over the compromises into which one feels himself to have been thrust. Too much perpetrated evil has been selfrighteously excused by this mode of being-guilty, which withdraws itself into its past and thereby resigns its present responsibility for the future. The authentic mode of 'making oneself responsible' is seen in the nature of care and the resoluteness to which conscience calls: it is making oneself responsible, not for the past, but for the future. '*Schuldigsein* constitutes the Being to which we give the name of 'care'. ... This calling-back in which conscience calls forth, gives a person to understand ... that [he] is responsible.'[49] To fulfill this call to responsibility in authentic resolution is to orient oneself to one's futurity, to those selected possibilities accepted as genuine and to which one decides to respond. This responsible exercise of freedom-for-the-future is what Heidegger has seen to be the foundation for morality in general.

   — But this suggests that all resoluteness is not authentic and much, even heroic, resoluteness is essentially inauthentic and not to be welcomed. Authentic resoluteness cannot subvert that fundamental freedom which makes it possible; authentic resoluteness is resoluteness-for-its-ground; in solicitous concern, it holds itself responsible for the freedom of others as well as for its own.

A founded existential ethic, then, of my responsible exercise of freedom would adumbrate the mode of my responsibilities to myself, to those 'others' who constitute my social world, and to the members of the 'they' — anonymous in my perspective but not in theirs — with whom I am in continually structured interdependence. It would speak to my responsibilities to the inhabitants of nature with whom I share my general environment and, for that matter, to nature itself. If, indeed, Being needs us, as Heidegger has come to urge,[50] then that relationship of each person to Being itself is also part of my complex of responsibilities and part of any ethical problematic.

Above all, the responsible exercise of freedom is a responsibility to responsibly structure one's time. As such, it involves an historic responsibility to one's heritage, to the fabric of relations constituting one's present, and most fundamentally, as Schutz urged, it involves a responsibility to those who are to come after. The authentically responsible use of freedom honors the *prospective* historic continuity of our existing together and treating that future we are now building with deference and respect.

Such an ethic would take the notion of stewardship, in the deepest sense of the word as the moral counter-part of Heidegger's root ontological concept of care. A founded existential ethic, then, would be an ethic of responsible, solicitously concernful stewardship over all that comes with one's ken.

Such a founded ethic would honor our own historicity by retrieving and appropriating the best of the tradition of moral philosophy — which, more than much traditional metaphysics, has in fact spoken to an ontology of personal existence. For moral philosophy has always worked on the unexplicated presumption of men as temporal beings-in-the-world. Even Descartes did not permit any epistemological alienation or methodological doubt to enter here. More than the metaphysical tradition, the history of moral philosophy has helped to prepare the way for the ontology of existing persons.

An existential ethic would learn from Aristotle that any description of human behavior is inherently normative just because all human behavior is value-laden. Men comport themselves, perceive problems to be solved, obligations to which conscience calls, and animate decisions to act in terms of value-judgements which they deem to be *true*; as he insisted in beginning both the *Politics* and the *Ethics*, all men act with a view to what they think is good. It would learn from Kant that we must, indeed, start with a universalizing formalism just to ground that kind of resoluteness which is authentic; but we must then proceed to a doctrine of content, or, as Kant termed it, a doctrine of political right that permits a doctrine of individual virtue. It would thus take from both Aristotle and Kant a lesson which Heidegger never developed (but which he might have learned from Peirce or Royce or Dewey): the essential unity of the double nature of the call of conscience — to a responsibility for our own free self-hood *and* for the structure of freedom in the social community in which we find our being.

A founded existential ethic would recognize historicity as a continuing condition of beings who are continually engaged in concrete situations, concrete individual and social concerns, decisions and allegiances, with specific conflicting obligations to sort out and conflicts of loyalties to resolve. It would not abrogate individual responsibility by dictating specific acts but it would show us how authentically to decide in the mulifarious situations in which we find ourselves and would delineate the considerations which are germane to our continuing task of resolving conflicts of value loyalties and evaluating the consequences of our own decisions. In its demand for authenticity, its own prime commitment must be a fundamental loyalty to the possibilities of freedom which provide its ground.

A founded existential ethic would not permit us, at any point, to disclaim 'moral judgement.'[51] It would not, out of disillusionment or despair, permit the suggestion that 'only a god can save us.'[52] It would take up that insight of folkwisdom: God helps those who help themselves. Rather than counselling quietistic resignation in awaiting what yet might come, it would urge on us that authenticity demands anticipation and appropriation of genuine possibilities for the enhancement of responsible freedom. It would teach us to exercise our freedom in loyalty to freedom — for others as well as ourselves; it would urge us to redeem the past by building the future in that kind of authentic resolution which takes responsibility for historical continuity as the horizon of its world.

Is this not the way we can make the meaning of what it means to-be our own in this our time? May we understand this call as the meaning of the call of Being to us today? As Heidegger has said, in speaking of our belonging to Being: 'This is the question. It is the world-question of thought. On its response is decided what will become of the earth and the existence of men upon this earth.'[53]

NOTES

1 Martin Heidegger, *Kant and the Problem of Metaphysics*, trans. J.S. Churchill, (Bloomington: Indiana University Press), 1962, p. 214. [Hereafter referred to as *KPM.*]

2 Immanuel Kant, *Kritik der praktischen Vernunft*, (Stuttgart: Reclam), 1966, p. 193.

3 See *KPM*, p. 162; see my *Heidegger, Kant and Time* (Bloomington: Indiana University Press), 1971, sec. VI. 3. [Hereafter referred to as *HK&T.*]

4 Martin Heidegger, *Being and Time*, trans. Macquarrie & Robinson, (London: SCM Press), 1962, pp. 347-8; cf. p. 238. [Hereafter referred to as *B&T.*]

5 In this paper, I have translated *Dasein* as 'person'. *B&T*, p. 339.

6 *B&T*, p. 323; cf. pp. 67, 254.

7 *B&T*, p. 313.

8 *B&T*, p. 324.

9 *B&T*, p. 322.

10 *B&T*, p. 354.

11 *B&T*, p. 325.

12 *B&T*, p. 327.

13 *B&T*, p. 328.

14 *B&T*, p. 329.

15 *B&T*, p. 332.

16 see *B&T*, p. 343.

17 *B&T*, p. 343.

18 see *B&T*, p. 358.

19 *B&T*, p. 347.

20 see *B&T*, p. 314.

21 *B&T*, p. 348.

22 see *B&T*, p. 355.

23 see *B&T*, p. 380.

24 *B&T*, p. 438.

25 *B&T*, p. 443.

26 see *B&T*, p. 157.

27 *B&T*, pp. 158-9.

28 *B&T*, pp. 332-3.

29 see *B&T*, p. 434.

30 *B&T*, p. 241.

31 *B&T*, p. 243.

32 *B&T*, p. 152.

33 *B&T*, p. 312.

34 Martin Heidegger, *Vom Wesen des Grundes* (Frankfurt: Klostermann), 1965, p. 38. [Hereafter referred to as *WG.*]

35 *KPM*, p. 166; cf. *HK&T*, pp. 165-66.

36 *B&T*, p. 360.

37 see *B&T*, p. 331.

38 *WG*, p. 53.

39 see *B&T*, p. 430.

40 see *WG*, p. 44.

41 *WG*, pp. 44, 53.

42 *WG*, p. 52.

43 Martin Heidegger, 'Letter on Humanism,' trans. Lohner; Barrett & Aiken, *Philosophy in the Twentieth Century*, (New York: Random House), 1962, vol. III, p. 297.

44 *Ibid.*, p. 295.

36

45 A. Schutz, *The Phenomenology of the Social World*, trans. Walsh & Lehnert, (Evanston: Northwestern University Press), 1967, p. 171.

46 quoted, Schutz, p. 97.

47 see Jean-Jacques Rousseau, *The Social Contract*, trans. C. Sherover, (New York: Meridian, New American Library), 1974, pp. 31-33.

48 see *B&T*, p. 327.

49 *B&T*, pp. 332-33.

50 Martin Heidegger, *The End of Philosophy*, trans. J. Stambaugh (New York: Harper & Row), 1973, p. 76.

51 *Der Spiegel* interview, trans. Alter, *Philosophy Today*, v. 20, No. 4/4, Winter 1976, p. 280.

52. *Ibid.*, p. 277.

53 Martin Heidegger, Der Satz vom Grund, (Pfullingen: Neske), 1957, p. 211.

THE MORAL WILL *

WILLIAM BARRETT

'When are you going to write an ethics?' The question was asked of Heidegger by a young friend shortly after the publication of *Being and Time* in 1927. Heidegger himself recalls the incident twenty years later. The question must touch a sensitive spot — one his critics had made sensitive — that he should remember it long afterward. The thinker must be allowed in the end to deliver judgment upon himself, even if indirectly. For there is a judgment implied here since he touches on the question that remains unanswered in the whole philosophy. Heidegger did not go on to write that ethics. That in itself would signify little; philosophers whose thought is morally saturated from beginning to end — William James would be an example — never bowed to the labor of producing an ethical treatise, and we are not the least troubled thereby. But this absence in Heidegger strikes us as more serious: It is not the incidental fact that he did not write an ethics that is troubling, but the doubt that he could write one and remain within the confines of his thought.

This may seen a strange accusation against a thinker whose effort, now that we are able to see it as a whole, was nothing less than a preparation to enter anew the sphere of religious existence. But all the preparation, so scrupulously and patiently carried on over the years, cannot reach its goal: It cannot enter the religious because it does not arrive at the ethical. To reach the ethical would require a leap to another level, a *metabasis eis allo genos* (a step into another region of existence).

This criticism might be fatal to another philosopher, but it does not, nor is it meant to, demolish Heidegger. It indicates, rather, the limits within which we have to measure his value to us. And right now such limits are particularly important to establish because in some circles Heidegger's name threatens to become the password of a cult, and his works the object of a pious scholasticism — which is all to the good so far as it helps disseminate his doctrine and serves to counteract certain narrower philosophic tendencies of the moment. The danger is that the scholastic pieties, oversensitive to any criticism, lead us eventually to believe that the philosophy accomplishes more than it actually does. Heidegger himself has stressed that the great philosophers of the past were always consumed by a single vision. They had only one thought, he tells us, which they were struggling to utter and which nevertheless remains unsaid

See notes at the end of this chapter.

or ill said through all they have written. We may allow his own beautiful words to be applied to himself: 'To think is to confine oneself to a single thought that one day stands still like a star in the world's sky.' He is the thinker of only one idea, Being, but this single star of his shines with a surprising radiance. We read the history of philosophy, and so history itself, differently now by its light. His thought undermines the subjectivistic constructions of modern aesthetics, and so enables us to think of a poem or work of art in at once a newer and more ancient manner. But rich as the bearing of his thought may be elsewhere, with the matter of ethics itself Heidegger does not come to grips.

This is not to imply that his thinking is somehow unethical or nihilistic; that was an impression carried away by his earlier critics, because his themes often seemed so austere and chilling. Here was a philosopher who took nothingness seriously and wrote about it openly; and surely that must hint at some strange and morbid trait in the man himself. A response like this is itself but the reflex of a superficial and socially acceptable nihilism that recoils from anything negative in our existence. And Heidegger is surely right that until we think through the 'nihil' (nothing) in nihilism we only continue to drift from one bogus 'affirmation' to another. No; the reason the ethical does not appear within the scope of Heidegger's thinking is not to be sought in these imaginary twists of his temperament. It lies much more fundamentally in the subject of ethics itself, and the obstacles that subject seems to place before him.

From its very beginning, in the hands of Aristotle, ethics has taken the will as its central fact. The will is 'deliberative desire,' the place in our psychic landscape where reason and appetite meet; where our wishes and emotions submit to reason, and reason in turn is activated by desire; hence the central pivot of the human being as a practical agent. The tradition has remained virtually unbroken ever since. Kant, the most systematic moralist after Aristotle, internalizes but remains fully within this tradition when he takes the moral will to be the center of the human person.

But in the fateful course of modern thought this essentially moral will was to become transformed into something else: the will to self-assertion and dominance; the will to power. Reason, under its sway, is pronounced legislative of phenomena, and eventually becomes technical reason. Nietzsche, because he consented to it and willed it as his own will, was able to probe this will in its tragic and demoniacal dimensions. In much less conscious but far more blatant manifestations, this will is everywhere around us in the modern marketplace. The Nazis had proclaimed their own vulgarization of the German philosophy of the will as the voice of national resurgence. Leni Riefenstahl's documentary on the rise of the Nazi movement, still extolled by *cineasts* as a model of its kind, was entitled *The Triumph of the Will*. If the matter of ethics is inseparably involved with the will, and the will has been compromised and even polluted at its source, how can one go ahead and write an ethics?

Yet freedom holds a central place in Heidegger's thought, and that would seem to have something to do with the will. Traditionally the question of freedom has been discussed by philosophers as the freedom of the will. To be sure, Heidegger's conception of freedom is detached from the will to action. Freedom is the condition of truth itself, for unless we are free to let be, to let things show themselves as what they are, we will only force our willful distortions upon them. But is not this detachment from willfulness a condition of the will itself? And is it not a moral state, since we praise people for it and attach blame to the opposite willfulness? Perhaps then there is another sense of the will, hidden in Heidegger's own pages, beyond that dissonant and self-assertive sense of the will he is seeking to avoid — a sense that we have to bring out into the clear. Perhaps we have to reach back beyond post-Kantian German philosophy to an older meaning of the will: to the meaning that *voluntas* had for some medieval philosophers, which goes back to St. Augustine and beyond him to the *Eros* of Plato. Perhaps the will, at its deepest, does not connote self-assertion and dominance, but love and acquiescence; not the will to power but the will to prayer.

In raising such questions, of course, we look beyond Heidegger to the whole of modern culture. To try to restore the moral will to a central and primary role in the human personality is bound to appear as an effort against the mainstream of this culture. After all, modernism began as a revolt against Victorianism, particularly the cramping moral code of the Victorians; and modernism has continued ever since in its goal of self-liberation. The great literature of the modern movement, on which we were raised, takes the side of Dionysian instinct against the moralist. 'Nothing is more characteristic of modern literature,' Lionel Trilling puts it very aptly, 'than its discovery and canonization of the primal, nonethical energies.' Freud and psychoanalysis were another powerful current flowing into the same mainstream. Whether it meant to or not, the psychoanalytic movement hardly strengthened the force of traditional morality. By dethroning the sovereignty of consciousness, by showing its weakness before the unconscious, it left people less able to believe in their moral freedom. When the conscious mind loses its potency, the will ceases to be a central governing agency. Our moral vocabulary was superseded by a psychoanalytic one. Instead of talking about the virtues and vices, people thought it much more profound and 'scientific' to talk about neuroses and complexes. The moral component of experience, no longer taken as primary and irreducible, was left at best the peripheral status of a social policeman. In trying to reassert the claims of the moral will against such formidable influences, one starts with an apologetic sense that one may be taken as a prig or a hypocrite.

Yet in all this disparagement of the moral will there remains one glaring discrepancy between this culture and our actual life; or, to bring the point closer to home, between ourselves as partisans of this culture and ourselves in the ordinary course of our private lives. We still go about our everyday business guided by this moral will, and we still discriminate in its terms. We do distinguish the people we know by their virtues and vices, and deal with them accordingly. We forgive an old friend who is sometimes odd and tedious by saying that, after all, she is a 'very dear person' and 'a good soul.' And with a brilliant and neurotic friend, on the other hand, for whom we have made psychoanalytic excuses over the years, if the friendship reaches the breaking point, we usually give up then all the jargon of the neuroses and declare simply that he has become so perverse, inconsiderate, and selfish that we do not care to see him again. It clears the air sometimes to say of someone that he is a stinker, period, as if coming out of the psychological clouds we were at least touching solid ground. In short, without being aware of it, we do follow Kant's view that the moral will is the center of the personality. And yet, amazingly enough, modern philosophers have yet to come to terms with this fact.

I

In attempting to disengage these points both within and against Heidegger, I am aware of a great deal of personal experience hovering in the background, and perhaps it will make matters clearer if I were here and now to avow this aspect of my enterprise. The late W.H. Auden once remarked that an important book is one that reads us, not the reverse. In this sense, I have been read by Heidegger for many years, and his response to my needs has varied. His German was simple and well within my ken, and so I was easily admitted past that barrier. The points on which I was rejected were particular obstacles of my own philosophical background, beyond which I had gradually to see my way. There followed a good many years of growing acceptance, closeness, and attachment. And this closeness was further heightened by the experience of teaching him, of putting him across over the resistances of students, having to recreate his meanings for them when they had, and perhaps fortunately in some ways, no English translation available. Nothing brings one closer to a thinker than to share his meanings with other people.

It was above all this experience of teaching him that added a vivid and adventurous note to our relationship. Over the years one found sympethetic students, and here for a philosophy text I had a singularly adventurous work to share with them. *Being and Time* had a dramatic story and a hero, Dasein, who went through some very powerful and moving experiences. 'Dasein' is Heidegger's word for human being — the being that each of us is in his or her own separate fashion. Since the word has such powerful connotations in German, we did not translate it, and in time used it as easily as if we were speaking of a familiar character in a novel. Dasein's story is this: He is thrown into the world, and loses himself in its various external trivia; but through the encounter with death, in the light of his own extreme possibility that death discloses to him, he may rise to the level of an authentic existence. He may even become aware of the unique and authentic sense in which his existence is historical, and so play a free and authentic part in the historical mission of his time. Since the class was in philosophy, it was not enough to follow this story; one also had to contrive and explore situations not in the text. 'What would Dasein do in such-and-such a case?' 'How does Dasein feel about so-and-so?' There were jokes attempted and made, of course, but our purpose was not flippant; we were talking in an easy and familiar way about someone who seemed to have become, in our imagination at least, a mutual friend. And so I continued in this happy state of companionship with the author and his character for a number of years.

And then I woke up one morning with a very disturbing feeling that there was, after all, something strangely empty about this Dasein. I did not try at first to wrestle intellectually with this feeling; the words that expressed it came spontaneously and forced themselves upon me, and they were these: 'Dasein has no soul.' To some philosophic sophisticates this may seem to simpleminded, or should we say simplehearted, reaction; but even now I find no more concise and compelling way in which to put my judgment. Nor was the feeling dispelled by the fact that I knew, and had known long since, the formal reasons against it: Heidegger's analysis is not intended to give us the actual person but only the structure of possibilities within which each of us has to enact his own finite and mortal drama of enlightenment. Even with allowance made for that self-imposed limitation, the same sense of a final emptiness seemed to stare back at me from Heidegger's text. Nor did it help that I chose to keep this feeling to myself before the class. They would have been confused, and I felt I could not then spell out for them clearly enough the source of my uneasiness. My task, after all, was to enlist their sympathy in the philosopher so that they might extract whatever insight they could from his text. To have placed this grave doubt, and one so inchoately formulated at that, before them would have immediately abolished every willing suspension of their disbelief and seriously undermined the rest of my pedagogical efforts. I chose therefore to hug my guilty secret to myself.

So I come at last to disburden myself of it here, and with the premonitory misgiving that I shall not probably produce any clearer statement than those instinctive words with which it originally forced itself upon me. For myself, I would prefer to leave it at that — that Dasein has no soul — trusting that there are still some uncorrupted readers around who will find such a judgment perfectly understandable. But philosophers distrust such instinctive responses; we are trained to distrust them, and so well sometimes that we lose, alas, the capacity for them. And so, in this professional capacity, the rest of this chapter will struggle to find reasons for a response that came spontaneously and will probably persist spontaneously whatever the reasons I shall give.

II

We may as well begin with the theme of death, since we have already alluded to this, and it also happens that some of Heidegger's boldest and most powerful pages are on this subject.

Philosophically, the key ideas here are those of actuality and potentiality. From an impersonal and public point of view, death is an actual event that happens every day in the world. We read about it in obituaries: It is something that happens to other people. To be sure, in the course of things it will happen to me, but not yet. As an actual event, or an event that will be actual sometime in the future, it is thus external to my existence now. But everything is changed if we shift our gaze from actuality to potentiality. My death will never be an actual event within my world; I will not be there to read my own obituary. This death, *my* death, the death that haunts me is the possibility that I shall lose that world. And as such an internal possibility, it pervades my existence now and at every moment. To be sure, it is the most extreme and absolute possibility, becasue it cancels all other possibilities. Yet if we do not turn away in panic, this vision of our radical finitude brings its own liberation. Free for our death, we are freed from the tyranny of petty worries and diversions, and thus open to the authentic self that beckons to us.

The thinking is straightforward, powerful, and cogent; and yet we get the feeling that something essential has been left out. What? It is not unusual to teach this part of Heidegger side by side with Tolstoi's great story *The Death of Ivan Ilyich*. Heidegger himself had learned from Tolstoi, and gives a footnote of approval to the latter for describing the breakdown of those impersonal structures with which we and society conceal the truth of death from ourselves. Placed side by side, Tolstoi's story and Heidegger's dissection form a powerful and corroborative parallel — up to a point; for in the end there is a whole world of difference between them. And this difference is not merely the greater immediacy of the artist's language, for Heidegger's existential analysis has a potent expressiveness of its own. The difference is the absence of the moral dimension from Heidegger's account. What, after all, is the transforming experience of death for Ivan Ilyich apart from the moral revulsion that assails him for the life he has led? That life, which had seemed 'normal' and acceptable to himself and his social peers, now shows itself to have been selfish, empty, vain, and therefore meaningless; and with this there comes also the vision of another and very different way in which men ought to live. That is the truth, the disclosure, the *Aletheia*, that the imminence of death brings with it. Heidegger's existential analysis makes explicit an ontological structure implicit in Tolstoi's story, but leaves out the moral message at its center. What we get is the anatomical skeleton of an organism without its beating heart.

To be free toward one's death? That is easier said than done. For the man who loves life, death looms as the supreme injustice. To submit to this injustice out of a sullen and stubborn stoicism is one thing; admirable perhaps, but not a reconciliation. To become genuinely reconciled, to assent to death as no longer unjust, is an infinitely farther step. That requires a leap as great as the medieval assent to Dante's inscription over the gate of Hell. 'Divine Love made me.' To be free toward one's death would require a conversion of the whole person, a transformation of heart and will. It could hardly be accomplished by the intellectual shift to viewing death as an internal possibility rather than an external actuality.

Tolstoi's is the case of the passionately religious mind struggling to make sense of the reality of death. But even for the passionately irreligious, where the confrontation with death is defiant, the moral will plays a central role. The nihilist or criminal, who sets his life at a pin's fee, is able to carry his pride and courage with him to the end only because he has taken up a certain stance toward life. He has established his style and he is morally bound to its gestures. He will play out his role to the end. Damning his executioners, he goes defiantly to the guillotine, like the antihero of Camus in *The Stranger*. The encounter with death remains the supreme adventure to test the moral will. No man dies freely save in affirmation of the values he attaches to life.

III

If we are liberated at all by death, it is in virtue of the light that it sheds on our human situation. Heidegger's theme throughout is this drama of truth and untruth, for which the pathos of our human lot only supplies the occasions. Indeed, his doctrine of truth — of the intrinsic connection of truth with Being, in the sense of evident presence — is his great and original contribution to philosophy. Yet even here, in the phenomenon of truth itself, do we find the will altogether absent? Let us see.

Freedom, he tells us, is the essence of truth. This does not, of course, mean that our will is free to legislate arbitrarily what is true or false. 'Essence' here signifies the ground — the condition that makes a particular phenomenon possible. We have to be free to let the things in question show themselves as they are. But of course, we say, everyone knows this; and so this thesis, which first struck us as paradoxical, might seem to be an idle platitude.

But viewed historically, far from being an innocuous commonplace, Heidegger's point is in fact an ambitious impeachment of the modern age and its doctrine of truth by conquest and rape. Francis Bacon proclaimed the coming time when mankind would put nature to the rack in order to compel her to answer our questions. Yet, however we twist her, we would still have to be free to listen to the answers that poor tortured nature gives us. And if we follow Kant, who says the same thing as Bacon in more gentle and reasonable words — that knowledge must organize our experience within the framework of certain categories and concepts — we have still to let experience, so organized, speak for what it is. More than this: We have to take the step backward and let that framework itself be seen for what it is.

This last step is one of the most difficult things to do, and scientists in this respect are as humanly imperfect as the rest of us. The history of science abounds in cases of scientists who cling tenaciously to their pet theory, refuse to be dislodged from it, twist facts to fit into it, or remain resolutely blind to whatever facts resist such twisting. The pet theory has become such an ingrained part of their vision of things that they cannot see it for what it is because they are always seeing everything else through it.

We suffer from the same willfulness in our ordinary life. Our traffic with other human beings is an endless tale of the obstacles we set before our seeing things as they are. We are all capable of a quite devastating perversity of will in distorting the situations we encounter daily. A man may go through life side by side with people whom he never sees truthfully and whose real relationship to himself remains hidden. He believes he loves when he really hates, hates when he loves, and alternately makes too much or too little of either. Se we go on in our blindness, twisting and distorting and obscuring what is so palpably there if we could only give up our hysterical meddling.

We begin to tread here on the familiar terrain of the psychoanalyst, to whom we may leave his own particular means of curing the cancer. Without intruding on the details of the clinic, we would only note in passing that whatever cure comes — and perhaps we should better say improvement, for our mortal condition never permits us to be totally cured of untruth — it does not come through the patient's acquisition of psychoanalytic theory. He could just as well have stayed home, read books, and spared himself the considerable expense of psychoanalysis. No; the significant changes come deeper down, though our intellectual views may also change in consequence. The patient comes to feel differently about the world, about himself and other people, and as a consequence he will see things differently.

No doubt, our vocabulary must be halting when we try to get close to this central region of the self where the great transformations occur; and we have learned little from Heidegger if we were merely to fall back upon some stock antithesis of will and intellect. The will — this volitional part of ourselves — is not to be understood as a mere organ of drives and blind desires. On the contrary, the will carries in itself its own enlightenment or darkness, as the case may be; and we move within this light and darkness in the most ordinary traffic of daily life. Freedom is not to be sought as a localized property that inhabits the will the way strength resides in our muscles. It does not show itself in some singular and violent leap, like an extraordinary feat of strength. Our freedom is the way in which we are able to let the world open before us and ourselves stand open within it. Our loves and hates disclose or conceal the world in this or that way. Far from being blind 'affects,' to which the intellect alone adds its light, they carry their own light within themselves. But this will is also a moral will; and not in the sense that we tack on 'values' and 'imperatives' that are extraneous to it; it is a moral will at its very source, in and of itself, for in its light we are called upon to bear ourselves thus and so within the world.

Clearly, the most important thing for us at this stage of history, according to the gospel of Heidegger, is to learn to let be. His word for this condition is *Gelassenheit*, which he uses also as a title of a slight but beautifully evocative dialogue that he devotes to this subject. How to translate *Gelassenheit*? Release, deliverance, self-surrender, the peace that passeth understanding? Perhaps we might remember Eliot's line,

Teach me to care and not to care,

to express the consummation of the self in selflessness that Heidegger's word intends. But however we translate it, *Gelassenheit* is central to the whole of the later Heidegger, and our natural human inclination is to ask how we may achieve it. We have to be will-less, but we cannot will to be will-less. And Heidegger leaves the matter at that.

But we cannot leave it at that. For we would be left with the quite paradoxial position that the human will, as willfulness, leads us into untruth; yet we cannot say that the will, in its positive and opposed sense, is in any way the source of truth. If we cannot will to be will-less, at least there should be something we can *do* about our willful condition. Otherwise we are left the helpless prisoners of our own perverse will to power.

We are caught in the old theological puzzle of grace and freedom. We cannot will the advent of grace, for we have to surrender the will if grace is to come at all; but how can we surrender this obstinate and perverse will unless grace itself enables us to do so? Perhaps we cannot penetrate farther into this mystery than the old theologians did, but at least we should go as far — we should not fall below their level. The traditional religions come to our aid with their ritual practices or codes of behavior that might possibly prepare the will for deliverance. For, contrary to many philosophers, Wittgenstein included, we can set about changing our will, and sometimes succeed, through the roundabout course of action. In any case, no workable religion can send us away empty-handed; there must always be something, humanly speaking, that we can do, though success (grace) is not assured. But this realm of the pragmatic does not concern Heidegger; the connection between Being and doing is not a central preoccupation, and attracts his attention chiefly in those situations where our frantic doing involves a loss of Being. The self-surrender, the *Gelassenheit*, that interests him is not the peace that might attend us as we set about an ordinary moral task — in the doing of which sometimes indeed the release of love may be born. He is drawn instead to the exalted rapture that may come to us in a walk through the woods or over a country path, and which, if we were poets, we could turn into a lyric poem.

What emerges here is the distinction between our ethical and our aesthetic existence, and the voice of Kierkegaard warning us against the aesthete suddenly sounds in the background. I do not wish to urge that distinction as Kierkegaard made it   I am not sure it is altogether satisfactory as he does make it — but I believe his point cannot be evaded. In the end, these two — Kierkegaard and Heidegger   are the ultimate antagonists. [1]

IV

To be sure, the concern with poetry is not an 'aesthetic' luxury to Heidegger, but a necessary and fulfilling step in his philosophic thought. In the technical era, when everything becomes an instrument at the service of the will, language is manipulated as a calculus. Poetry resists this will and thereby reveals a more fundamental dimension of language. Before the poem one must lay down one's self-assertion; one has to surrender onseself and enter the same circle of Being where poem and poet dwell. Thus the date 1936, when he published the first of his essays on the poet Hölderlin, is taken to mark the celebrated 'turn' in Heidegger's thinking, though this turn is not so much a reversal as a fulfillment, a direct step into what lay behind his earlier analyses of human existence.

We can understand then why poetry should be so central a subject for Heidegger. But why has he made Hölderlin his chosen poet? Heidegger himself voices the question. Why has he not chosen to explore the nature of poetry through some other more famous poet, Homer or Sophocles, Virgil or Dante, Shakespeare or Goethe? The immediate answer he gives is that Hölderlin writes about the poetic calling itself — poetizes about the nature of poetry — and we may therefore gather that nature more directly from him. But the deeper and the real reason for the choice follows a little later: Hölderlin is a prophet of our time, the 'time of need,' when the old gods have fled and the new god has not arrived. Standing between two worlds, he is the poet who speaks out of this void, and therefore Heidegger finds in him his spiritual kin.

All the same, he is a strange affinity, this Hölderlin, one of the greatest and loneliest of poets. Born in 1770 — the birthdate, as it happens, of Beethoven and Hegel — Hölderlin was part of the most brilliant and productive generation of Germans, but also was to undergo a sadder fate than any of his contemporaries. Toward the year 1802, when he was only thirty-two, he began to show signs of derangement, and by the end of 1804 had become incurably insane. The last thirty-six years of his life he spent as an amiable and harmless lunatic, being cared for in the household of a local carpenter and doing odd jobs as a gardener. Until we know enough about schizophrenia to settle such questions, we may continue to wonder in these cases of genius, as with Nietzsche too, whether the vision provoked the madness or was merely a consequence of it. With Hölderlin, in any case, the illness and the vision seem to go side by side. As the shadow darkens over the poet, the poems themselves become more daring, disconnected, schizoid — more 'modernist' in manner, as one critic aptly puts it. The great hymns are like magnificent and shining blocks of ice that detach themselves from a continent and float off into an empty sea.

And so our question persists: What if Heidegger had chosen another figure, a Dante or Shakespeare, as the paradigm poet from which to explicate the nature of poetry? Would not poetry itself look different to us then, and the will emerge as one of its themes? 'Hölderlin and the Essence of Poetry' was the first Heidegger I ever read, more then thirty years ago, and the question has never since left my mind. Why not Shakespeare or Dante indeed? With them the human person does not vanish into an empty presence. Here are real human agents, embodiments of the will in its sublime as well as its atrocious shapes — not the technical will, to be sure, but the moral will for good and evil. The antithesis to Hölderlin is, of course, Dante, and *The Divine Comedy* can be read as the great poem of the will in its various stages: the congealed will, fixed in its perversity, of the *Inferno*; the laboring and yearning will of the *Purgatorio*, and in the *Paradiso* the consummation of the will in prayer. In Hölderlin the voice of prayer sounds from beginning to end, but it is prayer that, finding no effective relation to the will, drifts off like a cloud thinning out into the void. For myself, I find Dante's Hell less terrifying than the alpine air of some of Hölderlin's poems. At least the damned are intensely alive in their perverted will, while Hölderlin's world rarefies off into the frightening and thin air of holy schizophrenia.

But Heidegger is able to look past these human aspects of Hölderlin and his poems that disquiet us. Is Heidegger humanly insensitive here? In any case, he is protected by the detachment of his philosophic calling. Intent on the single theme of Being, he has to look past our human pathology. He is guarded and protected by the thought he patiently builds. 'Poet and thinker are near akin,' Heidegger tells us; and perhaps they are, in the themes that preoccupy them, but in this particular case they are very different individuals with very different spiritual needs. One compares the philosopher going on into his seventh and eighth decades, serenely elaborating his meditation, with the youthful poet who succumbed in his early thirties. Heidegger writing about nothingness is the lucid and detached phenomenologist analyzing a datum. Hölderlin sounds a different note when he laments the fate of mankind that has lost its gods and is caught

In the grip of that Nothing which rules over us, who are thoroughly aware that we are born for Nothing, believe in Nothing, work ourselves to the bone for Nothing, until we gradually dissolve into Nothing ...

This is the voice of the actual man, not merely observing but also living through an anguish for which he must find a more sovereign remedy than philosophic meditation.

Is Being enough? Hölderlin evidently did not think so. Though he was caught in its grip and utters its encompassing presence more purely, if thinly, than any other poet, it could not sustain him. In search of the holy, he set off on the track of the fugitive god. Since the Christian god was no longer able to work for him, he sought to raise the antique gods to life again — an impossible task, as the Greeks themselves might have told him. After his first breakdown, which was brought on by overexposure to the sun on a trip through the South of France, he wrote to a friend that he had been stricken by the shafts of Apollo. It was really the absence of Apollo that finally struck him down.

The enchantment with Hellas has been one of the most profound but also of the most questionable features of the German spirit since the eighteenth century. The German interpreters of the Greeks number among them some of their greatest figures — Winckelmann, Goethe, Lessing, Schiller, Hölderlin, Nietzsche; and now Heidegger himself must be allowed to enter that august circle. We do not doubt the greatness of these interpreters; what we question is how much of this infatuation with Hellas has been prompted by romantic longing, by a nostalgia for a simpler and more vital stage of the human spirit; and how much of it, in consequence, tends to an 'aestheticizing' of the Greeks. We lose their reality for the dazzling image of them we would erect. But of all these German interpreters of the Greeks, Heidegger tells us, the greatest was Hölderlin. Why? Because he alone tried to take the gods of the Greeks seriously. But what is it then to take a god seriously?

I sat once on one of the stone seats of the theater of Dionysos at Athens, the relentless blue sky overhead and the sacred hill of the city beyond me, and tried to imagine myself two millennia earlier sitting as a spectator before a drama of Aeschylus or Sophocles. What was the response of the ordinary citizen of Athens to these plays? As I sat there, I began to have a sense of identity with that unknown whose place I now held. He is the forgotten man among all the interpretations, brilliant and varied as they have been, that we moderns have concocted of Greek drama. We have had the youthful Nietzsche expounding them in terms of Schopenhauer's metaphysics; Freudian interpretations under the leading idea of the Oedipus complex; and latterly Heideggerian readings of the Greek plays as the drama of revelation (*Aletheia*) and hiddenness. However stimulating to us, these interpretations inevitably pass that ordinary spectator by. As moderns, we come to the drama as literature and thus as part of our intellectual and aesthetic culture. But the city that put Socrates to death on suspicion that he taught against the gods would not have dug into the public till to sponsor performances that explore the intellectual themes that interest *us*. These dramas are 'morality plays,' as directly and completely so as the medieval morality plays, though the morality they teach, to be sure, is very different from the Christian one. Sophocles and Aeschylus are partisans of the gods, perpetually warning their audience that the power and prescience of the god is not to be discounted even when the course of events in the play seems to be eluding his prophecy. The long 'theological' debate that rounds out Aeschylus' cycle of the *Oresteia* strikes us on our first reading as prosaic, tedious, and altogether 'undramatic'; and it takes on life for us only as we acquire a scholarly interest in Greek religion. To the Athenian contemporary, however, these theological debates were supremely dramatic, since on their successful resolution depended the preservation of the city and its laws, and consequently the well-being of the citizens themselves.

The religious morality of the Greek bound him to the cosmos in its actual and local presence, to his city and region (*Polis* and *Chora*) in a way that Jewish and Christian faith were to terminate. If we sigh for these Greek gods, it is the dream of alienated men hankering to come home. We begin then to fancy that to the Greek his religion was only an aesthetic affair of beautiful images fashioned by sculptors and poets. When they are alive, however, these gods create *obligations*. They bind the moral will of the worshiper to their service.

Our era is the night of the world, Heidegger mournfully echoes Hölderlin, when the old gods have fled but the new god has not yet arrived. Perhaps. But what are we supposed to *do* during this sullen interregnum? In his interview with the magazine *Der Spiegel*, published only after his death, Heidegger declared against us and our civilization. 'Only a God will save you.' He too seems to have come around at last to believe that Being is not enough. But do we merely wait around until this unknown god strikes us like a bolt from the blue? This is to surrender too much to a kind of historicism, in the manner of Hegel, as if the prevailing climate of opinion were to decide our possible salvation. The individual who needs God will seek Him out, whatever the fashion of his age.

Heidegger is too great and restless a mind to remain chained to the mechanical rhetoric of 'the death of God.' He grumbles against the critics of his godlessness: Perhaps his 'godless thinking' is closer to the divine God than is philosophic theism, and he castigates the aridity and abstractness of the philosophic deity:

> Man can neither pray nor sacrifice to this god. Before the *causa sui*, man can neither fall to his knees in awe, nor play music nor dance.

Three centuries earlier, Pascal made a similar point: 'Not the God of the philosophers,' he cried, 'but the God of Abraham, Isaac, and Jacob.' But what a world of difference here from Heidegger, for this God of the Jews does not come to us through 'thinking' — not even that 'piety of thought' that Heidegger, mixing religious and intellectual vocabularies, recommends to us. We come to Him in faith, by a surrender of the will. And this God is perhaps more tenacious of life than Heidegger's historical scheme imagines. As the deity of a nomad people, He is not confined to his local shrines and natural sites, like the gods of the Greeks, but may still hunt us down in our modern homelessness. There are still those who pray through the Psalms of David; I know of no one who worships through a choral ode of Sophocles or Aeschylus. If I worship by means of a psalm, it has been something much less and much more than a poem. The living God binds me morally in my flesh and spirit. The ode of Aeschylus remains alive to me, through aesthetic appropriation, only as a great poem. Hölderlin knew he had come too late for those antique gods and he expired in the emptiness of his vision.

V

We come back to the moral will as the center of the human person. But in the history of thought, as in life, we never come back exactly to the point where we were and find ourselves unchanged. We are different as we return, and part of that difference has been made by Heidegger.

The moral will as our human center! How disappointing a message this must sound to our modern ears! How odd and simpleminded it seems against all the complex and sophisticated currents of modernity that have run the other way! But above all, how tame a cause this is to argue, how prosaic and stodgy, how positively hackneyed and old-hat! Ours has been an age of sensational discoveries, and if anyone is to bring us a message, we expect it to be revolutionary and spectacular, something that sets all our previous world by its ears. Intellectually we seem to have developed a fear of the commonplace and the truth that may reside there. So the very modesty of the message we seek may be after all a sign of its importance for us. And we have to insist on this modesty if we are to keep this moral will clear of the seductions of the will to power in any of its numerous disguises. The pervasiveness of this will to power throughout modern thought and modern life is one great lesson from Heidegger — so that he serves, even if he has avoided the matter of ethics, as something of a moral teacher after all. Whatever dominance we come to have over beings, we have in the end to bow before the mystery of Being. There, if at no other point, we have to learn to let be or else the tyrant will becomes its own slave. This saving grain of acquiescence is needed to preserve the moral will from the demon of its own earnestness, to restrain it from becoming overassertive of its own claims, so that it does not succumb to the temptations of hypocrisy or priggishness. In its modesty it will have enough to to in the days to come simply to keep alive the elementary decencies without which human civilization relapses into the jungle and human beings lose their meaning.

And perhaps it is just in this resistance to power in the world today that this moral will may bring a central message for our time. What else is the burden of Solzhenitsyn's life and writings? We may read his books as political reportage on the Soviet Union or to satisfy our sociological curiosity about the strange hierarchies of survival in the prison camps. But their deeper story is something else. They are above all moral documents — the story of a whole population struggling against the corruption forced upon them by a political regime. To survive under that regime is to practice continual duplicity, treachery toward one's neighbor, and to develop a brutal callousness toward life generally. And the miracle is that the moral will still survives in this people; that there are individuals who carry on the struggle for no more heroic reason than to stay decent — above all, 'not to become a scoundrel.' If dictatorship should become the wave of the future, then the doctrine of the moral will may not be so tame a thing after all; it might in fact have a genuine revolutionary content.

Our return to the moral will, however, is not a mechanical return to the doctrine of Kant. We have to burrow into the foundations that Kant, unknown to himself, really took for granted. He sought to make the sphere of the moral an autonomous and purely rational affair. The principles of ethics were to be certified on their intrinsic formal grounds alone. But are they really autonomous? Here Kant juggles in most legalistic fashion: yes and no. The laws of ethics are formally complete in themselves, but somehow he must tack on the assumptions of God and immortality. Practical reason, he tells us, if it is to be completely rational, must add the postulates of God and immortality. In short, it would be silly to practice the Kantian morality of duty if you did not also have faith in God or immortality. It required very little of Nietzsche to turn this about, and quite logically to point out that if you disbelieved in God and the immortality of the soul, then on purely rational grounds you would develop a different morality altogether. No; the moral will is not an autonomous function reigning in splendid and sovereign isolation. Man is a being in the world, if we remember our Heidegger; and each part of our being is caught up in our other multiple involvements with the world. For Kant these were the theism of his time and place. The Christian will, and its faith, has been there from the start in Kant's thinking. It is not the case in the Kantian system, as is commonly said, that 'Reason has to make room for faith,' as if the latter, once a place was made for it, slipped in independently. That faith is present and operant throughout the whole of the moral edifice that Kant constructs. Unknown to him, child of the Age of Reason that he was, he is as much a case of *fides quaerens intellectum* (faith seeking to elaborate itself intellectually), as the medieval St. Anselm, who coined that saying. And behind Anselm lies Augustine, as he also lies at a farther and less recognized distance behind Kant. The Kantian good will, which wills to submit itself to the moral law, is a descendant of the *voluntas*, the will in St. Augustine, which is restless until it rests in God.

Does our moral life then rest on a faith of some kind? Or to put the matter more pointedly, could we as existing individuals have the strength and courage to persist in our moral striving if we did not have a faith of some kind? And what kind of a faith, at the least, would it have to be? These are the ultimate questions to which the problem of freedom leads us.

52

NOTES

*   This has been published as Chapter Twelve of *The Illusion of Technique*, Garden City, New York: Anchor Press/Doubleday, 1978.
1   Kierkegaard makes the distinction between the aesthetic and ethical stages turn on the key notions of actuality and possibility, and the relative roles these play in our life.

The aesthete is in thrall to the lures of the possible. The actual person or situation with which he has to deal interests him only to the extent that his imagination can invest it with poetical possibilities. And if he is driven to move on restlessly, like Don Juan, from one woman to another, it is because he is in pursuit of the image of the Ideal Woman, a possibility that actual possession can never supply. In a less gross form, the aesthete emerges as the detached intellectual who seeks to contemplate actual existence as a purely aesthetic spectacle. The existing individual case, for this purely contemplative mind, is interesting only as it may be an instance of some possible universal or law.

The ethical man, on the contrary, is wedded to the individual and actual. The gritty, the humdrum, the ordinary reality of life are what he takes upon himself to live with and redeem if he can. And if he does find redemption, it is as this actual individual – this body, this flesh and blood, this spirit – who he is.

Now, on its surface, Heidegger's analysis of human existence might seem deeply ethical. His key terms are ones that normally have ethical connotations: care, solicitude, conscience, guilt, resolve, authenticity, and inauthenticity. Yet he himself has warned us against taking these in any explicit moral sense. His warning, however, seems to have fallen on deaf ears in the case of some avid but naïve Heideggerians who persist in trying to read *Being and Time* as if it were a moral tract. One would think that after the counter-culture of the 1960s it should be sufficiently clear to almost everyone that terms like 'authentic' and 'inauthentic' have no definite moral content at all.

The fact is that if we try to read *Being and Time* as an ethical work, we only come up with a parody of the ethical – a parody, moreover, that reveals itself as transparently aesthetic, in Kierkegaard's pejorative sense of that word.

Consider, for exemple, the matter of conscience:

Heidegger deals with this subject only as it illustrates the way in which Being and Nonbeing are woven inseparably together into the fabric of our human reality. He projects before us the instance of human being lost in the anonymity of its public and external roles, for whom somehow, and from somewhere, amid this drift of impersonality, the voice of conscience sounds. Who speaks in this call of conscience, and to whom? A self that is *not yet*, a more authentic self that is to be, calls to a self that, in its sheer diffuseness and anonymity, does not properly exist. A negativity calls to a negativity. And yet something significant has happened, for we become different in our being insofar as a new and different *possibility* of being beckons to us.

As a strictly ontological dissection of the peculiar enmeshment of possibility and actuality, of nonbeing and being, that we are, Heidegger's analysis here is both powerful and acute. But let us consider a living instance in its specifically *moral* aspect:

I have done something wrong: I have thoughtlessly hurt someone I love. (I am in fact thinking of an actual incident, which even now, twenty years later, still rankles). What overwhelms me here is the sheer particularity of the situation itself and my deed: that it was *I*, and no one else, who did *that* particular thing to *that* particular individual; and the grief and pain on the face of the beloved one whom I have wounded becomes my own pain in turn. No doubt, I shall resolve not to do anything like this again; and in that respect I am already differently oriented toward the future. But if I rush to such generalization; and if I take my juggling with concepts to convey the heart of what I have been through, then I have hardly felt very deeply at all. Unless I have been transfixed, as by a spear, by the particularity of that act, of the particular wrong I have done to that actual individual then I still remain as humanly and morally insensitive and callous as, unsuspected by myself

I had been before my treachery.

Now, let us imagine some young man, who, crammed to the full of Heidegger, has gone through such an experience and attempts to assay it in the master's terms. (Yes, I was almost, but thankfully not quite, that young man.) He is smitten by conscience, but what does this voice of conscience tell him? It speaks of the authentic self that may issue from this troubled incident. But what meaning has such authenticity if he has not been stung by the sheer moral wrongness of his act? The pain and suffering of the other person vanish before this narcissistic self-absorption in the self that he may become. I think we should find this young man's posture both offensive and ludicrous at once — the posture of the aesthete who stands at a distance from the actual experience and contemplates it simply as a stage in his self-development. And I think we should have to say too that so far as moral feelings are concerned, his conscience has really remained untouched after all.

With these matters of moral sensibility, with conscience as a strictly moral pheno- menon, Heidegger does not deal. His analysis moves in another and different dimension altogether; and to attempt to read *Being and Time* as a phenomenology of the moral con- sciousness is to produce something grotesque and monstrous.

2 *Being and Time* begins with a deliberate and audacious reversal of the whole Western tradition on the relation of the actual and possible: '*Possibility is higher than actuality.*' It is important to see why and how far this reversal can be carried through.

The Western tradition, from the first, grasped Being in terms of actuality and reality. What is, after all, is what is the case: what is real and actual. The German word for actua- lity, *Wirklichkeit*, connotes also that which is efficacious and urgent. Thus, Being is taken to signify what is real, actual, and urgent, in contrast to what is fictitious, merely possible, or of indifferent efficacy. But 'real' comes from the Latin *res*, which means 'thing'; and, accordingly, this Western understanding of Being had become too exclusively confined to the being of things.

And whether the things in question were taken as objects or subjects, depending on whether one was a materialist or idealist, Being was still understood as thing-being: the being of a thing.

It was against this exclusive notion of Being that Heidegger set out on his philosophic journey. Our human being, our ordinary concrete existence, cannot be grasped as the simple being of a thing. The axiom of traditional metaphysics had been: Actuality is prior to po- tentiality. The knife — to use Aristotle's example — has the potentiality of cutting because of its actual properties are what they are, and its potentialities derive therefrom. But that very peculiar being, the human being, is not a simple utensil or thing like a knife. Possi- bility and actuality are woven more intimately within the web of our human being. We are what we are through the horizon of possibilities that lies open to us. And Heidegger went on to make brilliant use of this insight to illumine the human condition in the light of certain regions of being in which we dwell or from which we are shut off.

But the thinker who challenges the tradition is bound to lose in the end. If he is great enough, however, his victory will have been to modify the tradition before it rolls back over him to correct his own onesided emphasis and strike a new balance. After Heidegger, the no- tions of the actual and possible cannot be universally invoked again with the same simplicity as when they are applied to things like utensils and tools. Nevertheless, his own formula 'Possibility is higher than actuality' belongs to his earlier thinking; and he never returned to qualify it in the light of his later themes. And now, having learned from him to acknowledge 'the silent power of the possible,' we have to come back in the end to give actuality its due priority. ...

The presence of this day, in which you and I are now, cannot be reduced to the things and objects encountered within it. But if this day opens as a field of possibility, it also encloses us within its definite horizon. It is *this* day and no other — a day that may call me to some decision or action that I cannot postpone. And if I lose it, I have lost part of my life forever. '*Temps le pressant*,' James Joyce puns: 'Time the pressing.' And he is right:

The present is also the pressing.

Finally, it is with question of cosmic Being that the issue of actuality becomes most crucial. The existence of the universe itself is the ultimate actuality with which thinking has to be engaged. That the world is, that there is anything at all rather than nothing – this is the supreme miracle and mystery, and also the supreme actuality within which our own existence has been cast. Here we face the fact of the All, the One, the unique and singular existence, as it was confronted by the ancient Parmenides; and the question of Being becomes perforce cosmological in its sweep. Heidegger brings us only to the threshold but does not enter into this cosmic question of Being.

Since Heidegger's thinking deliberately moves in certain ways parallel to Kant's, comparison with the latter becomes particularly relevant here. Thus Heidegger has written two books on Kant, as if checking his own progress at each stage by a backward look at the master; and each book, in turn, mirrors his own preoccupations at that step in his development. But these two books take us only through the first two parts of Kant's *Critique of Pure Reason*: the transcendental Aesthetic and the Analytic. There is no third book on the third and consummating part of the Kantian work, the Transcendental Dialectic, in which Kant deals with the enigmas to which cosmic Being gives rise: questions about the universe as a whole and the existence of God. Heidegger does not deal explicitly with these questions; at best there are two or three pages in his late essay *Identity and Difference* that touch on the question of the One, and that may be why he considered this little work the most important step in his thinking since *Being and Time*. But these few pages are only a faint beginning. Thus the absence of a third book on Kant corresponds to a real gap in Heidegger's thought.

And this gap consequently appears in his description of human existence, and particularly the moral aspect of our human condition. For these ultimate questions about the cosmos and God, as Kant rightly insists, are a part of our human nature that we cannot escape. We exist within these questions that reason cannot answer; and indeed the deepest part of our existence is involved with them. The man who says, 'I am going to die, and what meaning, then, has my life?' is asking in the same breath: 'What meaning has this world, this cosmos, in which I came to be?'

In short, the question of God remains unasked in Heidegger, however he may prepare *us* to set about asking the question anew. And for those who believe, with Kant, that our moral existence is inseparable from this question, this absence in Heidegger is one more reason for finding that his thought never finally arrives at the ethical after all.

LANDSCAPE

MARJORIE GRENE

The distinction between landscape and geography constitutes one of several major contributions made by Erwin Straus to the elucidation of lived spatiality and hence also to philosophical anthropology and in particular to the explication of the global conception of being-in-the-world. What I want to do here is first to remind you of this distinction, and then to consider its bearing on the concept of being-in as one might interpret it in the spirit of Straus' work in contrast to Heidegger's treatment of the 'in' of being-in-the world. The central issue in such a comparison is the question of the role of the lived body in existence. Straus had criticized Heidegger's treatment of the body in his essay on 'Philosophy and Psychiatry.' I could predict, I think, how faithful Heideggerians would respond to some of the points he makes; but the chief criticism is a clear, and, in my view, cogent one. Heidegger claims that one can deal adequately with *Leiblichkeit* in terms of Daseinsanalysis; he just isn't interested. Is this correct? Or, if one lays fundamental stress on the body at the start of one's account of being-in-the-world, has one made a move toward a philosophy of the person in part at least incompatible with Heidegger's? If this is so, finally, which is the more adequate account of human being? In this brief discussion, I cannot hope to provide a well-grounded answer to this basic question, but it is this issue I am basically concerned with, and I shall try to use the distinction between landscape and geography as a starting point from which to approach it.

Landscape is where I dwell, as distinct from geography, which locates me, or any one or any thing, in terms of an objective framework constituted by science as well as by common sense, which means, for most of us, common sense as mediated by science and technology. Granted that I don't have to be a sailor or a scientist in order to have some grasp of latitude and longitude. Yet I must have grown up in a society acquainted with the rudiments of the modern discipline of geography. On the other hand, everyone inhabits a landscape. To take an example: I was living in rural Ireland when Irish U.N. troops were sent to the Congo, and someone asked me, 'Mrs. Grene, is Congo in Belgium?' I was able to answer this question even though I'm so bad at geography that I once drew a free-hand map of the Mohammedan empire leaving no room for the Arabian peninsula. Still I do know a *little* about the subject, while my questioner had no conception of it at all. Yet she was, and is still, much more firmly rooted in a landscape than I have ever been. After a year or two working in an English factory, alongside other Irish laborers, she married one of these from her home village, and now lives in the council cottage where her late mother-in-law used to wash the family clothes by candlelight. Landscape, in this sense of inhabited place, it must be emphasized, moreover, has no connection with a sentimental return to 'nature.' It is where one belongs, whether rural or urban, or in any state from rags to riches. A person who has lived all his life in one particular district of Paris is at least as rooted in a landscape as any countryman. In short, landscape is one of the horizons of existence: not the narrowest one, of the lived body, nor yet the broadest, being itself, but somewhere in between. Geography, in contrast, is a frame of reference constituted by modern naturalistic thought. Because we ourselves are who we are as participants in modern western culture, we say that every human being is located geographically as well as in a landscape: every human being is born somewhere, in terms of latitude and longitude, as well as in terms of existence, and dies somewhere measurable geographically, as well as coming to an end as a personal history. But a landscape or a neighborhood is universal to lived existence in a way in which geographical location is not. Geographical location is constituted by objective thought. In terms of Heidegger's Daseinsanalysis it is clearly an aspect of *Vorhandenheit*, indeed, a paradigmatic expression of the Cartesian vision of things as *res extensae*. Is landscape constituted in an analogous way? And if not, what on earth is it (no pun intended)?

Let's see how if at all we could place landscape in Heideggerian terms (in particular, in terms of *Sein und Zeit*). As Straus reminds us in the essay I have already mentioned, Heidegger declares that, ontologically, whatever is not Dasein is to be understood in terms of categories, Dasein, by contrast, through *existentialia*. The categories are *Zuhandenheit* and *Vorhandenheit*. Geography, we have seen, belongs clearly under *Vorhandenheit*. Landscape, in contrast, is not *vorhanden*, spread out like a patient upon a table, but neither is it *zuhanden*. It is not there for use, as his leather and thread are for the cobbler, or her dishwasher for the modern housewife. Landscape is not *Zeug*. But then if landscape *is* neither as *Vorhandenheit* nor as *Zuhandenheit*, it must be an aspect of the being of Dasein. And certainly being-in-a-landscape is an aspect of Being-in. It has to do with spatiality — not the spatiality of what is *vorhanden*, but the more primordial spatiality of Dasein. Borrowing Merleau-Ponty's language, one would want to say that landscape is an aspect of lived spatiality. For Heidegger, however, any reference to 'life' or the 'lived' is privative with respect to Dasein. That's the problem I'll have to return to, at least in passing. The point here is that sptiality in terms of the analysis of *Sein und Zeit* is one of the aspects of being-in-the-world, yet it is not lived, and to call it so would be from Heidegger's point of view a demotion, a privation of a fuller meaning. For the moment, however, we are trying to go along with the Heideggerian analysis. So in his terms we could perhaps speak simply of Dasein's being-in, in a very neutral way, as different from the spatial containment of objects, as in a child's nest of hollow blocks. We could then take Straus's being-in-a-landscape, then, so far, as perhaps an aspect of the being-in of Dasein.

Moreover, we can perhaps make one other connection between Straus's concept of landscape and the being-in of Daseinsanalysis. Of the three fundamental Heideggerian propositions, *in*, *(sich) vorweg*, and *bei, in*, as *schon-Sein-in*, is associated with *Befindlichkeit*, as distinct, though of course not separable, from *Verstehen*. Similarly, one might want to suggest that the way of being-in-a-landscape, as distinct from one's orientation in a geographical locality, is, in Straus's terms, more pathic than gnostic. In-ness, of the neighborhood — or landscape-related — kind, is mood-saturated. It is how one is with things around one affectively, rather than in a cognitive or contemplative style. One doesn't *look* at one's neighborhood as one looks at a landscape to the second degree, a Constable or a Turner. One *is* in it, cozily, routinely, fretfully — usually, in any case, familiarly. So far, Strausian and Heideggerian Being-in seem to have a good deal in common.

But what of the landscape itself, as distinct from the way one is in it — or at least as distinct from this first approximation to the way one is in it? Here things get trickier, and it becomes evident, I think, that the Heideggerian concept of Being-in is not adequate to describe all the dimensions that in fact characterize Being-in-the world.

One might want, for exemple, to take landscape as roughly equivalent to Heidegger's *Gegend*: as neighborhood, the place where Dasein proximally is. In terms of *Sein und Zeit*, as we have seen, this would have to be (1) a tissue of *Zeug*, of the sort through which the worldhood of the world appears, or (2) the same, (mis)understood as merely *Vorhandenes*, and we may also add (3) *Mitdasein* insofar as it too appears within the horizon of the everyday. In thinking about landscape, however, we can omit reference to (3), *i.e.*, to other people. Our question is: what kind of *place* is it we are trying to describe? As we have already seen, neither (1) *Zuhandenkeit* nor (2) *Vorhandenkeit* will help us here. *Vorhandenkeit* is the category that fits geography, but *Zuhandenkeit* with the *Zeug* whose way of being it describes, is inadequate for landscape. Indeed, this is quite clear from Heidegger's own description of *Gegend*, a term which does indeed sound as it might be equivalent to landscape. Yet *Gegend*, Heidegger tells us, is the product of *Ent-fernung*, of Dasein's way of bringing beings within the world into its ken, into relation to itself. It is, again, a tissue of *Zeug*, and perhaps *Mitdasein*, produced by Dasein's activity of *Ent-fernen*, in short, a network of human relevances. But landscape is where one dwells in a richer sense; it is one's surroundings, the place where one is at home. Heideggerian spatiality lacks this component; there is simply nowhere to work it in.

If, therefore, being-in-a-landscape is an essential aspect of the milieu of human being, there is at least one such aspect that escapes the net of Heideggerian ontology, as expounded in *Sein und Zeit*. It *may* be that the 'Earth' of *das Geviert* might partly capture such a missing piece. But I doubt it, since in late Heidegger *Dasein* recedes, as it was always meant to do, in favor of *Sein*. Not a more adequate philosophy of the person is what interested late Heidegger, but a more prophetic proclamation of the question of Being. In any case, that's by the way. I am talking about the Daseinsanalysis of *Sein und Zeit* and asking how, there, a concept like Straus's landscape could be accommodated, and my answer is: not at all. There just isn't anywhere in the ontology of *Sein und Zeit* to fit it in.

Why not? I want to suggest two answers, or perhaps, two aspects of one answer. First, in his criticism of *Sein und Zeit* as a ground for therapy, Straus suggested that in addition to categories on the one hand and *existentialia* on the other, one needs *animalia*. Philosophically, there is something a little puzzling about his argument here, since he is addressing the question of the bearing of philosophy on psychiatry, and is introducing, quite rightly, a reference to the biological knowledge that the psychiatrist needs. But as ontologists of human being, as philosophers interested in the nature of the person, we are not concerned, directly at least, with advances in biological knowledge. At the same time, it seems to me, Straus is correct in finding Heidegger in this respect still surprisingly Cartesian. There is the order of the non-human, which is either related, for use, in *Zuhandenkeit*, to human concerns, or demoted to mere being there; and there is the human world, constituted by *our* way of being, but nothing in between — or nothing farther afield? Yet surely the peculiarly human transformation of being-in that Heidegger deals with is just that — a transformation, or transposition, into other terms of a more general way of being that characterizes both people and other animals. It takes no particular knowledge of biology to be aware of that. Human finitude may be as unique as Heidegger makes it out to be — it *is* certainly unique in some way — but it is a uniquely different instance of the finitude common to all that is born and dies. If we start, then, from a perspective that includes *animalia*, perhaps landscape will prove more tractable to our account of being-in-the-world and our way of dwelling in it. Let's try it.

We start, in Straus's fashion, with an I-allon relation common to all animals, if not all living things. Granted that human being-in, the human I-allon relation, is radically altered by the human constitution of symbol systems: yet this is, as I have suggested, a transposition of the more general I-allon relation, and it is from the more inclusive relation that we have to start. In general, then, every animal takes its place in an environment, rises up, as Straus puts it, over against an environment. It is there bodily, within its environment, yet bodily distinct from it. Now at the center of the I-allon relation, obviously, is the lived spatiality of the body itself, just the very incarnate being that Heidegger finds of such minor interest. Second, the proximal horizon of such centrally lived spatiality is the dwelling-place of the living thing in question, be it the fox's lair, the rabbit's burrow, the sailor's ship, or the town-dweller's condominium. Further, a slightly broader horizon of this horizon in turn is precisely the landscape, the general neighborhood where one belongs. I am not sure whether at this point one has crossed the boundary between animal and human. Of course an animal's niche, or its territory if it is territorial, is wider than its lair, den, burrow, nest or what you will. But if so, that is, if we take being-in-a-landscape as still common to all animals, there is also a human version of this dimension of being-in. Thus one can say, I think that one is, humanly, in a landscape somewhat as one is *in* one's mother tongue. And finally, remotest from the lived body in its individuality, yet still inherent in the I-allon relation, is the horizon of being itself, which is present, as Merleau-Ponty put it, as the background roar of a city is present to its inhabitants.

Note, please, however, that all these dimensions of being-in are bodily. The I-allon relation, however broadly or narrowly one takes it, is essentially incarnate. Witness the fact that it is, and must be, mediated by sense. Not for nothing was Straus's major work entitled *On the Sense of the Senses*: it is only through the senses that anything makes sense. Straus's pun on *Sinn* and *Sinn*, like Merleau-Ponty's on *sens* and *sens* — indeed, *sens, sens* and *sens* —, is fundamental to an understanding of the *in* of being-in-a-world. Embodied sensing, moreover, we have in common with all sensitive organisms. To understand the uniqueness of human sensing, and human making sense, with its peculiar artifact-dependence, we need *first* to grasp its rootedness in the I-allon relation as such, in its broader scope. If we put *Leiblichkeit* second, as a mere derivative from existence, we miss, not only the phenomenon of landscape, which I have been focussing on here, but the very ground of being-in-the-world itself. In fact, I would even hazard a guess that Heidegger failed to reach through to Being, as he had hoped to do, precisely because he had begun with a neutral, non-bodily, abstract Dasein. Only through incarnate existence can one reach Being. Hubert Dreyfus once argued, convincingly, that computers have to have bodies in order to be intelligent. Similarly, Dasein has to have a body in order to apprehend, and comprehend, the being of things or places or Being itself. In this respect Merleau-Ponty had started on a sounder course, ontologically, in his unfinished work, than Heidegger in his late writing. Dasein's preontological *Seinsverständnis* remains without development because it cannot make bodily contact with things themselves. True, Heidegger too, in *Sein und Zeit*, had presented a realistic theory of perception; but *how* it is realistic, yet without the dimension of embodiment, is very hard to grasp.

Let me suggest, finally, a reason why Heidegger's Daseinsanalysis may have neglected *Leiblichkeit* and with it not only landscape but a good deal more that is essential to being-in-the-world. Let us look once more at the three prepositions that characterize *Sorge*: *in*, (sich) *vorweg*, and *bei*. Since *Sorge* is to be read as temporality, one is inclined to identify these with the three temporal *ecstases*, past, future, present. But let's think of them for a moment from a different point of view. We have here a threefold unity: a *Dreieinigkeit*, but a *Dreieinigkeit* that is human-all-too-human rather than divine. Traditionally, of course, the being of man was grounded in the being of God. God was *causa essend*, *ratio-intelligendi*, and *ordo vivendi*, and these three aspects of divine being were reflected in human nature in so far as man was a creature, made by God the Father, insofar as the truth of God's being, and of Being as such, was revealed to him through Christ, and insofar as the order of human life was guided by the Holy Ghost. What is man with God's causality, revelation and grace removed? Instead of being made, he has been thrown into the world where he simply finds himself: *wo er als geworfen sich befindet*. His understanding, secondly, is not, as it was for Augustine, Christ the teacher teaching within, but the projection of his own existence, essentially in relation to his own non-existence (as *Sein zum Tode*). And, finally, the order he lives by is first and foremost keeping up with the Joneses: he is, not this very soul chosen by grace, but the They. (Unless, of course, swaying over the abyss of nothingness, he pulls himself up to authenticity and even, heroically, finds a Destiny.) Thus man, unprotected by the Trinity, is his own trinity. Orphaned by the Divine Father, he is not yet able to grasp his own being as one way among many others of living an embodied, animate life history.

One of the strangest sections of *Sein und Zeit*, it seems to me, is the *cura* story, which is fetched in, rather arbitrarily, in order to justify the term *Sorge* as shorthand for *sich-Vorweg-sein-im-schon-Sein-in-einer-Welt-als-Sein-bei-inner-weltlichem-Seienden*. But in that very story, it was clay, *humus*, from which man was fashioned, and that is why Earth demanded that he be called after *humus*, *homo*. Heidegger took up the cause of Care, who made the creature, but forgot the material it was fashioned from, which is after all just as necessary to shaping its existence as is the 'spirit,' the breath of life, that Jove infused in it. Without clay, without embodiment, there is no humanity, not only nowhere to be, in the sense of landscape, but no one to be there.

THE EMBODIMENT OF THINKING:
HEIDEGGER'S APPROACH TO LANGUAGE [1]

DAVID MICHAEL LEVIN

I

INTRODUCTION

One of the main directions in which I feel a need to carry on the work of think-ing Heidegger undertook and handed down, of course, unfinished, leads into the darkness that surrounds the problem of understanding just what constitutes the *embodiment* of thinking (i.e., of *Denken* and *Andenken*). If, as Heidegger says in his *Letter on Humanism*,[2] 'thinking is thinking of Being,' then we need to understand what it means, or what it is, to *embody* such a relationship with Being. What is the nature of the sensuous, perceptive, mortal body, insofar as it is susceptible to experiencing that relationship? How may we learn to body forth our ontological thoughtfulness? What experiential steps could we take, to exem-plify – visibly, tangibly, audibly – the attitude Heidegger calls 'thinking of Being'? The *Gebärde des Denken*, after all, must be taken seriously. And that means: we understand it as truly designating a way of being embodied.

We need to give the gift of thought to our embodiment.[3] Could it be that, when we open up to the body and become, in our thinking, more receptive to its ownmost nature, we can give to it this gift of thought in a way that *fills* it with the kind of thoughtfulness that will open us to a richer *perception* of the *sensuous presencing* of Being. What Heidegger calls 'dwelling' (*Wohnen*) is not other than thoughtfully *living* in this wonderful openness and undergoing an experience of this unfathomable presencing in everything we do, think, and say.

When we give to the body the gift of thinking, a thinking which thinks of Being, then the body becomes suffused with this thinking: ontological thinking fills and appropriates our posture, our bearing, our gestures, our movement. As thoughtful, the 'gates' of the human body are opened up to receive the glorious mystery of Being. Such thoughtfulness is embodied as a certain susceptibility to being moved, touched, affected, by the sensuous gifts that manifest the presen-cing of Being. And this susceptibility is also rejoicing and delight, since without these, our 'greeting' is not utterly open and receptive. Our senses receive the gift

See notes at the end of this chapter.

of Being in a way that appreciate its preciousness. Our sensing, thus transformed, no longer receives the gift by *reducing* it to mere 'sense data', dull, meaningless, and not at all satisfying. The opening of the sensuous is experienced as supremely meaningful, precisely because Being is no longer thought abstractly in the pain and suffering of re-presentational distance and control.

The capacity of our senses to receive what is granted *as a gift* requires the cultivation of our susceptibility to sensuous delight, and as much thoughtful openness as we are capable of developing. Without perceptive openness, the sensuous grant is refused, reduced to the 'fact' of a mere excitation. Openness also means surrender, submission: the kind that bends us very gently into an attitude of devotion and reverence. Unfortunately, so much of our experience, perhaps especially our encounter with other persons, is in the service of Ego. Consequently, our experience tends to be choked by anxiety. In defense of Ego's grasping nature, we become either aversively restrained and withdrawn or else very aggressive, willful and destructive. (Recall the 'rage' Heidegger writes of in the *Letter on Humanism*.) From an ontological standpoint, both of these gestures or movements inevitably bring us to the threshhold of pain and suffering. (See 'What Are Poets For?')[4]

According to Heidegger, re-presentation is at the root of this pain and suffering, inasmuch as it is precisely that mode of perception and bearing which is enthralled, and captured, by Ego. Re-presentation is a rigid and defensive strategy which imposes both temporal and spatial distance, temporal and spatial distortions: it willfully defers, postpones, or reduces the moment of thoughtful experiental presence. The re-presentational attitude projects dualities which restrict experiential openness — needlessly and fatefully. Although it emerged to defend against frustration, it is in fact this very attitude which is responsible for the *repetition* of pain and frustration. How will per-ception (*Wahr-nehmung*) receive what is given? With love and joy and thanksgiving? Or with the grasp and com-prehension of a will to power? And how will our bearing greet and carry the thought of Being? With arrogance, and in disgrace? Or with nobility, kindliness, and grace?

In this paper, we shall concentrate on the features constitutive of language: reading and writing, listening and speaking. And our concern is for the realization of the latent potential, borne by these powerful gestures. The realization of this potential may be characterized, quite succinctly, as openness. What is this process of opening, with regard, that is, for the gestures of language? And how is re-presentation, in language, a restriction of such openness?

II

HEIDEGGER'S HIDDEN THEMATIC

It is my conviction not only that Heidegger approved the development of a philosophy of the body, but that he cleared a place for such a philosophy to emerge. I will even maintain a stronger position, namely: that Heidegger constantly and consistently attempted to outline, in quite general terms, a philosophy of embodiment which would correspond to the unfolding of his thinking of Being. When you closely examine his work in light of this hypothesis, you may well be amazed to discover the intensity of Heidegger's pursuit, his single-minded perserverance, but also the depth and vastness of his accomplishment. There is overwhelming textual evidence to prove that Heidegger was wholeheartedly involved in an attempt to flesh out the immortal nature of thinking as the thinking of *mortals*, the calling of *sentient, corporeal beings* uniquely capable of a thinking open even to the sensuous presencing of Being. What Heidegger sought to understand is the essential nature and functioning of *human embodiment* in the light of Being.[5]

To be sure, we wish that Heidegger had been much more explicit, more concrete, more prosaically elaborate. But, if he needs an excuse, I suppose I would argue that, since he undoubtedly regarded what I have called sensuous thinking to be a dynamic process of continuous *never-ceasing* perfection, he must have thought it would suffice, for the time being, simply to propose some preliminary *norms* of embodiment.

To remind ourselves of Heidegger's sharp focus, we need only turn to *What Is Called Thinking?*, where, for example, he refers to walking, falling, standing upright, staying upon the way, face-to-face conversation, speaking, the qualities of the teacher's voice, screaming, listening, withdrawing, drawing, and calling. Similarly, in his studies on the pre-Socratics, especially Heracleitos, Heidegger unquestionably concentrates on such things as listening, hearing, and being attuned. He discusses the nature of sounds and their echoes, the functioning of the eyes and ears, qualities of color, and our capacity for seeing the luminous qualities of thinking. And let us recall his work on language, where he refers, for instance, to breathing, to the mouth and the tongue, and also the heart.[6] In still other works, Heidegger gives thought to such basic rural activities as plowing, sowing, reaping, skills of the hand, building, blazing trails, and gathering firewood.

III

THE EMBODIMENT OF THINKING IN LANGUAGE

According to Heidegger, the perfection of language is *Dichten*: the harmony of the stem of thought with the stem of song. In 'The Nature of Language,' he calls singing and thinking 'neighbouring stems.'[7] Thus, I think we may take language, in the sense of *Dichten*, to be an exemplary region where sensuous thinking takes place.

Many philosophers, of course, have considered language – or at least poetry, which is its idealization and perfection – to be a privileged kind of expression. On what grounds, if any, must we recognize such primacy, such authority? Descartes was certainly correct in pointing out that language is present only among human beings, and that, in consequence, the capacity to learn a natural language and enter into our world of communication will serve as a defining criterion of humanity. No other sentient beings are similarly gifted with the power of language. Nevertheless, I think this argument is not at all sufficient. After all, what other sentient beings can gesture expressively as do we? Furthermore, what is at issue here is *not* the privilege, or importance, of language in defining the human essence, but rather the privilege and power of language among the various embodiments of thinking. For thinking certainly can be embodied, can be bodily present, in the chopping of wood, for example; and also in cooking, mending old clothes, singing a lullaby, greeting your neighbourhood merchants, and repairing a stone wall. This is extremely important. Heidegger, as I understand him, wants to challange the intellectualistic tradition in philosophy, which introduces into human experience dualities that are painful and not fulfilling. This is the point of Heidegger's story, in his *Letter on Humanism*, about Heracleitos warming himself by a stove and welcoming his visitors with the words, 'Even here the gods are present'. Any activity whatsoever, no matter how domestic or humble, *can* be transformed into an embodiment of thinking open to Being. However, there is in fact a certain feature unique to language; and it is in virtue of this feature that language may be called a privileged form of sensuous thinking. Language – and only language – can adequately bring out, articulate and communicate the thoughtful nature of the sensuous by giving it the jewel of thought. Language possesses an exceptional, almost 'magical' power to present, or make manifest.

This means that language is, and must be, the principal medium for teaching. It is to language that we must turn in order to teach the way of embodied thinking. It is even true that we must turn to language in order to teach that language is not at all the only embodiment of thinking. So teaching is the function which ultimately grants to language its otherwise indefensible privilege.

Now, it is of the utmost importance that we understand the essential nature of language. Heidegger devoted much time to this question. To begin with, then, let us recognize, as does he, that neither the Cartesians nor the empiricists appreciate the essential nature of language. The mentalistic approach, and likewise the physicalist, do not even provide a *partial* access, since their reductionistic approaches introduce dualities which distort and repress our full experience of the true nature of language.[8] So Heidegger warns us, over and over again, against the dangers in our traditional approaches to language. These approaches, each one of which derives from a metaphysical system effective in closing off the openness of our experience with language, simultaneously reflect and encourage an unsatisfactory modality of experience. The consequences are indeed far-reaching.

So that we may develop an appropriate sense of these consequences, we need to consider our experience with language in the teaching situation. Teaching, surely, is an expression of compassion. The dedicated teacher always teaches out of compassion. Therefore, it is necessary that we give thought to the language of the teacher, the language of the teaching. If the heart of teaching is indeed compassion, then the essence of the language which teaches must lie in the *compassionate experiental qualities* of the language in which the teacher teaches. (And it should not be forgotten that the language a teacher 'uses' to teach is also something he is teaching. The socalled 'means' are always taught along with the teaching of the 'end', or the 'content'.) As Heidegger tells us in Lecture IV of *What Is Called Thinking?*, the 'how', or 'way', which he insists is *not* merely a question of 'style', is of the most fundamental importance. So he speaks of such qualities as intonation, melody, and vitality. These qualities need to be understood more concretely, however, and above all, as sensuous qualities of compassion.

What is compassionate language? More concretely, we must ask: what is the *sound* of such language? How can we experience the compassionate teaching of language? How can the teacher's experience with language — his speaking and listening, reading and writing — become so intensely expressive of his compassion that it not only encourages others to think and learn, but even holds the power to awaken in others that very same motive of compassion? — Let us not forget that one of the most important things we have to teach is compassion itself. Non-dualistic experiencing: the authentic way of being-with-others.[9] This involves an experiential openness which Heidegger conveys with such words as 'clearing' and 'lighting'. Compassion can be taught, or transmitted, only in a manner which embodies, manifests and exemplifies this very teaching.[10] The teacher must *embody* the non-dualistic openness of compassion in order to teach it as the root of thoughtfulness. When, in the course of the teaching process, the teacher needs to depend on language, his words must *audibly convey* the thoughtful *sound* of his compassion.[11] I do wish that Heidegger had said more on the related topics of teaching and compassion. But I am quite confident that what I have said here is not only coherent with Heidegger's explicit position, but in fact carries forward his approach to language.

IV

THE LANGUAGE OF HEALING

In his *Letter on Humanism*, Heidegger tells us that 'Thinking leads to the upsurgence of healing.'[12] Although Heidegger actually said very little about the method, or practice of healing, I now believe that the most fruitful approach to Heidegger's work is to regard it as an attempt to articulate an extremely radical and revolutionary philosophy aimed at liberating human beings from the cycle of sickness and health. I say his philosophy is extremely radical because it returns us to the phenomenologically primordial (pre-conceptual) ground of health, which is the absolute openness of Being. And I say it is liberating because, by returning us to the open ground of our being, *he helps us to effect a cure even beyond the ontic duality of sickness and health.*

The few direct and explicit remarks we have about healing are quite sufficient, however, to establish a crucial relationship between conditions of sickness and health, broadly understood, and the human being's capacity for grounding human existence in the openness of Being. Healing takes place, Heidegger wants to say, in the wholesome wholeness of a holy (or, let us say 'spiritual') life. Insofar as what needs to be healed are painful dualities such as mind/body, reason/heart, willfulness/willingness and activity/receptivity, the process of healing, which must ultimately transcend even the experienced duality of sickness and health, or the experienced difference between openness and closure, entails the perfect harmony, or integration, of 'meditative thinking' and its sensuous element, in an existential embodiment that manifests the holiness of thinking as a thinking of holiness which infuses and illuminates and fully opens the skillful functioning of every bodily organ, every breathing pore, every movement, gesture, and expression.

We cannot begin to appreciate the essential nature of language unless we understand it as a form of praxis — and, indeed, as a praxis of liberation. As such, language is intimately involved in the therapeutic process. We are familiar enough with the importance of what Freud called 'the talking cure'. But perhaps we need to see that the Freudian approach to therapeutic language, and the other professional approaches as well, are not entirely satisfactory. Are they really able to heal the pain, the frustration, the suffering which arise from experiental dualities? Judged from the standpoint of Heidegger's thinking, these approaches to language cannot completely heal: they are, at best, merely partial cures. Perhaps they are unsatisfactory to the extent that they are not grounded in thinking, not grounded in a praxis of thinking concerned with the opening of beings in Being. Heidegger's approach to language, then, is a courageous attempt to think a praxis of language which could be profoundly healing: a therapeutic language with the ontological power to cure the pain and suffering that accompany the most fundamental of all dualities, namely, the ontological difference between beings and Being.[13]

This primordial duality underlies the other dualities which we experience as painful and not fulfilling: the dualities of mind and body, thought and action, intention and accomplishment, intellect and heart, subject and object, this and that, and myself and other. Language is therepeutic — that is to say, healing and liberating — when it makes us whole. But this wholesome wholeness is possible, according to Heidegger, only when the language involved in human relationships makes contact with the Holy. (Perhaps I should communicate that I'm *not afraid* to say the word 'Holy' here, for Heidegger himself says it, but also because, more importantly, *it feels right* to me. On the other hand, I do think that we need a different conceptualization — one which is not burdened with the metaphysics of traditional theology.) Such language becomes a powerful presence which embodies and conveys holiness. It brings us closer to one another in, and through, the presence of Being. This closeness is essential to what is healing.

Let us consider the matter more concretely by focusing on speech. Speech has the power to heal when it echoes the sound of Being and conveys this gracious presence in, and as, its teaching through the openness, the responsiveness, and the compassion of its sensuous qualities.[14] Healing speech is a voice which breathes freely and sings. Singing is speech which is really joyful, spontaneous, moving. Singing is resonant with a meaningfulness that can be *felt*, even when it can't be *stated*. Singing is speech beyond duality: beyond the painfulness, for example, in speech which lacks sincerity and openness, or which expresses unrecognized fear, horror, embarrassment, or some other inner discord. Heidegger says: 'To sing means to be present: Dasein.'[15] In the voice which sings, there is no painful conflict between the content of meaning and the manner of utterance. The voice which sings opens joyously towards beings in Being. It receives and conveys the healing presence of the sound of Being, which silently echoes within it.

V

THE LIBERATION OF LANGUAGE

In order for language to liberate and be healing, language itself must be liberated, cured of the dualities which block its full healing power. Heidegger could not be more explicit on this point. Indeed, he seems to devote considerably more time to the process of liberating language itself than he does to the process of liberating beings through the powerful being of language. This concentration, is primarily pedagogical, and more seeming than real. Basically, the focus of his point is that we must learn to *release* our language from the rigidity and objectification of propositional grammar, and from an approach, or attitude so willfully instrumental and cybernetic, and so deadened, finally, by our unthinking technological clamour for absolute univocity, that even the soundings of our speech are restrained and muffled, or more like noise. (Univocity rules, for example, wherever the individual needs of authentic personal communication are reduced and standardized in order to fit the requirements of digital computer programmes or the pressures of institutional organizations. Within a context of totalitarian political tendencies, the 'polymorphous perversity' of Heidegger's philosophizing language — the uncanny sensuous anarchy of his thinking — is to be recognized as powerfully subversive. Like the language of our greatest poets, Heidegger's language will always resist the conformist pressures of authority and the tyrannies of the machine. Like the poets, he sings for us his gift of thought. This singing fills language with the breath of thought. Language belongs not to the society of mankind, but to the indwelling presence of Being.)[16]

While struggling to understand Anaximander's words, Heidegger discovered that he could actually begin to fathom their sense so soon as he allowed the words to 'resound' in their own way: he was learning how to let them be, to resonate fully and freely. He discovered that the strange Greek words opened up to him when he became *willing* to listen: when he became more open and attuned to their sensuous echoes and resonances. The words began to speak, he tells us, 'when spoken in a preconceptual way.'[17] Heidegger's discoveries point the way towards a very different approach to language: or a very different experience with language.

Heidegger's involvement with language, whether it be in the form of speaking, listening, reading, or writing, was constantly motivated by the desire to learn an attitude of releasement (*Gelassenheit*). For he understood that language could be liberating only insofar as it itself is released unto its own being. A thoughtful experience with language has two interdependent aspects: on the one hand, we must recognize the need to free language from the tyranny of our defensive and all-too-human will to power, while on the other hand we must recognize the power dwelling within language itself to free all sentient beings from the dialectical cycle of pain and frustration.

Heidegger, therefore, is never content merely to *discuss* the releasement of language from the chain of blind desire. Rather, his involvement with the language is always a relationship in which praxis actually *realizes* the experience of thinking. Thus, for example, his own philosophical writing, and the way he reads and listens to another philosopher's text, always paradigmatically *exemplify* his never-ending concern for the complementary aspects of releasement. Heidegger writes: 'If only once we could *hear* the fragment it would no longer *sound* like an assertion long past.'[18] Elsewhere, he comments, from the reader's standpoint, that 'a radiance all its own illumined what this sentence had to say.'[19] This is why his language is so powerful, so effective. Even when we don't understand the *sense* of his words, we can *feel* ourselves somehow *changed* by the experience of thoughtfully reading him, or thoughtfully listening to the crystalline clarity and purity of his speech. As Dr. Eugene Gendlin has demonstrated, significant changes can take place *very directly* when the sensuous qualities of the teacher's language embody and convey his liberating intentions in an exemplary way.[20] According to Heidegger, such directly healing language is exemplified in speech that joyfully bursts into song, and 'unexpectedly becomes a soundless echo which lets us hear something of the proper nature of language [i.e., lets us hear the being of language as the language of Being].'[21]

Let us now consider three areas in which Heidegger's extraordinary relationship with language is manifest. These are: first, Heidegger's attention to etymology; second, the metaphorical nature of his language; and finally the polymorphous, or polysemic 'perversity' of much of his language. In our examination of these topics, we will have an apportunity to see just how Heidegger's praxis of what I have called 'sensuous thinking' actually works (how it is embodied in an exemplary manner). At the same time, moreover, we will be able to see more clearly how sensuous thinking is also an involvement with language which directly contributes to its releasement, its consecration as a medium, or site, for the preservation and transmission of graceful healing through a mode of experience truly opened to the presencing of Being.

(1) In his 'Dialogue on Language', Heidegger tells us that the Japanese word for language is *koto-ba*, which means 'the petals that stem from *koto*.'[22] Considered in light of this poetic approach to the precincts, or being of language, Heidegger's etymological concerns take on a surprising and yet significant value. In 'The Way to Language,' he says: 'Everything spoken stems from the unspoken.'[23] My principal point is that Heidegger's etymologies and archaeologies exemplify, and thereby teach, his deliberate practice of *thinking by listening for (to) the echoes and reverberations which stem from the silent etymon: the root sound, or seed syllable. Heidegger's etymologies always* remind us to cultivate the root of the pure thought we have abstracted; they remind us that we need to move *towards the mystery, towards the wonder*, of thought's sensuous embodiment in some very simple and very humble form of 'practice': for example, in activities and expressive gestures such as giving, making handy, pouring water, turning, thanking, standing, and gathering. Heidegger's language – the language in which he *embodies* his thought, or the language to which he *gives* his thought – reaches us in a way that both heals and teaches, because he thoughtfully roots and secures his thinking in its sensuous (bodily) origin. This rooting consecrates even the simplest gestures, postures, and doings of human life as the embodiment, or ground, of 'meditative thinking.' Moreover, the language in which Heidegger teaches this practice is amazingly alive, resonant, strong and healthy, because it remembers to stay in touch with the mystery of

its creative seed. Heidegger's teaching is so powerful because it is entrusted to a language that freely breathes and sings. Within the realm of his language, the sound of the silent etymon resounds like distant thunder.

(2) Heidegger's language is, as we know, a vast treasure-house of thought-provoking metaphors, evocative figures of speech. How does Heidegger intend such language? How must we experience the manifestly poetic qualities of the language he thinks in, if we want to respond appropriately — that is to say, as his companions on the path of thinking? There certainly exists a very strong tendency, among philosophers bent on interpreting Heidegger's thinking, to assume that these stirring metaphors are merely the leaping flames of his poetic imagination.

But confusion prevails, since Heidegger himself takes great pains to warn us *against* the temptation to reduce his language to a mere embellishment of thought. For Heidegger, the metaphor is saying something which *cannot* be said some other way: it is essential for the thought, not only in virtue of its 'meaningful content', but also, and equally, because of the sensuous wisdom it protects and transmits. In his 'Letter on Humanism,' Heidegger unequivocally declares that Hölderlin's verse 'is no adornment of a thinking that rescues itself from science by means of poetry. The talk about the house of Being is no transfer of the image 'house' to Being. But one day we will, by thinking the essence of Being in a way appropriate to its matter, more readily be able to think what 'house' and 'to dwell' are.'[24]

On the same grounds, moreover, he enquires whether his way with language is motivated merely by the quixotic desire to play games with language, but follows his questions at once with a denial whose intended meaning leaves nothing to debate. In *What Is Called Thinking?*, we read: 'Is this return a whim, or playing games? Neither one nor the other. If we may talk here of playing games at all, it is not we who play with words, but the nature of language plays with us ...'[25] And he continues: 'Is it playing with words when we attempt to give heed to this game of language and to hear what language really says when it speaks? If we succeed in hearing that, then it may happen — provided we proceed carefully — that we get more truly to the matter that is expressed in any telling and asking.'[26]

So Heidegger's various figures of speech must be taken very seriously. They are intended to protect and preserve Being in its unconcealment. And they are concrete expressions of literal truth. In 'Letter on Humanism,' he tells us that 'the usage 'brings to language' employed here is now to be taken quite literally. Being comes, lighting itself, to language. It is perpetually under way to language. Such arriving in its turn brings ek-sisting thought to language in a saying. Thus language itself is raised into the lighting of Being.'[27] And he reminds us that 'To bring to language ever and again this advent of Being which remains, and in its remaing waits for man, is the sole matter of thinking.'[28]

But, if the figurative and poetical nature of Heidegger's language is indeed *essential* not only for the 'Sache' of his thinking, but also for the path, or 'way' of his thinking; and if, furthermore, his figures of speech are meant to be truthful, then it seems that we are called upon to recognize in Heidegger's language *a practice that teaches by example the bodying forth of thinking.* This interpretation is confirmed with special force, I believe, in Heidegger's approach to the translation of fragments from the pre-Socratics. With an insistence no reader can miss, Heidegger repeatedly writes of approaching the fragments by making a superhuman effort to *listen and hear* what they have to say. And he also writes of approaching them by reading them in such a way that the luminous presence of the thinking which inhabits them will be made visible. In his discussion of Parmenides' 'Moira', for example, where he pauses to reflect on the notion of *lumen naturale*,[29] Heidegger observes that 'Ordinary perception certainly moves within the lightedness of what is present and sees what is shining out ... in color; but is dazzled by changes in color, ... and pays no attention to the still light of the lighting that emanates from duality and is *phasis*.'[30]

We would be mistaken, however, if we were to understand Heidegger as saying merely that the fragments are *referring* to the lighting of Being. Numerous passages support a very different, and clearly much stranger interpretation, namely: that, just as 'What is heard comes to presence in hearkening.'[31] so too the mysterious lighting of Being *actually comes into exemplary presence* through the fragments of thought, and can be *seen* to shine within them when our eyes are thoughtfully opened.[32] But it is absolutely necessary to remind ourselves, here, that 'the golden gleam of the lighting's invisible shining cannot be grasped,'[33] and that the 'presencing of the near is too close for our customary mode of representational thought ...'[34] Only when thinking is *perfectly* embodied will our ears and eyes be fully open, fully capable of perceiving the sensuous presence of Being, which Heidegger characterizes as best he can by calling upon words such as 'lighting' and 'the ringing echo of stillness'.

This point is of the utmost importance. Our conceptual and representational approach to language keeps us closed off from the sensuous presencing of Being. Heidegger's acceptance of the challenge he met in translating the pre-Socratics taught him at least this: that only when our thinking is gracefully incarnate, and only when our bodily senses are thoughtfully open to receive what is granted, can the concrete sensuous presence of Being come forth in satisfying unconcealment. And I strongly suspect that the difficulty *we* encounter in meeting the challenge to develop our experiential openness is what basically underlies the overwhelming reluctance we feel to taking Heidegger's metaphors as concrete manifestations of truth. Let me put the point another way. We dimly sense that it would be unbearably frightening to open ourselves up to the extent required by the literal truthfulness of his language. And our response is therefore, not surprisingly, defensive. *We defend ourselves against anxiety in the presence of his metaphorical thought by interpreting his language as nothing but edifying poetry*, rather than the truthful sensuous presencing of Being. — But of course, the power of healing, in whose keeping Heidegger's language belongs, is not independent of the quality and openness of our response. What may we be granted to hear, when we listen with an openness and rejoicing that consecrates the human ears? — Heidegger calls this 'hearkening', and tells us that to hearkening may be granted and entrusted an echo of the very sound of Being, whose silence freely and spontaneously resounds in the liberated and deeply healing speech of the thought-filled philosopher, the compassionate teacher, whom the Greeks, in Socrates' time, called a 'physician of the soul.'

(3) Finally, we turn to consider, very briefly, the polymorphous, polysemic 'perversity' of Heidegger's language. Now, to be sure, Heidegger very graciously consents to weave his 'poetic' skeins of thought into a more 'prosaic' fabric of discourse, intertwining the older metaphysical language of re-presentation with his revolutionary language of immediate presence. But, although we may be thankful for the helpful *steps* of his propositional approach, we must respond with resolution and trust to the call of his challenge to *leap* into the openness, the lighting where Being presences. Speaking personally, I hear this call as it vibrates and resounds in the *sound* of his language: a language whose sensuousness is opened, and thus emptied, to receive the sound which Being grants. Such sounding is, in its very essence, fundamentally different from the sounds we normally hear, since what we normally hear has been *reduced*, by processes of defensive fixation and objectification, to an ordering configuration of sounds uprooted from their wholesome ground, the primordial silence from which they stem.[35] So what we normally hear is not a granting of sounds for whose sublimity and preciousness we would feel some spontaneous urge to rejoice, but rather something unfortunately much less healing, and not sufficiently different from what philosophers have called, thereby reflecting their own pathology, 'sense data' and 'acoustic waves'.

Heidegger tells us that he thinks *by listening*. And his way with language consistently exemplifies this practice and confirms the sensuousness of his thinking. He writes: '... our listening to the grant for what we are to think always develops into our asking for the answer.'[36] And he reassures us that he recognizes our problem by adding: 'Our characterization of thinking as a listening sounds strange ...'[37]

When we think by giving our thought to the sound of thinking — when we think, that is, by thoughtfully focused listening, or by hearkening unto the sound of thinking — it may be granted us to hear healing echoes of the primordial sound of the very language of Being. In 'The Nature of Language,' Heidegger writes:

And let no one suppose that we mean to belittle vocal sounds as physical phenomena, the [so-called] merely sensuous side of language, in favour of what is called the meaning and sense-content of what was said and is esteemed as being of the spirit, the spirit of language. *It is much more important to consider whether ... the physical element of language, its vocal and written character, is being adequately experienced*; whether it is sufficient to associate sound exclusively with the body understood in physiological terms, and to place it within the *metaphysically conceived confines* of the sensuous. Vocalization and sounds may no doubt be explained physiologically as the production of sounds. But the question remains *whether the real nature of the sounds and tones of speech is thus ever experienced and kept before our eyes.* We are instead referred to melody and rhythm in language and thus to the kinship between song and speech. All would be well if only there were not the danger of understanding melody and rhythm also from the perspective of physiology and physics, that is, technologically, calculatingly in the widest sense. No doubt much can be learned this way that is correct, but never, presumably, what is essential. *It is just as much a property of language to sound and ring and vibrate, to hover and to tremble, as it is for the spoken words of language to carry [the burden of] a meaning.* But *our experience* of this property is still exceedingly clumsy, because the metaphysical-technological explanation gets everywhere in the way, and keeps us from considering the matter properly.'[38]

So, if we really give thought to the sound of our language, and if we are truly *open* to experience that unto which we hearken, we should be able not only to confirm the validity of Heidegger's critique, but also to carry it forward to the clearing of Being — and indeed within the experiential dynamics of our own practice.

Heidegger's language exemplifies, and thereby shows forth, its *Sache*, the concern of thinking, in the perfection of its sensuous incarnation. Thus, the qualitative *way* Heidegger speaks and writes, whereby the sensuousness of speaking becomes the opening of thoughtful listening and the sensuousness of writing becomes the opening of thoughtful reading, is no less important for the teaching and transmission of his thinking than is the propositional content of meaning. Indeed, it would seem that, for Heidegger, the nature of his relationship with language is far more important. For this 'way' communicates and heals directly — and very effectively — by the grace of its concrete *exemplification*, its exemplary and, so to speak, 'poetic' *embodiment*. On the nature of this embodiment, Heidegger comments: 'By 'way', or 'how', we mean something other than manner [or literary style]. 'Way' here means melody, the ring and tone, which is not just a matter of how the saying [physically or neurophysiologically] sounds. The way or how of the saying is the [phenomenologically experienced] tone from which and to which what is said is [gracefully, or thoughtfully] attuned.'[39]

Among other things, we need to give careful thought to Heidegger's wordplays, which often seem to be generated by the sound of the words. And we need to listen without judgment to the sound of his alliterations; his repetition of words, phrases, and even entire sentences; the functioning of tautologies (which are likewise repetitions of sound); and utterances such as 'the proposition (*Satz*) of the ground is the ground of the proposition (*Satz*)', in which the sound of the words vibrates and rings with a vitality, or presence, that almost empties the words of their re-presentational, or cognitive content. These articulations of language are meant, I think, to be enchanting. They are soundings released from their egological work; so they are free to sing and enchant. More specifically, and in terms of the figure/ground *Gestalt* which Heidegger attempts to transmute into the more spiritually satisfying experience of 'the fourfold' (*das Geviert*), Heidegger's language gives itself in *figures* of sound that let there be heard a vibrant polyphony of echoes. These echoes, which stem from the mystery of a primordial silence, enable the mystery to come into presence and grounds the vitality of the echoes. However, the echoes also conceal their primordial *ground*, thereby protecting its holy mystery from our willful attempts to reduce it to the finitude of conceptually fixated grammatical figures of sound.

Heidegger's language *exemplifies and teaches*, in the most direct way, the embodiment of thinking in, and as, language. His thinking is sensuously embodied because he *gives* thought to the sensuous embodiment of his thought. He accepts and receives the sensuous element of language: like a poet, he rejoices in its treasures. As a thinker, he listens for the sound of spontaneity, the *thinking* sound which joyfully heals, the sound which resonates with all the echoes of Being.[40] As a thinker, he listens for the 'ring of truth' in the ancient voices of the early Greeks and he opens his eyes, eager to see the lighting, the 'radiance' which illumines the sentence he is reading.[41]

Heidegger is teaching us how to let our thinking go and be with its sound. He is showing us how to release our language from a repressive metaphysical grammar which refuses to accept the sensuous element as the bearer of a precious gift.[42] Heidegger's language is certainly not a mere Scrabble game of words; it is, however, very *playful*, for Heidegger's attitude towards language clearly expresses *in exemplary practice* the gesture he calls 'Gelassenheit'. Thanks to this playfulness, Heidegger is able to hear new thought resounding in the silence of ancient words.[43] His thinking receives the blessing of nourishment from the sounds through which his thinking breathes. His thinking does not forget to consecrate these sounds by releasing them unto the mystery of their own nature. Heidegger's celebration of language, opening the portals of the sensuous, cures the human body by teaching us the soundings of a language fully devoted to the concern of thinking. When we dwell together in the inner temple of language, sensuous thinking is the devotional practice of singing and rejoicing in the presence of Being.[44]

NOTES

1 I would like to express my heartfelt gratitude to Ted Kisiel, Roger Levin, Edward Sankowski, Calvin Schrag, and Steven Tainer, whose responses to earlier drafts of my paper especially helped me to say what I wanted to say.

2 Martin Heidegger, 'Letter on Humanism,' in *The Basic Writings of Martin Heidegger.* (New York: Harper and Row 1977), p. 196. The language of Being must be liberated from our dualistic grammar. When we speak of 'thinking of Being', the divisive preposition 'of' also means the *unifying* preposition 'with', for what we are talking about is something *more primordial and non-differentiated* than what the dualistic, representational (or typically conceptual) mode of thinking is able to articulate and express. The very *openness* of the presence of Being invalidates the claims of dualistic thinking, which regards Being as another object, and therefore as somehow opposed to us or hostile. What Heidegger calls 'meditative thinking' maintains our openness and balance with regard for the openness of Being. It helps us to *stay with* the ground of Being as well as to forget it. Meditative thinking calls for a new figure/ground relationship in visual and auditory perception. It calls for an experiential focusing of the bodily organs which is not fixated, but open.

3 Heidegger, 'Letter on Humanism,' p. 204: '*The human body is essentially other than an animal organism. Nor is the error of biologism overcome by adjoining a soul to the human body*, a mind to the soul, and the existentiell to the mind, and then louder than before singing the praises of the mind — only to let everything relapse into 'life-experience,' with a warning that *thinking by its inflexible concepts disrupts the flow of life* and that thought of Being distorts existence.' (My italics.) See also 'The Nature of Language,' in *On The Way to Language* (New York: Harper and Row, 1971), p. 101: 'When the word is called the mouth's flower and its blossom, we hear the sound of language rising like the earth. ... The sound rings out in the resounding assembly call which, open to the Open, makes World appear in all things. *The sounding of the voice is then no longer only of the order of physical organs. It is released now from the perspective of the physiological-physical explanation in terms of purely phonetic data. ... The indication* of the sound of speaking and of its source in Saying *must at first sound obscure and strange. And yet it points to simple phenomena.*' (My italics.)

4 'What Are Poets For?', in Albert Hofstadter (translator and editor), *Poetry, Language, Thought* (New York: Harper and Row, 1971), p. 120. Heidegger here translates *psychological* concepts such as objectification, defense, openness, and anxiety (or the need for security) into a pattern which he presents in *ontological* speech (poetical speech attuned to the presence of Being).

5 Martin Heidegger, 'The Nature of Language,' in *On The Way to Language* (New York: Harper and Row, 1971), p. 75.

6 Heidegger's most important reference to the mouth will be found in 'The Nature of Language,' p. 98. Once again, he warns us against reductionism: 'for the mouth is not merely a kind of organ of the body understood as an organism — body and mouth are part of the earth's flow and growth in which we mortals flourish, and from which we receive the soundness of our roots.' Breathing is discussed in 'What Are Poets For?', pp. 131-140. And the heart is mentioned, for example, on p. 140 of that same essay.

7 'The Nature of Language,' p. 98.

8 *Ibid.*

9 Concerning non-dualistic experiencing, see my essay, 'Freud's Divided Heart and Saraha's Cure,' in *Inquiry*, vol. 20, number 2 (Summer, 1977).

10 Eugene Gendlin has important things to say which pertain to this point. See his paper, 'Experiential Therapy,' in the anthology mentioned earlier: *Current Psychotherapies.*

11 See my essay, 'Self-Knowledge and the Talking Cure,' *Review of Existential Psychology and Psychiatry*, vol. XV, nos. 2-3 (1977) and also my 'Mantra: Sacred Words of Openness and Compassion,' in *Gesar: Buddhist Perspectives* (Tibetan Buddhist Nyingma Institute,

Berkeley), vol. VI, no. 1 (Spring, 1979). In regard to writing, see my paper on 'The Pheno-menon and Noumenon of Language,' in *Tri Quarterly*, vol. 38 (Winter, 1977). Ontologically understood, writing is the writing of light as it manifests in the radiance of our bodily gestures. It manifests when we write with eyes open to reading (gathering: *lesen*) the truth that the writing of mortals takes place only by grace of the primordial power of light. It manifests when we write giving thought to our gesture of writing, and our bodies become the joyously radiant medium through which the dazzling writing of light is read and con-veyed.

12 'Letter on Humanism,' *op.cit.*, p. 237. See also *op.cit.*, p. 230. Also see 'What Are Poets For?', in *Poetry, Language, Thought*, pp. 140-141, for some crucial comments on healing, the wholesome sound of wholeness, and the experience of holiness.

13 The dissolution of experiential dualities *does not abolish* the ontological difference. On the contrary, *it lets it be*. What *does* change with the cessation of duality is the pain, frustration, and suffering which normally accompany our various experiences of this dif-ference.

14 See *Aus der Erfahrung des Denkens* (Pfullingen: Neske, 1954, p. 25). See also my essay, 'Self-Knowledge and the Talking Cure,' in the *Review of Existential Psychology and Psychiatry*, vol. 15, no. 2 (Winter, 1978).

15 'What Are Poets For?', *op.cit.*, p. 84.

16 *What Is Called Thinking?* (New York: Harper and Row, 1968), p. 26. Also see *op.cit.*, pp. 116-125. Among other things, 'univocity' refers to the monotonous, lifeless, cold and colorless *sound* of speech.

17 Martin Heidegger, *Early Greek Thinking* (New York: Harper and Row, 1975), p. 39. See also p. 57.

18 *Early Greek Thinking* (New York: Harper and Row, 1975), p. 18. My italics.

19 *What Is Called Thinking?*, p. 180.

20 See 'Letter on Humanism,' p. 239. Also see Eugene Gendlin, *op.cit.*

21 'The Way to Language,' *op.cit.*, p. 113.

22 'A Dialogue on Language,' *On the Way to Language*, p. 46.

23 'The Way to Language,' p. 84.

24 'Letter on Humanism,' pp. 236-237.

25 *What Is Called Thinking?*, p. 119. See also p. 116.

26 *Ibid.*

27 'Letter on Humanism,' p. 239.

28 *Op.cit.*, p. 241.

29 *Early Greek Thinking*, p. 97.

30 *Op.cit.*, p. 100.

31 *Op.cit.*, p. 65.

32 See *op.cit.*, pp. 26-27, for example.

33 *Op.cit.*, p. 123.

34 *Op.cit.*, p. 121.

35 For an elegant and beautifully detailed phenomenological interpretation of *the normal range* of our auditory experience, I wholeheartedly recommend Don Ihde, *Listening and Voice* (Athens, Ohio: Ohio University Press, 1976). The more clearly one bears in mind the nature and functioning of our normal range of auditory experience, the more acutely one will realize how very different — and strange — is the auditory experience which Heidegger wants to teach. The contrast is thought-provoking; but it is also elucidatory.

36 'The Nature of Language,' pp. 75-76.

37 *Ibid.*

38 *Op.cit.*, p. 98 (My italics.)

39 *What Is Called Thinking?*, p. 37.

40 When reading Heidegger, one should be on the lookout for places where he seems to have received his thinking from *the free association of sounds*.

41 *What Is Called Thinking?*, p. 180.

42 From a political standpoint, therefore, Heidegger's language is extremely subversive: *its polyphony exemplifies Heidegger's resistance to the dogmatic standardizations and other processes of reification required by the technology of totalitarian societies.*

43 Heidegger's works abundantly confirm this fact. Consider, for example: (i) how his thinking progresses when he listens to 'es gibt'; (ii) how he hears the word for the notion of cognitive correspondence (*Abstimmung*) and reinterprets it as attunement; (iii) how he hears in the sound of 'Entschlossenheit' (which one would normally translate as 'resolve') the gift of a new kind of volition, a will which is not wilful, but open and willing; (iv) how he hears in the word 'gehören' the way that *binds* us and establishes our being as belonging to the sound of language; (v) how he hears in the word 'Entsprechung', not the familiar philosophical reference to correspondence, but rather a speech attuned to the *Sache des Denkens* by grace of its emptiness (the exhalation of breath); and finally (vi) how he hears in the word 'Ding' not only the archaic word 'dingen' (which means 'gathering') but also the sound of a ring, the enchanted 'Ring', the ringing of words which grant thought a new interpretation of thinghood, namely : the *thing* is that which gathers and unites the fourfold within the visible and audible ring of its gathering. I find it difficult to imagine the *Ereignis* of such thinking without these precious gifts of sound.

44 The opposite of what I call 'presence' is *not absence, which always enters into the hermeneutical* dynamics of presence, but rather *the experiential stasis* which Heidegger calls 'representation.' It is representation, and not presence, which defensively fixates, reifies, and demands totalization. Representation is the dualistic work of anxiety, whereas presence is the resolute openness of trust. Representation is never a completely satisfactory experience. Presence, however, is a bliss beyond the duality of a *painful* experience of absence.

TEMPORAL INTERPRETATION AND HERMENEUTIC PHILOSOPHY

OTTO PÖGGELER

(translated by Theodore Kisiel)

Fifty years ago, in 1927, Martin Heidegger published an admittedly fragmentary work which initiated a new epoch in the history of philosophy. Its title brings together being, the basic theme of Western thought, and time, which up until then was traditionally left out of any investigation of being. To be sure, 'time' had for some time become a catchword for philosophy. Bergson distinguished lived time from time as it is customarily understood. Dilthey sought to ground the human sciences in life as it is lived temporally and historically. Practically all of the human disciplines, ranging from theology to biology and physics, were engaged in rediscovering or reevaluating their concepts of time. As for Heidegger himself, he really was not out to contrast lived time with physical time, nor history with nature, but rather wished to revive the discussion of ontology, the determination and specification of the being of beings, in a radical and universal way, by considering its temporal implications.

The new ontology sought by Heidegger was in its method equated with phenomenology. Heidegger accordingly allied himself with Husserl. But he believed that Husserl's phenomenology was unilaterally oriented toward the paradigm of intuition. Husserl went from sense intuition to a non-sensuous or categorial intuition. Philosophical knowing thus becomes, in the spirit of the Platonic tradition, the seeing of a form, an *eidos*. Husserl even analyzed the 'consciousness of inner time' in the context of a phenomenology of perception. When we hear a melody or, for that matter, a triad of notes, we not only perceive the note just sounding but also retain the note just sounded and anticipate the note about to be sounded. Thus all three dimensions of time are involved. Only in this way can we apprehend a melody or a triad, in short a Gestalt or form. Without time, we would not perceive form at all.

Does this analysis not betray a certain partiality in the phenomenological approach? In pioneering fashion, Husserl placed the laws of logic out of the reach of psychologism — and yet, these same laws are then regarded as something in themselves, quasi-objects, as it were. Even the content of an ethical

See notes at the end of this chapter.

norm is interpreted as a value-in-itself. According to the modern turn given to the ancient philosophical tradition, this in itself must now be duly evidenced and authenticated in the ego. While Heidegger was studying and teaching Aristotle and Husserl's *Logical Investigations* together, he arrived at the thesis that the character of philosophical knowing had since the Greeks been defined by intuition. Theoretical truth, the truth which is 'seen', had usurped the claim to truth in general. In a radical break with the tradition, Heidegger took issue with this usurpation by making practical truth primary and by delving into the philosophical implications of religious truth. It is not tones and melodies or aesthetic forms originating from the flow of time, but rather phenomena such as destiny and grace, repentance and Kierkegaard's 'repetition', dread and fear, that lead to the decisive experience of time. The clues for such a phenomenology, which as a science of origins goes back to factic and historical life, no longer come from psychology, as in Husserl, but from history. These suggestions led Heidegger in 1922-23 to a hermeneutic phenomenology, which is essentially temporal interpretation. The philosophical tradition, Heidegger believed, could not do justice to the facticity and historicity of life – or of 'Dasein', as it was now called. Is not time, which makes facticity and historicity possible, the forgotten element behind the traditional philosophical approaches? With Aristotle, the philosophical tradition comprehended the multiplicity of being in terms of analogy, that is, as coordination and orientation of all possible senses of being to a leading meaning, on the basis of being as substance and accordingly as persistent presence. But if presence is regarded as the present, thus as a dimension of time, then traditional ontology approaches time unilaterally from one of its dimensions, from a present which becomes hypostatized into a permanent now. Can the sense of being be explicated into a multiplicity of meanings in a more adequate way, so that time in its fuller scope may be brought into play? What sort of time would this be? Would this 'temporal interpretation' give philosophy a new basis? Can such an interpretation be carried out at all?

In short, our concern in what follows is with the nature and possibility of temporal interpretation and of a hermeneutic philosophy based upon such interpretation. The paper is divided into three parts:

I   The basic traits of temporal interpretation.
II Difficulties in Heidegger's analysis of time.
III Difficulties in grounding hermeneutic philosophy upon temporal interpretation.

I

It is trivial to say that that which is can be in time. When I add two apples to two apples, this is a process which takes place in time. When I subsequently say 'two plus two equals four', such talk again takes place in time, right now and today, not tomorrow or the next day. But the equation $2 + 2 = 4$ does not hold just for today and then no longer. We speak here of a timeless validity or of an ideal being. What is here called ideality and contrasted with any occurrence in time, in temporal interpretation is to be made comprehensible precisely through time. It is to be demonstrated that even the mode of being of ideality is determined by temporal characteristics.

On the ontological level of being, entities become manifest in Dasein. Dasein, the openness of being, is that which makes a man to be a man. It is familiar to us only in man. 'Being' is thus not independent of some sort of human comportment, which reaches its term in the saying of 'is'. Being determines the ways in which something is given to us or encountered by us; it is accordingly articulated into different meaning. For example, something can be given to us in being-that and being-what, corresponding to the 'is' of an existential assertion and the 'is' as a copula. If the 'that' appears as a more or less accidental realization of the 'what', this pair of categories may be applicable to a table brought into being by a carpenter according to a pregiven conception or idea. But we resist characterizing man in the same manner and so designate man as 'existence' of a distinctive kind. Tables, men, and mathematical equations are encountered in different ways and in each case call for different meanings of being. If we take the world not as the sum-total of beings but as the totality of the ways of givenness, or the comprehensive how of encounter, then the various spheres in the world are ordered to respective guiding meanings of Being. If these distinctions are to be made comprehensible through a temporal interpretation, what sort of time are we talking about?

Heidegger paves a way for this question through an analysis of Dasein. Since modes of being are modes of givenness, Dasein is nothing other than the variegated openness of being. Since the world is the totality of the modes of givenness, Dasein is a being-in-the-world. The most natural world is taken to be the immediate environment considered as a context of relevances, in which everything has its meaning as something ready-to-hand and handy for the environment. For example, all things in a shoemaker's shop refer to one another in a network of relevances disclosed by the practice of his craft: the hammer refers to the leather to be nailed, the leather to the shoe to be made, and so forth. The act of knowing, in which an uninvolved and disinterested subject orients itself to an object as something merely on hand, is a deficient and derivative mode of this 'natural' way of being-in-the-world. Heidegger concretizes this radical departure from the tradition by developing a new determination of the basic structures of Dasein as being-in-the-world: Dasein always already finds itself in the world and accordingly is disclosed in the facticity and the trust of its situated state; at the same time, it must take charge of itself in a self-comprehension of its being-in-the-world, and in this way is existence and project; situatedness and comprehension belong together and constitute an articulation and a kind of 'discourse' which enable our being among (bei) things, with (bei) others and by (bei) ourselves. These basic determinations constitute a departure from the traditional view according to which man is immersed in the world of transitory things and through reason can escape the 'blindness' of the sense world to another suprasensible world of stability and permanence. Heidegger's departure from traditional views becomes even more apparent when he defines the natural or everyday being-in-the-world as 'care' or 'concern', thereby avoiding prejudgment of the way in which theory and practice are implicated in this care. But is the everyday caring Dasein really itself? It is truly what it is and how it is only when it expressly assumes its own Dasein in being-toward-death. It must through conscience allow itself to be called into this utmost possibility of its existence. The anticipatory resolve of willing-to-have-a-conscience, which reveals to each Dasein in its particular situation just what it means to be here in its staggering finitude, refers insuperably to time. Accordingly, at this point in the argument, in section 65, Heidegger formulates the crucial thesis that the being of Dasein thus unveiled, the sense which first makes all the details of the structure of Dasein comprehensible, provides the phenomenal content which 'fills in the meaning of the term 'temporality'' (*SZ* 326).*

What temporality means here is precisely what Heidegger wishes to show through his analysis of Dasein. His review of the ground covered up to that point in the argument shows that the entire analysis, down to its choice of structural terms, was already geared to an all-inclusive interpretation of temporality. The being-in-the-world of Dasein is comprehension, situatedness and articulation or discourse. Comprehension as a kind of know-how or skill draws its possibility from the fact that Dasein is ahead of itself and from this (ultimately, from the anticipation of death) comes back to itself. This state of being-ahead-of-itself is the future of Dasein's temporality. The state of already being in a situation is the having-been of the past, and the intimacy or familiarity (*Sein-bei*) of articulation or discourse is the present. Now, familiarity can insist on inhering in a situation or can seek to overcome its involvement by means of objective science. Dasein can be either authentic or inauthentic, owned or disowned, self-possessed or self-oblivious through absorption in matters contained within the world. In order to make sense of this modifiability, Heidegger, in a new tack upon the issue, distinguishes two equally primordial modes of the temporalization of time: historicality and the state of being within time.

In being situated in the world and thrust into life, Dasein is born into time. In being toward death, it deliberately assumes the finitude of this native condition and carries it into a concrete situation. Out of the 'freedom' which comes with being toward death, Dasein 'retrieves' from its future what it has been. When Dasein brings itself as an individual into its fate and as a people into its destiny, its origin and roots become a heritage. The assuming of fate and destiny is the authentic temporalization of time as historicality. Whenever things happen to come to the forefront in this primary historicality, whether things on hand or ready-to-hand (or, for that matter, a ring worn on the finger or a 'historical' landscape), Heidegger speaks of the 'world-historical', where world refers to the environment with regard to its historicality. But historicality includes more than the world-historical. Historicality can temporalize time only because it regards itself as already situated in time, only because historicality is connected with the state of being within time. Dasein, in being familiar with what it encounters, knows at first hand a 'then', 'now', and 'formerly'. It accordingly dates the beings which it discovers and in the course of such dating extends itself across a stretch of time, the 'during' of a duration. In being with others, such dating is public. The world time with which we reckon publicly can be read from the course of the heavens or from clocks. Dated time is first of all 'time to ...': time to get up, time to go to work, time to do this and that. It is very much a part of our environment. When this environmental condition is levelled, when this variegated world becomes remote, we can still salvage from this dating process a quantifiable and homogeneous sequence of nows. But all enumeration, according to Aristotle, points to the soul which enumerates. This soul, when it counts and enumerates, is always in time, wherein it applies itself to things on hand and ready to hand. But only the soul, or Dasein, really has the capacity to establish the framework of 'within-time-ness' and so to reckon physically and historically with time. Such reckoning can take place in oblivious disregard of itself and its historicality and so can lead to the assumption that the state of being within time is something given. But the state of being within time can also be established in conjunction with bringing about historicality. Dasein is therefore modifiable in its temporality.

In temporality, Dasein articulates its 'already' from its being ahead of itself and so stands out in the three ecstasies of past, present, and future. This 'precedenting and presenting future' first brings forth an 'openness' (*Da*) of being, reveals a world. In Heidegger's own words, 'ecstatic temporality originally clears its 'openness" (*SZ* 351). 'Temporality' here does not refer to the time which is viewed in conjunction with space. Rather, temporality as self-clearing first makes spatiality possible, so that space can then be taken together with time regarded as its fourth dimension. In the temporality of which Heidegger speaks the future does not come later than the past. Rather, both together and at once articulate Dasein as past and future. Heidegger thus can also speak of the future simply as 'advent' and 'coming'. For the same reason, he puts the past participle of being in the form of the present participle 'hav*ing*-been', (*gewesend*) in order to suggest by a breach in German grammar that what is at issue is the presence of the past. The fact that historicality belongs together with the state of being within time makes possible the physicist's time-measurements and the historian's chronology. Measured being-within-time and dated world-history are not possible without the measuring and dating Dasein. But being within time is not on this account merely 'subjective', inasmuch as it is basically a finding oneself in a situation and so not merely a matter of a subject isolated from things. Since Heidegger takes being within time to be implicated with historicality, only Dasein can in the strict sense be temporal. Things are in the time of Dasein. Whatever they themselves might be, they are not temporal in the sense of the temporality of Dasein. Physical assumptions can of course permit us to make time-measurements of those things subject to irreversible processes. Since Dasein is an already, an ahead, and an articulation at the same time, the terms past, future, and present do not refer to the states of being no longer, not yet, and now, as they traditionally did. The analysis of Dasein points out that Dasein in its temporality is finite, which is why Dasein is no longer tomorrow what it was not yet yesterday and is today. That 1981 is no longer, that it is now 1982, that the 'Now' is in fact now, are not matters for philosophy.

Heidegger regards Dasein as modifiable ecstatic temporality because he wants to work out the temporal characteristics inherent in being (which is open in Dasein). These characteristics would serve to distinguish one meaning of being from all the others and, for the first time, to articulate and structure the sense of being in a comprehensive manner. In obvious indebtedness to Kant's doctrine of schematization, Heidegger (in sections 69 a and c) orients the ecstasies to schemata which mediate time with what is temporalized in time or temporalizes itself as time. These schemata can thus point to the characteristics of the time of the being of beings. Dasein as temporal is carried away toward horizons which vary according to the ecstasy which transports Dasein. These horizons manifest their diversity in their schemata.

The schema of the horizon of the future is the 'for the sake of'. Dasein exists, authentically or inauthentically, for the sake of itself. From this 'for the sake of' naturally springs a 'for which'. The question 'what for?' receives an answer from the 'for the sake of'. That which is thus comes to have the 'in which' (*Wobei*) of involvement and relevance.

The schema of having-been is the 'in the face of which' through which Dasein is brought before its facticity, or else the 'on the basis of which' through which Dasein remains consigned to its facticity. From this 'in the face of which' or 'on the basis of which' springs a 'with which' of relevance and involvement.

The horizonal schema of the present is the 'in order to' in which something present is encountered. From it springs 'as' in which we take something as something. Heidegger expressly notes that this 'as' is modifiable. It can be a hermeneutic 'as' by which handy things are fitted and adapted to a working environment (or in a world-historical way to a historical world). But it can also be an apophantic 'as' which can regard something in a literal seeing and thus merely as something on hand.

But how can the schemata of the horizons of time yield characteristics for the different meanings of being and thus serve to distinguish things on hand and ready to hand as well as existent openness? Distinctions can arise because the temporalizing of time is modifiable, occurring in the authentic mode as historicality and in the inauthentic mode in the state of being within time.

The perspective provided by the schemata of authentic temporalizing pertains to a being whose characters reveal being as the being of factic and historical existence. Central to this is the schema of the future, the for-the-sake-of, which in the assumption of being-toward-death still proves to be the possibility of a finite capability of being, accepted in its finitude. The for-the-sake-of is thus tied to the in-the-face-to-which or on-the-basis-of-which, the schema of the past, whose facticity sets limits upon that capability. Together, the schemata of the past and future articulate a present situation which is explicitly assumed and, if need be, modified. The distinctive character of the being of existence points to an individuation which is achieved only in the moment of integration, the historical *kairos*.

But time can also become a perspective upon being in such a way that the condition of being-within-time prevails and historicality is obliterated. This happens, for example, when a craftsman is busy at his craft in self-forgetfulness, so that all beings are defined in terms of their handiness to his particular business. What here determines the for-the-sake-of is not the anticipation of death, which first frees finite possibilities, but the expectancy of an end or goal viewed as an undeniable fact and constant of life. The worker can in this way also reckon with his death, for example, by securing life insurance, seeing to his successor and the disposition of his property, and other such legalities. The on-the-basis-of-which taking facticity into account becomes a retentiveness derived from forgetting how to truly keep a tradition, where even the work relationships are considered self-evident matters of fact. The horizons which open up from the future as past are taken as something unquestionably present. That for the sake of which the entire labor occurs, namely, making a living, articulates the workman's world into an environment in which everything receives ist significance originally from a context of relevances and so does not first get its meaning superimposed upon it through supplemental values.

Heidegger maintains that handy things, whether immediately available or for the moment mislaid, stand in the light of the present, so that their being manifests a 'presential' sense. But this presential sense can still be modified when the guidance provided by the ecstacy of the (inauthentic) future is removed, in other words, when the motivation of the worker's interests and the orientation toward the goals of work are put out of play. Thus it happens that into the place of work steps a curiosity-seeker who wishes only to look around, who thereby can also say that this thing made of wood and iron gets its 'value' from the fact that one can hammer with it. Such curiosity, which assumes exaggerated form in Kierkegaard's aesthetic existence, alienates Dasein from itself, that is, from its primordial possibilities. Dasein is lured into such an alienation because it would like to avoid the unrest that comes with its finitude. In its leisurely repose and sojourn it lets itself be drawn into a mere 'regard' of the 'world' and so ends up in the restlessness of distraction and the loss of all sojourn (§ 36).

However, the accentuation of the present can also lead to scientific work, which as pure theory in objectifying thematization ultimately investigates the hammer without any intention of arriving at a good hammer. As noted above, the horizonal schema of the present is the 'in order to'. From it comes the 'as', according to which we take something as something. Heidegger expressly notes that this 'as' is modifiable. It can be a hermeneutic 'as' by which handy things are fitted and adapted to a working environment (or in a world-historical way to a historical world). But it can also be an apophantic 'as' which can regard something in a literal seeing and thus merely as something on hand. It is not the hermeneutic 'as' but the apophantic 'as' which guides and determines theoretical comportment, in which beings manifest themselves simply by being on hand. This does not exclude the possibility of theoretical research mastering the craft of working with its experimental apparatus or, in a second step, being applied to practical matters.[1]

II

Time as 'temporality' (here, the *Temporalität* of being as opposed to the *Zeitlichkeit* of Dasein) is the transcendental horizon in which beings are surpassed toward being itself and the sense of being is articulated and divided into various meanings. The unpublished third division of *Being and Time* was to have developed time as temporality and accordingly the doctrine of the horizonal schemata and their relation to the characteristics of being. Only a few preliminary indications in the published parts provide a sketchy outline of this project. But do these indications not show that Heidegger, in his intention to break with the dominant prejudice of the philosophical tradition, himself lapses into undemonstrated and untenable prejudices? This question governs the second phase of our considerations.

Heidegger emphasizes that while all three ecstasies are in play at all times in the temporality of Dasein, one of them assumes the lead (*SZ* 350). He presupposes that the 'primary sense' of temporality is the future (*SZ* 327). Future refers to the assumption of being-toward-death in which finite possibilities come over Dasein and thus define an insuperable limit for it. The sphere of the possible is limited in such a way that the 'already' articulates the ahead-of-itself (i.e., the past articulates the future) and brings Dasein into a situation. As comprehension or the capability of being, Dasein 'is' its possibility or possibilities. Possibility as an existential calls for a new concept of being and must not be confused with possibility as a category which, along with actuality and necessity, defines things on hand. But Heidegger does not particularly elaborate the contrast between possibility as an existential and possibility as a category. Nor does he relate the other ecstasies to the other modal categories or modal existentials.

Heidegger's elaboration (§ 68) manifests another remarkable feature with regard to possibility. The interpretation of comprehension or understanding out of temporality develops Dasein's ecstasies in a purely formal way. The interpretation of situatedness, by contrast, expressly employs the distinction between authentic and inauthentic temporalizing and so distinguishes authentic and inauthentic attunement, or dread and fear. Heidegger here notes the parallel with Aristotle's doctrine of the passions and especially with Christian asceticism, which distinguishes *timor castus*, the pure fear of God, from *timor servilis*, the servile fear of the world. In the same vein, should not the traditional doctrine of the virtues also be taken into account, where virtues would be regarded as stabilizations of comprehension or the capability of being? But since the future is regarded not only as the primary sense of temporality but also as the transmission of tradition, the disclosedness of Dasein is unilaterally located in attunement. The moment of comprehension in the phenomenon of 'willing to have a conscience' remains without structure. Historically as well as systematically, the 'royal road of ethics' is drummed out of philosophy.

Let it be noted in passing that the future as transmission of possibilities is likewise the denial of possibilities. In the same vein, what appears of the past is only that which persists from it and, as the 'already' which is to be 'retrieved' from the future, limits the project of that future. In *Being and Time*, the concept of the past as past (*Vergangenheit*) is with polemic fervor replaced by that of having-been (*Gewesenheit*). But is not the past deeper than just having-been? The past is dissipated in passing away; in departing, it retreats into itself.[2] It is only because of this self-withdrawal that it also persists in a transformed state and so can be 'repeated'. As past it is for us pure facticity. But *Being and Time* always links facticity with existentiality, the already with the ahead, and so only takes having-been into account. One can of course point out that the facticity of Dasein ultimately refers to the fact that this Dasein finds itself in a 'world' which has existed for 15 billion years. In the same vein, one might ask how far the concept of the past applies, whether, for example, it makes sense to wish to divide possible evolutions in other galaxies into past, contemporaneous, and future. In any case, it is still inappropriate in an analysis of Dasein to regard the past only in terms of having-been. Heidegger himself appears to pull back from his commitment to a futuristic interpretation of time insofar as he seems to want to return, at least philosophically, to the most ancient of ages. Philosophy, he declares, must be 'ancient' enough in order to be able to conceive the possibilities prepared for us by the 'ancients'. Does this not open the door to a romantic retreat back to a nostalgic past? However, the origin back to which the new appears to be projected is only the initial origin, as opposed to another origin. It is not to be taken for its own sake but only to the extent that it is an occasion for a new origin which is already present in the old.

Having-been and future in their interplay result in an articulation which, in Heidegger's words, 'implies the possibility and necessity of the most radical *individuation*' (*SZ* 38). In his reflections on the *logos* of philosophizing, Heidegger relates articulation as the exposition of situated comprehension to the assertion. He thus regards such articulation as 'discourse', a very remarkable form of articulation. Because Dasein can disregard the finitude of individuation and forget historicality in favor of being within time, this articulation, as a unity of having-been and future, can be modified. When Heidegger parallels this modifiable articulation expressly with the three temporal ecstasies, something unusual takes place. It is not discourse, first introduced as the third structural moment of Dasein, which is paralleled with the third ecstasy of presence, but decadence or fallenness, which is really a modification of the basic structure of Dasein in its entirety. Discourse thus seems to be but an extra fourth moment. In the discussion of discourse, only alienated temporalizing is taken into account, so that everyday chatter, but not genuine conversation, is attributed to the basic structure of Dasein. The voice of conscience speaks only in silence. Articulation as discourse converges conceptually with fallenness because all being-among-beings, or every form of being-present, seem to be but a fallenness. The authentic possibilities of being-with-others (e.g., of wearing a ring) are not explored. On the other hand, the for-the-sake-of-which of the future or in-the-face-of-which of the past appear to be, in expectancy and in retentiveness, merely something present.

Some of the imperfections in Heidegger's presentation can be attributed to the equivocations of the word 'present'. In Heidegger's sense of temporality, the present is the articulation of the already and the ahead taken as a whole, much like Bergson's *durée*. Europe in the present includes Christ insofar as Europe is Christian, anti-Christian and non-Christian, as well as the French Revolution, which determines our already just as much. In its individualized form, this present is finite and always changing in the passing away of customs and traditions. Europe now is the Europe of 1982. But neither 1982 nor this very second is the present Europe. The present Europe is a specific content, a dynamically articulated what. This is to be distinguished from the present understood as the bare that, in the sense of the traditional notion of existence, which distinguishes itself from a future understood as the not-yet and a past as a no-longer (not to be confused with advent and having-been). Inasmuch as Dasein in the traditional sense of the word 'existence' is not a 'real predicate', the present in this second sense seems to reduce itself to a mere point, a sheer limit between future as not yet and past as no longer. Ever since Aristotle, it has been asked to what extent time is really a nothing, for, after all, the future is not yet, the past no longer, and the present this empty limit.[3]

If the experience of time is developed in analogy with the intuition of space in our immediate field of vision and considered as an inner intuition, then this presumably empty limit can assume the proportions of a real predicate. In Husserl's example, the present (the middle note of a triad) belongs with the retained past (of the note just sounded) and the anticipated future (of the note to be sounded) in a threefold temporal dimensionality. Precise analysis of listening to music could in fact show that such consequences are not even implied. Although Heidegger does not take his point of departure from purely 'aesthetic' examples, he nevertheless falls victim to the 'spatialization' and the 'intuitive illustration' of 'time' in speaking of three dimensions in which, in the third place or position, the whole of the twofold articulation (i.e., of handing down and having been) is confused with a modification of this articulation as a whole — the modification of the *kairos* into the present as the bare that. Heidegger is thus led by the phenomena themselves when he finally, in his later work, corrects his initial mistake of giving precedence to fallenness rather than to discourse.

Acknowledgment of these two senses of the present brings a decisive thesis into play: present in the first sense (duration as articulation), as a content, a what, cannot be placed in opposition to present in the second sense (the that, the extant now distinguished from the not-yet and no-longer). Rather, articulation as finite comes to the already presupposed and existing now. So the what here originates, as it were, from the that, which accordingly becomes an ultimate how.[4] Since this how, as a way to be, is already in time, it can congeal into a mere that. As purely factic, a third sense of the present then pertains to it. Dasein physically and historically raises a screen or frame out of its being within time by way of a making present, for which it also uses time as its standard of measurement and dating. Since measuring always refers back to this measure, one can speak of a stable present (e.g., the year, the day, the second, etc.). But constant presence in this sense lacks precisely the present as articulation (e.g., 'Europe') as well as the now in its modal distinction from the not-yet and no-longer. Thus the factic presupposition of all measuring and dating falls out of the measurements and dates.[5]

The temporality of Dasein is originally an articulation of the past and the future. Since this articulation finds itself situated on the basis of the past, it comes to the 'legitimate task of grasping things on hand' (SZ 153). But the pursuit of this task need not lead to the establishment of a cognitive ideal which orients knowledge toward the already and assumes it to be absolutely eternal (the realm of ideas). Merely apprehending things on hand is rather a 'levelling' of the articulation which strips the worldly character from the individuated world to which Dasein is called. The guiding sense of being is thus taken away from an 'I am' which places every 'it is' over against itself, or rather, reduces it to itself.

But inasmuch as denial and departure are not experienced along with handing down (future as advent or coming) and having been, the 'I am' becomes shut up in itself while the sense of being is not at the same time stripped from the 'you are.' This leads to the much-discussed questions of whether the death of the other is not something else than what Heidegger makes of it, whether it is not just as important as the experience of one's own mortality, and whether or not the thou is completely absent from Heidegger's thought. It is precisely an analysis of the I-thou relation which could show that handing down and having been, with the denial and departure associated with them, must not be confused with future and past as the not-yet and the no-longer, which we set in relief from the contemporaneous. Heidegger typically juxtaposes my own existence with the 'they-self' and so bypasses crucial phenomena of the so-called 'objective spirit.' In the final analysis, the fate of the individual is tied to the destiny of a people. The people, once again as something ultimate, thus imposes obligations upon his capacity to be as a finite power. Being means bringing oneself into one's own finitude. Potential objections are thrust aside when Heidegger asks rhetorically: 'But 'does not time go on' in spite of my existing no longer? And cannot a great deal still unfathomed lie 'in the future' and come from it? The answers to all these questions lie in the affirmative. In spite of this, they pose no objections to the finitude of primordial temporality, since they are not at all pertinent to it'(*SZ* 330). Finitude is a characteristic of the 'I am,' whatever the 'I' might mean here, whether self or people. Whatever lies beyond the finitude of the I is not to be made a matter of curiosity. If Heidegger's philosophizing in its various phases commended itself through an eschatological sense of troubled times, this eschatological aura originated from the very heart of the matter. But isn't it possible that the finitude of individuation, which is the end at which the sense of being aims, is in its sense of being defined just as much by the 'you are' as by the 'I am', inasmuch as denial belongs to the handing-down in the I and departure to the having-been?

This one-sided orientation of the sense of being is expressed even more clearly in the formulations of horizonal schemata such as 'for the sake of' and 'in order to'. The temporal interpretation of exemplary modes of givenness brings out the consequences. When curiosity and science are related to the modifying of temporality into the state of being within time and so to falling into the already given, but science is made subject to the guidance and direction of resolve, then an authentic and an inauthentic falling or forfeiture would have to be distinguished, and the concept of falling as an inauthentic mode of Dasein would have to be abandoned. Since he never came to this differentiation, Heidegger could later, in a cheap polemic against 'calculative thinking', underrate the sense of the achievement of exact science, and not take into account that even counting can play a role in a framework which serves to interpret the given. The attempt to undercut Plato's theory of ideas does not see the validity which this doctrine could have in certain limited areas. From the perspective which he takes, Heidegger cannot even discuss the question of whether there can be 'archetypes' in the life of the soul or a 'natural law' in the life of law. To be sure, he does acknowledge that 'ideality' is phenomenally grounded in Dasein. But instead of making ideality comprehensible, he polemically exposes the danger of going from ideality back to a 'fancifully idealized subject' (*SZ* 229) as a parallel to his own return to a finite I. The comprehension of history, intended to introduce a finite-historical individuation into the sphere of other individuations, is related, along with such divergent figures as the Nietzsche of the Second Untimely Meditation and Count Yorck von Wartenburg, to his own undergoing of history. The sound insight that only he who endures history can really comprehend history, at the same time curtails historical comprehension to the dimension of decision.

III

To conclude, at least a summary inquiry should be made into whether the attempt to ground philosophy anew through temporal interpretation is not on the whole erected upon untenable presuppositions. Being — which was Heidegger's point of departure — has been thought as presence, which refers to the present, which is only one of the dimensions of time. If we go along with the literal translation of *ousia* as presence, then we must also allow that the words 'presence' and 'the present' are interchangeable. The phrase 'in the presence of many guests' can be said in at least two ways in German: 'In Anwesenheit zahlreicher Gäste' and 'In Gegenwart zahlreicher Gäste'. Does *Gegenwart* here refer to only one dimension of time, the present in contrast with the past and the future? Does the discovery that being has been thought as *Anwesenheit* and therefore as *Gegenwart* necessarily lead to the question of being and time? Certainly not. We can surely say 'yesterday, in the presence of many guests', but yesterday's presence cannot be apprehended as past, permitting us to say 'in the past of many guests'. 'In Gegenwart', 'in Anwesenheit' or 'in Beisein' (a third way of saying 'in the presence of' in German!) refer to the affiliation of different parties in an activity. This presence is enabled as much by space as by time. Beyond that, it requires that the guests actually be 'there', and as guests, so that they may act accordingly in such a context and not like 'stones', for example. All of these meanings are implied in the notion of presence. If I were to say, 'He spoke in the presence of stones', everyone understands that this presence was not the desired and appropriate one, it was not the fulfilled presence. Language is clearly more clever than the philosopher who appeals to it and relies upon it.

It can now be noted that Heidegger gives precisely this unusually broad connotation to the temporality which he discusses. He believes himself justified in doing so because the philosophical tradition has always spoken in the same way, for example, when it characterized being as apriori, and so in the light of time. The question nevertheless remains whether Heidegger does not confuse temporality of this sort with other representations of time. This is indicated by the thesis that the tradition, using intuitively given things as its guiding clue, has defined being in terms of a 'presential' sense. But here as well, the 'presential' is not really a temporal characteristic, since intuition takes place as much in space as in time. If we wanted to examine the temporal aspect rigorously, we would instead have to speak of a 'perfect' tense. With the apriori, thinking arrives at something that cannot be modified, and thus at something which has already been in the fullest sense, that is to say, 'perfectly'. This having-been in its perfection can then be regarded also as an eternal present. Plato's doctrine of *anamnesis*, or his call to the statesman immersed in his times to return to the realm of essences, manifests this interpretation of being in the perfect tense just as does Hegel's parallel between *Wesen* and *gewesen*, between 'essence' and 'having been'.

When Heidegger attempts to extract a futuristic interpretation from this interpretation of being in the perfect tense, does he not have to take seriously the fact that temporality in the sense meant by him is itself temporal, that his ontology not only must take historicality into account, but also must understand itself as historical? He says as much in his programmatic statement of

§ 6: since the tradition took being as presence and placed it in the unexamined light of time, the question of being and time must now be explicitly raised. This questioning and the ontology thus formed is historical. But since the historical part of *Being and Time* was to follow the systematic part and then did not appear at all, the work failed to do justice to its hermeneutic intentions. Many ambiguities therefore remain: Can the craft commerce with the handy, which had its historical hour, be indicative of the 'natural world' in a paradigmatic way, even though not even the world of the primitives can be illuminated by it? Is the talk of historicality not related to the historically experienced man of our transitional period, who has gone through Christian eschataology and modern historicism? Concrete investigations must be undertaken to determine what in the meanings of being already propounded is historical and what perhaps points to a basis which underlies historical change. Instead, in conformity with the Aristotelian doctrine of the analogy of being, the exemplary meanings of being are related to a dominant meaning. Heidegger, like his teacher Brentano, follows the medieval version of the doctrine: In a genealogy of being, the various meanings are obtained by way of derivation and privation from a leading meaning — no longer the divine being, but the historical being of Dasein. The thesis of the historicality of ontology formation can go together with this conception of the analogy of being, because in an eschatological atmosphere an individuation is sought which secludes itself in itself as something ultimate and does not comprehend itself as one individuation among others.

Programmatically, Heidegger maintains throughout that an idea of being can be obtained only when, along with existing Dasein, all the beings not like it are also investigated in their being, not only things on hand and ready to hand but also those which simply 'persist' (*SZ* 333). However, this program is countermanded by the doctrine of the analogy of being, which gives existing Dasein a leading role. Heidegger can also support this interpretation by a retrospective glance at the monadological metaphysics of Leibniz. And so the concept of being on hand or 'present-at-hand' remains obscure. Does it refer to the thinglike entity which refuses to be situated in Dasein's kind of world, or does it mean the state of being given to the Dasein who simply 'looks'? If it is the latter, then even world-historical matters would be given to the historian who simply observes, and personal matters would be given to Kierkegaard's aesthete in the mode of being on hand. But Heidegger does not draw this consequence. Instead, from the polemic of Christianity and life philosophy against the Greek 'lust of the eyes', he draws the myth that the orientation toward thinglike beings allowed Greek philosophy to take being as an idea and so as appearance or 'look'. Great significance is given to existential possibility but we are given no hint of how it differs from categorial possibility. Excluded from consideration from the start are metaphysical questions such as how life can emerge at all from inert matter; how, of the specific forms that are possible, some are suddenly realized in evolution, such as the beauteous world of blossoming plants and the insects; what sort of meaning the emergence of 'spirit' has in this world (for that matter, what does 'death' mean in this context?). Heidegger labels such questions as 'metaphysical'. He does not rule them out entirely, but the preliminary question of how ontology is formed at all takes precedence over them. And yet this would have been the place to ask whether or not the orientation of the sense of being toward an ultimate 'I am' is likewise charged with prejudices of a 'metaphysical' kind. Heidegger's position is clear: to distinguish regions of entities and to construe existing Dasein as one of these regions would result in directing oneself toward the 'it is' and thus missing the governing role of the 'I am'. If, however, the 'I am' were understood as the individuation among individuations, then, from the ensuing self-differentiation between beings like Dasein and those which are not, not only the 'you are' but also the 'it is' could be given the meaning which is appropriate to each. (Here I can refer to Hans Jonas' book *The Phenomenon of Life*).

Does Heidegger's discourse of temporality not involve an unclarified metaphorology? We speak of a metaphor when a familiar word receives a second meaning from its use in a certain context. But what takes place here is not simply a matter of a simile between what is signified in the second location and that of the first. Talk of a 'lion in battle' is a metaphor only if the one who does the fighting is not really a lion but a king, for example. When a primitive man said 'I am this animal', no metaphorical language was involved for, in his mythical consciousness, he is in fact the totem animal. Even the talk of an electric current initially meant just that, since it was assumed that something really flowed through the metal. The progress of physics made this language metaphorical. But nowadays we no longer experience its metaphorical character. What we have is a dead metaphor, which gets its meaning immediately and not as a second meaning mediated by a context. It seems as if the talk of temporality and temporalizing has already, in some phenomenological works, likewise become a suppressed or dead metaphor. To some, the insistence with which authentic time is sought in Heideggerian circles itself betrays a quasi-mythical consciousness. Inasmuch as Heidegger still expressly seeks the transition from familiar time to the temporal characteristics of being in the horizontal schemata of the temporal ecstases, he suggests that the language of temporality must have a metaphorical character for our customary ways of speaking. The question remains whether it is possible to avoid such a metaphoric, if phenomenology is regarded as a science of origins. Theologians have said that we do not call God a 'father' from our experience of earthly fathers. It is rather the reverse: because we experience God as father, we can also know what an earthly father is. In the same vein, Heidegger can maintain that it is only because we experience being in its ecstatic or 'temporal' character that we can know time in the ordinary sense. But the question still remains whether that which is sought in asking the question of being — the *sense* of being, which 'calls for a unique set of concepts' (*SZ* 6) — is not obscured by conceptions of time which, though familiar, are nevertheless used in an unclarified way. This seems to be the case, even though such a metaphoric is at the same time illuminating for the purpose for the purpose for which it is used, which is to think of being in a way which permits movement to be attributed to it. Time distinguishes itself from the traditional representations of space by giving prominence to the finitude of movement in its irreversibility and in its uniqueness, its character of 'one time and never again'. It is precisely this concern with the finitude of the movement of being which became the new and dominant theme in the philosophy of time of the last century.

It was Heidegger himself who, a few years after the appearance of *Being and Time*, discovered unclarified prejudices in his approach and accordingly modified it. There it was asserted that various modes of the temporalization of time results in Dasein taking beings in a differentiated being. Such talk presupposes that the sense of being develops itself in different meanings. But this development — for example, the exposition of the mode of givenness of being handy or ready to hand — is by and large already presumed throughout history. But prehistorical man was not familiar with a tool in our sense and today we can no longer transpose the old-fashioned world of the shoemaker and carpenter into technical civilization. If being as a mode of givenness is the openness or truth of beings, then the movement of Being, in which it explicates itself into different modes of being, can be taken as the truth of being itself. Heidegger now calls this truth 'history' of a unique kind, namely the history of being. Temporality, which with its schemata was regarded as the ultimate principle of differentiation of the modes of being, now fades away in the movement of this history. Heidegger explicitly retracts the way in which he had at one time made *Temporalität* the Platonic idea of ideas. When the tradition took being as presence, it was characterized by an oblivion of being which failed to question it precisely with regard to the temporal character of this presence. The experience which leads to the new phase of Heidegger's thought indicates that this oblivion cannot be abrogated once and for all (by the application of the principle of temporality), inasmuch as it belongs to the 'essence' (to be taken verbally) of being itself. Being itself is in its truth not a determinable ultimate ground but rather groundless, like an abyss, since no reason can be specified for the fact that it gives this truth at all; likewise, it is ungrounded, since the single leading meaning of being, which perhaps dominates an entire epoch, obscures other possible meanings. 'Finitude' is now rooted in this abyss-like state of being without ground. The abysslike ungrounded ground of the truth of being is a happening in an extraordinary sense, but it is not movement which can be unilaterally read in time. But while he speaks of a history of being, Heidegger still emphasizes that the finitude of being, as a possibility of the most radical individuation, is always thought out of the utmost radicalization in historicality.

It is still the custom to distinguish a Heidegger I from a Heidegger II and to execute a 'turn' from the first to the second, that is, from the analysis of Dasein to the history of being. Heidegger himself has spoken of three decisive phases in his thought: the question of the sense of being, the question of truth as history or the history of being, and the question of the clearing. Indeed, he lamented the fact that the second phase accentuating history had been slipped in between the first and the third. The experience which leads from the second to the third phase and so to Heidegger's later work can be formulated in the following way: the truth of being cannot be thought as history, because history in the non-metaphorical sense is in fact but one of the realms opened up by the truth of being. If the truth of being itself as abyss-like ungrounded ground reveals being in different ways as the truth of beings, so that it holds itself back in its inexahaustibility, even obscuring other meanings by the governing meaning of being that is put forward, then this double selfwithholding or concealing (the so-called 'epoche' of being) also enables the epochal character of history, as distinct from nature as well as from what is called 'ideal' being. (This distinction between history as a realm of beings and what is called the history of being must not be covered over by a premature doctrine of the analogy of being.) Heidegger takes pains to expunge the metaphoric which seems to resonate, for example, in his discussion of the mission of being. Such a mission is not to be understood from history, but from a transmission or sending as a consigning and adapting-itself-to, the assignment or allocation of a leading meaning on the basis of obscuring other meanings, thus a revelation together with a concealment.[6] Obviously, a metaphoric of space now comes to the fore in characterizing what in *Being and Time* was called the 'transcendental horizon'. This metaphoric gains prominence when Heidegger speaks of a regioning region, a countering country, or a prespatial place. The dynamics and finitude of the mobility of this horizon is suggested when the region is regarded as the locus of thought and thought in turn is regarded as a way, so that the regioning of this region is that which enables the way, 'makes way' for thought, as it were. This metaphoric also includes Heidegger's long-standing favorite, *Lichtung*, or 'clearing', first of all thought in terms of a clearing in the woods wrested from the forest enclosure as an opening upon the earth which lets the sky break in and form its horizon. (With this in mind, 'lighting' might then be used as a second, though derivative, translation of *Lichtung*.)

But nowhere does Heidegger try to clarify whether the language of thinking may or perhaps must use such metaphors. The unclarified metaphoric of time admitted that time or, more precisely, temporality and historicality in *Being and Time*, is, on the one hand, used as a principle of the differentation of the modes of being and of Dasein and, on the other hand, functions in the discussion of the historicality of the construction of any ontology as the medium in which that differentiation occurs.[7] The ensuing aporia induce Heidegger to give up the temporal interpretation and to try other approaches. Thus, in the second phase of his thought he explores the history of the truth and in the third the clearing as the issue of his thinking.[8]

In these different approaches, Heidegger contributed to recent attempts to wrest a futuristic interpretation from the traditional 'present-tense' — or better, 'perfect-tense' — interpretation of being. Heidegger's way was to relate 'being' in a positive sense to finite individuation. In circling this issue under the leitmotif of 'Being and Time', Heidegger wished to purge this approach of the unconscious prejudices which traditional metaphysics had not expressly overcome. Perhaps because of this, a scholasticizing of the original motive took place when the traditional schemata entered into the approach and together with what was actually sought produced an unclarified metaphoric. The same thing happened to Hegel when he took his goal to be a dialectic, which he interpreted as a move counter to traditional logic. Marx likewise ultimately distorted what is justified in his motives by relying upon this dialectic.

When Heidegger applied the motive of his thinking to the question of being and time, he understood his thinking as 'hermeneutical'. Insofar as he articulated the sense of being from an ultimate 'I am', he interjected a metaphysical motive into his thinking, a bias that distorted hermeneutics, which is intended to go with life as it is and so also with scientific work. So it was not by chance that Heidegger finally ended in a thinking which remained alone and wanted to remain alone. This was likewise Husserl's fate, with whom he worked for long years in the same city, although between these two, who had wanted to work together, no further word was exchanged, and worlds in fact separated their respective endeavors. Heidegger's thinking became a way which was intended to lead Western thinking irrevocably beyond itself. Hence the key to the way, namely the transformation of the dominant presuppositions of thinking, was not intended to be merely something of interest psychologically or heuristically, but the very 'logic' of thinking. Heidegger has always made his position clear: when thinking becomes the 'way', it does not remain a mere self-exposition or historical exploration of a self-changing individuation. Thinking must rather forego existential, religious, or political decisions and hermeneutically investigate only the underlying structures. Heraclitus already said it: the way up and the way down — as you go and as I go — are one and the same. The question remains how philosophy is able to apprehend the same. To this question Heidegger has made a decisive contribution.

NOTES

* Numbers prefixed by 'SZ' and placed in parentheses in the body of the text refer to the pagination of *Sein und Zeit*, which is given in the margin of the English translation.

1 The distinction between the hermeneutic and the apophantic 'as' which Heidegger discovered in his study of Aristotle leads to the project of philosophy as hermeneutic. Provisionally introduced in § 33 of *Being and Time*, the distinction really belongs in the doctrine of the schemata of the temporal ecstases. For details, especially with regard to how temporal interpretation is essentially hermeneutic philosophy, see the introduction to my anthology, *Hermeneutische Philosophie* (Munich: Nymphenburger, 1972) pp. 18ff. Ricoeur's thesis that *Being and Time* ontologizes the notion of comprehension or understanding distorts the significance of this work for the development of a hermeneutic philosophy.

2 In poetic constructions of the experience of parting and leavetaking, therefore, the question of eternity is raised. See the work (in fact oriented toward Hegel) of J. Hoffmeister, *Der Abschied* (Hameln, 1949). Heidegger clearly wishes to leave eternity to theology; he has always refused to take temporality and finitude quasi-theologically as something ultimate.

3 On Aristotle, see Heidegger's *Die Grundprobleme der Phänomenologie* (Frankfurt: Klostermann, 1975) p. 331; on Augustine, see his *Was heisst Denken?* (Tübingen: Niemeyer, 1954) p. 41.

4 On the reduction of the distinction of being-what and being-that to that of what and how, see *Grundprobleme*, p. 170.

5 Oskar Becker, *Grösse und Grenze der mathematischen Denkweise* (Freiburg/Munich, 1959) pp. 58, 61. Heidegger brings together Einstein's 'revolution' in physics and Dilthey's 'revolution' in the historical sciences. See his *Logik: Die Frage nach der Wahrheit* (Frankfurt: Klostermann, 1976) p. 17. The thesis that even Einstein is concerned with 'measuring' obstructs inquiry into the philosophical significance of Einstein's theory, since Heidegger develops what he means by measuring from the paradigm of Newtonian physics. Later, Heidegger compares Heisenberg's quantum mechanics understood as a collapse of the subject-object separation with his own efforts in *Being and Time*, but leaves undiscussed just how it differs from Heisenberg's Pythagoreanism. See my obituary *Martin Heidegger* in *Zeitschrift für allgemeine Wissenschaftstheorie* VII (1977).

6 If philosophers since Hegel have tried to mediate the transcendental approach with history, Heidegger here – contrary to the usual opinion among exegetes – takes leave of this endeavor. See my lecture 'Historicity' in Heidegger's Late Work', *The Southwestern Journal of Philosophy* IV (1973) 53-73, as well as the chapter 'Philosophie und Geschichte' in my book, *Hegels Idee einer Phänomenologie des Geistes* (Freiburg/Munich, 1973).

7 See my lecture 'Heidegger's Topology of Being', Joseph Kockelmans (ed.), *On Heidegger and Language* (Evanston: Northwestern UP, 1972) 107-146.

8 "Historicity' in Heidegger's Late Work', esp. 65-73.

COMMENTS ON PROFESSOR PÖGGELER'S PAPER

KARL-OTTO APEL

I am not prepared to go into the details and do justice to the subtle points of Professor Pöggeler's interpretation of Heidegger's philosophy of time. Instead I take the licence of focusing on a very general point of his paper.

Professor Pöggeler, at the beginning of his paper and at the end of it, states that Heidegger's philosophy is *epoch-making*. He does so in spite of many criticisms. Thus the question arises: what precisely makes Heidegger's thought epoch-making?

Professor Pöggeler introduces a distinction between three phases or stages of Heidegger's thought: 1. Philosophy of 'Dasein'; 2. History of Being as 'history of truth'; 3. the happening ('Ereignis') of the clearing or lighting of (the truth) of being. In view of this tripartition, I would like to raise the question: by which of these 3 phases is Heidegger's thought epoch-making? Or better: in the sense of which phase can the epoch-making contribution of his thought be definitely formulated?

It seems to me that Professor Pöggeler, notwithstanding his critical remarks, sees an inner consequence in the development of Heidegger's thought, such that even his critical remarks may be integrated into his reconstruction of the internal logic of Heidegger's way of thought. Hence it seems that also the epoch-making contribution of Heidegger's thought can only be found out and/or brought out through following (tracing) the turns or changes of Heidegger's thought from the first into the second and finally into the third phase.

This would mean that, on Pöggeler's account, the temporal interpretation of the meaning of being from the view-point of 'Dasein' has to be transcended, at least in a sense, by the insight that the apparent systematics of that analysis, i.e. the idea of 'existential ontology' as 'fundamental ontology', is itself only a paradigmatic Gestalt in the history of the truth of being. And again, that even the history of the truth of being, in as far as it is a history, must still be conceived of as only one of the ontological realms or regions that are opened up through the happening of the clearing or lighting of being.

Hence it seems that the notion of the happening of the clearing or lighting of being definitively makes up (presents) Heidegger's epoch-making contribution to philosophical thought. I would, in a sense, agree with this thesis.

See notes at the end of this chapter.

And such a comment is even made easier or more plausible to me by the consideration that Heidegger in his last (final) notion of the 'lighting of being' comes again closer to his original question concerning the constitution of the meaning of being, whereas in the second phase he was rather guided by the claim that he had detected the original meaning of truth by his tracing that idea back to the idea of opening or uncovering ($\acute{\alpha}$-$\lambda\gamma\sigma\epsilon\iota\alpha$) and hence could speak of a history of the happening of truth. As is well known, Heidegger corrected himself in this respect after the publication of Tugendhat's book, *The concept of Truth in Husserl and Heidegger*[1], and made clear that he in fact did not discover the original meaning of truth but something different – viz. the 'lighting of being' – that must precede truth, viz. propositional truth, being the condition of its possibility.[2]

I think that, by this clarification, Heidegger has summarized the meaning of his contribution to philosophical thought in the sense of his 3rd and last period of thought. And I would in fact agree that he thereby has outlined the essential core of his epoch-making contribution to philosophical thought, but, I would suggest, also the limits of this approach.

Let me try to elucidate (or illustrate) the point of this remark:

Plato, in his progress from 'Kratylos' to 'Theaithetos' and 'Sophistes', seems to have won the insight that truth is not a matter of words (of the $\acute{o}\phi o\acute{o}\tau\gamma\varsigma$ $\acute{o}\nu o\mu\acute{\alpha}\tau\omega\nu$), but a matter of the 'logos', i.e. of the proposition as connection of words reflecting a connection of ideas. This was the very foundation of propositional logic and classical epistemology and ontology. Now, in a sense still to be clarified, we must stick to this conception of propositional truth. In an other sense, still to be clarified too, we have to go back behind Plato's step along with Heidegger.

This, I suggest, makes up the significance of Heidegger's discovery of the opening of being and, on the other hand, of his late self-correction. What does this mean?

Heidegger, through his discovery of truth as 'opening' which is at the same time 'concealing', has in a sense come back to a notion of truth that lies already in the words, supposing that the words are not taken as abstract linguistic entities ('Wörter-Dinge') but as embodiments ''incarnations'') of meaning-happenings, so to speak ('Worte' in the sense of 'Wortungen', as it was called in the tradition of German 'Logos-Mystik'[3]).

I think in fact that each word of a living language can in this sense be considered as a paradigm of that opening and concealing of being that fixes itself in so called natural language as 'house of being' and 'housing of the human being'[4] and as such precedes and makes possible the truth and falsehood of propositions. (One may, in this context, think of the modern linguistic theory of 'meaning-fields' as a realisation of Wilhelm von Humboldt's vision concerning the truth – or falsehood – provided through the immanent world-views of languages[5].)

Formerly, I tried to develop along these lines the program of a Transcendental Hermeneutics of Language from a Heideggerian vantage-point[6]. But in the meantime Heidegger had discarded Hermeneutics as well as transcendental philosophy in his later work. At present, I believe indeed that transcendental hermeneutics cannot be grounded on the basis of Heidegger's philosophy; but this does not mean that I would side with Heidegger against transcendental hermeneutics. Heidegger came to reject hermeneutics and transcendental philosophy as part of metaphysics. I myself have come to reject a foundation of transcendental hermeneutics exclusively on Heideggerian premises because this would amount, in my opinion, to exchanging 'oblivion of being' ('Seinsvergessenheit') for 'oblivion of the logos' ('Logosvergessenheit'). This point of view led me to depart from Heidegger, at least in some very fundamental respects, and to project rather a transformation of transcendental philosophy[7]. Let me elucidate on this point.

As Heidegger himself reconfirms by his late self-correction, opening the meaning of being is not yet truth; it is only a condition of the possibility of truth. What does that mean? Talk about a condition of the possibility of truth sounds like transcendental philosophy. Is Heidegger's discovery of the opening or lighting a discovery by transcendental philosophy? How then does this discovery fit in with classical transcendental philosophy?

In order to answer these questions, it is useful to turn back to 'Being and Time'. In its context Heidegger's late declaration that the opening or lighting of being is not yet truth but a necessary pre-condition of truth has a rather precise pre-figuration: There it is said that the primary disclosure of being ('Seinserschliessung') is not accomplished through the 'predicative synthesis' of judgments but through a 'hermeneutic synthesis' of understanding that precedes the predicative synthesis of judgments or, respectively of 'apophantic statements' ('Aussagen'). The hermeneutic 'as' must precede the apophantic 'as' in the sense of a quasi-transcendental meaning-genesis, so to speak.

Now, I still think, this was an important new insight which opened up the hermeneutic dimension of the transcendental pre-conditions of propositional truth, or, in other words: the dimension of those transcendental pre-conditions of intersubjectively valid truth that cannot be traced back to Kant's functions of understanding in the sense of pre-communicative and pre-historical consciousness in general. Instead of these Kantian pre-conditions of world-understanding or instead of Husserl's noetic-noematic achievements of intentional acts, a sphere of preconditions of world-constitution was disclosed that precedes all subjective achievements in so far as it is bound up with the existential structure of human being-in-the-world which in its part is bound up with the socio-historical structure of the epochal disclosure of being itself.

However, does this mean that the hermeneutical synthesis of world-understanding qua opening or clearing of being can be completely disconnected from the (subjective) pre-conditions of the validity of predicative synthesis of judgments in the Kantian sense? In other words, can it be supposed that the 'lighting of being' in Heidegger's sense is a necessary and sufficient condition of propositional truth in such a sense that this notion can render obsolete the traditional type of transcendental-philosophy?

This seems to be indeed Heidegger's contention at least during the second period of his way of thought, since he proclaimed the surmounting or dissolution ('Verwindung') of the traditional philosophy of 'Subjectivity' ('Subjektivität').

This turn was already prepared during the first period, I think, since Heidegger already in 'Being and Time' suggested that the apophantic 'as' of propositions as formulations of theoretical knowledge is merely a deficient mode or privation of the hermeneutical 'as' in the sense of the 'as' of world-disclosure in the context of practical world-commitment. From this it followed that also objectivity or objective validity of scientific knowledge is to be conceived of as merely a deficient mode of the significant openness of world-understanding within the context of practical world-commitment ('Umgang'). Now this, I think, was one of Heidegger's most exciting, most influential and most problematic contentions. And, according to my feeling, the thesis was never really discussed with respect to its plausible and implausible aspects; rather it became a reason for a parting of minds ('Scheidung der Geister'). (Thus e.g. N. Hartmann refused Heidegger's pre-predicative or pre-theoretic understanding of the world as relevance-connection ('Bewandtnis-Zusammenhang') of the 'ready at hand' as being a 'geistloses Bewusstsein' (spiritless consciousness)).

I would suggest that this crucial epistemological question has to be discussed in close connection with the more general question whether the 'lighting of being' is in fact the necessary *and sufficient* condition of the possibility of propositional truth, such that a history of the truth of being, or at least a philosophy of the happening of the lighting of being may transcend and relativize classical transcendental-philosophy.

The answer to this question cannot be unambiguous, I should think. I will try to sketch an answer in the following in terms of a philosophy that considers Heidegger's philosophy not as a surmounting of transcendental-philosophy, but rather as part of a necessary transformation of 'transcendental philosophy'.

Starting out with Heidegger's contention that scientific knowledge, or rather theoretical-objective knowledge, is merely a deficient mode of world-understanding within the context of practical world-commitment, I would first emphasize that there is a truth-kernel in this contention, but also an overstatement that may be explained, I suggest, as a consequence of a phenomenological confusion.

The truth-kernel in Heidegger's contention seems to me to lie in the insight that a pure mind or consciousness, so to speak, that would only glare (or stare) at things as pure objects could not discover any-thing as something, i.e. understand it according to its being, because it would not have any view-points from which to discover the significance of things. Thus it turns out, that the apophantic 'as' of the predicative synthesis is in fact grounded in the hermeneutic 'as' of a synthesis of world-understanding that is bound up with the practical world-commitment of being in the world.

Now, one important consequence of this fact of transcendental hermeneutics seems to me to lie in the circumstance that scientific knowledge itself is not to be conceived of as possible without presupposing certain cognitive interests (or knowledge-leading interests) that spring from the relationship of our world-understanding to the 'for the sake of' of our practical committments of life, which thus may provide view-points for different questions underlying different types of possible inquiries[8]. In this respect the structure of care, i.e. of 'Dasein's being ahead of itself', seems to me in fact to be even a pre-condition of fundamental view-points of research-guiding questions, and in that sense even a pre-condition of the categories in the Kantian sense. (For example, one may make this clear with respect to the category of causality which presupposes our practical commitment to intervening in the course of nature and bringing about something through doing something.[9])

However, this internal connection between the view-points of scientific questions and the pre-predicative synthesis of world-understanding shows also that the apophantic attitude of theoretical knowledge is not just identical with glaring at things as beings that are merely 'on hand' (*vorhanden*). In fact, on the basis of this limit-case attitude — which has its exact parallel in the later Wittgenstein's caricature of pure naming of things without any context of a language-game[10] — no scientific theories could constitute themselves any longer. Hence the secret of existential pre-conditions of the constitution of scientific theories on the basis of a certain modification of our (practical commitment of) 'being-in-the world' can not yet be disclosed by the talk of 'being on hand' ('Vorhandenheit') as a deficient mode of 'being ready at hand' ('Zuhandenheit').

In fact, the answer to this question, I would suggest, must rather take its vantage-point from the fact (also stressed by Heidegger and Pöggeler) that our world-understanding can and must become a *public* one with the aid of discourse. To suggest the point more precisely, I would try to interpret the modification of being-in-the-world that constitutes the basis of science in terms of a crucial modification of the demand for the publicness of our world-understanding, such that the publicness of the shared meanings of everyday language is no longer satisfactory, but has to be superseded by the postulate for strict *objectivity*, i.e. *intersubjective validity* of formulated knowledge, i.e. of its propositional truth. Thus, on my account, it is not the phenomenological limit-case of pure being-on-hand (*Vorhandenheit*) of beings, but rather the limit-case of a radical universalisation of publicness that provides the crucial meaning of objectivity of scientific knowledge. And this latter demand of a radicalization of the demand for publicness into that of strictly intersubjective validity is an implicit demand of the truth-claims of every-day statements, I would suggest. The consequences of this move with respect to the idea of transcendental hermeneutics are rather interesting with regard to a further argument concerning Heidegger's departure from traditional transcendental philosophy.

First, it has to be stressed that the demand for radical publicness qua intersubjective validity (which is implicit even in every-day statements) is a common original concern of science and philosophy. It is identical, I suggest, with the discovery of the *logos*, as it is testified to e.g. by Herakleitos who said that the sleeping people have different worlds but the awakened have only one world, due to the deep logos in their souls.

Second, it has to be stressed that Heidegger himself in his own philosophical claims must presuppose and make use of the universal validity claims of the propositional *logos*. This topic, by the way, is implicitly touched upon by Heidegger himself in 'Being and Time' where he suggests the need and the possibility of a 'radicalisation' of the 'pre-ontological' (i.e. existential) world- and self-understanding into a fundamental-ontological understanding of being'. It was Theodor Litt in 1948 who emphasized – from a neo-Hegelian standpoint – how Heidegger's claim of a 'radicalization' of understanding presupposes the universal *logos*[11]. But a thorough discussion did not really come about even in this case.

I would suppose, from my present stand-point, that Heidegger in fact never seriously considered the question what it should mean for himself, i.e. with regard to the pre-conditions of his philosophy, that he, after all, had to presuppose the universalistic truth-claim, and that is to say, intersubjective validity-claim of the (scientific and philosophical) *logos*. It means, among other things, that all insights into dependencies of world-views and philosophical ontologies (and, for that matter, of paradigms of scientific theories) on epochs of the history of being transcend in principle the possible scope of relativization. For philosophical hermeneutics may progressively discover new mediating conditions of a historical world-constitution; nonetheless, it cannot thereby meaningfully relativize itself, i.e. its own truth-claim, by claiming the possibility of quite another epochal logos, so to speak.

If I see things rightly, precisely this attitude of total relativizing and even obsoletizing philosophical truth-claims, especially transcendental philosophical truth-claims, by way of socio-historical imagination and linguistic-structuralistic speculations has become fashionable in our day, along the lines of either a quasi-Heideggerian, or a quasi-Wittgensteinian, or a quasi-structuralist way of thinking. Now, it must be said quite strictly, I think, that to assert that human thought could imagine quite other types of thought than itself amounts to what I would call 'oblivion of the *logos*'; and that means that such thinking is not self-critical at all but, quite to the contrary, deeply uncritical and even nonsensical, in a sense.

Now, in order at least tentatively to show the bearing of these considerations with regard to O. Pöggeler's topic, let me finally take up the question of authentic and inauthentic temporality, as it was discussed by Heidegger in 'Being and Time'. I would claim even today – in fundamental agreement with Heidegger – that forgetting about the authentic temporality of human 'Dasein', including its historicality, in favor, say, of a scientistic objectivism, which would dispose of human actions and history as of change-processes within the frame of the data-time, amounts to presenting a paradigm of inauthentic temporality of human 'ek-sistence'. (I would even go farther and claim that the logical-semanticist attitude of dealing with truth in as far as it illegitimately abstracts from the transcendental-pragmatic pre-conditions of propositional truth amounts to the same type of 'fallenness'[12])

However, Professor Pöggeler also claims — if I understand him rightly — that there must of course be a possibility of practicing science, and, for that matter, logical semantics and finally philosophy (in as far as it is bound up to the common logos of science and philosophy) without falling a victim to inauthentic temporality. But what would that way look like?

Heidegger, as far as I can see, in 'Being and Time' knows only one other mode of authentic temporality of human 'Dasein' besides that of being oneself in taking over one's own being unto death in one's radical individualisation ('Vereinzelnung'). The other mode is represented by belonging to the destiny of one's nation ('Volk') and thereby participating in an authentic 'we' (wir) and taking over a heritage of history.

Now, I would suggest that there is a *third* mode of *authentic temporality* which Heidegger seems to overlook or disregard in the same sense as he overlooks the necessary radicalisation of publicness in his account of scientific, or even philosophical, knowledge-claims. The third mode I have in mind has been represented, in a still somewhat one-sided and scientistic way, e.g. by Ch.S. Peirce's demand of joining the indefinite community of scientific investigators and thus the collective enterprize of progress towards the truth as universal consensus through a moral 'surrender' of all private interests of life, including even one's soteriological interests[13]. This paradigm of joining the temporality of a human enterprise in history might be called one-sided, and even scientistic, as I suggested. Nevertheless, it provides a paradigm of temporality of 'Dasein' that is not simply based on 'fallenness' within time; it rather is based on a resolute surrender of one's concern with one's own individuality.

I would suggest that there must be some mode of joining the progress of an indefinite communication-community towards realizing the idea of the transcendental subject (which is anticipated counterfactually in our arguing) that may transcend the scientistic limitations of the Peircean conception. It would be relevant not only for the scientific mode of 'Dasein', but even with regard to the problem of realizing practical reason in the sense of ethics[14]. It might thus represent an alternative to Heidegger's surmounting of transcendental philosophy and the very *logos* of philosophy — an alternative in the direction of a *transcendental-hermeneutic and transcendental-pragmatic transformation of classical transcendental philosophy*.

106

NOTES

1 E. Tugendhat, *Der Wahrheitsbegriff bei Husserl und Heidegger*, Berlin: W. de Gruyter, 1967.

2 Cf. M. Heidegger, *Zur Sache des Denkens*, Tübingen 1969, p. 76 f.

3 Cf. K.-O. Apel, *Die Idee der Sprache in der Tradition des Humanismus von Dante bis Vico*, Bonn: Bouvier, ²1975, index.

4 Cf. Heidegger, 'Brief über den 'Humanismus'', in: *Wegmarken*, Frankfurt a.M.: Klostermann, 1967.

5 Cf. e.g. G. Gipper (ed.), *Sprache – Schlüssel zur Welt*, Düsseldorf; Schwann, 1959.

6 Cf. K.-O. Apel, *Die Idee der Sprache* ..., loc.cit. (see note 3), Einleitung.

7 See K.-O. Apel, *Transformation der Philosophie*, two volumes, Frankfurt a.M.: Suhrkamp 1973, (Eng. trans. *Towards a Transformation in Philosophy*, London: Routledge, 1980.

8 Cf. K.-O. Apel, 'Types of Social Science in the Light of Human Interests of Knowledge', in: *Social Research*, 44/3 (1977), pp. 425-70.

9 Cf. K.-O. Apel, *Die 'Erklären/Verstehen'-Kontroverse in transzendentalpragmatischer Sicht*, Frankfurt a.M.: Suhrkamp, 1979.

10 Cf. K.-O. Apel, 'Wittgenstein und Heidegger: die Frage nach dem Sinn von Sein und der Sinnlosigkeitsverdacht gegen alle Metaphysik', in: Apel, *Transformation* ..., vol. I. loc. cit. (see note 7).

11 Cf. Th. Litt, *Mensch und Welt: Grundlinien einer Philosophie des Geistes*, München: Federmann, ²1961.

12 Cf. K.-O. Apel, 'C.S. Peirce and the Post-Tarskyan Problem of an Adequate Explication of the Meaning of Truth', in: *The Monist*, vol. 63/3, July 1980.

13 Cf. K.-O. Apel, *Der Denkweg von C.S. Peirce*, Frankfurt a.M.: Suhrkamp, 1975 (Eng. trans. *The Development of Peirce's Philosophy*, Univ. of Mass. Press, forthcoming).

14 Cf. K.-O. Apel, 'Das Apriori der Kommunikationsgemeinschaft und die Grundlagen der Ethik', in: *Transformation der Philosophie*, vol. II, loc.cit. (see note 7). Cf. also 'Types of Rationality Today', in: Th. Geraets (ed.): *Rationality Today*, Univ. of Ottawa Press, 1979.

SECTION III

PHENOMENOLOGY AND PRAGMATISM

A FRESH LOOK AT JAMES'S RADICAL EMPIRICISM

RICHARD COBB–STEVENS

'... the entire field of experience ... is constituted as a room full of mirrors.'
Wm. James, 'The Notion of Consciousness'[1]

In his introduction to the critical edition of *Essays in Radical Empiricism*, John McDermott recalls Bradley's challenge to early disciples of William James, '... to make an attempt in earnest to explain and to develop his doctrine of Radical Empiricism.'[2] Even the most enthusiastic followers of James have found it difficult to meet this challenge, since they have all considered some aspect or other of his theory as untenable. The strongest negative criticism has been directed against his thesis of the ontological neutrality of the data of pure experience. In several passages James contends that the primal 'stuff' to which he gives the name 'pure experience' is neither mental nor physical as it is originally given, but comes to be classified in these categories only by subsequent reflective acts. Moreover, he claims that, just as the same mathematical point may be situated at the junction of two intersecting lines, so also the same originally neutral unit of pure experience can later be viewed as belonging to two radically different contexts, in one context functioning as a solid physical object and in another as an element in a stream of consciousness (*ERE*, 7). Ralph Barton Perry was the first to observe the ambiguity in this usage of the term 'experience' which ordinarily refers to the conscious life of an individual, but is here taken as a comprehensive expression designating '... an aboriginal form of being, embracing consciousness, together with non-conscious or non-mental forms of beings, such as bodies.'[3] Johannes Linschoten, the first commentator to approach James's thought from a phenomenological point of view, also deplores this confusing tendency to use the same term to refer both to the act of experiencing and to that which is experienced.[4] More recently, Bruce Wilshire attempts to make sense out of his ambiguity by suggesting that the confusing language in the early pages of the *Essays* becomes at least partially comprehensible in the light of James's later recognition that the point of intersection between subjective and objective is the experience of the lived-body as the harmonious amalgam of psychic and physical.[5] This mitigated version of James's thesis has the double merit of restoring to 'experience' its more obvious meaning, and of explaining the ambiguity in James's usage of the term as a result of

See notes at the end of this chapter.

his imperfectly articulated insight that the human body may be considered in one context as a part of the experienced world, and in another context as the focal center from which the world is experienced. Hence, what is strong about James's theory is his anticipation of Merleau-Ponty's phenomenology of the body-subject; what is weak is his 'neutral monism' which derives both the individual stream of consciousness and its referents in the physical world from the primordial stuff of pure experience. From a different perspective, A.J. Ayer similarly softens James's thesis by remarking that he should have limited himself to a defense of the more viable position that '... our conception of the world can be exhibited as a theory with respect to our experiences.'[6] In this view, physical objects are not derived from the data of experiences as if from some primordial *Urstoff*, although it must be admitted that our only access to the physical world is through experiences which do interpret reality.

My purpose in this brief paper is not to question the validity of these two different but complementary efforts to salvage worthwhile aspects of James's theory. Nor shall I repeat the now well-established points of affinity between James's analysis of consciousness in *The Principles of Psychology* and Husserl's phenomenology.[7] Rather, I propose to offer a new reading of the most controversial doctrine of Radical Empiricism, i.e., the 'derivation' of physical reality and of consciousness itself from pure experience, in the light of certain texts of the later Husserl concerning the status of transcendental subjectivity, texts which have heretofore not been considered in the literature comparing James and Husserl. My method will be first to gather under several headings James's principal observations about pure experience and then, using as a guide Husserl's reflections on the transcendental sphere, to construct an interpretation of what James may have meant by this seemingly bizarre theory.

PART I: A SKETCH OF JAMES'S THEORY OF PURE EXPERIENCE

1. *The flux of pure experience is not the same as the stream of consciousness, recognized as the psychological flow of thoughts and feelings of a given individual.*

This point is made frequently by James when he insists that the flux of experience is absolutely anterior to the distinction between subject and object, or interior life and external reality. As originally given, pure experiences are neutral:

> ... let us suppose that primary reality is of a neutral nature, and let us call it by some name also ambiguous, such as *phenomenon, datum* or *Vorfindung*. As for me, I would willingly use the plural, and I give it the name *pure experiences. (ERE*, 268)

Another variation on the same theme is his distinction between pure experiences as mere *thats* and their subsequent classification as *whats* by further pure *thats* which themselves may later undergo a similar classification. A simple *that*, a given datum of pure experience, takes on the status of a *what* when it is thematized in reflection as belonging either to the interior realm of conscious life or to some objective zone of reality. (*ERE*, 8-9, 57) It should be noted that James is careful to distinguish various types of objectivity: perceived things, imagined realities, dreamed events, mathematical objects and logical idealities. (*ERE*, 10)

2. *Pure experiences are characterized by the conjunctive relation of continuous transition which grounds the possibility of cognition.*

The *thats* of pure experience are not atomically isolated units but are linked by transitional elements which are as immediately given as the parts which they join. Of the many relations that connect pure experiences the most significant, according to James, is the conjunctive relation of continuous transition which assures the possibility of cognition. (*ERE*, 27-31) As part of his strategy of debunking the view of consciousness as a spiritual entity transparent unto itself and endowed with a mysterious power of self-transcendence, James goes so far as to refer to cognition as a '... kind of external relation.' (*ERE*, 14) Cognition can be defined without the notion of consciousness as a '... leading towards ... and terminating-in percepts, through a series of transitional experiences ...' (*ERE*, 14) Thus, knowing is nothing but a relationship of experiences interconnected by transitional intermediaries which lay out a direction towards a terminus. This choice of the spatial imagery of extrinsic alongsidedness is confirmed by James's claim that cognition of a unit of pure experience comes about '... *by way of addition* – addition to a given concrete piece of it, of other sets of experiences ...' (*ERE*, 7) Bruce Wilshire rightly wonders if this description of knowing is compatible with James's earlier interpretation in the *Principles* in terms of the correlation between act of thought and intentional object. I shall attempt to resolve this apparent contradiction in James's thought after a fuller consideration of the characteristics of pure experience.

3. *The continuous transition of pure experience is a temporal life.*

The key to James's understanding of the cognitive relation as a 'union by continuous transition' (*ERE*, 30) may be found, I believe, in those passages where he describes this conjunctive relation in the language of temporality. Consider, for example, the following text:

> Life is in the transitions as much as in the terms connected; often indeed, it seems to be there more emphatically, as if our spurts and sallies forward were the real firing-line of the battle, were like the thin line of flame advancing across the dry autumnal field which the farmer proceeds to burn. In this line we live prospectively as well as retrospectively. It is 'of' the past, inasmuch as it comes expressly as the past's continuation; it is 'of' the future in so far as the future, when it comes, will have continued *it*.
> These relations of continuous transition experienced are what make our experience cognitive. (*ERE*, 42).

In another passage he makes it clear that pure experience in its immediate givenness is a kind of *present*, and that the retrospective designation of a *just-past present* as subjective or objective by a new experience involves a continuous transition of past and present:

> Its [a pure experience's] subjectivity and objectivity are functional attributes solely, realized only when the experience is 'taken,' i.e., talked-of twice, considered along with its two different contexts respectively, by a new retrospective experience, of which the whole past complication now forms the fresh content.
>
> The instant field of the present is at all times what I call the 'pure' experience. (*ERE*, 13)

We must ask what is the relationship between this basic flux, the union by continuous transition of elemental pure experience, and the time of the stream of consciousness as described in the *Principles*. Moreover, if it be true that the primal flux is temporal, then we must try to understand why James frequently uses resolutely spatial imagery to describe it.

4. *The continuous transition of pure experiences is an impersonal or anonymous life.*

James Edie has convincingly demonstrated that James's theory of consciousness in the *Principles* is non-egological and corresponds roughly to similar positions taken by the early Husserl (in the first edition of the *Logical Investigations*) and by Sartre (in *Transcendence of the Ego*.)[9] Moreover, Edie points out that this interpretation is supported by texts from the *Essays*, and in particular by a prolonged footnote to the essay, 'The Experience of Activity.' (*ERE*, 85-86) I should like to add a terminological note to Edie's analysis. When James distinguishes in this text between '... the elemental activity involved in the *that* of experience,' and the further specification of this anonymous *that* into '... two *whats*, an activity felt as 'ours,' and an activity ascribed to objects,' he is clearly talking in the first instance of the pure experience of activity. When he does refer to the field of consciousness later in the same passage, he describes it as a retrospectively apprehended *what*: 'The individualized self, which I believe to be the only thing properly called self, is part of the content of the world experienced. The world experienced (otherwise called 'the field of consciousness') comes at all times with our body as its center ...' (*ERE*, 86) Thus, the stream of consciousness is described as a *what* which is derived by reflective appropriation from the more elemental pure flux of experience which can only be called a *that*. Selfhood belongs to the experienced field and is therefore a retrospective achievement of the flux of pure experience which is itself impersonal or anonymous. Edie makes this same point, but uses the term 'consciousness' as a substitute for James's pure experience of activity and for the parallel phrase in the *Principles*, 'the pure activity of our thought taking place as such.'[10] Of course, this usage of 'consciousness' is perfectly justified by James's treatment of the term in the *Principles*. Then why make an issue at all of this nuance? I am convinced that the language of the *Essays* is much clearer. 'Pure experience' is the term reserved for the functionality of consciousness, the absolute anonymous and automatic flow which makes manifest both objectivity and subjectivity. Properly speaking, this elemental flux should not be call a *con*-sciousness or a *subjective* life. No doubt, this is what James meant in the *Principles* by his reference to the stream of thought as '... a stream of *Scious*ness pure and simple.'[11]

5. *Pure experience cannot be described in itself but can only be indicated obliquely.*

James denies the existence of consciousness as an entity only to reaffirm the life of consciousness as a functional flux of pure experiences. In itself, this flux is neither mental nor physical but a kind of function which generates the appearance of these forms of being. It would seem, therefore, that the crude term '*stuff* of pure experience' is an expression of the fact that pure experience cannot be described appropriately either in objective language or in the traditional language of subjectivity. James is particularly uncomfortable with language derived from the tradition of soul-theory which, he claims, makes the consistent mistake of substituting spiritual entities (e.g., 'self-transcendent' acts of consciousness) for real experienced transitions. The 'pointing' of one element of pure experience towards another is one such immediately given conjunctive relation. If such transitional experiences are given prior to the reflective designation of subjective and objective contexts, then traditional epistemology has created a false problem in asking how subjective experiences can transcend themselves towards objective reality. (*ERE*, 121-122) Thus, it is the use of the term 'subjective' to refer to the original pure experience of cognition that creates the so-called epistemological problem.

Every time James himself tries to describe the original stuff of pure experience more precisely, he is obliged to evoke unusual situations where the flux of experience might be imagined as totally disassociated from reflective activity:

'Pure experience' is the name which I give to the immediate flux of life which furnishes the material to our later reflection with its conceptual categories. Only new-born babes, or men in semi-coma from sleep, drugs, illnesses, or blows, may be assumed to have an experience pure in the literal sense of a *that* which is not yet any definite *what*. (*ERE*, 46)

In ordinary adult life we are always already engaged within a reflective mode which interprets lived *thats* as belonging to a contextual framework of *whats*. No doubt, this is why the primitive flux seems to be experienced as emanating from a stable center of selfhood, rather than as the source of all objectivities including the self. Nevertheless, the fact that pure experience can be indicated at all, even in this indirect manner, shows that the primitive flux is in some sense still an experience. What might James mean by an experience that is neither subjective nor objective?

6. *Elements of pure experience reflect or mirror one another.*

The themes of continuous transition and of temporality are related to a final and perhaps more fundamental characteristic of the flux. According to James, units of experience naturally mirror or reflect one another. Let us consider carefully the following text:

> At bottom, why do we cling so tenaciously to this idea of a consciousness superadded to the existence of the content of things? ... Is it not in order to preserve this undeniable fact: that the content of experience has not only an existence of its own, as immanent and intrinsic, but also that each part of this content fades, so to speak, into its neighbors, gives an account of itself to others, in some fashion issues from itself in order to be transparent from part to part, or is constituted as a room full of mirrors? (*ERE*, 268)

This succession of metaphors (fading, giving an account, issuing forth, transparency, mirroring) seems to refer to a relationship between parts of experience that is more primitive than cognition. Experience is first a system of units which naturally refer to one another, and the mirrored 'trace' (to borrow an expression from Jacques Derrida) of one unit within another is the source of the conjunctive relation of cognition.[12] Could it be true that mirroring is prior to knowing? If this be the case, it would explain why James gives priority to conjunctive relations as the central theme of *Radical Empiricism*, and why he subordinates the relation of cognition itself to the theme of conjunctive relations in general. Cognition is a 'kind of external relation,' (*ERE*, 14) because tracing or mirroring of one unit of pure givenness in another is the condition of the possibility of knowing, rather than the inverse. Every unit of pure experience is a differential within a system; every unit leaves traces of itself on its neighbors. In other words, the system of pure experience is constructed like a language. The tracing process effects a union by continuous transition (i.e., the temporal flux). It is as though the overlapping succession of pure experiences are linked with one another not by reason of the form of time which holds them together as a unity of experience, but rather it is because elements of pure experience first picture one another that the temporal flux itself is generated. This position seems to be a frontal assault on the primacy of conscious presence. Cognition is a function within a more general referential structure, the mutual mirroring of elements of pure experience. Fundamental mirroring is a process of differentiation and union, an original continuous transition which is more elementary than, and the source of, the function of cognition.

PART II: COMPARISON WITH THEMES FROM HUSSERL'S TRANSCENDENTAL
PHENOMENOLOGY

Let us now consider three themes developed especially in Husserl's later works:
the danger of transcendental psychologism, absolute inner-time consciousness as
primal flux, and the elementary structure of this flux. It is my conviction that
the conjunction of these Husserlian themes will provide a framework for interpreting James's theory of pure experience in a coherent and comprehensive
manner. I shall make a brief exposition of each of these topics, suggest comparisons with Radical Empiricism where it seems pertinent, and conclude with a
unified view of James's theory.

1. *The danger of transcendental psychologism.*

What is psychologism, and in particular, what is meant by its more subtle manifestation which Husserl called transcendental psychologism? His polemic against
psychologism in the *Logical Investigations* is directed against any theory which
derives the necessary laws of logic from empirical observation of mental processes considered as mundane events. Gradually, the term 'psychologism' comes
to mean any consideration of acts and processes of consciousness as taking place
within an already given world. Thus, in so far as Bergson or James understand
the stream of consciousness as a flux occuring within the psyche of an individual
in a manner parallel to other mundane events, their analyses are psychologistic.
Bruce Wilshire has already demonstrated how the *Principles* moves from an
initially psychologistic point of departure to a final phenomenological break-
through, when James sees the stream of consciousness as a field of absolute
givenness rather than as an unusual mundane event.[13] According to Husserl,
more subtle forms of psychologism continually threaten the progress of phenomenology and are particularly dangerous in the final stages of transcendental
phenomenology. For example, whenever the reflecting philosopher asks questions about the ontological status of the ultimate life of subjectivity, he is liable
to slip back into psychologism if he construes subjectivity in any way as a being
alongside of other beings. Or the philosopher may succumb to the 'illusion of
transcendental solipsism,' if the transcendental domain is taken as an ultimate,
but nonetheless empirical, source of everything mundane.[14] Thus, subjective
idealism is a clear instance of transcendental psychologism.

James's frequent attacks against theories of consciousness as a kind of
ethereal stuff alongside of material realities and his rejection of the spiritual
space of the soul as the locus of conscious life may be understood as efforts to
avoid considering experience as a mundane event, even as a 'spiritual' mundane
event. The *Essays* continually refer to pure experience rather as an 'event'
through which both material and spiritual worlds are made manifest. Pure

experience is not a subjective psychological occurrence, but an absolute given-ness which precedes the distinction between subjective and objective, and which makes this distinction possible. The pure *thats* of the concatenated flux are constituted as subjective or objective *whats* by retrospective pure experiences, which themselves are pure *thats*. The continuous transition of *thats* by which *whats* are made manifest is not an ontic event. It does not take place *in* a body, or *in* a psyche, or even *in* a subjectivity.

During his lifetime James was accused of solipsism by a contemporary American philosopher, Boyd Henry Bode, who clearly interpreted the data of pure experience as subjective events locked within a private psyche.[15] We are fortunate in having James's response to Bode as part of the text of *Radical Empiricism*. Bode had argued that unless our experiences are endowed from the outset with the power of self-transcendency ('... the self-transcendent function of reference to a reality beyond itself.' *ERE*, 119), then no motive will occur within the series of experiences for supposing anything beyond it to exist. James's critique reveals that he considered the flux not as a series of subjective events but as a transcendental zone of absolute givenness. He first remarks that Bode has misunderstood the status of conjunctive relations, and explains his misunderstanding as the result of a substitution of retrospectively grasped acts for the original living flow of experience:

> I suspect that he performs on all these conjunctive relations (of which the aforesaid 'pointing' is only one) the usual rationalistic act of substitution — he takes them not as they are given in their first intention, as parts consti-tutive of experience's living flow, but only as they appear in retrospect, each fixed as a determinate object of conception, static, therefore, and contained within itself. (*ERE*, 120)

James's expression in this text, 'the usual rationalistic act of substitution,' is his term for transcendental psychologism. He next quotes a saying attributed to Kierkegaard that we live forwards and understand backwards, and notes that understanding backwards is a typical fault of philosophers. (*ERE*, 121) I think that he touches here upon the profound reason why philosophers fall back into transcendental psychologism: retrospective experience (or reflection) is liable to confuse pure *thats* for *whats*. He concludes that Radical Empiricism strives to resist this tendency of reflective reification of the flux:

> Radical Empiricism alone insists on understanding forwards also, and re-fuses to substitute static concepts of the understanding for transitions in our moving life. A logic similar to that which my critic seems to employ here should, it seems to me, forbid him to say that our present is, while present, directed towards our future ... (*ERE*, 121)

This reference to the presence of the anticipated future within the present may serve as a transition to our second Husserlian theme.

2. *Absolute inner-time consciousness as primal flux.*

Husserl's analyses of the primal flux of inner-time consciousness are the result of his reflections on the possibility of reflection itself. In *Ideen I*, he observes that every lived experience can become the object of subsequent reflection, and explains that this reflective reconstruction of originally unreflective experience is possible because of a structural unity which holds reflecting and reflected together, the flux of experience itself. Thus, in the case of reflective acts, the flux assures what he calls an 'unmediated unity' between perceived and perceiving.[16] In his *Lectures on Internal-Time Consciousness*, he argues against Brentano that lived experience, while it is being lived through, is not objectified. The act of perception is not thematized as a second object of the perception during the perceiving.[17] Moreover, it is important not to confuse the subsequent reflection with the inner awareness of lived experience which we have while it is being lived through. The structure that makes possible both the non-objectifying awareness of lived experience and its subsequent reflective appropriation is inner-time consciousness. When objects are experienced, the process of experiencing is also experienced in an indirect and oblique way, and moreover the experiencing of the process is retained in such a way that a subsequent experience can take it as a direct object. The present awareness embraces within its scope the traces of the just-past precisely as past. This process is somewhat akin to what we ordinarily refer to as the temporal flow, when we mean by that expression the stream of conscious life reflectively apprehended as ours. According to Husserl, the primal flux can only be spoken of by analogy with this more familiar temporal experience.[18] The ultimate structure of the ego's life is such that the primal flux only shows itself in the background of, and in inseparable unity with, the constituted time of the stream of consciousness.[19] It would seem, however, that the primal flux is still a consciousness:

> Consciousness is necessarily consciousness in each of its phases. Just as the retentional phase has the preceding one in consciousness without making it an object, so also the primal datum is already in consciousness – and moreover in the peculiar form of the 'now' – without being objective. It is precisely this original consciousness which goes over into retentional modification, which then is retention of this consciousness itself and of the datum which was originally conscious in it, since both are inseparably one.[20]

Thus, the link between the primal flux and the constituted stream is retention which holds onto the preceding phase in a conscious but non-objectifying manner and grounds the subsequent objectifying reflection. This process of objectification links the transcendental source of the primal flux and the constituted stream, and is called by Husserl in the *Crisis* the 'self-objectification' of the transcendental ego.[21]

James's treatment of time-consciousness in the *Principles* has already been shown to be perfectly parallel to Husserl's analysis of immanent time consciousness. I am suggesting here that the flux of pure experience refers to a more primitive temporality comparable to that 'pre-phenomenal, pre-immanent temporality' which Husserl designates as the primal flux.[22] In this interpretation, the stream of consciousness recognized as 'mine' is a constituted flux, retrospectively grasped as a personal flow of moods, feelings and cognitive activities. The more primitive flux of pure experience is the transcendental source, the constituting flow from which the stream of consciousness is derived by retrospective experience. The two streams are intertwined and in fact are identical as *whats*, but are distinguished from one another as a *that* is distinguished from a *what*. This distinction is James's manner of expressing the peculiar form of identity in difference that obtains between constituting and constituted or between transcendental source and psychic stream of consciousness.

Incidentally, this interpretation might help clarify certain obscurities in James's treatment of the relationship between ego and self in the *Principles*. As constituted flow, the stream of consciousness is designated as belonging to a self, whose central nucleus is the body. As constituting flow of pure experience, the flux is pre-personal, although it is still in some sense a consciousness. Pure experiences of conjunctive relations are *felt* relations, but by whom are they felt? James's 'passing Thought' as momentary *subject* of the flux (or should I say 'dative' of pure experience?) is somehow other and yet the same as the self constituted in reflection.[23] The trouble is that the term 'subject' or 'ego' is always construed as an entity and hence ultimately as an object. James's theory of the ego's life as a functional succession rather than a substantial unity shows his understanding that transcendental life cannot be adequately expressed in language which takes for granted the distinction between subject and object.[24]

3. The elementary structure of the primal flux.

The question of the 'subject' of transcendental life leads to the issue of the deep structure of the primal flux. On the one hand, Husserl refers to the constituting flux as an ego's life. For example, in the *Crisis* he speaks of a '... reduction to the absolute ego as the ultimately unique center of function in all constitution.'[25] Yet we know from Klaus Held's analysis of the C-manuscripts that Husserl sometimes refers to the originary temporal process as anonymous and automatic.[26] Whatever may be meant by these expressions, it does seem logical to affirm that the underlying process which grounds reflection must be pre-personal in some sense, since the very distinction between subjectivity and objectivity is derived from reflection. In this regard, Robert Sokolowski remarks that it is unfortunate that Husserl refers to the foundational level in terms of *inner*-time consciousness, '... because it is neither inner nor outer but prior to both.'[27] It might be added that the description of the primal flux as a life of transcendental 'subjectivity' is equally confusing, for it would seem that the theme of subjectivity belongs to the order of constituted reality. James's language in the *Essays* is more consistently unambiguous. Everything 'inner' and 'outer,' everything subjective and objective has its absolute source in neutral pure experience.

Leaving aside the issue of appropriate language, let us consider the linkage between just-past and the present, which for Husserl is clearly the key to the structure of the primal flux. This linkage makes the concatenation of the flow possible; without it there could be no life and no reflection. In short, the fact (ontological rather than ontic fact) that disparateness or otherness can be brought into unity is the structural condition that makes temporality and reflective life possible. Could this be what James means by treating knowing as 'a kind of external relation,' or by his intriguing remark that cognition is possible because '... the entire field of experience is constituted as a room full of mirrors?' Could this 'external' language of mirroring refer to the fact that there must first be an interplay of difference and togetherness in order that consciousness might be?

In conclusion, this brief study has attempted to establish that pure experience is a transcendental theme. Pure experience is the transcendental primal flux that grounds the retrospectively appropriated stream of consciousness. *Radical Empiricism*, therefore, represents a transcendental turn only partially accomplished in the earlier *Principles of Psychology*. Only this interpretation makes sense of the following enigmas of Radical Empiricism:

1. how pure experience may be said to be prior to the distinction between subjective and objective.

2. why pure experience is the primal stuff and yet cannot be described as it is in itself, but only designated obliquely by comparison with its subjective and objective manifestations.

3. how the ground of cognition can be a kind of external relation, a mirroring that is prior to knowing.

The same answer may be given to each of these problems: pure experience is a transcendental source, and therefore not something alongside of other things, not a subjective stream confronting or containing an objective reality, but a pure *that* by which various *whats* (subject, object, self, other) are made manifest.

NOTES

1 William James, 'The Notion of Consciousness,' in *Essays in Radical Empiricism. The Works of William James*. Introduction by John McDermott (Cambridge: Harvard Univ. Press, 1976), p. 268. This quotation is from an article originally composed in French by James. For the original text see p. 113 of the same volume. Subsequent references to the *Essays* will be taken from this critical edition, and will be indicated by the abbreviation *ERE* followed by the page reference.

2 *Ibid.*, xlvii.

3 Ralph Barton Perry, *In the Spirit of William James* (Bloomington: Indiana Univ. Press, 1958), p. 100.

4 Johannes Linschoten, *On the Way Towards a Phenomenological Psychology*. Translated by A. Giorgi (Pittsburgh: Duquesne Univ. Press), p. 248.

5 Bruce Wilshire, *William James: The Essential Writings*. Edited and with an introduction (New York: Harper, 1971), xlix-lviii.

6 A.J. Ayer, *The Origins of Pragmatism* (London: Macmillan, 1968), p. 303.

7 For an excellent critical review of various phenomenological interpretations of James's work, Cf. James M. Edie, 'William James and Phenomenology,' *Review of Metaphysics*, XXIII (1970), pp. 481-526.

8 Wilshire, *op.cit.*, liv.

9 Edie, *op.cit.*, pp. 509-519.

10 *Ibid.*, pp. 516-517. Cf. William James, *The Principles of Psychology* (New York: Henry Holt, 1890), Vol. I, p. 333.

11 James, *Principles*, I, p. 304.

12 Jacques Derrida, *Speech and Phenomenon*. Translated with an introduction by David B. Allison. (Evanston: Northwestern Univ. Press 1973), p. 85.

13 Bruce Wilshire, *William James and Phenomenology* (Bloomington: Indiana Univ. Press, 1968), *passim*.

14 Edmund Husserl, *Formal and Transcendental Logic*. Translated by Dorion Cairns. (The Hague: Nijhoff, 1969), pp. 241-243. Cf. Edmund Husserl, *Formale und transzendentale Logik*. Edited by Paul Janssen (The Hague: Nijhoff, 1974 (Husserliana XVII), pp. 213-214.

15 The following comment of Bode's is cited in the notes to the critical edition of the *Essays* on p. 185. 'To conclude, the philosophy of pure experience does not account for our awareness of a world beyond our individual experience; and it also fails to show how there can be a world that is common to a multiplicity of individuals.'

16 Edmund Husserl, *Ideas*. Translated by W.R. Boyce-Gibson. (New York: Collier, 1972), p. 112. Cf. Edmund Husserl, *Ideen zu einer reinen Phänomenologie und phänomenologischen Philosophie*. Vol. I. Edited by Walter Biemel (Husserliana III), (The Hague: Nijhoff, 1950), pp. 85-86.

17 Edmund Husserl, *The Phenomenology of Internal Time-Consciousness*. Translated by James S. Churchill (Bloomington: Indiana Univ. Press, 1966), pp. 57-60. Cf. Edmund Husserl, *Zur Phänomenologie des Inneren Zeitbewusstseins*, Edited by Rudolph Bohem (Husserliana X), (The Hague: Nijhoff, 1966) pp. 35-38.

18 *Ibid.*, p. 100. Cf. *ZB*, pp. 74-75.

19 Husserl, *Ideas, op.cit.*, p. 128. Cf. *Ideen I*, p. 104.

20 Husserl, *The Phenomenology of Internal Time-Cinsciousness, op.cit.*, p. 162. I have made slight alterations in Churchill's translation at the suggestion of a colleague, William Vallicella. Cf. *ZB*, 119. 'Bewusstsein ist nötwendig *Bewusstsein* in jeder seiner Phasen. Wie die retentionale Phase die vorliegende bewusst hat, ohne sie zum Gegenstand zu machen, so ist auch schon das Urdatum bewusst – und zwar in der eigentümlichen Form des 'jetzt' – ohne gegenständlich zu sein. Eben dieses Urbewusstsein ist es, das in die retentionale Modifikation übergeht – die dann Retention von ihm selbst und dem im originär bewussten Datum ist, da beide untrennbar eins sind ...'

21 Edmund Husserl, *The Crisis of European Sciences and Transcendental Phenomenology*. Translated by David Carr (Evanston: Northwestern Univ. Press, 1970), p. 186. Cf. Edmund Husserl, *Die Krisis der europäischen Wissenschaften und die transzendentale Phänomenologie*. Edited by Walter Biemel (Husserliana VI), (The Hague: Nijhoff, 1954), p. 188.

22 Husserl, *Time-Consciousness, op.cit.*, p. 109. Cf. *ZB*, p. 183.

23 Cf. Robert Sokolowski, 'Picturing,' *Review of Metaphysics*, XXI (1977), p. 3. Sokolowski uses the expression 'dative of manifestation' in an analogous manner.

24 Cf. my analysis of the functional continuity of pure egos in *James and Husserl: The Foundation of Meaning* (The Hague: Nijhoff, 1974). pp. 74-81. Cf. also Edie, *op.cit.*, pp. 509-519.

25 Husserl, *Crisis, op.cit.*, p. 186. Cf. *Krisis, op.cit.*, p. 190.

26 Klaus Held, *Lebendige Gegenwart. Die Frage nach der Seinsweise des transzendentalen Ich bei Edmund Husserl, entwickelt am Leitfaden der Zeitproblematik* (The Hague: Nijhoff, 1966), pp. 118-122.

27 Robert Sokolowski, 'Ontological Problems in Phenomenology: The Dyad and the One,' *Review of Metaphysics*, XXIX (1976), p. 700.

LEWIS'S PRAGMATIC KANTIANISM:
TOWARD DIALOGUE WITH PHENOMENOLOGY

SANDRA B. ROSENTHAL

The linkage of pragmatism with empiricism and naturalism has been a crucial factor in the historical alienation of pragmatism and phenomenology, for such a linkage has led to the interpretation of pragmatism as a form of reductionism which views man in terms of Watsonian behaviorism or stimulus response mechanisms. Such reductive interpretations in turn have led to a second but closely related type of reductionist interpretation which views meanings of objectivities as reducible to basic elements from which the meanings are originally built.

It is precisely these points which converge to provide the key focus for the often presented interpretations of pragmatism as a philosophic first cousin of analytic philosophy, more specifically, some form of positivism. And, it is precisely such a reductionism in any of its related forms to which phenomenology is reacting in its objection to scientific or natural or empirical methodology in understanding man's relation to his world. Thus pragmatism is seen to have strong positivistic leanings and to have nothing of interest to offer to or gain from the alien movement of phenomenology. However, such interpretations have for too long distorted the significance of the pragmatic response to enduring and deep rooted philosophic issues.

Pragmatism is indeed naturalism in that man is within nature. But, nature is not the mechanistic universe of the Newtonian world view. Such an assertion that it is has confused lived experience with the 'experience', or rather, the inadequate substitute for experience, that results when one takes a type of naively realistic view that allows the abstractions of a particular science to become the building blocks of reality. It is precisely the scientism of the 18th and 19th centuries, which arose from a projection of the contents of physics and psycho-physics as the ultimate building blocks of physical and psychical realities, against which pragmatism is so strongly reacting. Thus, pragmatism is indeed empiricism, but an empiricism which returns to the richness of lived experience. And, when one turns to lived experience, one comes to see that though man emerges from the richness of nature as a unique part of nature which has the ability to know and to relate in other unique ways, yet nature, for man, is constituted by a system of meanings, and only through such meanings does that reality from which man has emerged reveal itself to man.

See notes at the end of this chapter.

Pragmatism brings the being of man in the world and the knowing by man of the world together, and if either one of these interwoven strands, as understood within the framework of pragmatism, is assimilated to analytic philosophy, then the entire fabric of the pragmatic position disintegrated, leaving nothing to view but a few insignificant threads. Such an assimilation to analytic philosophy is evinced in interpretations of all of the classical American pragmatists, but nowhere is such assimilation evinced with the exclusiveness to be found in the literature on C.I. Lewis' philosophy.[1] And, Lewis' relation to Kant is frequently taken as the basis for such assimilation of his position into the framework of analytic philosophy — either into the Vienna Circle type of positivism and constructionalism or the British ordinary language analysis of the post Wittgensteinian variety. As the standard script goes, Lewis, like Kant, distinguishes what is given in sense experience from the concepts under which it is subsumed or through which it is thought. However, he departs from Kant in his position that no conceptual scheme is forced upon us, but rather we can choose conceptual schemes, which are applied to the sensory manifold on purely pragmatic grounds. Thus, according to the standard script, there is, on the one hand, the presentation of sensations or sense data of some sort and, on the other hand, a somewhat arbitrary, or, at best, conventional use of conceptual schemes in organizing the brute data. Such a standard script leads inevitably to the fashionable conclusion that there is 'something wrong' with Lewis' thought: his distinction between the analytic and synthetic is untenable; his concept of the a priori is empty; his construction of objectivities out of sense data doesn't work, his depiction of the verification of empirical beliefs is self-defeating, and on and on it goes.[2] And, indeed, the fashionable conclusion is, in a certain sense, quite right. Lewis' 'analytic philosophy' is open to all sorts of reasonable objections by reasonable critics. However, Lewis' position yields such inadequate analytic philosophy precisely because neither pragmatism in general, nor Lewis' pragmatism in particular, has a philosophic kinship with analytic philosophy.[3]

To correct the script, one must return to the place where it began; that is, to Lewis' relation to Kant. Thus, we will turn to Lewis' acceptance of or departure from each of two crucial points in Kant's philosophy, but they will not be the points from which the standard script begins. Rather, they will be the points relating to Lewis' dispositional theory of meaning, which is perhaps the key factor in coming to grips with his pragmatism. First, his appropriation of Kantian schemata within his dispositional theory of meaning will be seen to contain within itself a radical rejection, rather than acceptance, of the notion of brute data, brute sensations, sense data, or any other uninterpreted bits as the starting point for knowledge. Rather it will be seen that for Lewis, as for the phenomenologist, the return to lived experience incorporates a rejection of the atomistic or building block theory of knowledge and, with it, a rejection of the relation of sensation, object, and world which underlies the building block theory. It is precisely this reversal of the relation of datum, object, and world, which is central to both the pragmatic and phenomenological returns to lived experience, which binds them together in a rejection of any sort of positivistic reductionism. The examination of Lewis' pragmatic appropriation of the Kantian schematism will show that for Lewis, as for the phenomenologist, apprehended appearances are appearances for conscious awareness only as they emerge within a world of appearing objects.

Secondly, Lewis' dispositional theory of meaning, when developed, will show the significance of Lewis' departure from the unalterability of Kantian conceptual structures, a significance which is far removed from the conceptual conventionalism found within the framework of analytic philosophy. Such a departure from Kant will be seen to stem from a more fundamental departure which also reveals itself through Lewis' dispositional theory of meaning, that is, Lewis' rejection of the Kantian distinction between noumena and phenomena in favor of the pragmatic category of interaction. It will be seen that for Lewis as for the existential phenomenologist[4] there is no existential or ontological gap between appearance or phenomena and reality or existence. Rather, the phenomenon is the phenomenon of something. We reach the ontological reality or being of a thing through the phenomenon within the perceptual field.

With this somewhat general overview of the direction to be followed, we can now turn to the first of the two issues raised, Lewis' appropriation of the Kantian schematism within his dispositional theory of meaning. Lewis stresses in many places and in many ways that meaning is not limited to language or linguistic meaning. Rather, the basic sense of meaning for Lewis is sense meaning. He stresses that meaning 'cannot be literally put into words, or exhibited by exhibiting words and the relations of words.'[5] Lewis does not consider this a required function of language, for he holds that 'Patterns of linguistic relation can only serve as a kind of map for the location of the empirical item meant in terms of sense experience.'[6] Such an inability to express meanings exactly produces the result, recognized by Lewis, that an examination of linguistic entities can give us no exact understanding of meanings and their relationships.[7]

It is precisely this focus on sense meaning, however, which leads to the interpretation of Lewis as putting forth a phenomenalistic reductionism which views meanings as reducible to the sense data out of which they are built — that original Kantian manifold. This interpretation, however, is oblivious to the two key features of Lewis' pragmatic theory of sense meaning: its dispositional nature, and its unique incorporation of the Kantian schematism. Though meaning is derivative from the sensuous, and though meanings themselves can be termed sensuous insofar as they refer to experience, yet meaning, even in its sensory aspect, cannot be reduced to the content of experience. The difference can perhaps best be clarified by stating that the sensuous aspect of meaning provides, literally, the 'sense' or principle or form by which man interprets and organizes the sensory. It is sense meaning as an interpretive principle, then, that must be examined.

For Lewis, meanings are neither Platonic entities in the metaphysical sense, nor are they psychological facts. Lewis does not want to give meaning an existence independent of purpose, yet he does not want to reduce meaning to psychology. Meanings, for Lewis, are to be understood as relational structures emerging from behavioral patterns, as emerging from the lived-through response of the human organism to that universe with which it is in interaction. Or, in other terms, human behavior is meaningful behavior, and it is in behavior that meaning is rooted. What, however, is meaning as a relational pattern? A purely relational pattern devoid of sensuous criteria of recognition would be a pattern of relationships relating nothing that had reference to the world, while a pure datum, devoid of the relational pattern, could not be an object of thought. Lewis does not have purely abstract categories of the understanding on the one hand,[8] and a brute sensory manifold on the other. Rather, sense meaning, as the inseparable mingling of the sensuous and the relational is, for Lewis, the vehicle by which we think about and recognize objects in the world. And, for Lewis, sense meanings are developed as schemata in the Kantian sense. An implicit sense meaning for Lewis is a disposition or habit by which man interacts with the environment, while an explicit sense meaning is a precise 'imaginatively inspectable' schema or criterion of recognition of the sensuous.[9] It is to the interrelation of implicit or concrete sense meaning as dispositional, and explicit sense meaning as Kantian schemata, that the ensuing discussion will turn.

An explicit sense meaning for Lewis is a schema — a rule or prescribed routine and an imagined result. However, there must be within the schema not only the prescribed act or routine and imagined result, but also the sensory cues which leads to the instigation of the act. And, if the act is dependent upon the cue, then different cues will give rise to different acts. Thus, there is not one act but an indefinite number of acts corresponding to an indefinite number of possible cues or appearances. (For example, varying perspectives yield varying appearances or cues and hence varying resulting acts.) Indeed, even if one considers only one essential property, so that the application of the physical object meaning is determined solely by the presence of one property, the use of test routine leads to an unlimited number of possible tests. Yet, this indefinite number of cues and acts radiate from one intended objectivity. Precisely what it means to apprehend an object or objective structure rather than an appearance only is to have 'filled in' the result of a particular act with the results of other possible acts given other possible cues. Thus, in a sense there are an indefinite number of cues, acts, and resulting appearances. Yet, in another sense, though there are an indefinite number of cues and acts, they are all 'part of' the one result, an objectivity having certain characteristics. The difference between an apprehended appearance and an apprehended object for Lewis is not the difference between internal and external, or between subjective and objective, but rather precisely this difference in levels of meaning organization.[10]

Thus, if we are to meaningfully assert the existence of physical objects, or, in other terms, to preceive a world of objectivities, then there must be, in addition to sensory cue, act, and further sensory appearance, that which binds into a system the set of possible sensory cues and possible resultant acts which as a system give rise to the resultant objective structure. Here it must be remembered that although Lewis speaks of the result of a schema as an image, the image, as part of the schema, is general as opposed to particular.[11] Yet, Lewis emphatically rejects the traditional notion of abstract general ideas. His position can perhaps best be clarified by taking the term 'image' as 'aspect'. For example, one may say, quite correctly, that a mountain range presents a majestic image or aspect. And, while the specific empirical content of experience is best understood as one particular among many, the image of the schema as criterion of recognition is best understood as the one which applies to the many. Indeed, the importance of the content of the image of the schema lies in the way in which it comes into being. Such an image represents an aspect of the structural order by which it is regulated, whether the resultant image is taken at the level of appearance or objectivity. This regulative order requires further examination.

The emphasis on an indefinite number of cues and acts stresses a variability of sense meaning in that an indefinite number of schemata is needed to exhibit fully the totality of appearances implied in attributing even one character to an object. Yet, the variability is limited, and in some sense the totality of the range is brought to bear in the apprehension of an objectivity. In addition to the diversity of specific schemata, then, there must be that which limits the range of varying schemata and imaginatively 'fills in' the resultant appearance of a particular act with the results of other possible acts, thus giving objectivity to that which is produced via the schema. There must, in short, be what Lewis calls a 'fixity' to meanings. What is 'fixed' is precisely that which determines the nature of and governs the range of the inexhaustible variety of specific schemata. Thus, what is 'fixed' is a structure or rule of generation of explicit schemata, and this, for Lewis, is the concrete disposition or habit. Concrete sense meaning, as the disposition or habit, is the source of the generation of explicit schemata, each of which makes precise for conscious awareness, some aspect of the concrete sense meaning; some selection from the inexhaustible range of possibilities.

Further, and perhaps most important within the context of the general purpose of this essay, there is the consideration that the generality of the image lies precisely in the fact that as an aspect of the dispositional structural ordering, it reflects, in its very generation, the generality of such an ordering. In brief, appearances come to awareness only within a world of appearing objects, for appearances as generated by schemata are generated as appearances of intended objectivities because of the functioning of the concrete disposition or habit as the rule of generation of explicit schemata. The most adequate model, for Lewis, to indicate the relationship intended is that of a 'mathematical rule generating a number series.'[12] What are the characteristics of such a model? First, a mathematical rule cannot be reduced to the number series nor constructed out of the series, for it is necessary to the formation of the series and to the character which each member of the series possesses. Like a mathematical rule, a dispositional rule of generation cannot be reduced to nor constructed out of the series generated, nor can it be separated from that which it generates, for that which is generated represents an aspect of the structural order by which it is generated. Not only is the meant objectivity fixed in its character through the functioning of habit in 'filling in' the results of an act with the results of other possible acts given other possible cues, but the appearance which is apprehended by a change of focus which attempts to 'withhold' this 'filling in' is itself partially fixed in its character precisely by that which is attempting to be 'withheld.' Apprehended appearance is not brute uninterpreted content but is shot through with the dispositional structural orderings of objectivities. Appearances are meanings which emerge via abstractive attention from the context of meaningful objectivities, for the focus on appearance is the focus on that which is generated indirectly through the functioning of habit. At every level, man's response enters into the very character of the data.

Secondly, the number series generated by the mathematical rule has the capacity for indefinite expansion. Just as a mathematical rule may generate an unlimited series of numbers, or just as a continuum may generate an unlimited number of cuts within itself, so a disposition as a rule or organization contains within itself an unlimited number of possibilities of specific schemata to be generated. Furthermore, the inability to exhaust via enumeration all possibilities is not a contingent fact, but rather is intrinsic to the nature of the generating rule. Meaning as dispositional, then, is the source of the concrete unity of objectivity as more than a collection of appearances. Such an objective concreteness which transcends any indefinite number of appearances is built into our very sense of objectivity, for meaning as dispositional is the source of a sense of a reality of physical objectivities whose possibilities of being experienced transcend, in their very nature, the experiences in which they appear.

We have seen, then, that the series of possible schemata for the application of a meaning to experience is 'fixed' prior to the imposition of a linguistic structure. Yet it is 'fixed' not by any eternal ontological order, but rather by the concrete, biologically based, disposition or habit as the rule of generation of explicit schemata. Such meaning cannot be reduced to the 'merely psychological' for what is bound together into a unity is a triadic relationship of factors emerging from organism-environment interaction. Meanings emerge from organism-environment interaction as precise triadic relational structures unified by habit as a rule of organization and as a rule of generation of specific schemata, and it is only within the backdrop of such a functioning that appearances come to awareness.

Before turning to the second issue, or, perhaps it should be said, as a bridge to the second issue, some implications of Lewis' dispositional theory of meaning should be briefly noted, implications which accentuate the affinity with phenomenology. First, Lewis' dispositional theory of meaning requires the concept of time as process. What occurs within the present awareness is not the apprehension of a discrete datum in a moment of time, but rather the time-extended experiential 'feel' within the passing present of a readiness to respond to more than can ever be specified. As Lewis observes, 'It is not the time-extended cognition but the chopping of it up into unextended instants which is fictitious.'[13] Or, as he elsewhere states, 'There is only one given, the Bergsonian real duration. ... The absolutely given is a specious present, fading into the past and growing into the future with no genuine boundaries. ...'[14]

Second, it is the awareness of habit as a disposition or readiness to respond to more than can be specified which gives a concrete meaning to the concept of unactualized possibilities, of a reality of potentialities which outruns any experienced actualities. That readiness to respond to more than can ever be made explicit, which is 'there' in the functioning of habit, is immediately experienced in the passing present and gives experiential content to the concept of the 'more than' of objectivities which can never be exhaustively experienced, to the concept of unactualized possibilities of being experienced which pervade every grasp of the world around us and which belie any attempt at phenomenalistic reductionism.

Thirdly, meaning as dispositional brings a sense of real alternatives − the could do otherwise − into the heart of perceptual awareness and leads away from deterministic hypotheses and toward a recognition of what Lewis refers to as a 'primordial sense of probable events.'

Finally, Lewis' dispositional theory of meaning becomes the tool by which Lewis, throughout his theory of empirical truth in terms of verification in sense experience, avoids the extensionalist confusion of meaning and evidence.[15] Lewis does not hold that meanings are reducible to the experiences which verify, for as indicated by his dispositional theory of meaning, meanings outrun in principle any number of experiences, and in fact help give structure to the experiences. The possibilities of experience contained within the meaning structures may be progressively fulfilled, but they can never be completely and finally fulfilled. Meanings for Lewis are rooted in experience, and verified by experience, but not reducible to experience.

Further, though meaning applications are verified by experience, or fulfilled within experience, there remains the significant issue as to the nature of the experiences which verify. For Lewis, as for the pragmatists in general, experience is that rich ongoing transactional unity between man and his environment. Only within the context of such an interactional unity does what is given emerge for conscious awareness. Indeed, one of the most distinctive, most crucial, but most often ignored aspects of Lewis' position is the concept of experience as having the character of an interactional unity between man and his environment.[16] The philosophic attempt to view experience in terms of a reduction to any type of atomic elements loses the very nature of experience, for it loses the ongoing dynamic process of man's interaction with his world and hance it loses the characteristic features of lived experience which such a dynamics incorporates, characteristics which are 'there', which are experienced, but which are lost to the philosophic awareness which tries to understand experience in terms of what remains after the reductionist axe has murderously chopped it to bits. But, this statement brings us precisely to the systematic significance of those pervasive textures of experience as lived before interpreted by science, textures of experience implied already by the discussion of meaning as dispositional. And, this leads directly into the second issue to be discussed, the significance of the possibility of alternative meanings as this relates to Lewis' rejection of Kant's noumenal-phenomenal distinction. It is to these pervasive textures of experience, and to a coerciveness which is the foundation for, rather than partially determined by, the alternative meanings we bring to experience, that we will now turn.

The stress on alternative conceptual schemes for interpreting experience may seem to harken back to the conventionalism of analytic philosophy. Indeed, later analytic philosophers have rejected much reductive analysis and are rather concerned with identifying, classifying, and describing the most general features of our conceptual structures. Yet, even those who focus on the aspect of alternative conceptual schemes in Lewis' philosophy as the basis for viewing him as an analytic philosopher have at times been led to note a 'nonconformity' in Lewis' thought, since for Lewis certain fundamental principles, such as the if-then order of potentialities and real connections, and the serial order of time, are not partially determined by alternative conceptual schemes, but rather are necessary for the very possibility of the applicability of any conceptual scheme to experience. Indeed, the awareness of just such a coerciveness has led at least one Lewis critic to observe that certain fundamental principles in Lewis' philosophy are categorial in the sense of being illustrated in every possible experience, and thus hardly conform 'to the typical positivistic model of a relativistic theory of categories.' Such a coerciveness is then held to imply a heritage from Kant of an unalterable a priori necessity which has not received due recognition by Lewis or his critics.[17] However, this 'puzzlement' from the framework of analytic philosophy cannot be solved by bringing in the baggage of Kantian fixed categories of the mind, for in addition to contradicting Lewis' explicit and emphatic rejection of fixed, necessary categories of the mind, it negates a critically important aspect of Lewis' position towards which this element of coerciveness, when properly located, directly points. For Lewis, as for all the pragmatists, man is a natural organism in interaction with a natural environment.[18] It is from this backdrop that his entire philosophy must be understood. And, if experience is such an interactional unity, then the nature of experience reflects both the responses man brings and the pervasive textures of that independently there, ontologically real surrounding natural environment from which man has arisen and which reveals itself to man through the meaning structures he has established by his behavioral interaction with it.[19] There is, thus, for the pragmatist in general, and for Lewis in particular, a 'two directional openness' within experience. What appears opens in one direction toward the structures of the independently real or the surrounding natural environment and in the other direction toward the structures of man's modes of grasping that independently real, for what is experienced is in fact a unity formed by each in interaction with the other. There is, for Lewis, an ontological dimension of what appears which reveals itself in experience and which forms a limit on the empirically relevant meanings we establish.[20] The pervasive textures of experience which are exemplified in every experience and without which our responses to the world could not be as they are, are not some Kantian necessary structures which close us within the phenomenal, forever cut off from the noumenal. Rather, such pervasive textures of experience are at the same time indications of the pervasive textures of that independent, ontologically real universe which, in every experience, gives itself for our responses and which provides the touchstone for the adequacy of the meanings through which it reveals itself to us. Thus, the basic textures of experience lead to the outlines of the basic textures of the ontologically real, to nature,[21] but not to the nature of the natural scientist. Rather, it is the sense of nature before natural science, the level of nature to which I, in my lived experience, am fundamentally bound.

Lewis, in rejecting the role of man as spectator, in viewing experience as shot through with the dynamics of purposive activity, in understanding the perceived world as a unity of interaction between man and that facticity which gives itself in experience, holds at once that the content of knowledge is the real, that the real has an independence from mind, and yet that the object of knowledge is partially dependent upon the noetic act and is thus relative in its nature to the mind. Indeed, Lewis holds that the supposed incompatibility of these three characteristics of the relation of thought to reality stems from a failure to radically and once and for all reject the presuppositions of a spectator theory of knowledge.[22] What appears within experience is also the appearance of the independently real; there is no ontological gap between appearance and reality. Further, it is at the same time 'to me' to whom it appears and reflects my intentional link with the externally real. What appears, then, opens in one direction toward the structures of the independently real and in the other direction toward the structures of our modes of grasping the independently real. Or, in other terms, what appears within experience is a function of both in interaction and thus 'mirrors' neither exactly, though it reflects characteristics of each.

Indeed, it is precisely because the brute facticity of the ontologically real universe which man comes to know is independent of man's meanings and the possibilities of fulfillment they allow that meanings, for Lewis, must be determined on pragmatic grounds; those meanings which endure do so not because they are fixed in the human mind from all eternity, nor because they have been conventionally or arbitrarily chosen, but because they allow reality to reveal itself to us, allow us to interact with that which gives itself to us in ways which work, in ways in which the possibilities contained within the meaning structures can be progressively fulfilled, in ways which allow the ongoing conduct of the human organism, immersed in a natural world, to proceed according to expectations rather than to be frustrated.

It was noted at the start of this essay that pragmatism brings the knowing by man of the world and the being of man in the world together, and that if either of these aspects is forced into an alien analytic framework, the significance of pragmatism is lost, while, on the contrary, when properly understood, each of these aspects can be seen to have an affinity with phenomenology. It has been seen that Lewis' dispositional theory of meaning with its pragmatic incorporation of the Kantian schema is the basis for understanding both aspects. If one misinterprets his theory of meaning, forcing it into some kind of reductionism or into some kind of linguistic framework, then his pragmatic theory of meaning cannot allow for the grasp of precisely those pervasive textures of experience which his pragmatic naturalism asserts. It is meaning as dispositional which allows for the grasp, at its most basic level, of time, process, continuity, real relations and real potentialities; for a sense of an anti-deterministic world in which one grasps real alternative possibilities, a sense of the 'could be otherwise' without which real value orientation becomes meaningless; for the 'feel' of the surd, brute, otherness of the environment to which one must successfully respond. These subtle tones of experience which make man's awareness of a world of appearing objects possible are at once the subtle tones, or modes of being, of that which enters into all experience, for as has been seen, experience opens in one direction toward the structures of the independently real, and in the other direction toward the structures of our modes of grasping or interacting with the independently real, and thus experience incorporates characteristics of each.

Finally, it should be noted that it is the interactional unity of man with that ontological reality which reveals itself in experience and from which man has emerged which is, in fact, the world in which man lives.[23] For Lewis, the world within which specific meanings and beliefs arise, and within which objects and qualities emerge for conscious awareness, is not some copy of an independent reality, nor is it a spectator grasp of an independent reality in its character as independent. Rather, such a world is the encompassing frame of reference or field of interest of organism-environment interaction; the ultimate backdrop of rationality within which emerging facts are situated; the 'outermost' horizon of meaningful rapport by which man is intentionally linked with the independently real. Thus, our world of appearing objects, from the most immediate grasp of 'what appears,' to the most all inclusive comprehension of what facts conceivably may be, is a function of the interaction of the noetic act and the independently real, and, as a function of both, 'mirrors' neither exactly, though it reflects characteristics of each. If one returns to Kant for an understanding of the full significance of Lewis' dispositional theory of meaning, one finds that the worlds of C.I. Lewis and the existential phenomenologist are not so alien after all. On the other hand, it is not an overstatement to say that those who ignore Lewis' dispositional theory of meaning have truly lost his world.

NOTES

1   In *The Philosophy of C.I. Lewis* (La Salle, Illinois: Open Court, 1968, ed. by Paul A. Schilpp) interpretations of Lewis as some type of analytic philosopher abound throughout the book.

2   Almost without exception, the interpretations of Lewis' position in terms of analytic philosophy of some variety wind up by showing the inadequacy of his basic concepts.

3   His influence on analytic philosophy is not here denied. However, there is a difference between what a philosophy is asserting and how it influences those who assimilate it within their own framework.

4   This limitation to existential phenomenology is not intended to necessarily exclude the possibility of affinities with Husserl in this area, but rather to avoid taking a definitive stand within the ongoing debate as to whether Husserl does or does not wind up in idealism and/ or subjectivism.

5   C.I. Lewis, *An Analysis of Knowledge and Valuation* (La Salle, Illinois: Open Court, 1962; orig. 1946), p. 140. (Hereafter referred to as *AKV*.)

6   *AKV*, pp. 140-141.

7   Such meaning relationships are, of course, the foundation for Lewis' analytic, a priori structures which underlie and make possible all empirical knowledge.

8   Lewis holds that a pure conceptual pattern of relations 'is, of course, an abstraction; no such concept ever existed apart from imagery and sensory material, in any human mind.' (C.I. Lewis, *Mind and the World Order* (New York: Dover Publications, 1956, orig. 1929), p. 80. (Hereafter referred to as *MWO*.)

9   Although Lewis usually speaks of sense meaning as a precise, explicit schema, yet sense meaning is, for Lewis, intensional or conceptual meaning, and this he frequently identifies as a disposition or habit. He clarifies this dual aspect of sense meaning when he observes that 'A sense meaning *when precise and explicit* is a schema.' (*AKV*, p. 134) Furthermore, though he speaks of sense meanings as being 'in mind,' he observes that though 'we have thought it well judged to take sense meaning as criterion in mind,' yet 'the important character connoted by 'in mind' here is 'entertained in advance of instances of application which are pertinent' ... One may consider such criteria of application, as meanings entertained in advance, in terms of incipient behavior or behavior attitudes if one choose.' (*AKV*, pp. 143-144)

10   As Lewis notes, appearing qualia are apprehended 'not by introspection, nor by extrospection, but simply by *spection*.' (*AKV*, p. 444)

11   For Lewis, it will be remembered, the schema is an intrinsic part of meaning and thus partakes of the generality of meaning. (See *AKV*, pp. 161-163 for Lewis' discussion of this point in relation to the Kantian synthetic a priori.)

12   *AKV*, p. 110.

13   *AKV*, p. 330.

14   *MWO*, p. 58.

15   As a related point, it should be noted that knowledge, for Lewis, must not only be verified as true; it must be justified as rationally credible. Lewis rejects what he considers the over-emphasis on future experience contained in empiristic theories which put forth an account of the verification of knowledge as if it were the whole story. It is precisely the function of empirical judgment to save the hazards of action without foresight. In this fact lies the significance, for Lewis, of the justification of knowledge as distinguished from the verification of it. Lewis is led thus to define empirical knowledge not as verified belief but as justified belief.

16   The pragmatic focus on scientific *methodology* as the lived activity of the scientist, as opposed to any focus on scientific contents and their illicit projection as the building blocks of reality, leads precisely to the pragmatic focus on the creative interaction between man and his environment through purposive, goal oriented modes of response. (The pragmatic

understanding of scientific methodology and its philosophical significance has been developed by me in some further detail in my article, 'Pragmatism and Phenomenology: The Significance of Wilshire's Reply,' *Transactions of the Charles S. Peirce Society: A Quarterly Journal of American Philosophy*, XIII, 1977, pp. 56-66, see esp. pp. 60-62.)

17   Lewis White Beck, 'The Kantianism of Lewis,' *The Philosophy of C.I. Lewis*, pp. 274-284.

18   Lewis' theory of knowledge is usually analyzed by his critics in complete oblivion to any tendency towards naturalism which may direct his thoughts in epistemology. If such a tendency is recognized, it is sometimes dismissed by taking note of Lewis' statement that 'To make it clear that *empiricism in epistemology* and *naturalism in ethics* do not imply such relativism and cynicism has been one main objective in the writing of this book.' (*AKV*, viii) However, precisely what is at issue is the nature of the experience in which knowledge is rooted for Lewis and hence the nature of the empiricism which Lewis espouses. Pragmatism can claim to be a 'radical empiricism' precisely because it returns to the richness of lived experience which has been lost by past empiricism's erroneous focus on scientific contents as opposed to scientific methodology as lived interactional activity.

19   Lewis makes the distinction between the 'order of being' and the 'order of knowing', and stresses that an epistemological analysis does not make superfluous analyses of other sorts. He stresses that the mistake of too much philosophy, 'since Kant, and perhaps particularly amongst idealists, is the tendency to attach to epistemological analyses a kind of *exclusive* truth.' As he further observes, 'In some one of the innumerable meanings of the word 'is' it must be true that a thing is what it is 'known as,' identifiable with its *ratio cognoscendi*; but it is also the effect of its causes, the cause of its effects, the organized whole of its physical or other constituents, and a hundred other significant things besides.' (*MWO*, pp. 149-150) Though Lewis' main emphasis is usually on the epistemological aspect, the other senses of 'is' are always there in the background providing the context for his discussion.

20   Thus Lewis stresses that he is not advocating phenomenalism, but rather is presenting a 'phenomenology of the perceptual.' C.I. Lewis, 'Autobiography,' *Collected Papers of Clarence Irving Lewis*, ed. by John D. Goheen and John L. Mothershead, Jr. (Stanford, California: Stanford University Press, 1970), p. 18.

21   As Lewis states, 'Empirical reality does not need to be assumed nor to be proved, but only to be acknowledged.' *AKV*, p. 361.

22   *MWO*, p. 154. Lewis holds that 'The history of philosophy since Descartes has been largely shaped by acceptance of the alternatives; either (1) knowledge is not relative to the mind, or (2) the content of knowledge is not the real, or (3) the real is dependent on mind. Kant, and phenomenalism in general, recognizes the relativity of knowledge, the dependence of the phenomenal object on the mind, and hence the impossibility of knowing the real as it is in itself. Idealism, taking the impossibility of knowledge as its main premise, argues to the unqualified dependence of reality upon mind. ... Realists in general seek to reconcile the possibility of knowing reality with its independence of the mind by one or another attempt to escape the relativity of knowledge.' (*MWO*, p. 154) (Although Kant is considered the beginning of 'the rejection of the spectator,' he himself was not immune to some of its presuppositions.)

23   Lewis' concept of 'world' is developed in some detail in my article, 'The 'World' of C.I. Lewis,' *Philosophy and Phenomenological Research*, XXIX (1969), pp. 589-597.

'A THING OF MOODS AND TENSES' — EXPERIENCE IN JOHN DEWEY

VICTOR KESTENBAUM

Dewey began *Experience and Nature* not once but twice, in 1925 and 1929. The first chapter of each edition is called 'Experience and Philosophic Method,' but they afford distinctively different beginnings for Dewey's metaphysics of experience. I believe that *Experience and Nature* is one of the great statements of, and approaches to, what Husserl in the *Crisis* calls 'the antagonism between the 'life of the plane' and the 'life of depth.''[1] In his original first chapter, Dewey begins his metaphysics of experience on a 'level of depth,' of pre-predicativeness and pre-reflectiveness, which seems to all but eclipse not only the 'life of the plane,' but the life of reason and judgment. His beginning, then, was not an introduction, for he had advanced too deeply too quickly. In the Preface to the second edition he remarks that 'the first chapter was intended as an introduction. It failed of its purpose; it was upon the whole more technical and harder reading than the chapters which it was supposed to introduce.'[2] Indeed, it was technical and hard reading because it presented as beginnings what really were achievements of the entire book. Thus, though Dewey's original beginning was not an adequate act of introduction, it supremely well records the state of mind or kind of consciousness which informed *Experience and Nature*, and which found its fulfillment nine years later in *Art as Experience*. I would like to reflect on this beginning, to see what it requires of us, and what it probably required of Dewey.

I will concentrate on two aspects of this beginning. First, I will follow Dewey's return to the life-world, what he variously calls direct experience, primary experience, gross experience, vital experience, macroscopic experience, or lived experience. Secondly, I will outline some of the features of Dewey's return to the pre-predicative world funded and founded in the pre-objective, anonymous intentionality of habit. These two steps, you will notice, are the same Husserl takes in beginning *Experience and Judgement*, in his interrogation of transcendental subjectivity. The first step involves, Husserl says, '*retrogression from the pregiven world* with all of its sedimentations of sense, with its science and scientific determination, *to the original life-world*.' Noting that the life-world is not simply pre-given but allows questioning regarding its modes of constitution, Husserl identifies the second step as 'the regressive inquiry which

See notes at the end of this chapter.

goes from the life world to the subjective operations from which it itself arises.'[3] I do not seek to argue the philosophical significance regarding the similarities and differences between *Experience and Judgment* and *Experience and Nature*, though these are more interesting and more important than many suppose. Rather, I prefer to consider how Dewey accomplishes his own journey from the 'life of the plane' to the 'life of depth.' In discussing this journey, I will quote fairly extensively from Dewey, both to assure your that he really said these things, and to provide some texts for consideration.

To return to experience as it is had or lived through, signifies, Dewey says,

> beginning back of any science, with experience in its gross and macroscopic traits. Science will then be of interest as one of the phases of human experience, but intrinsically no more so than magic, myth, politics, painting, poetry and penitentiaries. The domination of men by reverie and desire is as pertinent for the philosophic theory of nature as is mathematical physics; imagination as much to be noted as refined observation.[4]

Dewey's empirical, experiential, or what he calls 'denotative' method, requires the philosopher to begin 'back of any science.' 'Any' must be emphasized here, for not only does Dewey explicitly exclude the reduction of experience to physiology, he pointedly denies that psychology provides a better beginning for the interrogation of experience. What Dewey calls 'coarse and vital experience,' lived experience, is he says, 'Protean; a thing of moods and tenses.'[5] For this reason, the determined meanings of science, or philosophy for that matter, are poorly suited to describe experience, to 'seize and report' it, as Dewey says. Not only is there a natural difficulty in subjecting experience to the objectivations of reason, there is a social dimension. It is probably inevitable he comments,

> for the philosopher to mix with his reports of direct experience interpretations of it made by previous thinkers. Too often, indeed, the professed empiricist only substitutes a dialectical development of some notion about experience for an analysis of experience as it is humanly lived.[6]

Even empiricism has failed, Dewey believes, in its fidelity to lived experience. Cogently, not cutely, he remarks that 'not safely can an 'ism' be made out of experience.'[7] Interpretation, even by empiricists, simplifies, and simplifies in directions usually set by custom, convention, or conviction, which, Dewey says, 'one assumes to be natural simply because it is traditionally congenial.'[8] This interrogation of the 'natural attitude' — of what 'comes naturally' to us through scientific sense or common sense — is a constant theme of Dewey's chapter, and of course of his entire philosophy of experience. Though there certainly is warrant in so much of his writings for viewing Dewey as an uncritical naturalist overwhelmed by the success of scientific method and rationality, this perspective is just too narrow and too simple.

Dewey, then, knew well the meaning of Husserl's conviction in the *Crisis* that the life-world is the 'forgotten meaning-fundament of natural science,' as Husserl says. But Dewey also knew the deeper meaning of Merleau-Ponty's lesson that 'reflection is truly reflection only if it is not carried outside itself, only if it knows itself as reflection-on-an-unreflective experience, and consequently as a change in structure of our existence.'[9] Thus, although the philosopher reflects, he is, Dewey says,

> prone to take the outcome of reflection for something antecedent. That is to say, instead of seeing that the product of knowing is *statement* of things, he is given to taking it as an *existential equivalent* of what things really are 'in themselves', so that the subject-matter of other modes of experience are deviations shortcomings, or trespasses — or as the dialectical philosopher puts it, mere 'phenomena.'[10]

In Dewey's regression to the life-world, it is not only scientific rationality which must recover its foundation, reason itself must be grounded in the life-world and more fundamentally, in the pre-predicative world. Dewey simply will not have philosophers deducing experience from their favorite reasoned concepts. The experiential method requires us, he says, to 'go behind the refinements and elaborations of reflective experience to the gross and compulsory things of our doings, enjoyments and sufferings.'[11] To uncover structures of experience requires forms of articulation which respect the world-founding character of lived experience. How, though, does Dewey see lived experience? What is it like for him? His discussion of two aspects of lived experience provides the transition from his regression to the life-world, to his consideration of the pre-predicative foundations of its 'subjective operations' as Husserl calls them.

Dewey's first characterization of lived experience is that it is not primarily a knowledge affair: our relationship to the world, our most basic affinity to it, is not a series of positings of distinct intellectual objects. The human being is not an 'epistemological subject,' and 'epistemic nucleus' in some Piagetian sense. Intentional objects are found and dealt with in many other ways than those of knowledge and belief. The rationalism and intellectualism of Dewey's day was quite disturbing to him, for it seriously narrowed the scope of experience to ideas, beliefs, and concepts, equating, in short, being and being known. Dewey says this all in one of the great paragraphs of this beginning chapter:

> *being* and *having* things in ways other than knowing them, in ways never identical with knowing them, exist, and are preconditions of reflection and knowledge. *Being* angry, stupid, wise, inquiring; *having* sugar, the light of day, money, houses and lands, friends, laws, masters, subjects, pain and joy, occur in dimensions incommensurable to knowing these things which we are and have and use, and which have and use us... All cognitive experience must start from and must terminate in being and having things in just such unique, irreparable and compelling ways.[12]

Meanings are had in a variety of ways and press toward a variety of fulfillments in experience. Some fulfillments are more adequate than others, and this too is discovered in experience, but for Dewey it is a betrayal of the possibilities of experience to insist that a fulfilled meaning must be a validated meaning. Conversely, though, Dewey did believe that a validated meaning, or one claiming this status, must be fulfilled, must be 'had' in such a way that its meaning may compel, and as I next suggest, it is on the level of the pre-predicative, of anonymous habit, that we are compelled.

The second characterization of lived experience by Dewey concerns its ambiguity. Because it is 'Protean; a thing of moods and tenses,' lived experience must be approached as a field with a focus and a fringe. Dewey was here of course influenced and convinced by James: a field theory of meaning is required by the facts of experience, for it is not only the face of experience which we live. Thus, similar to Merleau-Ponty, Dewey refuses to accept what he calls the 'reduction of experience to states of consciousness.'[13] Experience, he says, 'is something quite other than 'consciousness,' that is, that which appears qualitatively and focally at a particular moment.'[14] Every text of consciousness exists in a field, horizon, or context. This text-context relationship is fundamental to Dewey's metaphysics of experience. The eighth chapter of *Experience and Nature*, 'Existence, Ideas, and Consciousness,' contains Dewey's theory of consciousness and is built around this text-context relationship. Dewey, no less than James, wished to reassert for philosophy the importance of what James called 'the backwater of consciousness.' Thus, Dewey says that,

> it is important for a theory of experience to know that under certain circumstances men prize the distinct and clearly evident. But it is no more important than it is to know that under other circumstances twilight, the vague, dark and mysterious flourish.[15]

The self, the ego, the subject as subjectivity, cannot be identified with, or reduced to, judgement or consciousness. The theater of the subject's experience is darker, more mysterious, than the accomplishments of predicating reason suggest or allow. The metaphysics of the text-context relationship moves Dewey in two directions at once: into the world of existence in search of personal, historical, and social contexts of experience, and deeper into the subject, into the pre-predicative context of habitual meaning.

After the epoche of objective science, and after the epoche of objectivating reason, Dewey is better positioned to grasp the deepest source of the pregivenness of the world. The pre-predicative is the source and the ground of the texts of experience and their horizons. The horizons of pre-predicative meaning are present yet absent in experience. Dewey states:

> Because intellectual crimes have been committed in the name of the subconscious is no reason for refusing to admit that what is not explicitly present makes up a vastly greater part of experience than does the conscious field to which thinkers have so devoted themselves.[16]

The 'conscious field' recedes, silently, anonymously, into a 'subconscious field.'

Dewey is not attempting another revision of a Freudian taxonomy of levels of consciousness, though later in the book he does refer again to the 'conscious,' 'fore-conscious,' and 'sub-conscious.' Instead, he is really seeking the source of that affinity between self and world, the ground of memory, knowledge, and judgment, which pre-exists the distinction between self and world, subject and object.

In perhaps the most important three sentences of his beginning, Dewey says,

> Experience is no stream, even though the stream of feelings and ideas that flows upon its surface is the part which philosophers love to traverse. Experience includes the enduring banks of natural constitution and acquired habit as well as the stream. The flying moment is sustained by an atmosphere that does not fly, even when it most vibrates.[17]

In a mild rebuke to James and a profound indictment of philosophy, Dewey summarizes the point of view he had been developing for 25 years and would develop for another 25 years: *habit*, not reason, is the world-founding principle. The already constituted world, the life-world, is rooted in the anonymously functioning intentionality of habit. The 'life of depth' which Husserl sought, the invisible persistence of meaning which Merleau-Ponty sought, are, for Dewey, the hidden achievements of habit. Dewey of course cannot match the brilliance of James's accounts of the intentionality of the body, what Dewey calls here 'natural constitution.' But it is Dewey, not James, who closes in on the pre-reflective intentionality of habitual, taken-for-granted meaning, making it the foundation of his philosophy of experience. Any epoche or reduction for Dewey must be a discovery and revealing of the pre-objective intentionality of habit, for habit is both the foundation of our creativity and transcendence, as well as the source of those prejudices of the natural attitude and determining reason which blind us to the world.

Dewey's regression then, to habitus, is not a return to primordial experience, or to the origin of origins. It is certainly not a return to an absolute beginning or even a secure beginning. It is a return to that accord between self and world which reveals the proximity of eidos and habitus, habitus and epoche, and yet this return to experience suggests why habit is not so easily disengaged from the world and transformed into a rationalized beginning. We live the world in our habits, and the world lives in our habits. Habits, those pre-predicative structures of meaning which are the basis of our 'life of depth,' both cultural and perceptual, are beginnings with a history of entanglements. Individual and collective habitus is the beginning for Dewey not in the sense that a new ordering idea, concept, or 'first principle' has been proposed to 'explain' experience. Rather, human experience reveals, quite unmistakably, the persistence of meaning we call habit. Dewey requires us, then, to return to experience mindful of at least two things. First, the beginning embodied in habit is the object and the agent of the elucidation of experience. Secondly, the beginning which is embodied in implicit habit is not a first thought which can be undone and then reconstituted as an explicit origin. What other responses Dewey's own beginning requires of us, I will leave for discussion. Thank you.

NOTES

1   *The Crisis of European Sciences and Transcendental Phenomenology: An Introduction to Phenomenological Philosophy*, trans. David Carr (Evanston: Northwestern University Press, 1970), pp. 118-121.

2   *Experience and Nature*, 2nd edition (Illinois: Open Court Publishing Company, 1929), p. xiii.

3   *Experience and Judgment: Investigations in a Genealogy of Logic*, trans. James S. Churchill and Karl Ameriks (Evanston: Northwestern University Press, 1973), pp. 50, 52.

4   *Experience and Nature* (Illinois: Open Court Publishing Company, 1925), p. 6 (Hereafter EN)

5   EN, p. 3

6   EN, pp. 3-4

7   EN, p. 4

8   EN, p. 4

9   *Phenomenology of Perception*, trans. Colin Smith (New York: Humanities Press, 1962), p. 62.

10   EN, pp. 15-16

11   EN, p. 16

12   EN, pp. 18-19

13   EN, p. 7

14   EN, p. 7

15   EN, p. 7

16   EN, p. 7

17   EN, p. 8

SECTION IV

PHENOMENOLOGY AND THE THOUGHT OF MERLEAU-PONTY

UNCONSCIOUSNESS: REFLECTION AND THE PRIMACY OF PERCEPTION

ROBERT D. ROMANYSHYN

I. INTRODUCTION

Physics is an implicit psychology and a theory of things is also already a theory of the body. Uncritically adopting its conception of the world from the natural sciences, modern psychology has more or less understood the body as a thing, and as a consequence of this view of the body has more or less either ignored consciousness as an illusion (Skinner, 1971), or treated it as a derivative of biological processes. Mind, then, has been reduced to brain until this reductionism is forced back upon itself where a dualism of mind *and* body re-emerges (Pennfield, 1975). Such a view, it seems, is the line of development of modern psychology: the body is conceived in the image of things, and consciousness is derived from this image of the body.

Psychoanalysis, however, seems to be an exception to this view, and Freud's work appears to restore an understanding of body, things, and consciousness which is prior to psychology's vision. Recognizing and developing the symbolic character of things, Freud also transforms the meaning of the human body. 'The body is enigmatic ...' in psychoanalysis, Merleau-Ponty says, and with Freud's work '... mind passes into body as, inversly, body passes into mind (1964a, p. 229).' Mind or consciousness, therefore, is also changed, and Freud recovers '... between the body's anonymous life and the person's official life ... (Ibid)' a consciousness which neither fully knows its ignorance nor is fully ignorant of its knowing, an *unconsciousness* which Merleau-Ponty calls the 'Protean idea in Freud's works (Ibid).' But just when this psychoanalysis seems to be an exception to much of modern psychology, it becomes the very epitome of its expression. Unconsciousness becomes the repressed, and the Cartesian consciousness whose influence Freud has rightly circumscribed (Cf. Freud, 1961, XIX, p. 16, n. 1) reappears *beneath* consciousness as a silent but all knowing witness of life's forbidden wishes. Thus, it is small wonder that Merleau-Ponty says that 'we have only to follow the transformations of this Protean idea ... to be convinced that it is not a fully developed idea, and that ... we still have to find the right formulation for what he (Freud) intended by this provisional designation (Ibid).'

See notes at the end of this chapter.

Merleau-Ponty's work offers, I think, a possible direction for such a formulation. Reconsidering the Freudian unconscious from the point of view of perception, Merleau-Ponty challenges Freud's Protean idea, and in such a fashion that a challenge is also offered to the notion of the Cartesian *cogito*. Beginning with perception Merleau-Ponty offers an understanding of human subjectivity which radicalizes the meaning of *reflection*, and which integrates the notions of the lower and the higher into a dimension of *lateral depth*. More specifically, I mean that Merleau-Ponty's thesis of the primacy of perception, according to which perception founds thought but only as thought finds itself being founded in this way, offers a critical consideration of 'Freud'[1] which moves toward 'Descartes', but toward a 'Descartes' which is also critically re-understood in a movement toward 'Freud'. Perceptual consciousness, therefore, is not merely a hybrid of Cartesian consciousness *and* Freudian unconsciousness, but a transformation of each for the sake of a new beginning.

My intentions in this paper are to consider *first* this double movement of Merleau-Ponty's thought, *second* the understanding of subjectivity which emerges from it, and third a difficulty which remains in the path of these reflections. Thus in parts two and three of this paper, I will consider respectively the movements from consciousness and unconsciousness to perception, where in each case a notion of lateral depth will be seen to emerge. Then in part four I will take up this notion of perceptual consciousness and lateral depth to indicate its presence in Merleau-Ponty's work and its relation to a changed and deepened meaning of reflection. Finally in part five I will raise what I think remains at issue in Merleau-Ponty's analyses and suggest some directions for its consideration.

II. FROM CONSCIOUSNESS TO PERCEPTION: THE PHENOMENOLOGY OF PERCEPTION

The chapter entitled 'The Cogito' in the *Phenomenology of Perception* is Merleau-Ponty's first attempt to work out the ontological consequences and implications of his thesis of the primacy of perception. While some of his thinking in this chapter will later be revised and/or abandoned, its position in the work bears witness to how the thesis of perception radically alters the notion of the *cogito*. For example, having already provided phenomenological descriptions of the perceived world and the body, Merleau-Ponty says: 'What I discover and recognize through the *cogito* is not psychological immanence, the inherence of all phenomena in 'private states of consciousness', [and] ... not even transcendental immanence, the belonging of all phenomena to a constituting consciousness, the possession of clear thought by itself (1962, p. 377).' On the contrary, what perceptual consciousness reveals about consciousness in general '... is the deep seated momentum of transcendence which is my very being, the *simultaneous* contact with my own being and with the world's being (Ibid., my italics).'

Immediately, however, Merleau-Ponty challenges himself because maybe the case of perceptual consciousness is unique and maybe it prejudices this re-consideration of the *cogito*. Are there not, he asks, instances which sustain the absolute privilege of consciousness, instances like one's awareness of 'psychic facts' which demonstrate consciousness' transparency to itself? Do not experiences like love and will, for example, show consciousness in full possession of itself, and if not these then surely does not the case of 'pure thought (Ibid., p. 383)' demonstrate that consciousness is identical with its own self-awareness?

Using the example of the feeling of love, Merleau-Ponty says that it seems to be the case that love, like any psychic fact, is the same whether its object is '... artificial or real ...', and apart from the fact that its object may or may not have the value one now gives to it. I love, I think about love, I remember being in love, and in each of these instances it seems that one is within '... a sphere of absolute certainty in which truth cannot elude us (Ibid., p. 378).' Of course, one can be mistaken about the *one* he loves, and about *what* he remembers of his love, just as one can be foolishly mistaken in his *thoughts* about love. But in the acts of loving, remembering, and thinking, within consciousness itself, it seems that error is not possible: one either loves or does not love, just as one either thinks or does not think. About one's *feeling* of love and/or about one's *thinking*, therefore, there can be no doubt. Within consciousness one is in perfect contact with himself; within consciousness everything is true. 'A feeling, *considered in itself*, is always true once it is felt (Ibid., p. 378, my italics).'

Such certainty, however, masks an illusion, for as Merleau-Ponty points out it seems quite clear that '... we are able to discriminate ... between 'true' and 'false' feelings ... (Ibid.),' and that 'Besides true love, there is false or illusory love (Ibid.).' In time, for example, I may discover that I do not love this other, and that what I thought to be love was in fact a mistaken illusion. Dis-illusioned, *now*, and trying to understand what has happened to me, I may either convince myself that indeed I really already knew *then* that I was not in love, or I may accept that I was fully deceived. In short, discovering myself *now* as mistaken in love *then*, I also discover within myself a zone of either absolute knowledge or absolute ignorance.

Neither 'solution' however is appropriate, for in the first instance my love from the beginning was never really true love so that now there can be no question of an earlier mistake, and in the second instance I was so fully deceived, that it is now impossible to know with any certitude if I am deceived about my deceiving, if I am mistaken about that mistake. Indeed both 'solutions' come down to the same thing: *an absolute separation of the true and the false and a disregard of time*. In the first case the lover is absolutely present to himself and is never deceived or mistaken, and in the second he is absolutely absent from himself and always deceived or mistaken. Moreover in both cases there is the same 'retrospective illusion (Ibid., p. 381),' that same *substitution* of a present knowledge *substantialized into a higher consciousness* for the continuing ambiguity of experience, that same tendency to stop time and canonize one privileged moment.

The fact, however, is that *then* I was in love and *now* I find I was mistaken, and thus the issue is to understand *how* one can not know what he knows and/or know what he does not know. The issue is *how* one can hide from himself even while knowing he is hiding. On the one hand, I could not have fully known *then* that this love was an illusion, for then I would and could not have loved. Thus Merleau-Ponty rightly says that '... it is impossible to pretend that I always knew what I now know, and to see as [always, already] existing, a self-knowledge which I have only just come by (Ibid., p. 380).' But on the other hand, I could not have fully *not known*, for then how could or would I ever love, how could I ever know that I am not deceived again? On the contrary, therefore, what I *now* discover is that indeed I did know *then* that my love was mistaken by not knowing it, and that by not knowing it I knew. What I discover is an ignorance at the heart of my knowledge, but also a knowledge at the heart of this ignorance. Thus 'The love which worked out its dialectic through me, and of which I have just become aware,' Merleau-Ponty says, 'was not, from the start, a thing hidden in my unconscious, nor was it an object before my consciousness, but the impulse carrying me *towards* someone ... a matter of experience not knowledge from start to finish (Ibid., p. 381, my italics).' I could not have known *then* what I know *now*, but neither could I not not have known.

Perceptual consciousness, therefore, is not for Merleau-Ponty a special case, for even 'psychic facts', like this experience of love as well as the other examples considered in this chapter, reveal a consciousness (a subjectivity) which knows itself only in and through the world and over time, a consciousness which neither creates nor discovers itself (which amounts to creation) but *recovers* itself from the world. Indeed in this work Merleau-Ponty says that he has restored a 'temporal thickness (Ibid., p. 398)' to the *cogito* which is after all only another way of saying a consciousness which knows itself through its participation in the world. There is neither endless doubt nor absolute certainty, and consciousness is neither total presence to nor total absence from itself. On the contrary, consciousness is present to itself only by its absence, and in its absence it is present to itself. Or as Merleau-Ponty says of his own reflections in this work '... presence to oneself and presence in the world ...' are linked together, and '... the *cogito* (is identified) with involvement in the world ... (Ibid., p. 433).' In Sallis' (1973) terms, Merleau-Ponty has radicalized '... the bond between presence to self and transcendence so as to integrate the former into the latter (p. 66).' Thus if 'The primary truth is indeed 'I think' ...,' then this is true '... only provided that we understand thereby 'I belong to myself *while* belonging to the world (Merleau-Ponty, 1962, p. 407, my italics).'

There is, then, in this analysis of the *cogito* as exemplified in these passages a first suggestion of another meaning of consciousness or subjectivity, a suggestion which to be sure still exists side by side with a notion like the 'tacit cogito', that 'retreat of non-being (Ibid., p. 400)' which still haunts the *Phenomenology of Perception* and will remain with Merleau-Ponty until *The Visible and the Invisible*. But despite this spectre of 'Descartes', the thrust of perceptual conciousness has already forced a new beginning — even if that *explicitly* comes later. The thesis of the primacy of perception has lowered consciousness into the world and in such a way, moreover, that 'Descartes' is *infected* with 'Freud', but with a 'Freud' which is also transformed. There is in other words an echo of 'Freud' in these criticisms of 'Descartes' so that if consciousness is not transparent to itself it is '... because the subject that I am, when taken concretely, is inseparable from this body and this world (Ibid., p. 408).' It is, therefore, no accident, nor is it surprising to find after the *Phenomenology of Perception* increasing references to and considerations of Freud and psychoanalysis, for it is as if these first suggestions of another meaning of consciousness and subjectivity are already foreshadowed in Freud, even while Merleau-Ponty's phenomenology of phenomenology is the latent meaning in Freud's work, '... the philosophy implicit in psychoanalysis itself ... (1970, p. 31),' the thrust of Freud's genius when shorn of its own inadequate mechanistic assumptions. And yet as much as this movement from 'Descartes' is also a movement toward 'Freud', as much as Merleau-Ponty praises Freud's '... increasingly clear view of the body's mental function and the mind's incarnation (1964a, p. 230),' as much as he admits that 'Freud is soverign in his ability to listen to the hushed words of life (1970, p. 30),' we can neither ignore nor forget his criticisms of Freud. In short his critical re-consideration of the *cogito*, his critical re-examination of what he calls 'high altitude thought (1968, p. 13),' already affects his consideration of the unconscious, or what one may call low altitude thought. 'Our age,' Merleau-Ponty says, 'is as far from explaining man by the lower as it is by the higher, and *for the same reasons* (1964a, p. 240, my italics).' Merleau-Ponty is no Freudian, therefore, and indeed in following out this double movement of his thought the justifiable suspicion emerges that 'Freud' is a 'Descartes' of the depths, and 'Descartes' a 'Freud' of the heights, that is, while 'Freud' reasons the dream 'Descartes' dreams a new reason.[2] Thus Merleau-Ponty already says in the *Phenomenology of Perception* that 'The idea of a form of consciousness which is transparent to itself, its existence being identifiable with its awareness of existing, is not so very different from the notion of the unconscious ... (1962, p. 380).' His critique of one, therefore, is also a critique of the other, and in this process each is transformed for the sake of a new beginning. In the next section, I want to consider this second movement, and in the subsequent section I will consider this new beginning which is foreshadowed in each of these critical analyses.

III. FROM UNCONSCIOUSNESS TO PERCEPTION: *THE VISIBLE AND THE INVISIBLE*

Most of Merleau-Ponty's considerations of the unconscious from the side of perception are to be found in the working notes to *The Visible and the Invisible* (1968), and in another place (in press) I have discussed these issues in a slightly different way. For this paper, however, what seems essential in these considerations is that '... perception qua wild perception is of itself ignorance of itself, imperception ... (Merleau-Ponty, 1968, p. 213).' Perceiving effaces itself in favor of the perceived, much like 'Expression fades out before what is expressed (1962, p. 401).' Like speaking, therefore, perceiving, which is for Merleau-Ponty a 'nascent logos (1964b, p. 25),' '... promotes its own oblivion ... (1962, p. 401).' Between perceiving and the perceived there is a kind of natural unconsciousness, an unconsciousness at the heart of perception. *I* am not present to the birth of my own perceiving, *and yet* in another sense I must be there in order to perceive. This natural unconsciousness at the heart of perception is not, therefore, a total ignorance. On the contrary it is another kind of knowledge, and the perceiving subject, like the speaking subject, is *present* to his perceiving and speaking because he is also *absent* from them. His absence, then, is a kind of presence just as his presence is through this absence. '*I* do not perceive any more than *I* speak — Perception has me as has language — (1968, p. 190, my italics)' Merleau-Ponty says.[3] But then most importantly he adds that '... as it is necessary that all the same *I* be there in order to speak, *I* must be there in order to perceive — (Ibid., his italics).' The question is, however, in what sense I am there by not being there, and Merleau-Ponty's answer is 'As *one* (Ibid.).' It is not I who perceive but *one* who perceives in me, a way of being present then which is indefinite, ambiguous and indeterminate.

Merleau-Ponty's work makes it quite clear of course that this *one* who perceives is the embodied subject, and hence also that his re-consideration of the Freudian unconscious is a *resurrection* of the body toward consciousness, a notion that is implicit in Freud's descriptions but ruled out by his metapsychology. Thus through the example of the woman in the street who grips her coat together because she feels others are staring at her breasts but who could not say what she has just done or tell us why, Merleau-Ponty indicates that this sensitive body can know what *I* do not (want to) know, that it can be a knowing which *motivates* ignorance.[4] What seems not so clear, however, is 'how' this body knows what I do not know, not however in the sense of an explanation but rather in the sense of a more adequate description. That woman in the street indeed may be absent from her presence to the others' looks, but it is a question then of a better understanding of how this body is a presence by virtue of absence, of how it can foster a knowledge of which *she* is ignorant.

Here Merleau-Ponty's reflections on the Freudian unconscious are deepened in this last work, for it is here that he suggests as Lingis says that '... the invisible substructure of the visible is the key to the unconscious structure of consciousness (1968, p. liii).' The invisible, he says, '... is not the contradictory of the visible (Ibid., p. 215),' a negative defined in its opposition to the positive. Nor is it a potential visible, a '... possible visible for an other ... (Ibid., p. 229).' Neither a category nor an inference from the visible, as Freud's unconscious is at times presented and justified as an inference from the data of consciousness, it is rather '... the secret counterpart of the visible, ... the Nichturpräsentierbar

which is presented to me as such *within the world* ... (Ibid., p. 215, my italics).'
The invisible therefore, is the visible's only way of being visible (... an Urpräsentation of the Nichturpräsentiebar ... Ibid., p. 254), the '... *other side* or the *reverse* of sensible Being (Ibid., p. 255, his italics).' Like the light, the invisible is a level or system of levels, which are not *what* we see but are that '... *with which, according to which*, we see (Ibid., p. li, his italics).'

But for Merleau-Ponty all of this is also to be said of the unconscious of consciousness. It, too, is not *what* we see but is that through which there is the perceived. Speaking of consciousness he says that '*what* it does not see it does not see for reasons of principle, (and that) it is because it is consciousness that it does not see (Ibid., p. 248, his italics).' It is, in other words, *because* consciousness does not see itself seeing, or because it never fully touches itself touching, that it sees (and touches) the world. Or said in a positive way it is because consciousness sees itself only in seeing things, because in touching things it manages to touch itself, that consciousness is consciousness. This central blindness of consciousness, then, is a blindness in principle, and hence the only way of consciousness being consciousness is by not being conscious of being conscious of the world. *Consciousness is not an act*, Merleau-Ponty says, *but a being at (être à) the world.*

Unconsciousness is the *other side* of consciousness, therefore, like the invisible is the *other side* of the visible. But what is related in this way is related as a *pivot*, and the reversal of visibility/invisibility, of consciousness/unconsciousness, is around an *axis* or *hinge* without which *either side* is mistakenly understood as a thing or an idea. Consider, for example, the phenomenon of depth. It is not the visible and yet as invisible it has no other way of appearing except as *of* the visible. The painter who paints depth paints things, and it is between and among these things that depth appears. Understood in this way, things are not real facts nor ideas, but pivots around which the visibility of their surfaces and the invisibility of their depth gravitate. To capture depth, to capture the invisible, then, the painter must paint things as these pivots, as Merleau-Ponty's reflections on painting in 'Eye and Mind' (1964b) eloquently affirm.

A thing is a pivot, a crossing of the invisible and the visible. But so too is the human body a pivot, and the example of the woman in the street suggests that her body is a *hinge* around which consciousness and unconsciousness, knowledge and ignorance revolve. That woman, then, is neither conscious nor unconscious, nor a body *and* a mind, but one subject who as embodied is conscious of her sexuality in a particular way, *as a secret and forbidden sexuality*, by virtue of her being unconscious of it. Her body, therefore, knows the world in a way in which *she* does know it, and yet *she* is this body. This body, therefore, is the crossing of this knowledge *and* this ignorance, and to erase one in favor of the other, or to privelege either knowledge over ignorance or ignorance over knowledge, is to lose both, and to lose the body as this pivot. 'Define the mind as the other side of the body,' Merleau-Ponty says, and further say that 'There is a body of the mind, and a mind of the body and a chiasm between them (1968, p. 259).' There is, therefore, no other way for this woman to know her sexuality *in this way* except to not know it, and yet conversly in this not knowing she nevertheless knows it as a face of the world. The look of others reveals her sexuality because she conceals it *and* because her body offers itself to be seen in this manner. The eyes of others penetrate her garments because those eyes already reflect what her body desires *and* what she forbids. The gaze of others already disrobes her because between her hand which unknowingly closes the coat and this gaze there is already a secret knowledge.

The unconscious is neither the absence of knowledge nor the absence of the subject from himself, but rather this pivoting of knowledge and ignorance, this crossing of absence and presence. In this light, therefore, the unconscious is a phenomenon of *ambiguity*. Thus, where there is ambiguity there is a consciousness which is also unconsciousness, and an unconsciousness which is also consciousness. But as the double movement of Merleau-Ponty's thought has already shown, this ambiguity is really only another way of speaking about the 'body of knowledge,' and while Merleau-Ponty's reflections on the unconscious do not equate the Freudian unconscious with the body, they nevertheless do suggest that the body as a 'knowing' of the world is the starting point for any notion of unconsciousness. Indeed what one finds in these reflections is a *resurrection* of the body which compliments the previous incarnation of mind, a relation between me and my body which is neither one of absolute identity nor absolute difference. Moreover, one also finds in these reflections a suggestion of *lateral depth*, that is suggestion that the *unconscious is in the world between us*, and hence '... is to be sought not at the bottom of ourselves ... but in front of us, as articulations of our field (Ibid., p. 180).' In the next section I want to briefly consider these suggestions but in doing this I do not want to bypass a difficulty which emerges as a consequence of them. Despite this new beginning the fact remains that ambiguity does not equal ambivalence, and if Merleau-Ponty's unconsciousness shows us the paradox of *being* conscious while not being conscious, then Freud's unconsciousness shows the problem of *becoming* conscious. This is the problem of *repression*, and in the final section of this paper I want to briefly consider how Merleau-Ponty's suggestions affect this issue.

IV. PERCEPTUAL CONSCIOUSNESS AND REFLECTION

In a paper written in 1912 and entitled 'A note on the unconscious in psychoanalysis,' Freud justifies his conception and use of this term within the context of a definition of consciousness. He says: 'Now let us call 'conscious' the conception which is present to our consciousness and *of which we are aware*, and let this be the *only* meaning of the term 'conscious' (1958, XII, p. 260, my italics).' Beginning with this definition which equates consciousness with its awareness of itself as consciousness, Freud is correct in *inferring* that there is more to psychological life than meets the mind. But beginning in this way, Freud already

accepts this Cartesian image of consciousness and thereby infects his own beginning. As Descartes' *cogito* already presumes a Galilean world (Husserl, 1970,
p. 70), so too does Freud's unconscious presume a Cartesian *cogito*. Despite the
genuine insight in Freud's notion, therefore, his speaking of the unconscious
vitiates its most important contributions, as the previous sections have indicated.

Merleau-Ponty's phenomenology of perception, however, offers a new beginning which is best described in his last published work, the essay 'Eye and
Mind (1964b).' A sustained meditation on the notion of depth, this work opens
up the dimension of a *lateral depth* as the pivot or axis of the above and below.
The painter, he suggests, struggles to capture not the world as it is for profane
vision, and his effort is not to portray on canvas a resemblance to that world.
Indeed to the extent that the painter achieves this *representation* of the visible,
to that same extent does he fail to paint, since the achievement of painting is
that 'It gives visible existence to what profane vision believes to be invisible
(Ibid., p. 166).'

But what does profane vision believe to be invisible? In the context of this
essay, one of the examples which Merleau-Ponty uses provides the best illustration of an answer. Looking at some water in a pool, he acknowledges that that
water inhabits that space, and yet it most certainly is not contained there,
because '... if I raise my eyes toward the screen of cypresses where the web of
reflections is playing, I cannot gainsay the fact that the water visits it, too, or
at least sends into it, upon it, its active and living essence (Ibid., p. 182).' What
the painter sees but what profane vision forgets, therefore, is this water which
is in the pool because it is not there, this water which is in the pool because
it is also in the trees. It is this relation of *reflection*, this relation of mirroring in
which a thing is what it is by virtue of the others which surround it, '... this
radiation of the visible ... (Ibid., p. 182)' which painters, like Matisse in his early
canvasses, paint but which everyone does not see.

It is clear, however, that this relation of reflection, this 'dehiscence' of the
visible, this '... system of exchanges ... (Ibid., p. 164)' also includes the painter
himself, because his body which sees the spectacle is also of the visible. 'The
painter 'takes his body with him' ...,' Merleau-Ponty says, and 'It is by lending
his body to the world that the artist changes the world into paintings (Ibid.,
p. 162).' We must understand, however, that this lending is not a conscious act,
nor only a gift of giving. On the contrary, it is also a possession or a being pos-
sessed by the world, or perhaps best said it is a lending which is also a borrowing,
a lending because it is a borrowing. The world, then, borrows the painter's body
as much as he gives it, and indeed the things of the world are already 'encrusted'
into one's flesh, much like the sculptures of Henry Moore indicate. Painting's
interrogation of the world, therefore, '... looks toward this secret and feverish
genesis of things in our body (Ibid., p. 167),' which is why, I guess, Merleau-
Ponty hears the artist Paul Klee when he says that 'Perhaps I paint to break out
(Ibid., p. 167),' and also why he says himself that 'There really is inspiration and
expiration of Being, action and passion so slightly discernible that it becomes

impossible to distinguish between what sees and what is seen, what paints and what is painted (Ibid., p. 167).' A circularity of sorts exists, therefore, between the painter and the world, and there is a human body and a human world when '... between the seeing and the seen, between touching and the touched, between hand and hand, a blending of some sort takes place ...(Ibid., p. 163).'

The painter *recovers* what profane vision forgets, this '... metamorphosis of seeing and seen which defines both our flesh and the painter's vocation (Ibid., p. 169).' 'Man is a mirror for man (Ibid., p. 168),' Merleau-Ponty says, but, of course, it is also true that things reflect man back to himself just as they reflect each other. The mirror, the playing of light and shadow, the use of water as a reflecting surface, and indeed the example of painting itself in this essay, are, therefore, 'only' particular illustrations of this more general theme, of this eruption of lateral depth by mirroring. In Raoul Dufy's painting 'Old Houses at Honfleur' (See Fig. 1)[5] for example, the houses in the distance are reflected in the water, and it is the water which gives these houses their place in the world. Indeed what would these houses be without this reflection? Surely they would not and could not be human things, things of this world, because in truth they would then have no place. They would exist no-where, they would be without anchorage in the world, they would simply float away. But they are *houses in the distance* because and only because they are also in the water, because and only because they are closest to the seer in the water which nevertheless also gives them their distance. Through their reflection in the water they are present to the seer, but through that reflection they are also absent and far away. The water, therefore, is the depth of the houses their 'inside' as it were made visible, just as conversly the houses are the depth of the water.

'The mirror itself,' Merleau-Ponty says, 'is the instrument of a universal magic that changes ... myself into another, and another into myself (Ibid., p. 168).' It is, however, also the instrument of a *lateral depth* which announces a presence by absence, and which indicates that the world already has its hold on me. When I look at myself in the mirror, for example, I do not simply discover an image of myself at the surface of the glass. On the contrary, what is reflected to me is a ghostly presence which inhabits that world on the far side of the mirror, at a distance which is as great from the mirror's surface as *I* am from it on this side of the mirror. What the mirror betrays is that secret life that I already live amongst things, that distant presence which is somehow both familiar and strange. Indeed, the mirror often betrays a relation with things which may be unacknowledged and not yet known, so that sometimes for example when one looks in the mirror he discovers a look which reflects an attitude and a style of which he is unaware. '*I* am not this *one*,' the individual wants to say, and yet I am this one who is in the mirror, this one who is already captured and known by the world in this way. The mirror holds and reflects, therefore, the way in which others see me, even while it betrays a way in which I do not see myself. It reflects the *one* who I am, and indeed the surprise of the mirror is in its displacement of me from myself, in that discovery that I possess myself only in this dispossession by things. The surprise of the mirror is that the one who I am belongs as much to those things on that side of the mirror as it does to me here on this side. Like Dufy's houses in the water, therefore, which are present in their place in the distance only because they leave that place and are absent from it, the subject who is reflected in the mirror is one who is present to himself only because of this absence, a subject who is present to himself only at a distance.

But the mirror as instrument reveals only more explicitly what things and others do to and for me more confusedly. For the woman in the street, for example, the eyes of others are a mirror of who *she* is, and although in this case *she* does not acknowledge or recognize that reflection, the fact remains that others, like the mirror, present me to myself by keeping me from myself. In this context, then, the unconscious can be understood as a phenomenon of the mirror, and the mirror can be understood as the most explicit example of the fact that the world is the other side of my consciousness, that is that others are the visible expression of my unconsciousness. The unconscious is in the world between us as I previously said, and the mirror merely expresses this fact most clearly, for it indicates that I have already been taken over by the world even while it also offers the possibility of recovery. The unconscious can be understood as a phenomenon of the mirror, therefore, because the mirror reflects a dialogue of absence and presence.

Already in the *Phenomenology of Perception* Merleau-Ponty had written that 'It is through my relation to 'things' that I know myself ... (1962, p. 383),' and in *The Visible and the Invisible* he has said that 'There is an *Einfühlung* and a lateral relation with the things no less than with the other ... (1968, p. 180).' Both statements announce a *philosophy of reflection* in which the double sense of this term and the tension which this double sense raises are maintained. On the one hand reflection is a 'being given back by' which presumes an initial *absence* of the subject from himself. But on the other hand reflection is a 'bending back upon' which presumes an initial *presence* of the subject to himself. Distinguished but not separated from each other, these two senses of reflection indicate that although the subject's first presence to himself is only through the world, in another movement this initial presence by absence can be recovered and transformed. Situated within this context of a 'philosophy of reflection,' therefore, the unconscious as a phenomenon of ambiguity finds its depth in the unconscious as a phenomenon of the mirror. The dialogue of absence-presence, which was the outcome of Merleau-Ponty's double critique, is fleshed out in the mirror, in that mirror of others and the world, in that mirror whose magic and significance is that is presents me to myself as a *familiar-stranger*. The consideration of consciousness and unconsciousness from the side of perception becomes, therefore a 'philosophy of reflection' in which the dialogue of absence and presence is transformed from a conversation of the subject with himself to a dialogue between a subject and his world. In short, the primacy of perception in Merleau-Ponty's work is a radical alteration of the notion of reflection, and within the context of this new beginning the descent of consciousness back toward the world and the ascent of the body toward consciousness converge toward the body as an axis of knowledge and ignorance because the subject is a pivot of I and Other.

The unconscious as a phenomenon of reflection is not, however, without its problems. Although Merleau-Ponty's 'reflections' do suggest that the unconscious as the other side of myself in the world seems to be a necessary condition for any notion of unconsciousness which would not simply be a *negation* of Cartesian consciousness, a 'mirror image' of the cogito, a question can be raised about whether or not Merleau-Ponty's view is adequate to what Freud means by this term. In the final section, therefore, I want to consider a difficulty which remains in the path of these 'reflections.'

V. CONCLUSION: REFLECTION AND REPRESSION

'I borrow myself from others ... (1964a, p. 159),' Merleau-Ponty says, and to be unconscious is to be absent from oneself while being present in the world. This is the direction of Merleau-Ponty's reconsideration of the Freudian unconscious, and while this direction has the merit of describing the unconscious as in the world between us, it also seems to bypass or to ignore what is most central about the Freudian unconscious, the notion of repression. For Freud (1957) the unconscious is very much tied to the task of *becoming* conscious, a task moreover which is constantly beset by *resistance*, whereas for Merleau-Ponty 'becoming conscious' seems to occur too easily. Indeed with Merleau-Ponty one seems to miss the sense of *effort* or of *work* which is involved in overcoming *resistance*, and thus one seems unable to grasp the *labor of recovery* which is involved in becoming conscious. Stated in terms of the examples of this paper, Merleau-Ponty's 'reflections' seem not to sufficiently distinguish between the painter and the patient (the woman in the street). Each, it is true, is absent from himself in being present to the world. But the painter recovers this absence in his creative expressions, and thus he returns to himself from the side of the world. This *recovery*, however, is precisely what the woman can not do. Her sexuality is repressed and not expressed, and indeed her repression can be seen as a failure or an absence of expression. Hence the question which Merleau-Ponty's understanding of the unconscious as a *moment of reflection* raises is if this woman *is* understood within the context of Merleau-Ponty's 'reflections'. Expressed in more general terms the question is if the unconscious as a phenomenon of the mirror does justice to Freud's notion of repression. My position is that it does provided however that one draws out the implications of this altered meaning of reflection.[6] The conclusion of my paper, therefore, is addressed to two of these implications both of which offer a way of understanding repression within this context of reflection.

First, Merleau-Ponty's reconsideration of the unconscious suggests that the initiative for repression is neither initially nor primarily with the subject nor on the side of the subject alone. Repression is not an intrapsychic event, but is on the contrary initiated *between* a subject and his world, *between* me and you. In other words, repression is an absence and a failure of reflection.

As an absence of reflection, repression characterizes a condition of living in which a subject faces a world which provides no mirrors of reflection for this or that experience of human life. Consider, for example, that moment in 1897 when Freud and the beginning science of psychoanalysis are thrown into a crisis because the stories of sexual seduction of the child by the parent are not actual events. It is a decisive time because at that moment psychoanalysis is transformed from a science which interrogates the psychological in time and in the world to one which now uncovers the natural and universal conditions of human life which are older than time and prior to any world. Faced with these false accounts, Freud reasons that psychoanalysis is not a discipline of the real but of the fictional. The child has not been seduced by the parent; on the contrary he has *wished* to be the seducer. The father now is innocent and it is the child who is guilty. The child is no longer the *passive* victim of a sexual trauma but the *active* instigator of it.

It would seem, however, that Freud misreads Oedipus, since the stories of his patients do not necessarily reflect a universal drama of instinct and incest. Indeed they are heard in this way only because there are already operative in Freud's view the *dichotomies* of the real versus the fictional, and the individual versus the other. In other words, given the Cartesian ground of Freud's thinking, he is already predisposed toward the psychological as an individual rather than a relational phenomenon, and toward a notion of reality (and history) as a given in itself. Thus *either* the parent *really* seduced the child *or* the child *wished* to seduce the parent and *between* these two alternatives there was nothing to choose, nothing to see. Given the context of his thought, therefore, it was not possible for Freud to hear his patients' stories as descriptions of the parent-child relations of his time, as indications of how relationships *between* people in that age concealed and did not reflect the sexual dimension of human life. Given this context, there was no way for Freud to hear these tales as a witness of the unconscious side of Cartesian consciousness, that is as an expression of how the life of passion finds no reflection in the Cartesian dream of reason. Given this context, Freud was not able to understand these stories as an indictment against an age and a culture.

In 'Eye and Mind' (1964b), Merleau-Ponty notes that 'A Cartesian man does not see *himself* in the mirror (p. 170).' On the contrary, '... he sees a dummy ... which, he has every reason to believe ... is not a body in the flesh (Ibid.).' The stories of Freud's patients describe this situation. These tales of sexual trauma do not express a real, actual event – as Freud discovered –; but neither do they express a forbidden, repressed instinctual wish – as Freud imagined. On the contrary they describe an intentional relation toward the world which has found no *reflection* in that world. They reveal, in other words, a world in which the relations between individuals, as well as the things of that world – the styles of dress, of furniture, of architecture etc. –, conceal more than they reveal the flesh of the living human body. Repression, therefore, is an absence of reflection in this first sense of the term.

But what is absent for reflection in this way is also unavailable for reflection in the second sense of this term, and hence repression also characterizes that condition of living in which experiences, which find no anchor in and/or reflection by the world, slip away from the world and are buried beneath it. Of course, this is where Freud begins, with the maintainence of repression, and this is where the strength of psychoanalysis lies. His patients' stories do reveal that a passion which slips away from the world does reappear as a fantasy above life or as a symptom from below it. But, as we have already seen, his unacknowledged acceptance of a Cartesian universe leads him to inquire about the *origins* of repression in a predetermined way. The origins are destined to be found *within* the individual rather than *between* himself and others, and as a consequence what is *below* life is destined to take on a priority over what is within life and in the world.

Paradoxically, however, the *praxis* of psychoanalysis seems at odds with this theory of repression, and the praxis seems to support an understanding of repression within the context of reflection. For example, there is a passage in one of Freud's works where he recommends that the analyst be like a perfect reflecting mirror to the patient. But why should Freud use this image, if there is not the intuition of the *origins* of repression as the *absence* of a reflection, and further an intuition of the *maintainence* of repression as the *failure*, that is the impossibility, of reflection in the second sense of this term? This recommendation, therefore, may be an acknowledgement of repression as a relational phenomenon, an acknowledgement of repression as originating at the *interface* or at the *boundary* of two worlds, particularly where the world which is emerging finds no reflection for certain of its dimensions in the world which already exists. As such, moreover, this recommendation may also be an acknowledgement of the necessity for the analyst to bring to reflection, in the first sense of this term, what has slipped away in order that the failure of reflection, in the second sense of the term, may be reversed. In other words, the recommendation may in fact acknowledge that what is recovered for reflection in the mirror of analysis becomes available for reflection as expression. This point, however, leads directly to the second implication of Merleau-Ponty's reconsideration of the unconscious.

Repression is the other side of expression, and indeed it is both the *outcome* of expression and *overcome* by expression. As the outcome of expression, repression refers to a situation of dialogue in which what is being expressed *does not allow* the possibility of some other expression. It is the situation described in the previous point, and one which is distinguished from that situation of dialogue in which what is being expressed merely leaves unnoticed some other possibility. The point, therefore, is that repression as the absence and failure of expression, is a particular kind of dialogue which moreover builds on expression's natural tendency to conceal even while it reveals meaning. As the outcome of expression, then, repression is a conspiracy of two, the result of a particular style of dialogue between me and others, and/or between me and the world. Repression is constituted in partnership.

But what is constituted in partnership is also recovered from in partnership, albeit of a different style, and in this sense the repressed unconscious can not be detached from the dialectic of the interpretative work which defines the analytic situation. The repressed unconscious originates in dialogue and is recovered in dialogue, and either to ignore this or to forget it is to accept a definition of the repressed unconscious as an *intrapsychic* domain. The praxis of dialogue in the analytic situation, the procedure of interpretative recovery, is not incidental to what the repressed unconscious is, and in this light it is well to recall that Freud himself admits that repression is an inference from resistance. *He* met resistance in the work of recovering what had slipped beneath life, but this situation does not logically nor phenomenologically mean that the patient has repressed *within himself* what is resisted. On the contrary, what it shows, I think, is that in its origins and in the analytic situation repression is inseparable from the dialogue. Indeed without the *work* of recovery, without the *effort* of overcoming the resistances, which defines the analytic situation, there would be no repressed unconscious. It is the labor of recovery which announces the repressed, and the patient represses *in relation to* a situation of dialogue. Repression is the obverse of expression, therefore, and repression without the situation of dialogue presumes a subject apart from the world.

Drawing out these two implications of Merleau-Ponty's reconsideration of the unconscious from the side of perception indicates, I think, that the unconscious as a moment of reflection does take into account the Freudian concept of repression. Indeed it goes further insofar as Merleau-Ponty's 'reflections' describe the *origins* of Freudian unconsciousness from the side of the world. The unconscious is in the world between us, the invisible substructure of the visible, and it is on this basis that it can slip away from the world and be buried beneath it. Within Merleau-Ponty's work, therefore, the unconscious does not signal a subject layered within himself. On the contrary it describes a subject's relation with the world, a relation in which the absence of reflection expresses a dialogue which finds no support in the world.

VI. POSTSCRIPT

I began this paper with the notion that a theory of things is a theory of the body which in turn leads to a theory of the psychological. Freud's psychology, I have tried to suggest, reflects and is a reflection of a particular world, and consequently the repressed unconscious is a historical phenomenon. Thus when the world changes the unconscious changes. Today it is questionable whether things conceal the sexual dimension of human life, and hence whether there remains a sexual aetiology to neuroses. Indeed if one considers a phenomenological work like Husserl's *Crisis* (1970), in which there is expressed a deep and abiding concern over the loss and/ or absence of subjectivity in the modern world, then a different picture of the unconscious emerges. The crisis of the sciences are most fundamentally the crisis of the psychological in the sense that the mathematization of nature and the human body leads to an *interiorzation* of the psychological, to an image of the psychological as equivalent to the mental, and to an understanding of it as on the other side of the world. Matter, it seems, no longer mirrors man, and it is questionable what we reflect in our relations with each other. Indeed, it seems that today we may be living in a situation in which there is a world without the psychological and the psychological without a world. Perhaps, therefore, the unconscious today is the absence (and the failure) of the psychological. Certainly the very curious situation of a modern psychology without the psychological bears some reflection.

NOTES

1   Names in parenthesis indicate that Merleau-Ponty's considerations refer as much to a way of thinking as they do to these thinkers themselves and/or their specific works.

2   I am referring here to Descartes' fateful dreams on the night of November 20, 1619 which he claimed presented him with the new philosophy. My point, then, is that Freud makes the dream subject to reason while Descartes makes his new reason subject to a dream. Each starts in the other's domain as it were and each achieves a kind of ironic reversal. On the one hand, Freud's project ends up 'infecting' reason with the irrational – reason is contaminated by the dream –, while on the other hand Descartes' project ends up 'sterilizing' the rational of the irrational. In their respective starting intentions, then, Freud is more Cartesian than Descartes, and Descartes more Freudian than Freud. Each, however, winds up where history has placed them: Freud 'below' life and Descartes 'above' it.

3   To be perfectly consistent Merleau-Ponty should have said here that the perceived has me etc. Perception is an abstraction, and the issue really concerns the notion of 'Einfühlung (1968, p. 248).' But this inherence of the subject in the world, this presence to the world which is also however a presence to oneself, presumes the later part of my discussion.

4   I write the sentence with the parentheses in order to call attention to an important point which I will discuss later in this paper. This is the notion of repression. Placing the words 'want to' in brackets indicates that while the structure of habit is a different relation between I and my body than the structure of repression, the two structures have the same source. In each case it is a question of a knowing by not knowing, but in the one there is a *motivated* 'ignorance'. In one case, therefore, this 'mindful-body' gives itself over to the world, and in the other case it chooses a world to give itself over to. In each case it is a different relation of activity/passivity.

Indeed Merleau-Ponty himself speaks of repression in this way (See Romanyshyn, in press) when he discusses the phantom limb (1962, p. 82ff). '... the phenomenon of the phantom limb is absorbed into that of repression ... (Ibid., p. 82)' he says, and just as one's body can project and sustain habitual situations, it also can project and keep alive previous intentions, phases and of one's history which are no longer supported by the world. There can be, in other words, a 'phantom history' just like there is a phantom limb, because this body through which one perceives, this sensitive flesh is a history and this history is embodied. Indeed what Merleau-Ponty's consideration of repression suggests is that in the human psychological world the dichotomy of a biological organism *and* a historical subject is erroneous. Considered psychologically the human body, this *one* who perceives is neither biological nor historical, nor a combination of the two. Considered psychologically the biological-historical distinction has to be re-thought.

5   This illustration is taken from a book entitled *Fauvism: The 'Wild Beasts' and its Affinities* by John Elderfield (1967). The particular painting is only one illustration of this theme of reflection, of things mirroring each other, which is found in many of the Fauvists works. In another piece by Dufy, 'Street Decked with Flags at Le Havre' (p. 77), for example, a flag mirrors the people in the street. Here too, therefore, one also finds an expression of this *lateral depth*.

6   Of course, Merleau-Ponty has not entirely neglected the issue of repression, and in the *Phenomenology of Perception* he says that repression is '... the transition from first person existence to an abstraction of that existence ... (1962, p. 83),' a point which he demonstrates in suggesting that repression is like the phenomenon of the phantom limb. In each case there is a suspension of time, a disruption of it, as one tries to live his life *as if* a particular moment of it were privileged. In each case, there is a privileged moment of existence abstracted out of the on-going current of one's life. But as one reads these passages, the suspicion emerges that Merleau-Ponty glides too easily from this notion of repression as *abstraction* to the notion of repression as the upsurge of an *impersonal* existence, and that

in fact he understands the former in terms of the latter, and/or confuses the two. Thus repression as abstraction seems to be understood as an idea of one's life which is no longer supported by or reflected in the world, and indeed repression as abstraction, with its image of an arrested time, becomes repression as the impersonal, with its image of a time that *one* lives, and/or a time that is lived through me. There seems, therefore, already to be a foreshadowing of this later tendency in Merleau-Ponty to understand the repressed unconscious in terms of the unconscious as a *moment of reflection*. There seems to be already this preference for a phenomenological *description* of unconsciousness, that is for an understanding of it primarily as an index of this first moment of reflection. The Freudian unconscious, however, is an index of something more, an index of a reflection which resists recognition, recovery and expression. In terms of the discussion in the *Phenomenology of Perception*, the unconscious as impersonal is like a reflection neither noticed nor expressed, while the unconscious as an abstraction is like a reflection which as unnoticed and not expressed is nevertheless expressed and lived out in another way. In each instance there is a dialogue of absence and presence, but in the latter the dialogue is also fixed at some given point, a dialogue therefore which continuously repeats itself. In summary, Merleau-Ponty's unconscious as a moment of reflection leaves no symptom. One can, so to speak, live with this unconscious, a notion which is however foreign to Freud's view.

Again, however, these difficulties appear, I think, because in this early work the radical alteration of the meaning of reflection has not yet occurred.

BIBLIOGRAPHY

Elderfield, John, *Fauvism: The 'Wild Beasts and Its Affinities*, New York: Oxford University Press, 1976.

Freud, Sigmund, 'A Note on the Unconscious in Psychoanalysis' in Volume XII of *The Standard Edition*, translated by James Strachey, London: Hogarth Press, 1958.

— 'The Unconscious' in Volume XIV of *The Standard Edition*, translated by James Strachey, London: Hogarth Press, 1957.

— 'The Ego and the Id' in volume XIX of *The Standard Edition* translated by James Strachey, London: Hogarth Press, 1961.

Husserl, Edmund, *The Crisis of European Sciences and Transcendental Phenomenology* translated by David Carr, Evanston: Northwester University Press, 1970.

Merleau-Ponty, Maurice, Preface: *L'Ouvre de Freud*, by A. Hesnard, *Existential Psychiatry* No. 28, 1970, pp. 29-34.

— *Phenomenology of Perception* translated by Colin Smith, New York: The Humanities Press, 1962.

— 'The Philosopher and His Shadow' in *Signs* translated by Richard C. McCleary, Evanston: Northwestern University Press, 1964a.

— 'Man and Adversity' in *Signs* translated by Richard C. McCleary, Evanston: Northwestern University Press, 1964a.

— 'Eye and Mind' in *The Primacy of Perception*, Evanston: Northwestern University Press, 1964b.

— 'The Primacy of Perception' in *The Primacy of Perception*, Evanston: Northwestern University Press, 1964b.

— *The Visible and the Invisible* translated by Alphonso Lingis, Evanston: Northwestern University Press, 1968.

Penfield, Wilder, *The Mystery of the Mind*, Princeton: Princeton University Press, 1975, p. 13.

Romanyshyn, Robert, 'Phenomenology and Psychoanalysis: Contributions of Merleau-Ponty' in *Psychoanalytic Review*, in press.

Sallis, John, *Phenomenology and the Return to Beginnings*, Pittsburgh: Duquesne University Press, 1973.

Skinner, B.F., *Beyond Freedom and Dignity*, New York: Knopf, 1971.

Toulmin, S., and Janik, A., *Wittgenstein's Vienna*, New York: Simon & Schuster, 1973.

COMMENTS ON PROFESSOR ROMANYSHYN'S PAPER

MIGUEL ITURRATE

I begin my comments on Professor Romanyshyn's paper, *Unconsciousness: Reflection and the Primacy of Perception*, by declaring that its consideration has been a very stimulating experience for me. There are two main reasons for this personal reaction. The first reason is that Professor Romanyshyn calls our attention to some of Merleau-Ponty's ideas concerning psychoanalysis in a very effective way, since these ideas about psychoanalysis have been somewhat neglected by our philosophers and by our psychoanalysts until the present time. The second reason is that, after more than fifteen years of experience as a psychoanalyst and as a professor of philosophy, I have become convinced myself — in accord with Merleau-Ponty — that phenomenology *is* 'the implicit philosophy of psychoanalysis.'[1]

Merleau-Ponty's persuasion that 'experience anticipates a philosophy and philosophy is merely an elucidated experience,'[2] led his phenomenological convictions to a natural encounter with Freud's empirical discoveries. Professor Romanyshyn's paper is a serious testimony of this encounter, by giving us his personal conception of an approximation between Merleau-Ponty's phenomenology and the unconscious as conceived of by Freudian psychoanalysis.

Although it could be a worthwhile effort to discuss and evaluate its original standpoint and all of his ideas, some of which I am not in agreement as will be manifest at times, I believe that the most effective expression of my respect regarding Professor Romanyshyn's paper consists — in a sort of constructive critique — of following the initiated route with my own suggestions about *the* phenomenology and about *the* psychoanalysis which are Merleau-Ponty's concern. This constructive critique requires a cautious, albeit necessarily concise answer to the two fundamental questions contained in this approach, namely, what must be understood by 'phenomenology' and what must be understood by 'psychoanalysis' in the context of Merleau-Ponty's ideas.

During the year 1960, Merleau-Ponty wrote a brief but extremely dense essay about the relations of phenomenology and psychoanalysis, where he declared that, even though they complement each other, 'phenomenology and psychoanalysis are not parallel; much beter, they are both aiming toward the same *latency*.'[3] This rather enigmatic expression is the bond that links our considerations to Professor Romanyshyn's center of attention in his paper, that is,

See notes at the end of this chapter.

the unconscious.

Merleau-Ponty's above mentioned essay is his *Preface* to Dr. Hesnard's publication about the importance of Freud in our time. In this essay, Merleau-Ponty explicitly determines that phenomenology must be understood in the line of Husserl's last conceptions, where he resolutely left behind the Cartesian direction, and initiated the peculiar trend of his last works. Here we find the starting point of Merleau-Ponty's own ways. This specification of Merleau-Ponty's idea of phenomenology is important, because it gives us the unequivocal direction of his considerations in the *Preface* to Hesnard's publication.

Under the inspiration of Husserl's final and decisive search for the ultimate foundation of human activity, that which led him to his definitive notions of 'genetic constitution' and of the *Lebenswelt*, as the natural development of his basic conception of *fungierende Intentionalität*, Merleau-Ponty assumed this 'operative intentionality' to discover and recognize that, in any experience in the world, 'the relationship between subject and object' – as he says – 'is no longer that relationship of *knowing* postulated by classical idealism, wherein the object always seems the construction of the subject, but *a relationship of being* in which, paradoxically, the subject *is* his body, his world and his situation, by a sort of exchange.'[4]

On the other hand, we must recall that Merleau-Ponty began one of the most important stages of his career as a Professor of psychology and pedagogy at La Sorbonne (1949-1952). As such, he was already familiar with Freud's conceptions to the extent that, all throughout his writings, he appears as one of the philosophers who has most profoundly penetrated into the very nature of psychoanalysis as a psychological theory,[5] except that Merleau-Ponty's opinions about Freud's ideas evolved until he arrived at the interpretation that he establishes in his *Preface*.

In this context, 'psychoanalysis' must be understood as a comprehensive psychological theory whose purpose is to help us understand man's place in the world: the psychoanalysis which, as Merleau-Ponty affirms, is in accord with Husserl 'precisely in describing man as a timber yard, in order to discover, beyond the truth of immanence, that of the *Ego* and its acts, that of consciousness and its objects, of relations which a consciousness cannot sustain: man's relations to his origins and his relations to his models. Freud points his finger at the *Id* and the *Superego*. Husserl, in his last writings, speaks of historical life as *Tiefenleben*.'[7]

The man who is described 'as a timber yard' by Merleau-Ponty, is the man of our daily life: the man who lives in Husserl's life-world; the one who, as a constant self, we name 'I,' 'you,' 'he' and 'she;' the one who is an I-subject, not only because he consists of consciousness, i.e., of self-presence for whom things of the world are present too, but also because he consists of the obscure and almost bottomless unconscious; the one who can no more be identified with the Cartesian cogito because, as consisting of consciousness and of unconsciousness, as Freud discovered, does not coincide exactly with himself; the one who exists as operative intentionality, as life-experiencing-world, where the subject-object relationship, as a relationship of being, comes to be *a dialectical situation* where subject and object mutually require one another as the subjective and the objective double polarity of *reality*, which is the *a priori* necessary and universal condition for all possible experience.

These considerations help us to clarify, even though in an extremely succint way, Merleau-Ponty's apparently obscure formulation of phenomenology and psychoanalysis as complementing each other as they are 'aiming toward the same *latency*.'

When we consider Husserl's description of the life-world, the first characteristic that we find is that it is the world of our ordinary experience, the world in which man does exist, live, think and act, and not the abstract 'objective' world through the sciences. Reflection led Husserl to the conclusion that this life-world is the pre-given original source and necessary universal condition, not only of knowledge, but of all possible activity. This life-world, however, is some sort of universal 'taken for granted' that remains concealed in 'anonymity,' as Husserl says, that is, latent, *unconscious*, and which can come to be manifest for us only thanks to a very special effort.[8]

After this first 'latency' indicated by Husserl, he reveals another one which is important. In every experience, says Husserl, *intentionality* is protention and retention at the same time, because we discover that in every perception there is some sort of anticipation − we grasp the object in and through the projection of its possible explicitations − and some sort of sedimented tissue resulting from preceding perceptions, in such a manner that there are always 'latent' and implicit modes of consciousness which remain unnoticed at first. Thus, the same type of 'anonymity' discovered in the life-world is discovered in intentionality. We recognize here the anonymous 'operative intentionality,' determined by Husserl as to indicate the constant and unconscious character of its constitutive functioning, which led him to his conception of *genetic constitution* by means of which man is revealed as the *meaning-giver* in the world.[9]

I decided to recall these last ideas of Husserl, because Merleau-Ponty identifies phenomenology with them in his *Preface*. These ideas are so clearly indicative of several of the most important of Merleau-Ponty's own conceptions, that there is no need now for further elaboration. So, when Merleau-Ponty maintains that Freud's *libido* is man's general power of taking root in the world by actualizing himself as an incarnated-I,[10] we understand that Freud's libido is, for Merleau-Ponty, Husserl's operative intentionality, mainly after Freud's explicit declarations that libido is 'synonymous with psychical energy in general,'[11] and that it is an original 'neutral energy' as regards aims and objects in man's life.[12]

Finally, psychoanalysis conceives human behavior as depending on the fact that man acts and behaves in conformity with his own knowledge of reality, save that this knowledge of reality must be interpreted here, not as a system of strictly objective correlations, but as *a system of meanings*. The reason is that Freud characterizes our psychic activity as having the purpose of satisfying the natural needs of the individual, inasmuch as things found in the world are experienced as *meaningful as objects for the libido*, regarding either the sexual level of the Id, or the level of the socalled Ego-interests, conditioned by the moral dimension proper to the Superego.

According to psychoanalysis there are some aims and objects of the libido which are determined as such by the sexual nature of our own body. There are, however, aims and objects different from those of the level of sexuality or corporeality, and which satisfy the libido in the level of socio-cultural dimensions named Ego-interests in psychoanalysis. These aims and objects are chosen by the Ego *free from* impositions external to itself and *free for* determining them by itself. The Id, the Superego and the Ego's own habitualities as the subjective *a priori*, and external reality as the objective *a priori*, are necessary conditions for the Ego's own determination, acting in *latency* by means of unconscious and also conscious processes. In this manner, psychoanalysis' revelation of man as the meaning-giver, is also the revelation of man's *freedom* as being-in-the-world. In other words, the meaning of an object comes to be the manner in which one establishes oneself and the not-self in a framework of mutual respectivity so that, the subject-object relationship is secured as a true dialectical situation that — in latency — ties up man and things together as being-in-the-world. Moreover, man is thus able to change some factual situations which, externally pregiven as a field of objects and internally sedimented as a field of intentions, offer him a variety of meanings which challenge him to take up one of them as his own, by himself.

Thus, and with Merleau-Ponty, I am convinced that phenomenology is the actual philosophical ground of Freud's empirical discoveries, 'aiming toward the same *latency*,' that is, aiming toward the life-world, conceived as reality itself, as the *a priori* necessary and universal condition for all possible experience, toward the original libido functioning as operative intentionality and, finally, toward most of the psychic processes of man.

At the end of my comments on Professor Romanyshyn's paper, and in coherence with the spirit of his ideas in a sort of constructive critique, I dare affirm that phenomenology's and psychoanalysis' message to our century is a message of optimism and a message of dignity that attempts to remind us of man's role as meaning-giver in the world.

NOTES

1   'Phenomenology and Psychoanalysis, Preface to Hesnard's *L'Oeuvre de Freud*,' in *The Essential Writings of Merleau-Ponty*, ed. by A.L. Fischer (New York, Harcourt, Brace & World, Inc. 1969) p. 84. Hereafter to be cited as *Preface*.

2   M. Merleau-Ponty: *Phenomenology of Perception* (London. Routledge & Kegan Paul. 1962) p. 63. Hereafter, *Phen. of Perc.*

3   *Preface*, p. 87.

4   Merleau-Ponty: *Sense and Non-Sense* (Evanston, Northwestern University Press, 1964) p. 72. Hereafter *Sen. Non-Sen.*

5   See: *The structure of Behavior* (Boston, Beacon Press, 1968) pp. 177 ff.; *Phen. of Perc.*, pp. 158 ff. and passim; 'Cezanne's Doubt' in *Sen. Non-Sen.*, pp. 22 ff.; 'Man and Adversity,' *Signs* (Evanston, Northwestern University Press, 1964) pp. 227 ff.; 'The Child's Relations with Others,' *The Primacy of Perception and Other Essays* (Evanston, Northwestern University Press, 1964) passim; 'Working Notes,' *The Visible and the Invisible* (Evanston, Northwestern University Press, 1968) pp. 332, 240-241, 243, 269-270; 'Phenomenology and Psychoanalysis, *Preface*.'

6   *Preface*, p. 83.

7   *Ibid.*, p. 86-87.

8   Husserl: *The Crisis of European Sciences and Transcendental Phenomenology* (Evanston, Northwestern University Press, 1970) pp. 111-114.

9   Husserl: *Formal and Transcendental Logic* (The Hague, Martinus Nijhoff, 1969) pp. 177 ff.

10   *Phen. of Perc.*, p. 158.

11   Freud: *New Introductory Lectures*, in *The Complete Introductory Lectures* (New York, W.W. Norton & Company, Inc. 1962) p. 567.

12   Freud: *The Ego and the Id* (New York, W.W. Norton & Company, Inc. 1962) p. 34.

EXPERIENCE AND CAUSALITY
IN THE PHILOSOPHY OF MERLEAU-PONTY

WESLEY MORRISTON

The philosophy of Merleau-Ponty is, above all, an attempt to chart a middle course between the extremes of realism and idealism. The central question of philosophy in our time, he writes, is '... that of man's relationship to his natural or social surroundings.'

> There are two classical views: one treats man as the result of the physical, physiological, and sociological influences which shape him from outside and make him one thing among many; the other consists of recognizing an a-cosmic freedom in him, insofar as he is spirit and represents to himself the very causes which supposedly act upon him. On the one hand, man is a part of the world; on the other, he is the constituting consciousness of the world. Neither view is satisfactory.[1]

The problem, as Merleau-Ponty sees it, is to do justice to the insights of each position while avoiding the errors of the other; to do justice to the fact of embodiment and to the situated character of human freedom without depriving man of his freedom and transcendence; and at the same time to do justice to man's consciousness and freedom without placing them completely outside the world of which he is conscious. The problem, in other words, is that of avoiding realism without falling into idealism, and vice versa.

In this paper, we will be concerned with Merleau-Ponty's rejection of the realist claim that man is merely one object among others in the midst of the physical world and that human experience is the outcome of objective causes interacting with the physiological mechanisms of his body. Specifically, we will examine the reasons Merleau-Ponty gives for insisting that '... an experience can never bear the relation to certain factual conditions that it would bear to its cause ...'[2] A careful exposition and critique of his arguments on behalf of this claim will throw light on his own view of the relation between man and world. But at the same time it will show that he escapes realism only at the price of accepting a view which is subject to some of the same difficulties as the idealism that he rejects.

See notes at the end of this chapter.

I

Before we can consider Merleau-Ponty's arguments in any detail, something should be said about the meaning of his claim that an experience cannot have a cause.[3] The problem words, of course, are 'experience' and 'cause.' Merleau-Ponty does little to give either a precise meaning, but the following remarks have ample textual support.

'Experience' should be taken in a very broad sense. It encompasses not only perception, but thought, feeling, and action as well. When Merleau-Ponty denies that an experience can have a cause, he is denying that anything can *cause* me to do whatever I do or to be aware of whatever I am aware of.

But what, then, does Merleau-Ponty mean by the word 'cause'? Nowhere in his writings is there an explicit analysis of the concept of a cause. But several key elements of an analysis can be gleaned from those passages in which he presents his arguments against realism.

1) The cause of something is a condition or set of conditions which is *sufficient* for the existence of that something. If the causal conditions are met, the effect does not fail to occur.[4]

2) If a condition or set of conditions is the cause of something, then *whenever* conditions *of the same type obtain*, a *similar* effect will be produced.[5]

3) A cause is 'external' to its effect. This is a difficult claim to interpret, but I take it that Merleau-Ponty is accepting something like the Humean claim that cause and effect are logically independent of one another. Thus if event *a* is the cause of event *b*, it is logically possible that *a* occur but not *b*, and vice versa. To say that cause and effect are 'external' to one another is therefore to say that they are definable independently of one another.

4) The relation between cause and effect is asymmetrical. If event *a* is the cause of *b*, then it cannot also be the case that *b* is the cause of *a*.

These four points by no means constitute a complete analysis of the relation of cause to effect. Numerous question remain unanswered. Is there some non logical necessity in the connection between cause and effect? Must the cause always be an event? Does it necessarily precede its effect in time? Are the standing conditions without which the effect would not be produced to be considered part of its cause or not? Merleau-Ponty does not answer any of these questions, Fortunately, however, what he does say is sufficient to enable us to state and evaluate his arguments for the claim that an experience cannot be caused. Each of them can be taken as arguments for conclusions which refer to one or more of the features of the causal relation mentioned above.

The first of the three arguments we will consider is an attempt to show that an experience cannot be *externally* related to the motives that explain it. The second hinges on the *asymmetrical* character of the causal relation. And the third is an attempt to show that the necessary conditions for an experience are never *sufficient* to produce that experience.

II

The first argument is most clearly presented in Merleau-Ponty's discussion of depth perception. There he argues that the clues to depth on which we normally rely — eye convergence, apparent size, disparity of the retinal image, etc. — are not causally related to perceiving in depth. On the contrary, they are related to it in a way that is inconsistent with their being causes. They are *internally* related to depth perception, whereas a cause is a 'determining factor *external* to its effect.'[7] Or, to put the argument in another way, a cause is *definable* independently of its effect, whereas the clues to depth are not definable apart from the experience they motivate. What is convergence, if not an effort to see in depth? And what is the apparent size of a tree that I see in the distance, if not the size of a 'tree-seen-in-the-distance'?

> ... the convergence of the eyes is not the cause of depth ... it itself presupposes an orientation towards the object placed at a distance.[8]
>
> Apparent size is ... not definable independently of distance; it is implied by distance and it also implies distance. Convergence, apparent size and distance are read off from each other, naturally symbolize or signify each other, are the abstract elements of a situation and are, within it, mutually synonymous ...[9]
>
> ... the experience of convergence, or of apparent size, and that of depth ... do not act miraculously as 'causes' in producing the appearance of organization in depth; they tacitly motivate it insofar as they are both already a certain way of looking at a distance.[10]

The question that must be raised about this argument is clear: are the clues to depth definable independently of the experience that they motivate? The argument appears to assume that they are not, but it is far from obvious that this is so.

Consider, for example, the way in which eye-convergence is related to depth perception. Let us grant that Merleau-Ponty is right in suggesting that the eyes converge *in order to* see at a distance. It hardly follows that convergence is definable *only* in terms of my actually seeing something in the distance. It would be easy to imagine a case where my eyes converged, but where I failed to see anything at all.

Consider an analogous case. I move my arm in order to move the axe in order to chop wood with the axe. The movement of my arm can be described in terms of what it accomplishes: I am 'swinging the axe,' 'chopping wood,' etc.

Under these suggested descriptions, it is implied that the axe moves. But it doesn't in the least follow from this that the movement of the axe and the movement of my arm are not definable independently of one another or that they are not causally related. On the contrary! Only because the arm-movement *is* a causal condition of the desired effect do I move my arm in order to accomplish that end. Similarly, one *might* argue, only because eye-convergence *is* a causal condition of depth perception do the eyes converge in order to see in depth. But, in any case, eye-convergence and depth perception are not 'internally related' in any way that would be *incompatible* with their *also* being causally related.

This point will be clearer if we turn to another of Merleau-Ponty's examples, this time an example of voluntary action and its motives. The death of a friend, he tells us,

> ... motivates my journey *because* it is a situation in which my presence is required, whether to console a bereaved family or to 'pay one's last respects' to the deceased, and, by deciding to make the journey, I validate this motive which puts itself forward, and take up the situation. The relation between motivating factor and motivated act is thus reciprocal.[11]

The most important sentence is the last one: 'The relation between motivating factor and motivated act is thus reciprocal.' The sequence of events — first the recognition of the situation as one in which a journey is required, and then the taking of the journey — is one in which the earlier event *motivates* the later one, and the later event *confirms* the anticipation which was implicit in the earlier one. As Merleau-Ponty puts it in another context,

> One phenomenon releases another, not by means of some objective efficient cause, like those which link together natural events, but by the meaning which it holds out ... To the degree that the motivated phenomenon comes into being, an internal relation to the motivating phenomenon appears; hence, instead of the one merely succeeding the other, the motivated phenomenon makes the motivating phenomenon explicit and comprehensible, and thus seems to have preexisted its own motive.[14]

One phenomenon — the motive — 'holds out' a certain meaning. The situation is perceived *as* one which requires my presence at the funeral, and that in turn suggests a journey. When I take the journey, I am explicitly doing something which was already implicitly suggested by the situation as I perceived it. The act makes it clear and explicit just what this situation required, and it constitutes itself as an act with this situation as its motive. The motive and the act that it motivates are thus 'reciprocally' related; each is to be understood in terms of its relation to the other.

It is clear that Merleau-Ponty is describing a genuine phenomenon. The situation is apprehended as one that makes a certain demand, and my act is experienced as satisfying that demand. My act and the situation which motivates it are in *this* sense 'internally' related. Nothing quite like this is true of a *merely causal* relation. The effect does not 'satisfy' a 'demand' made by the cause (thought it may confirm the expectation of some witness who perceives the cause). Motivation, therefore, is not the same as causation. *But that is not the issue.* The question is *not* whether the *relation* of motivation is the same as the *relation* of causation, but whether the *terms* related as motive to motivated act may not *also* be causally related; whether in other words, a motive can *also* be a cause. To make his argument plausible, Merleau-Ponty would have to demonstrate that the motive (the situation in which a death has occurred) is not definable independently of the journey, that the journey is essential to its identity. Unfortunately, there are two sound reasons for denying that the journey is essential to the identity of the situation that motivates it.

First, and most obviously, the demand presented by the motive might go unsatisfied. It is *at least* logically possible that this situation obtain but no journey take place. As Merleau-Ponty himself says, the motive only 'suggests' the journey – it makes a journey more or less probable, but it does not 'necessitate' it. This feature of motivation alone is enough to assure the logical independence of the motive from what it motivates.

In the second place, the motive does not 'suggest' *precisely this* journey. This journey includes a virtual infinity of acts and features that were not suggested by the motive. Whether, for example, I should put my right foot or my left foot forward first when boarding the train was in no way part of the 'meaning held out' by the motive. An infinity of possible 'journeys' would have satisfied the demand made by this situation equally well.

It thus becomes clear that motivation is an *intentional* relation. Just as, when I seem to see an ox, the ox may turn out not to exist, so too, when the situation makes a certain 'demand,' that demand may not be satisfied. And just as the ox that I seem to see may, *for my seeing*, be indeterminate in many respects ('Does it have a scar on its other side?' Just how large are its teeth?'), so too the journey demanded by the situation may be unspecified in any number of details. And the analogy can be pressed even further. 'I see an ox' entails that there is an ox that I see. But that is only to say that we would not call my experience of seeming to see an ox a case of 'seeing' unless we thought that there was indeed an ox to be seen. We would not take it as evidence for saying that my experience of seeming to see is not 'externally' related to the ox. Even though *under the description* 'seeing the ox,' the existence of an ox is logically implied, the *experience* which is *described as* 'seeing an ox' is definable independently of any actual ox. Similarly, to describe a particular situation as the motive of a particular journey logically entails that the journey have taken place. If the journey did not take place, then that description of the situation would be incorrect. But it by no means follows that the situation itself is not definable apart from the journey.

We must therefore conclude that Merleau-Ponty's analysis of motivation does not yield a satisfactory argument to the effect that motives are not (also) causes. Let the relation of motivation be ever so intimate. It does not follow that the *events* (and/ or standing conditions) which motivate an experience are not *also* causal conditions of that experience.

III

A second argument calls attention to the fact that perception is what first gives us access to the world:

> The alleged conditions of perception precede perception itself only when, instead of describing the perceptual phenomenon as the first way of access to the object, we suppose round about it ... a realm of truth, a world. In doing so we relieve perception of its essential function, which is to lay the foundations of, or inaugurate, knowledge, and we see it through its results.[13]
>
> ... experience ... gives us access to being, in which case it cannot be treated as a byproduct of being.[14]

In these passages, it is claimed that our original mode of awareness of the world — perception — cannot be caused by anything within the world of which we are aware. The 'alleged conditions of perception' *appear* to precede it only when we forget that the 'essential function' of perception is to 'lay the foundations of, or inaugurate, knowledge.' To give a causal explanation of perception would therefore be to explain it in terms of 'its results.'

Although Merleau-Ponty stresses this argument in a number of passages, it seems to rest on a confusion between knowledge and the object of knowledge. Perception may very well 'lay the foundation of knowledge' (at least knowledge of the physical world) in the sense that it yields the premises for all our subsequent theoretical knowledge of the world. But from this it follows at most that perception is not caused by our *knowledge* of the world. It does not follow that perception is not caused by events — known or unknown — within the world.

Of course, if perception were said to be the ground, not only of our knowledge, but of the world known, it would follow that no intramundane object could cause us to perceive. It may be that Merleau-Ponty is committed to saying that there is a sense — very difficult to define — in which this is true. But that is a point better dealt with in the context of the argument to be treated next. In the context of the present argument, the suggestion is only that perceptual experience is what first 'gives us access to being,' and no clear reason is given for saying that this 'access' cannot be caused by that to which it gives us access. Granted that all knowledge begins with experience — why can't it be a 'byproduct of being' all the same?

IV

The final argument that I want to discuss is rather cryptically stated in the following passage:

> To experience a structure is not to receive it into oneself passively: it is to live it, to take it up, assume it and discover its immanent significance. Thus an experience can never bear the relation to certain factual conditions that it would bear to its cause ...[15]

What Merleau-Ponty has in mind will be clearer if we consider some obvious examples of 'experiencing something.'

Consider, for instance, the pain I feel when a falling rock crushes my foot. We say that the falling rock causes my bones to break and that it causes me pain. But it does not cause me to experience my pain *in the particular way* that I do experience it. To experience pain is necessarily to experience it *as* something: *as* an obstacle to the completion of some task; *as* a reason for rushing to the hospital; *as* bearable or unbearable, and so on. Which way I experience it depends, not on any 'objective cause,' but rather on how I 'live it,' 'take it up,' or 'assume it.' The rock may cause my bones to break, but it does not cause me to experience the breaking of my bones. On the contrary, it is my experience which 'discovers' the rock *as* an obstacle to be overcome, etc. Because experience always determines the significance (in the context of my life) of its object, the object cannot be a cause of the experience which is directed upon it.

But isn't some part of my experience caused by the fall of the rock? Isn't it possible to isolate some moment of awareness which is directly caused by the falling rock? Merleau-Ponty's answer would surely be 'No.' His insistent rejection of the 'constancy hypothesis,' i.e., his rejection of the view that there must be elementary sensations which correspond, point for point, to elementary objective stimuli, leads directly to the conclusion that there is no layer of sensations directly *caused* by external stimuli. But that is not to deny that the falling rock which crushes my foot is a *necessary* condition of my experience. The claim is rather that it is not *sufficient* either for the experience as a whole *or for any part of it*. No 'part' retains its identity in abstraction from the experienced whole.

A further illustration of this claim may be drawn from one of Merleau-Ponty's many discussions of experimental results which, in his view, refute the 'constancy hypothesis.'

> If a given area of the skin is several times stimulated with a hair, the first perceptions are clearly distinguished and localized each time at the same point. As the stimulus is repeated, the localization becomes less preceise, perception widens in space, while at the same time the

sensation ceases to be specific: it is no longer a contact, but a feeling of burning, at one moment cold and at the next hot. Later still the patient thinks the stimulus is moving and describing a circle on his skin. Finally, nothing more is felt. It follows that the 'sensible quality', the spatial limits set to the percept, and even the presence or absence of a perception, are not *de facto* effects of the situation outside the organism, but represent the way in which it meets stimulation and is related to it.[16]

The objective stimulus does not determine the character of experience — that depends on how the perceiving body 'meets' it. Localization, felt temperature, etc. — all are a function of the way in which the organism responds to the situation, and not a simple function of the objective stimulus. In this case too there are no 'factual conditions' which are causally responsible for my experience. And there is no layer of sensations which remains constant while undergoing varying interpretations. What I experience depends upon the way my body meets the 'objective situation.'

The argument thus has only one premise: to experience something is to take it up into the context of my life, to understand it in terms of a significance which I bring to bear on the situation. From this Merleau-Ponty seems to think it follows that an experience cannot be related to *any* set of factual conditions as effect to cause. But it *doesn't* follow. At most it follows that some particular condition — the hair touching my skin, the rock falling on my foot, the death of a friend — is not *sufficient* to produce the experience in question. It by no means follows that there is no other condition or set of conditions sufficient to produce that experience. Nor does it follow that the particular event in question is not *one* of these conditions. The falling rock does not *by itself* cause us to experience it in any way — granted. But it may nevertheless be one of a set of conditions, including, perhaps, facts about my personal history, which *is* sufficient to produce my experience. The way in which I take up the situation may have its causes. And the falling rock may be one of the causal conditions of my experience even if it is not the only one. Similarly the rubbing of the hair on my skin does not by itself cause the feeling of heat. But we have been given no reason for denying that it is one of the causal conditions of that feeling, the others presumably including the physical state of my body.

The upshot of these remarks is that it won't do to conclude from the fact that one thing isn't the cause of something, that nothing is. Nor will it do to conclude that, because something isn't a sufficient condition of something else, it isn't one of the causal conditions of that something. If we avoid these two errors, it is very difficult to see how an argument to the effect that an experience cannot have a cause can be derived from the (correct) observation that what experience I have depends as much on me as on the factual situation that I must 'assume.'

But it may be felt that we have failed to pursue matters far enough. If something is the cause of my experience, then it must be definable independently of my experience; it must have some features of its own, independently of me and my experience, in virtue of which it can cause me to have that experience. This is an implication, as we have already seen, of the claim that cause and effect are 'external' to one another. But now it might be suggested that the putative causes of experience do not meet this requirement because, like everything else, they are objects encountered or encounterable within the human world; and because they, like every other object, *are dependent for their meaning and significance* on the way in which I 'take them up' and 'discover their significance by integrating them into my world. Whatever characteristics they might seem to have, they have *only in relation to* a 'world' which is inseparable from me since it is the all-embracing interpretive framework which I, as perceiving subject, bring to bear on any perceptual situation. It follows that objects have no characteristics of their own (i.e., independently of my experience of the world) in virtue of which they could cause me to have the experience that I have. Once we understand the all-embracing character of the way in which I 'take things up' and 'discover their significance,' we will see that experience could not be causally related to any object within the world of experience.

Merleau-Ponty never puts matters in quite this way. But something like the above does seem to be an implication of his general view of the relation between man and world. When, in an often-quoted passage, he asserts that 'I am the absolute source,'[17] he seems to mean that my existence is wholly responsible for the meaningful structure of the world, and that the things I encounter within the world have the determinate characteristics that they do only in virtue of the fact that I understand the world in the way that I do.

We must be careful in interpreting Merleau-Ponty here, however. He does not mean to suggest that I am the absolute source of the *existence* of the world, that my experience literally creates the world, or that the *esse* of the world is simply *percipi*. On the contrary, he is trying to chart a middle course between a 'realist' metaphysics which would explain experience in terms of objective causes, and an 'idealist' metaphysics which would simply identify the being of the world with its being an object for 'transcendental consciousness.' The world and the perceiving subject, he tells us, are *inter*dependent.

> The world is inseparable from the subject, but from a subject which is nothing but a project of the world, and the subject is inseparable from the world, but from a world which the subject itself projects. The subject is a being-in-the-world and the world remains 'subjective' since its texture and articulations are traced out by the subject's movement of transcendence. Hence we have discovered, with the world as the cradle of meanings, direction of all directions, and ground of all thinking, how to leave behind the dilemma of realism and idealism ...[18]

Still, it must be conceded that self and world depend upon one another in somewhat different senses. Entities within the world *receive* their meaningful structure from the perceiving subject, whereas the perceiving subject depends upon the world in the sense that it *must* project a world for itself. Kant might have said as much about the relation between the activity of the human mind and the phenomenal world which is the product of that activity. The parallel can be pushed even further. If we ask what, if anything, there is independently of the perceiver, we find Merleau-Ponty unwilling to deny that there is anything at all, but equally unwilling to say *what* it is. All of which is reminiscent of the Kantian doctrine of the thing-in-itself. But whereas Kant held that it is meaningful to subsume things-in-themselves under the unschematized categories, though such subsumption can never be theoretically justified, Merleau-Ponty seems to hold that it is strictly meaningless to say that there is a world of entities apart from any perceiver.

> ... what precisely is meant by saying that the world existed before any human consciousness? An example of what is meant is that the earth originally issued from a primitive nebula from which the combination of conditions necessary to life was absent. But every one of these words, like every equation in physics, presupposes *our* pre-scientific experience of the world, and this reference to the world in which we live goes to make up the proposition's valid meaning. Nothing will ever bring home to my comprehension what a nebula that no one sees could possibly be. Laplace's nebula is not behind us, at our remote beginnings, but in front of us in the cultural world.[19]

Laplace's nebula exists only in a context of scientific thought. And scientific thought is carried forward by a human being, the scientist, who continues to live in a pre-scientific world, a world to which he has access through ordinary perception. In this sense, science presupposes ordinary experience, and every word in a scientific proposition refers us back to this perceived world. It is this reference which, as Merleau-Ponty says in the passage quoted above, 'goes to make up the proposition's valid meaning.' If, then, the perceived world is the fundamental order of reality, and if the perceived world is ontologically dependent on human existence, it is not only impossible to determine what there is independently of the human perceiver — it is meaningless to ask what sort of things exist apart from us.

Given this assumption about the relation of the perceiver to the perceived world, we can reconstruct Merleau-Ponty's argument for saying that experience cannot have a cause as follows:

1) Independently of me and my experience, things within the world have no characteristics.

2) But a cause must have some characteristics of its own in virtue of which it produces its effect.

3) Therefore things as they are independently of me do not cause my experience.

4) But insofar as they do have characteristics, they are dependent on me and my world — I am not dependent on them.

5) Hence I am not caused to experience the world by anything within the world.

The trouble is that if things as they are independently of me are literally characterless, it is as difficult to see how they could *limit* my experience as to see how they could *cause* it. But limit it they must. For otherwise the meaning I give them would be wholly arbitrary. World-projection would be indistinguishable from world-creation. All of which, as Merleau-Ponty never tires of insisting in his critique of 'transcendental idealism,' is inconsistent with the manifestly finite and situated character of human life.

V

At this point, two related objections must be met: first, that we have overlooked the preeminent place of the 'subject-body' in Merleau-Ponty's account of the relation between man and the world, and second, that we have neglected the distinction between the subject-body's 'operative intentionality' and the 'act-intentionality'[20] of the fully conscious intellect which explicitly posits the universe of objects that it constitutes. If we keep these doctrines in mind, it might seem that there is no difficulty in distinguishing Merleau-Ponty's view from the idealism that he rejects. For Merleau-Ponty, the world is always already structured by the subject-body's 'latent knowledge.'[21] It is not explicitly constituted 'at this moment'[22] by a transcendental consciousness which is of, but not in, the world that it constitutes.

All of this is true and important. Merleau-Ponty does want to emphasize the distinction between the act of judgment and the 'transitional synthesis'[23] involved in the perceptual process. But this distinction does not address the point at issue. In order to shore up the arguments against the realist view that experience has its causes in the objective world, Merleau-Ponty needs to say that objects within the world have no characteristics of their own apart from their relation to the human world. Moreover, this is exactly what he does seem to say in the passages cited above. But that leaves him with one of the problems endemic to the idealism that he rejects: how do we account for the non-arbitrariness of the way in which entities are assimilated to the categories of the human world? It makes no difference to this point whether the subject of experience is conceived as an 'a-cosmic freedom' or as an embodied perceiver — on either view, experience is wholly structured by an interpretive framework (a 'world') which the subject brings to the perceptual situation, and the problems inherent in this conception are as pressing on Merleau-Ponty's view as on the view of the idealism that he rejects.

The source of the confusion may be a failure to distinguish between idealist metaphysics and idealist epistemology: between the idealist claim that beings are ontologically dependent upon the subject who experiences them, and the related, but logically distinct, claim that perceptual experience consists in explicit synthesis and judgment. The *Phenomenology of Perception* abounds with criticisms of the second claim, but little is said against the first. On the contrary, Merleau-Ponty is quite explicit in his rejection of the independent reality that the realist wants to talk about. At most, his view allows for a pinpoint reference to an uncharacterizable being independent of the human world.

For all the talk in phenomenological circles about 'undercutting the subject-object dichotomy' and 'bypassing the dilemma of realism and idealism,' there is still a dilemma to be faced and a problem to be solved. No matter how anonymous the perceptual process and no matter how tacit our knowledge of the network of relations in terms of which objects are 'automatically' experienced, we cannot regard it as the contribution of the subject to experience without being prepared to distinguish it from what is *not* the contribution of the subject – unless, of course, we are prepared to say that everything is contributed by the subject, in which case it would be impossible to account for the situated character of human life.

NOTES

1 Merleau-Ponty, *Sense and Nonsense*, tr. by Hubert Dreyfus and Patricia Dreyfus, (Evanston: Northwestern University Press, 1964), pp. 71-72.

2 Merleau-Ponty, Maurice, *Phenomenology of Perception*, tr. by Colin Smith with revisions by Forrest Williams, (New York, Humanities, 1974), p. 258. Cited hereafter as PP.

3 Lest there be any doubt that, in the passage quoted above, Merleau-Ponty means flatly to deny that an experience can have a cause, he footnotes the passage as follows: 'In other words: an act of consciousness can have no *cause*. But we prefer not to introduce the concept of consciousness, which Gestalt psychology might challenge and which we for our part do not unreservedly accept. We shall stick to the unexceptionable notion of experience. (PP, p. 258, n. 1).

4 Cf. PP, p. 259.

5 This seems to follow from Merleau-Ponty's identification of 'causal thinking' with 'inductive reasoning.' Cf. PP, p. 116.

6 Cf. PP, pp. 49, 258.

7 PP, p. 49.

8 PP, p. 259.

9 PP, p. 261.

10 PP, p. 259.

11 PP, p. 259.

12 PP, p. 50.

13 PP, pp. 16-17.

14 PP, p. 258.

15 PP, p. 258.

16 PP, p. 75.

17 PP, 'Preface,' ix.

18 PP, p. 430.

19 PP, p. 432.

20 PP, pp. 428-429.

21 PP, p. 223.

22 PP, pp. 238, 326.

23 PP, p. 265.

A REPLY TO PROF. MORRISTON'S PAPER –
'MORRISTON'S MERLEAU-PONTY'

JOHN FLYNN

Morriston claims that Merleau-Ponty's arguments against realism lead him to accept premises which would commit him to idealistic conclusions. The particular premises Morriston has in mind are the following:

1) Independently of me things within the world have no charateristics.

2) Insofar as they do have characteristics, they are dependent upon me and my world – I am not dependent upon them. Or, alternatively, the perceived world is ontologically dependent on human existence.

From these premises Morriston thinks that an idealistic conclusion is unavoidable. His Merleau-Ponty is then committed to saying that

3) experience is wholly structured by an interpretative framework which the subject brings to the perceptual situation.

This, according to Morriston, gives Merleau-Ponty the typical idealist difficulty of having no way to account for the non-arbitrariness of the way entities are experienced.

I must confess considerable uneasiness over the account Morriston has given of Merleau-Ponty's thought. It appears that Morriston would reduce the phenomenology of perception to a version of the very intellectualism which Merleau-Ponty takes such pains to criticize. If this is the result of Morriston's argument, then what is distinctive and original about Merleau-Ponty has been obscured and misrepresented.

Much of the misrepresentation is due to the indirect and unclear route that Morriston takes to a characterization of Merleau-Ponty's position. The whole first half of his paper is devoted to showing that Merleau-Ponty is driven to accept idealist premises in order to shore up a weak case against realism, in particular against the claim that experience can be caused. There are a number of serious and related problems in Morriston's approach here which skew our perception of Merleau-Ponty's position from the start. First, we are asked to look at Merleau-Ponty through the very narrow lens of one claim, 'experience can never be caused.' We are not placed within the intentional horizon of Merleau-Ponty's philosophical motivations. There are a number of questions which Morriston fails to raise, an omission which serves to suppress the radical picture which Merleau-Ponty's trying to express.

For example, what would a successful critique of realism accomplish philosophically for Merleau-Ponty? And how is this critique related to the purpose and method of a phenomenological account of perceptual experience? In the course of my discussion, I will suggest answers to these questions. For the present, I will just state dogmatically that in the absence of the context which such answers would provide, we will lack the philosophical perspective needed to properly evalutate both the meaning and success of Merleau-Ponty's project.

A second and related way in which Morriston's presentation skews our perception of what is at stake is that his own reconstruction of Merleau-Ponty's critique of realism is ambiguously focussed and needlessly complicated.[1] It is clear from Merleau-Ponty's writings that his opponent had shifted from realism in the *Structure of Behavior* to empiricism and intellectualism in the *Phenomenology of Perception*. Even if Merleau-Ponty's opponent had remained the same, Morriston fails to distinguish between two importantly different versions of realism, a distinction which has important bearings on the precise meaning of the cause which, Merleau-Ponty argues, cannot produce experience. Morriston's initial statement of realism in which it is characterized as positing 'experience as the outcome of objective causes interacting with the physiology of the body', is a materialist sense of cause. To reject this sort of realism is to reject the view that all relations (including the relation of experience to its objects) are ultimately reducible to merely spatio-temporal relations of constant conjunction between physical event-types. Yet in his reconstructive account of the logical conditions of Merleau-Ponty's concept of cause, Morriston nowhere mentions the restriction of cause to repeatable spatio-temporal relations between physical events. In this context, he commits Merleau-Ponty to a wider Humean-type conception of cause which would leave open the possibility of a realism which countenanced both any non-physical causal interaction as well as the more typical mental/physical interactionism. This ambiguity of focus muddies things considerably so that it is never clear what Morriston takes Merleau-Ponty to be rejecting when he says that realism is mistaken and that experience can never be caused.

The troubles I have in following Morriston's account of this matter are compounded when he indicates that an experience can be caused by someone's personal history. One natural reading of this assertion would be to suppose that it means that a person's experience is motivated by how he takes up a situation, how he lives it. If this is what Morriston means by a motive which can also be a cause, then we have entered the world significances, of operative and act intentionality which Merleau-Ponty claims is the only way we can properly characterize experience. Cause becomes indistinguishable from motive. The motivated act or experience is now seen as intelligible only against a background of intentionally characterizable conditions to which it is internally related.

Despite evidence that he is fuzzy about this issue, I am inclined to think that on the whole Morriston agrees with Merleau-Ponty that experience intentionally characterized, can never be caused. He cites discussions which he believes show that the relation of experience to its antecedents displays intentional characteristics of internal relatedness which causal relations, in any strong sense of the term, can not display. This is all that is needed to make good on Merleau-Ponty's point.[2]

Since all that would be needed is to show that one necessary condition of a causal relation cannot be present in a motivational relationship, it is puzzling to me why Morriston goes on once he thinks this fact has been established. The discussions which follow concerning the bearing of the sufficiency and asymmetry of cause to experience are only artificially related to Merleau-Ponty's philosophical concerns and do not advance Morriston's argument. The only reason I can think of for Morriston to include them is that he wants to bring Merleau-Ponty's account of experience out of the vagueness in which it was unaccountably left in the beginning of the essay. But that task would have been more usefully accomplished directly, to begin with. For it is only after we have a precise explication of the philosophical function of his notion of experience, of how the body-subject is related to the world, that we can begin to consider whether Merleau-Ponty is committed to idealism.

Nothing that has been said so far settles the question of whether Merleau-Ponty is unwittingly committed to some sort of idealism. However, the issue over materialistic realism which dominates the discussions of the *Structure of Behavior*, and to which Morriston's remarks are usually directed, is not the most natural setting for considering this question. It would be more fruitful to turn to Merleau-Ponty's objections to empiricism and intellectualism in *Phenomenology* as a background for locating where he himself stands.

Merleau-Ponty regards empiricism and intellectualism as generic names for tendencies of philosophic thought which carry traditional prejudices about the nature of perceptual experience. They are related as thesis to antithesis. Roughly speaking, the former construes perception as the passive reception of sensations impressed upon us by objects to which we are externally related. Since the mute atomistic sensation is taken as the explicative factor in experience, there is no way, even with the aid of postulated mechanisms of association, for us to account for the significance and continuity of experience on this basis. Intellectualism recognizes that the conscious subject must be supposed to have some initiative and so introduces the notion of judgment as what is required if experience as we know it is to be possible. On the intellectualist account, judgments of the understanding, whether *a priori* or conventional, are posited as the way in which the 'meaning' of passively received sensations is interpreted. Experience has meaning and continuity only through us as subjects of experience who provide this 'meaning' through operations of the understanding.

There is no doubt that Merleau-Ponty sees intellectualism to be an advance over empiricism as a theory of experience. Many areas of our experience, especially scientific knowledge, are constituted by judgments of the understanding.

But even if intellectualism might be assimilatable to a more adequate account of some areas of experience, it is no better than empiricism as an account of perception. Merleau-Ponty does not think that intellectualism can account for how experience can exhibit a world which is less than the clear and distinct concept which structures it. Intellectualism leaves no room for the ambiguity, the spatial and temporal openness and the resistence of the world as we live it in perceptual experience.

Even beyond this, the general trouble with empiricism and intellectualism as obstacles to an adequate phenomenology of perception is that both participate in 'the prejudice of the world.' They are both variants of objectivism. For both, the world is *assumed* to exist independently of our awareness of it. The world is taken to produce our sensations through an external relation with our bodies. Objectivism thereby formulates the habitual prejudice about the world carried by our natural, unreflective attitude. As Richard Schmitt points out, objectivism is being attacked because it uses the notions of 'for us' and 'in itself' in the familiar sense in which we say that events and objects exist in nature in themselves, independently of any human awareness and are, as such, describable by true statements in science.[3]

For Merleau-Ponty, when we discard the notions of sensation and judgment as products of analytical reflection and look afresh at perceptual experience as it is lived, we will find no justification for this prejudice of the world. We will then see that the world is exhibited in actual perception neither as the dead letter of sensation nor as the transparency of the concept. Perception yields access to being immediately, intentionally, ambiguously and incompletely. Science constitutes the second order expression of this lived world, it fixes the world; it abstracts from the fluidity of perception by means of the understanding.

So Merleau-Ponty is not denying that relations in the world *can* be expressed in the way that science presupposes. He is not denying that the abstract constructions of scientific judgment are *taken* to exist independently of us or that we might have good reasons for such representation. Such judgments constitute a world which is 'in-itself' and can be represented as causally related to us in a realist sense of cause. However, Merleau-Ponty *is* claiming that there are legitimate ways of representing man and the world which do not require the independence presupposition characteristic of objectivist thought. Second, he is claiming that a phenomenological description of lived perception does not justify the introduction of the independence assumption in the field of primordial experience. And, finally, he is claiming that the structure of lived bodily experience expresses the original and originative relation of experience, a structure which is presupposed by other legitimate, but secondary, representations of experience.

Now we have the question of Merleau-Ponty's alleged idealism in clearer focus. To answer it, we need to know what he thinks the structure of lived perceptual experience is. We will want to know in what precise sense he means to say that the world in perceptual experience is 'for us' and not 'in-itself' and yet also 'in-itself' and *not* simply 'for-us'. Is he committed to some analogue of intellectualism as Morriston suggests or to some original conception which transcends both empiricism and intellectualism without falling into still another form of idealism?

For the sake of definiteness and because he speaks of the subject's interpretive framework as wholly structuring experience, I will suppose that Morriston is attributing an idealism which is an analogue of the intellectualist variety to Merleau-Ponty. I have just sketched the rationale for Merleau-Ponty's return to lived perception which indicates his opposition both to intellectualism and to the objectivism it entails. However, it still might be true that, despite his intentions, Merleau-Ponty did not succeed in extricating himself from either the intellectualist's account of perception or from its presuppositions.

This is the line Morriston takes. He attempts to support it in two ways. His first way is to try to show that Merleau-Ponty's critique of realism requires a commitment to the view that the world has no character of its own except as we constitute it through the interpretative concepts of our understanding. I have argued already that the critique of realism requires no such premises. Merleau-Ponty's critique is carried through quite effectively by an eidetic analysis which exhibits the divergent structures of causal and motivational relations, a fact which Morriston recognizes but from which he fails to draw the appropriate conclusions. What I will grant, however, is that the phenomenological account which Merleau-Ponty develops as a replacement for a discredited objectivism, contains statements which taken in relative isolation, might be interpreted in an idealist way.

This is the second and mostly undeveloped tack that Morriston takes. He says, 'Merleau-Ponty needs to say that objects within the world have no characteristics of their own apart from their relation to the human world'. (and) This is exactly what he does seem to say in the passages cited above.' The passages to which Morriston is referring summarize Merleau-Ponty's distinction between the operative intentionality of the body-subject and the act intentionality of higher orders of consciousness. Morriston does not develop an interpretation of these passages, but he obviously thinks that Merleau-Ponty's distinction between orders of intentionality will not help him to avoid idealism. What is clear, however, is that the idealism being attributed to Merleau-Ponty can no longer be counted as intellectualism. Since the body-subject does not operate intentionally 'from the understanding', the description of the operation of the body-subject, if it is idealism at all, must yield a new form of idealism.

Morriston's interpretative claims would be more concrete and, hence, more cogent if he had explored this matter in some detail. Since he uses the idealist placeholder phrase 'contributes an interpretative framework' to range indiscriminately over a subject's thetic and non-thetic experience, he does not put us in a position to see if he has missed something important in this distinction.

If Morristion had explored this distinction in detail, he would have seen that he is using 'experience' in a way that makes the distinction impossible to draw and which therefore make his claims about perception and experience difficult to evaluate. He says that, for Merleau-Ponty, to experience something is to ... understand it in terms of a significance which I bring to bear on the situation. And 'I, as perceiving subject, contribute an all-embracing interpretative framework' which I 'bring to bear on any perceptual situation.' The perceptual experience to which Morriston refers is what he calls 'A prescientific world' to which we have access through 'ordinary perception' or 'ordinary experience'. It is this thematized world of ordinary perception which Morriston equates with the non-thematized world of the lived body. Nothing could be further from Merleau-Ponty's meaning. Ordinary perception, ordinary experience and the ordinary use of perception language all participate in the objectivizing prejudice of the world characteristic of the material attitude. Far from being identical with the subject of ordinary perceptual experience and its objectivizing interpretative framework, the incompleteness, ambiguity and indefiniteness of the world as perceived by the body/subject is explicitly contrasted with it.

Merleau-Ponty proposes that access to the lived experience of the body-subject yields access to a world in which the objectivist assumption has not yet been constituted. Morriston seems to have completely missed Merleau-Ponty's claim that there is a set of transitions in the genesis of experience from the pure perceptual experience slowly constituted through the body's operative intentionality to the constituted product of operative and act intentionality which we call the world of ordinary perceptual experience.

There is a place, however, where Morriston does engage in a bit of explicit exegesis to support his claim that there is direct textual evidence for Merleau-Ponty's idealism. He cites Merleau-Ponty's assertion, 'I am the absolute source'. Morriston's translation of this statement is as follows:

> 'My existence is wholly responsible for the meaningful structure of the world, and that the things I encounter have the determinate characteristics that they do only in virtue of the fact that I understand the world the way I do'.

It is from this paraphrase that Morriston draws the implication that he thinks leads Merleau-Ponty into his idealist difficulties. He is quite right that from this 'translation' of 'I am the absolute source' one can draw out the desired idealist and intellectualist implication which reads, 'Independently of my interpretative framework, things within the world have no characteristics.' The question remaining is whether Morriston's purported translation is correct.

This matter cannot be settled straightforwardly by an appeal to the context in which 'I am the absolute source' was stated. The context is clear about intending a distinction between man, as body-subject, as he stands primordially within lived experience and the constructed 'man' who is either a product of scientific analysis or who, as the epistemological subject, is the product of intellectualist reflective analysis. But the remark is made in the Preface of *Pheno-*

menology where one would hardly expect Merleau-Ponty to be able to fully spell out exactly what he meant. The context therefore is too incomplete and hence ambiguously open to alternative readings.

If Morriston feels sure of his idealist interpretation, it can only be because he believes that it is supported by the detailed discussions in the rest of the book. Since we cannot attempt a full scale interpretation here, we must make some smaller, yet still significant, steps in the direction of resolving this interpretative issue. I think that a persuasive textual case can be made against Morriston's interpretation. Toward this end I have assembled four passages from *Phenomenology* which will let Merleau-Ponty speak for himself and will serve to exhibit the gestalt of Merleau-Ponty's non-idealist thinking on a small scale.

1) The real has to be described, not constructed ... Which means that I cannot put perception into the same category as the syntheses represented by judgments, acts or predications. My field of perception is constantly filled with colors, noises, fleeting tactile sensations which ... I place immediately in the world, without ever confusing them with my daydreams ... The real is a closely woven fabric. It does not await our judgment before incorporating the most surprising phenomena ... Perception ... is the background from which all acts stand out; and is presupposed by them. The world is not an object such that I have in my possession the law of its making ... *Phenomenology of Perception* (PP p. x, xi)

2) The first philosophical act would appear to be to return to the world of actual experience which is prior to the objective world ... (to) *restore to things their concrete physiognomy*, (and) to subjectivity its inherence in history ... The field is not an 'inner world', the 'phenomenon' is not a state of consciousness ... (underlining mine)
The sensible configuration of an object ... is not grasped in some inexpressible coincidence, it is understood through a sort of act of appropriation which we all experience when we say that we have 'found' the rabbit in the foliage of a puzzle. Once the prejudice of sensation has been banished, a face, a signature, a form of behavior cease to be mere visual data whose psychological meaning is to be sought in our inner experience ...
More generally, it is the very notion of the immediate which is transformed: henceforth the immediate is no longer the impression ... but the meaning, the structure, the spontaneous arrangement of parts. (*PP* pp. 57-58)

3) ... The gestalt is recognized as primary. Form is the very appearance of the world ... It is the birth of a norm and is not realized according to a norm; it is the identity of the external and internal and not the projection of the internal in the external ... If a universal constituting consciousness were possible, the opacity of the fact would disappear (*PP* pps. 60, 61)

4) We witness every minute the miracle of related experience, and yet nobody knows better than we do how this miracle is worked, for we are ourselves the network of relationships. The world and reason are not problematical. We may say, if we wish, that they are mysterious, but their mystery defines them: there can be no question of dispelling it by some solution ... True philosophy consists in relearning to look at the world. (*PP* p. xx)

It is clear from these passages that Merleau-Ponty does not 'solve' the dilemma of realism and idealism by finding a middle way which does justice to the insights of each. Such a middle way would be as much a product of analytical reflection and as much committed to the prejudice of the world as the extremes it tried to mediate. The phenomenology of perception is not intended to be a theory of what perception must be, but rather a phenomenological description of the material essence of perception as it is lived.

It is not easy to state in precise general terms what Merleau-Ponty's picture of the perceived world finally comes to. I sympathize with Morriston's difficulties here. The meaning of the passages I have quoted are not immediately assimilatable to any familiar category. Yet there is a temptation for us to want to reduce the cognitive dissonance and to see Merleau-Ponty as an idealist or a realist after all. This is a temptation to which Morriston has yielded and as a result he misunderstands the distinctive character and result of Merleau-Ponty's philosophical project.

Let me close with a few interpretative and also speculative remarks about what I think the Merleau-Ponty's philosophical project comes to.

What is clear to me is that the *Phenomenology of Perception* is an attempt to place the discussion of perception in a different conceptual setting than the ones we have inherited from the realist/idealist controversy. For him, it is not just a matter of eliminating the prejudice of the world or of discarding the category of sensation. Merleau-Ponty is making a deeper demand. He is asking us to give up the idea that the subject of experience and the world are in some sense fundamentally alienated from one another. Causal thinking tends to alienate us from the world by representing our relation to it as contingent and external. Yet despite Hume's attempt to repress it, the notion of cause retains an aura of power, of the idea of bringing something about. To be caused by the world is to be completely *dependent* upon the world; it is to be in its power and to have this power be quite literally senseless.

Idealism pictures us as alienated from the world in another way. Here the world is dependent upon us. In this framework, we have regained our command, our power over the world. The world is now pictured as a distanced consequence of our mental agency; we bring it about by our acts of judgment. Regardless of the philosophical reasons, even good reasons, that may have led to these results, both idealism and realism reflect a relationship of alienation which is carried by the very concepts of self and world which form their basis. In psychological terms, we could look at idealism as an overcompensation against a fear of the alienating power of the world. There is a fear of the engulfing power of the world in both realism and idealism.

Against these pictures of alienation, I think that Merleau-Ponty wants to capture an intimacy in our body's relation to its world which cannot be captured in the terms of either causal or agential dependence. Each of these latter terms suppresses the subjectivity of the body in experience. There is no doubt that for Merleau-Ponty our world has power and presence for us which must be given its due. Our being-in-the-world constitutes a field of meaning which is generally magnetized in varying degrees of strength toward the side of the world. Yet what has been overlooked is that the presence of the body-subject is required if the circuit of meaning is to be animated and completed, if geographical environment is to be intelligible as behavioral environment.

The world as perceived by us is not without character, but we are required to complete the gestalt. The gestalt is the norm of the perceived world. Merleau-Ponty seems to understand it as a bi-lateral gestalt which requires the co-presence of body-subject and an already organizable world. This bi-lateral field of meaning cannot be said to be the sole result of the operative intentionality of the body acting as a sufficient condition. Nor can it be regarded as solely the product of the insistent presence of the world. If the body and the world depend upon each other, it is in a sense entirely different from the dependence of exclusive power. It is an attunement and reliance which is much more like that of a true and intimate friendship. There is a mutual support and fittingness between body and world which constitutes and defines their relationship. The lived body and the phenomenal world belong together. One might say that Merleau-Ponty's distinctive and original contribution to the philosophy of perception is his attempt to recall us in detail to the special sort of friendship between our bodies and that world which is our natural and original home. Although the project was never finished and its implications never fully clarified, it is nonetheless the case that it is a position for which the traditional dilemma of realism and idealism does not arise.

NOTES

1 One example of this which I do not have the space to explore in my discussion is carried by Morriston's claim that 'Motives can also be causes.' Since Morriston does not add the disclaimer 'under different descriptions', I take him to mean that descriptions of causes (realist sense) and of motives (intentional sense) are intensionally as well as extensionally equivalent. This is obviously false. But there are also grounds for thinking that they cannot be extensinally equivalent either. If event individuation is tied to properties of events, it could not be otherwise in this case.

2 Morriston is not at all clear on the central issue of internal relatedness. He treats it as synonymous with logical dependence. Even here he sometimes speaks as if events could be logically related rather than propositions describing the events. He fails to consider the similarities and differences between the various sorts of internal relatedness which Merleau-Ponty recognizes: sign vehicle to significance; intentional act to intentional horizon; and proposition to proposition.

3 R. Schmitt, 'Merleau-Ponty II' *Review of Metaphysics* Vol. XIX, No. 4 June 1966 p. 729.

SOCIAL ENCOUNTERS AND DEATH:
HERMENEUTICAL REFLECTIONS

C. PAX

In an essay entitled 'Hegel's Existentialism' Merleau-Ponty has commented that the nearest approximation we have to the understanding of death lies in the meeting of another person.[1] Surely, at first, this seems to be a strange observation. Are we not in the very midst of life in the give-and-take of the exchange of ideas, in the company of friends and in the effort to create a viable society? And yet, there is truth in what Merleau-Ponty says. A hint of this truth is given in the experience of alienation, an experience sufficiently common to have generated a quite extensive body of literature. Without need at present of following this literature into its many interesting avenues, we can acknowledge that it is often with a certain apprehension and fear of failure that we approach one another, even after the sometimes awkward initial attempts at understanding. Behind this apprehension lies the knowledge that we have no certainty, but only a hope, that we can achieve a moral world and no certainty that we can, either as individuals or as nations, learn to live in peaceful coexistence.[2]

My purpose in this essay is to investigate briefly the similarities between social encounters and the act of dying in order to see how the two experiences might be mutually revelatory.

'To meet another person' embraces a wide expanse of experiences, both positive and negative, ranging from the briefest and most casual encounter to the complete dedication to or the complete destruction of another person. Furthermore, these meetings are both personal and societal, i.e., mediated through various institutions. In all of these meetings with another person, however, we place ourselves in a radically different situation from the situation from which we look out upon the things of the world or encounter its forces. Meeting another person places us in a situation of *personal* vulnerability. In order to meet another person we must present ourselves not merely physically but personally and this necessitates making ourselves available to the *person* of the other. This availability is appropriately called responsibility inasmuch as it rests upon the recognition that the other person has a kind of claim against me as a person. It is, of course, possible to neglect or to deny this responsibility to the other person. This denial of responsibility, however, does not take me out of the position of being vulnerable but rather serves as a means to protect myself

See notes at the end of this chapter.

from the power of the other person; when regret or shame follows such an act, the very fleeing from responsibility brings to light my vulnerability. If the denial of responsibility goes further and wounds the other person, the action makes explicit *his* vulnerability. If the wound strikes at the very life of the other person, the vulnerability is complete and the other person dies. The other person can, of course, be myself if the situation is reversed.

Because the heart of personal vulnerability lies in human freedom, the vulnerability which characterizes our relations with one another can be clearly distinguished from the vulnerability we experience in the threat of natural catastrophe. No one can be held responsible for the damages of a flood or a hurricane whose power goes beyond our ability to forestall its damages. Contrary to this, in the breakdown of human relations we do want to know who, or whose interests, were responsible for the breakdown. A person is said to have acted irresponsibly precisely when it was in his power to avert harm to others and he failed to do so.

Reflection on responsibility indicates clearly the ambiguous character of our experienced freedom. The experience of freedom is a complex experience embodying two diverse movements. On the one hand, there is a movement from oneself, from one's own decision to act, and this movement gives to freedom the note of spontaneity. On the other hand, there is the movement *from the other toward our power to act.* This second movement of freedom is related not to spontaneity but to the deeper notion of respontaneity and, because of the claim of the other person upon us, expresses itself as responsibility. I call the notion of respontaneity deeper because even the power to act from oneself is always experienced as a spontaneity in reference to a situation, i.e., in reference to what is other than one's self. Freedom as sheer spontaneity would imply both absolute power and absolute irresponsibility, and is, as a matter of fact, never experienced. The term re-spontaneity keeps the notion of action from oneself but calls attention to the fact that our freedom is also an opening to another person and another powerfulness. It is this openness to the powerfulness of the other which gives the mark of personal vulnerability to our encounters with others. More specifically, it is the openness of freedom to the powerfulness of another freedom which distinguishes personal encounters, even when mediated through objective economic and political institutions, from the encounter with the powerfulness of natural forces.

To speak of a demand made against us by another person need not imply, of course, that the other person is against us as a contender. Rather, because freedom is more profoundly re-spontaneity than it is spontaneity, the demand indicates a lack of complete autonomy in the individual freedom and a need for fulfillment from the other.

Our need of the other person is two-fold, and apart from taking note of and living within this twofold need we have no self-presence as a person. The first need for the other person is for our fundamental self-identity as a person. The second need is the need for a world, for a common place, and even for objectivity. This twofold need shows itself frequently in experience and is not difficult to find. Our lives are least worth living when we are isolated, when we are in exile or without the love and respect of our fellows. If this isolation becomes complete and unbearable the result may be suicide or, on the level of consciousness, a giving way to the ever-present threat of despair and of letting go of all worth in one's self and in others. When a person becomes thus incapable of recognizing any worth whatever in others he becomes brute-like and society rightly and by necessity guards itself against such a one as it does against other impersonal forces.

The need for others must not be confused, however, with a mindless gregariousness, as Marcel correctly points out.[3] Privacy is compatible with respect given and received. One might even say that privacy is a necessary condition for mutual respect because without the observance of the uniqueness of each person, mutual respect is dissolved into identity. The irreducible multiplicity of unique human individuals reveals, paradoxically, that our need for the other has its roots in a common ontological situation, namely, the situation of experiencing our individual freedom, our individual consciousness and our individual existence as participations in freedom, consciousness and existence which belong to others as well as to oneself.

The second need for other persons is, as said above, the need for a common world and for objectivity. Even beyond the question of whether objectivity has any meaning apart from the community of subjects (a question which goes beyond the purpose of this paper) we have a great need for the confirmation of our insights by others. This is especially true in the moral and political orders because only if values are held in common, and efficaciously held in common, can a society continue to exist.

But how does this reliance upon the other person for self-identity and for a common world help us to understand the act of dying? How is the meeting of persons an exercise in the art of dying? And, equally important, how can a philosophical awareness of death help us to understand personal relations and social institutions?

By the philosophical awareness of death I mean the appropriation by reflection of human life precisely insofar as it is experienced as being a life that reaches toward death. Thus, a philosophical awareness of death is to be clearly distinguished both from the physical experience of dying and from any subjective concerns. As an attempt to reach eidetic knowledge, the search for a philosophical understanding of death is similar to the search for a philosophical understanding of other modes of experiencing such as perception, corporeity, historicity, etc.

Meeting other persons can be (although it need not be) an exercise in the art of dying because in both experiences we are brought face to face with a power that is other than ourselves and which makes a radical demand upon persons. The experience of freedom as re-spontaneity is the cognition of a calling by the powerfulness of the other upon our freedom. In meeting another person we bring to revelation a power which is not present for our control but which, at least in part, defines our worth as a person. In the experience of dying we likewise bring to revelation a power that is beyond us and which defines us as persons. It is only in dying (and in the reflective understanding of dying as a defining dimension of life) that our life in its entirety, and our persons in the totality of our actions and freedom, become present to ourselves. Up to the time of dying only a segment of our lives has been present and up to that time our power of altering the direction and meaning of our life is at least to some extent within our own power to choose. The advent of death is the advent of a powerfulness from beyond us which establishes who we are in a definitive way. One fundamental similarity between the experience of dying and the experience of meeting another person is that in both experiences we find ourselves placed in the presence of a power that is other than ourselves and which is at the same time so intimate to our own being that it acts as a defining power in reference to our own persons.

This power is from the other. It is not a power over which we have any fundamental control. In the presence of the other person we have to wait upon his opening of himself to us; we are not able to force his good will but must wait upon his making the opening. Indeed, the necessity of waiting, arising from the recognition of the *personal* claim of the other upon us, distinguishes this encounter from the encounter with brute forces. In those relations mediated by social institutions the same issue of respect for persons provides a basic means to distinguish humanitarian laws, governments, economic policies from those which are oppressive.

This power which is revealed in the personal encounter is a power which makes us wait with our own being somewhat in abeyance and in this way is a creative power which is not of ourselves but which invites and makes possible our own creative response. This dependence upon the creative power of the other is most clearly evident in friendship, since friendship is available to me only upon the willingness of the other, but in an analogous way the creative energy of freely concerted action becomes available only in the socially mediated acceptance of ourselves by other members of a community.

In dying we are faced with a demand made upon us which appears even more radical than the demand made by our fellows. In the reflective awareness of our own being-unto-death we are in the presence of a power which is absolute in the sense that it claims our entire presence as a person. It is a power that is factually overwhelming but a power which we have to respect as the only power that can enable us to reach the entirety of our self-presence as free agents. Until the act of dying the meaning and worth of our lives is characterized by the 'not yet'. The meaning of *my life*, as the whole of my life, is held in abeyance both for others and for myself until it is made available to myself and others by the removal of the uncertainty contained in the 'not yet'. Only in the creative powerfulness which we name death, whether one freely accepts and participates in the power or is simply overwhelmed by it, is man able to become himself in the totality of the meaning of his life and his freedom.

To speak, as we have been doing, of a reflective appropriation or understanding of death is to speak of something other than death as a biological termination of life. It is to speak of dying and of being-unto-death as a structure of human life which allows us to raise the question of the meaning of the *whole* of one's life. Because this question is raised only from within the on-going creative effort to live one's life well, we have, perhaps with some propriety, referred to this effort of thinking as the practice of the art of dying. This art, like the art of meeting other persons, entails the presence and cultivation of an appropriate habit of consciousness. It demands the ability to uncover and cultivate an intellectual stance of wonder and questioning in the presence of a powerfulness which is experienced as other than myself. Both other persons and death have the power to influence my life and do so even against my wishes. What the meeting of others *means* and what dying *means*, however, are not simply matters of the power of the other. Their meaning is determined also, in part, by the way in which one actively and existentially interprets the encounters with the power in question. When it is made concrete, this interpretation is nothing less than a participation or a failure to participate in the power that is present. How I interpret and participate in the power determines in some degree what the power of the other does to and in me and how it changes the meaning and value of my person as a participant in the power.

To participate fruitfully and fully in the powerful presence of another person requires an active receiving of the power by means of a recognition of the rightfulness of the other person's claim against me. And beyond this respect for the other is required a willingness and ability to trust the other person if one is to operate creatively in his presence. Because of my own powerfulness toward the other person I can cancel out or at least diminish the power of his presence by refusing to open myself to him. I can refuse to trust and even refuse to recognize any worth whatever in his person or even any worth in the whole human condition. To do so, however, affects not only the other person but condemns me to isolation and eventually to a lack of meaning in my own life.

In the presence of the powerfulness we name death it is also possible to refuse to participate creatively, even though this power is such that I cannot overcome it. We do not have the power to overcome death. We do have the power to refuse to participate in this powerfulness and thus to make the act of dying into nothing more than the termination of my whole life. To a certain mentality, this is the only fact of dying. But it is important to notice that death is this 'fact' of termination precisely to a certain mentality, that is, death becomes this 'fact' only by reason of a particular interpretive stance taken by the one confronting this power. The one taking this noetic stance does so, of course, with the claim that this is the only reasonable stance to take. The claim is based on the apparent lack of any objective evidence which could invalidate the claim. It is, nevertheless, a claim and the price that must be paid for taking this stance is that the last meaning of human experience is that it is *no* meaning, inasmuch as (within this interpretive stance) meaning for that life is no longer existent. The attempt to understand meaning *simply* within the actions of a life is analagous to the attempt to find meaning simply within the isolated self. Both attempts are abstracted from concrete experience, which always includes the others (other persons and the power called death), and both lead to the futile affirmation of absurdity.

There is a great difference, however, as well as a similarity between the act of dying and the act of meeting other persons. The encounters with other persons never or rarely, and then only when it is a matter of life and death, engage the totality of our persons. Meetings with other persons can be duplicated both because they take place in time and time provides 'another chance,' and because there are a multiplicity of other individuals. The ability to carry on two conversations at once is not only an expression of a certain versatility but an indication of a profound characteristic of the human condition. Such a double conversation indicates, as do many other experiences, not only that we as individuals are radically incomplete without the presence of the other person, but that this 'other person' presents himself as a multiplicity. This aspect of our condition makes it possible to disregard some individuals or even to cancel them out completely without losing our self-identity or completely destroying a common world.

The power to which the name death is given, however, *does* claim our whole person; this encounter is a single encounter alongside of which there are no other possibilities. Each person must die his own death and in death becomes radically individualized, even though others may be in his company and attempt to provide aid. This power of death to individualize radically, lies in the fact that all other persons, each and the whole race, is subject to the powerfulness of death. The power of death does not need to respect the powerfulness of individual persons because it is a powerfulness over *all* persons.

This utter powerfulness of death makes it difficult to accept the possibility of a creative participation in this power. Even when particular personal relationships are very dear to us (and at the same time very fragile) we can enter into them with the realization that life can go on beyond the possible failure of the relationship. On the other hand, even after we have become convinced of the necessity of trust as a condition for meaningful and fruitful encounters with others, and even after we have achieved a degree of ability in structuring our habits of life in accordance with this need for prior trust, even then we have difficulty accepting a similar condition in the face of death. Because *all* is at stake and because the power of death is overwhelming, an active and trusting participation in this power is immensely more difficult than participation in the powerfulness of another person. It is the immensity of this difficulty which, perhaps, makes it advisable to seek a field for practicing the art of dying in the exercise of the art of meeting other persons.

The suggested field of practice, namely, personal encounters, is itself an arena of sufficient difficulty. Both experience and history testify to the difficulty of fruitfully meeting others and of constructing a viable society. Aristotle is undoubtedly correct in teaching us that man is social by nature and Marx in teaching that man is species-being. But it must be further noted that, of all the kinds of species-beings, man is least comfortably species-being; he is *initially* least fully species-being, least willing to fit into this definition. It is, in fact, man's refusal to fit comfortably into this definition which gives rise to the problems of individual and societal rights and duties and which brings about the possibility of a conflict among the classes. Man is species-being only under protest. He is the one species-being who is not only species-being but also individual value, beyond but not separate from his membership in the species.

The clarification of this dual role of man is perhaps the primary gain to be won from a philosophical appropriation of death. Above we said that the power of death radically individualizes man; now it must be said that this same power places man *equally radically* within the community of men. Because death faces *each* person *and the species as a whole* (and our own power is now such as to make this threatening), it defines man both individually and as a species-being. *In being-unto-death man is at once radically individual and radically communal.* Because the power of death is such that it defines man both communally and individually, there is a profound lack of *social* understanding in any humanism, whether dialectical or not, which in its understanding of man and human well-being neglects in principle the structuring and defining role of death. This is why Merleau-Ponty, in the essay already referred to, can identify the major sin of Nazism not in the atrocities and slaughter which it perpetrated, but in the fact that it caused men to forget death.[4] What new forms of thinking and understanding it may be necessary to learn or to re-learn in order to participate creatively in the powerfulness we name death is a theme which must be taken up in another essay.

NOTES

1 'Hegel's Existentialism' in *Sense and Non-Sense*, translated by Hubert L. Dreyfus and Patricia Allen Dreyfus, Northwestern University Press, 1964, p. 68.
2 *Ibid.*, 'Concerning Marxism,' p. 125.
3 Cf. 'An Essay in Autobiography,' in *The Philosophy of Existence*, translated by Manya Harari, Books for Libraries Press, Freeport, N. Y., 1969.
4 *Op.cit.*, p. 67.

SECTION V

PHENOMENOLOGY AND THE THOUGHT OF MEINONG

MEINONG'S THEORY OF OBJECTS AND ASSUMPTIONS

JANET FARRELL SMITH

INTRODUCTION

What is an assumption and how is it related to an object in Meinong's mature philosophical theory? My method in this paper will be to isolate what can be stated as some paradoxical or puzzling situations which arise in Meinong's theory. Then I will attempt to show how these apparent paradoxes arise from misconceptions of Meinong's method. I shall first state what might appear to be a lack of integration between Meinong's object theory and theory of apprehension. Then I shall give some examples which might be thought to be troublesome cases of contradictory objects, but when understood correctly can clarify Meinong's method.

An assumption in Meinong's theory is like a judgment. It is an experience in which an Objective [state of affairs] is entertained with an attitude of acceptance or rejection. It differs from judgment in that it lacks the element of conviction. I am most interested in the relation of Meinong's analysis of assumptions to his analysis of their correlated objects. In order to examine this problem I must first address some general questions.

In his *Gegenstandstheorie* published in 1904[1] Meinong proposed a new, distinct and separate field of philosophy which we call 'object theory'. Object theory was new in the sense that its scope included the nonexistent and nonactual objects, going beyond traditional metaphysics and ontology. Meinong called it *daseinfrei*, free of existence presuppositions. The question I want to ask is 'How separate is object theory? So separate and distinct that its insights have no integral connection with the theory of apprehension [*Erfassungsweise*]?'

Meinong may overargue his case in order to establish a separate and distinct field of philosophy hitherto unrecognized by the constricting categories of traditional philosophy. The objects, however, are distinct in more than this sense. Meinong says explicitly in both the 1904 essay and in his *Selbstdarstellung* written at the end of his life in 1920, that the objects 'are' or 'obtain' entirely independently of the psychological act which is correlated with them. They correspond to different types of apprehension. *Objekte* correspond to the type of apprehension known as *Vorstellen* (presentation), while *Objektive* correspond

See notes at the end of this chapter.

to *Denken*, which includes both judging and assuming. Meinong says: 'These experiences should not however be seen as constitutive for the object in any way.'[2]

Meinong himself was sometimes drawn to paradoxical modes of expression. He says of the *daseinfrei* or 'pure' objects studied by object theory 'There are objects of which it is true that there are no such objects.'[3] Now the paradoxical situation which arises with the independent and separate status of object theory concerns the insights one expects should derive from it in relation to theory of apprehension. Yet how can an object which is entirely independent of its apprehending experience yield any insights about the experience?

The question here arises from the following two claims:

1) Meinong explicitly states that the characteristics of the four types of objects [*Gegenstände*], *Objekte, Objektive, Dignitative, Desiderative*, are not derived from the characteristics of the apprehending experiences. He continues to insist on the independence of these objects from psychological acts.

2) On the other hand, one wants to take seriously the overview of Meinong's philosophy which sees object theory and theory of apprehension as complementary, and at the very least, not unrelated aspects of a unified undertaking. If we are to see object theory as illuminating the structure of intentional acts, then we must find some connection between the object and the act which allows this integration to take place.[4]

On the one hand we seem to be bound by the restriction that objects are independent, both in their creation or coming into being, and in their resultant eternal status. On the other we are drawn to the view that something about the objects reveals to us the structure of our own intentional acts. For what is the purpose of object theory if not to reveal the unlimited range of human imagination? Surely Meinong was not content with giving a taxonomy of objects spilled forth by the accidental peculiarities of language. It is human thought which for Meinong makes language comprehensible.

Meinong's first claim on the independence of objects is heightened by noting his assertion in *Über Annahmen, Second Edition*, that the object 'airship' had objective status before the human mind conceived it. It is also reinforced by Meinong's tendencies to speak of the human imagination as pulling some object out of the endless domain of *Aussersein*, even though he had doubts about this notion. In these passages Meinong speaks as if the objects 'are' in some eternal pre-ordained realm; they become objects of human apprehension only when by chance or stimulus some imaginative mental process seizes them and catches them within the human domain. The 'pure objects' [*Reine Gegenstände*] are then truly lost entities, belonging neither in rationalist realism such as one finds in Plato or Frege nor in the domain of empirical observation.

We might state the paradoxical situation briefly thus: Objects' independent status insisted on for the purpose of giving object theory autonomy and for establishing Meinong's peculiar brand of 'realism' precludes making the connections necessary for claiming that objects illuminate the fundamental intentionality of human thought. So Meinong's most characteristic positions seem strained one by the other. Denying the first claim leaves the objects dependent on some psychological process, collapsing Meinong's 'realism' back into psychologism. ['Realism' is strictly speaking a misnomer, since Meinong insists on the independent status of nonexistent as well as existent objects.] Yet the very purpose of Meinong's philosophical investigations as they issued from Brentano's influence would seem defeated by denying the latter claim.

It seems then that there is a gap in Meinong's theory about the objects.[5] He requires that they be detached from their psychological moorings in order to conduct his philosophical investigation. He requires this so that they will be more than merely subjective ideas in some particularized mental state instantiated in some individual mind at some particular time. However, they are so decisively detached that it is unclear how they reflect back on the intentional processes which Meinong claims are fundamental to human thought. It is as if Meinong, motivated like Frege to distinguish the 'associated idea' from the objective factors of sense and reference, tried, unlike Frege, to bring back the sense and reference as the intentional objects of thinking. Frege, however, disavowed psychology, while Meinong claimed that his philosophy had continued relevance to psychology.

Having now isolated what appears to be at least a lack of integration in Meinong's theory, I will proceed to make some observations on how Meinong's theory best makes the connections necessary to integrate the object and the apprehension of the object, how to integrate object theory and theory of apprehension.

First some general remarks about the preceding considerations. They misconceive Meinong's entire philosophical enterprise. The allegedly separate examination of objects is merely another method of examining the structure of the experience, or intentional act. The object distills and crystallizes the nature of the act. So when we study the object we discover the nature of an experience or at least what could be an experience.

Certainly these corrective remarks indicate the direction in which we must go to understand Meinong's entire philosophical system. One feels at least however that some point of integration should be made between the act and the object, and that Meinong, being as careful and as thorough a philosopher as he is recognized to be, would have more to say on the particular way in which the act is revealed by the object. Let us entertain two possibilities. The first is the content-object distinction. The second is the factor of language.

It is important to note that in 1899 Meinong made a break with his early psychologistic method, which coincided with the general anti-psychologistic trend of the late nineteenth century.[6] Object theory is evidence of this break. For this reason, as well as his avoidance of the Kantian doctrine that the subject's act is somehow 'constitutive' of the object, he may have been shy of making connections between act and object so that mental acts have any 'determining' influence on objects.

There is one doctrine however, where Meinong does make a direct connection between the structure of the mental act and the object toward which it is directed. The content-object distinction, adopted from Twardowski,[7] enabled Meinong to sever his ties with psychologism and adopt a separate theory of objects. The object of an act is entirely distinct in properties and independent of the content lived through by the subject who entertains that object. There is no qualitative resemblance between the properties of the content (psychic state) and the properties of the object. So the object may exist or fail to exist, yet there is no question about the existence of the psychic state which entertains the object. This distinction allowed Meinong to make the fruitful division between the *Sein* and *Sosein* of the object, without denying the empirically verifiable nature of the mental state which entertains the object. Objects admit predicates of existent or nonexistent, blue or green, but contents do not share these predicates. The content of the act, though unlike the object in its properties, is yet 'adequate' to the object, or 'corresponds' to it in some way.

Does the distinction between content and object provide a basis with which to explain the structure of the connection between act and object, and thus to integrate object theory with theory of apprehension? In one way it does since the relation between content and object is asserted to be one of structural correspondence. The contents serve as 'connecting links' as Twardowski calls them; to carry certain mental acts toward certain objects. Contents are the factor which serve to answer the question 'How did this object *a* [not *b*] become intentionally related to this mental experience? How is it that we experience in a way that we do not confuse mountains with trees? Or red with white?' Yet simply to state that the notion of content answers this question may be merely a designation and not an explanation.

If the content is only subjective mental process then by definition it cannot supply the factors which serve to link mental process with an independent objective entity. This is so especially since Meinong says that the known object is not affected by the knowing or intending. On the other hand, if the content is not merely subjective, but possesses properties which serve to link the subjective process with the object, then to be efficacious, it must possess some measure of objectivity. But if it does possess some measure of objectivity, how do we decide where the content ends and the object begins? If we retreat from this suggestion to save our distinction, and assert that content is only subjective mental process then how does the apprehended independent object participate in or infuse its nature into the content to make this efficacious connection?

These observations may explain why Meinong called the relation between content and object an ideal one, a priori and necessary. He did not assert that the contents were efficacious in bringing about the relation.[8]

The attempt to explain how the apprehending experience and the object are 'adequate' or structurally correpondent with each other can perhaps only be successful by introducing the factor of language. Language mediates between the subjective contents and the objective entity by functioning as a provocateur of subjective associations (what Meinong calls *Ausdruck*) and simultaneously standing in the relation of denoting objects (what Meinong calls *Bedeutung*). These two aspects of language, however, may be powerless to unite the apprehending experience with its object unless we view language as conditioned by its use, which Meinong calls *Meinen*. Although I do not have space here to give arguments for this view, I suspect that *Meinen*, or reference, must always be viewed as intentional reference, if it is to accomplish the task of uniting the apprehension with the object. In a consistently Meinongian framework, then, language must be viewed as a live instrument, a series of speech acts which are profoundly intentional. Meanings of words and sentences cannot be divorced from their intentional context. This is a matter for further exploration. I will say no more about it here.

Let us now take a specific example of an object which can be shown to have properties which are structurally related to a set of assumptions made about it. In what follows I take up an example of an apparently contradictory object in order to make some observations about contradictions and assumptions. The example also shows, (although it does not explain) how apprehending act and object share certain characteristics.

In Act III Scene iv of Shakespeare's *Macbeth*, the ghost of the recently murdered Banquo is seen by Macbeth to sit in the King's place at the table. To the Lords who request that Macbeth be seated and are puzzled at his mutterings, Banquo's ghost does not exist, a fact to which Lady Macbeth attests when she excuses her husband for his strange behavior. In the exchange between the latter it is clear that Banquo's ghost exists as far as Macbeth is concerned. For we who witness the spectacle and understand the behavior of Macbeth, Lady Macbeth, and the Lords, it is not enough to say simply that a ghost appears to one character and not to the other. To understand the fateful unfolding of the drama we must comprehend that Banquo's ghost exists for Macbeth's perspective and not for the others. This situation then produces three mutually incompatible Objectives regarding the object Banquo's ghost, (which appears to be the same continuous object throughout): 1) Banquo's ghost exists, 2) Banquo's ghost does not exist, and 3) Banquo's ghost both exists and does not exist. These Objectives of being are in turn required for the being-so (Sosein) of the object and for the ensuing development of the tragedy. They are required as well for the truth of the statements made in the sequel by Macbeth, the Lords, and by the spectators.

Now I must make a warning here that I am not about to construct a theory on the nature of fictional objects in literary contexts. I have chosen this example for one simple point. Banquo's ghost appears to be an object with contradictory properties regarding its existential status. However, it is clear to the least sophisticated that these contradictory predications (I take existence predication here only in the grammatical sense) are not made on the same level. We might even say that they are not made on the 'same logical level' if we had a theory about the nature of assumptions involved in dramatic literature. The clearest case is the logical difference between a subject (Macbeth) only 'assumed' to exist and the spectator-subjects who do exist (ourselves).

Indeed one might suspect that the points one is led to make about the different levels on which these predications of existence or nonexistence are made might recur in similar form when one begins to talk of the 'assumptions' held respectively by Macbeth, the spectator-characters (Lords), by Lady Macbeth, and by the spectators of the drama. Each set of assumptions is respectively more complex since it may recognize (or 'assume') the previous set of assumptions. We have in effect a set of interlocking hypotheses on which the comprehension of the drama rests. In the case of Banquo's ghost then we might want to say that the apparently contradictory properties *of* the object could be represented as contradictory assumptions *about* the object. This is not to say that properties simply are assumptions. But in this case there is a clear structural relationship.

My point here is that the apparently contradictory properties determining existential status arise on different levels of predication just as the contradictory assumptions arise from different vantage points within the drama. The contradictory assumptions are in fact necessary to the artistic unity and complexity of Shakespeare's drama. In certain cases then, contradictory properties are not only comprehensible, they are necessary.* This particular set of contradictory properties does not result in contradiction since each property occurs on a distinct logical level. When it might be the case that some of these properties do occur on the same logical (or artistic) level, as one might want to argue they do in the case of Macbeth and Lady Macbeth, there is a purpose and a point to their predication. In other words, we might even grant that a contradiction exists in *Macbeth*, yet not consider it a devastating result of our analysis.

How then, some dubious critic might say, even if I grant your points in the case of this unusual example, does your observation apply in cases of more mundane non-fictional objects? Very simply put my reply here amounts to questioning whether the case with non-fictional objects is very much different from the fictional or literary object in the preceding case. Or, even, different from cases of objects which have been thought to present logical difficulties to Meinong's theory. Contradictory properties arise easily and constantly in everyday life, in science, in mathematics, in ways that depend on our purpose of investigation. I am claiming here that these contradictory properties can in some cases be seen as arising from contradictory assumptions, which in turn might allow the 'contradiction' to make sense. When we see the properties and assumptions as structurally parallel, the 'contradictory objects' may even make sense. Failure to perceive the intentional context in such cases may lead to the charge of paradox when none is present. The purpose of introducing the literary example lies in dramatizing the role of assumptions which may be more easily forgotten in other contexts.

Often, as in the example from Macbeth, distinct conscious subjects make assumptions which contradict one another, but which are useful or necessary in the context. We need to keep in mind, however, that one conscious subject will often make contradictory assumptions within one context for various purposes. These might include the careful scrutiny of a scientific or mathematical theory. If this were not possible, or not explicable, we might say that we have failed to give a theory which accounts for the dialectic of human thought. I see Meinong as providing a philosophical basis with his theory of assumptions to account for just such features of novelty and creativity in thinking and speaking.

Even if we cannot always construe or analyse contradictory properties as arising from predications which occur on different logical levels, I think we can construe straightforward contradictions in cases such as the infamous round square (or the existent non-existing round square) as harmless. This will perhaps require suspending full application of some classical logical laws in some contexts, but I think a case can be made for doing that. I have not considered here the possibilities for fully rigorous logical treatment of such examples as Meinong's Triangle, which is neither isoceles nor scalene, and thus evades the Law of Excluded Middle. But that is a matter for another, more strictly logical investigation.[9] As a final word, let me say that I do think that, with some effort, Meinong's theories can be presented as internally coherent. I have tried here to advance some considerations to make them more plausible.

212

NOTES

*   Aesthetically necessary, i.e., necessary for the purpose of the artwork.

1 Über Gegenstandstheorie, *Gesamtausgabe*, Volume II, Editor: Rudolf Haller, (Graz-Austria: Akademische Druck-u. Verlagsanstalt, 1971), pp. 481-586. Translated as 'Theory of Objects,' in *Realism and the Background of Phenomenology*, edited by Roderick Chisholm, (New York: Free Press, 1960), pp. 76-117.

2 Selbstdarstellung, *Die Philosophie der Gegenwart in Selbstdarstellung*, edited by R. Schmidt, (Leipzig: Felix Meiner Verlag, 1921), p. 12.

3 'Theory of Objects,' in *Realism and the Background of Phenomenology*, p. 83.

4 In this part of my paper I am keeping in mind the following remark by Professor J.N. Findlay: 'It is strange that many people do not know how closely Meinong's contributions to Object-theory centre in his analyses of various sorts of conscious intentions, and how he even said that what was peculiar in [his?] philosophy lay in its pervasive relation to psychology, by which he means the categorial facts of subjectivity.' 'Meinong the Phenomenologist,' in Meinong Issue, *Revue Internationale de Philosophie*, No 104-105, 1973, p. 164.

5 Perhaps the 'gap' between object theory and theory of apprehension results from Meinong's strategy of placing the question of the existential status of objects upon the objects themselves rather than upon the type of act directed toward those objects. Or, perhaps it results more from placing the question of the *Sosein* of objects on the objects themselves. Perhaps Husserl's notion of epoche could avoid the problems we have noted in Meinong's theories. On the other hand, Husserl's strategy throws the problem back upon the apprehending subject, which leaves his philosophy open to the charge of idealism or solipsism, a charge which Meinong surely would have wanted to avoid.

6 This break is marked by the publication of 'Über Gegenstände Höherer Ordnung und deren Verhältnis zur inneren Wahrnehmung,' ['Objects of Higher Order and their Relation to Inner Perception'] *Gesamtausgabe*, Volume II. I have found the question of Meinong's relation to psychology treated in great depth in David Lindenfeld's 'A. Meinong and the Reinterpretation of Positivism,' Dissertation University of Chicago, 1973.

7 Kasimir Twardowski, *Zur Lehre vom Inhalt und Gegenstand der Vorstellung*, (Vienna: Alfred Holder, 1894).

8 See *Über Annahmen, Second Edition*, (Leipzig: Barth, 1910) section 44, pp. 265-268. Cf. J.N. Findlay's treatment of this question in his *Meinong's Theory of Objects and Values, Second Edition*, (Oxford, 1963), Chapter I., especially pp. 35-41.

9 See my 'Theory of Reference and Existential Assumptions' Dissertation, Columbia University, 1975, and my paper 'The Russel-Meinong Debate'.

MEINONG'S CRITICISM OF HUSSERL'S *IDEAS*, VOL. 1

MARIE-LUISE SCHUBERT-KALSI

Meinong's critical commentary on Husserl's 1st volume of *Ideas* in its 1913 edition has not yet been published.[1] It exists in typewritten manuscript form, a few of its portions illegible.[2] The German original will be published eventually in Meinong's *Gesamtausgabe*.

Meinong was six years older than Husserl. Both were students in Vienna of Brentano's psychological analysis. The two men were friendly for a number of years until about 1902.[3] Husserl sent his writings for appreciation and criticism to Meinong, who had long been established as author and full professor in Graz, when he himself was still struggling along as *Privatdozent*. At that time, the letters between them were amicable and constructive. Their friendly relationship seems to have broken off through angry disputes over alleged plagiarisms, and over ignoring each other's works, which both claimed needed recognition.

It is important, then, to realize that Meinong wrote his comments after their friendship had ended. Meinong did not read Husserl's text sympathetically, but with harsh criticism imposed his own meaning on Husserl's terminology.

Meinong, in contrast to Husserl, remains a strict empiricist — at least as far as the foundations of his philosophical analyses are concerned. The theory of knowledge is basically experiential; psychological analysis and testing are employed. By that token, consciousness is, for Meinong, an existing entity and therefore an object of experiental knowledge. And in this manner, he understands Husserl's term 'consciousness'. Consciousness and, of course, its contents are strictly differentiated from their objects which can be of all modes of being and corresponding modes of knowledge. This is crucial for our understanding of Meinong's criticism of Husserl. And I must spend some time describing Meinong's concepts as far as they are relevant to his Husserl critique.

In his notes, Meinong proceeds as follows: he goes through Husserl's book and refers to certain pages — intending the content of the whole page, or a passage thereof, or single expressions — and goes on to analyse them with the just mentioned attitude.

In the beginning, Meinong generally discusses the discipline Phenomenology, with particular focus on 'essence' before he enters into a direct discussion of Husserl's book. (I do not deal with that general discussion.) The main points of

See notes at the end of this chapter.

his criticism considered in my paper are the vagueness of Husserl's subject matter, his idealism or solipsism, as Meinong calls it, then, in particular Husserl's treatment of consciousness and pure consciousness, the *a priori*, doubt, the General Thesis and *hyle, epoche*, and *noema*. Of course, there are a variety of other items which can not all be considered.

This paper evolved from the chapter on Meinong and Husserl in my book on Meinong containing translations of selected papers by Meinong and his critical notes on Husserl's phenomenology of the 1ste vol. of his *Ideas*[0].

There is no time to say everything I would like to say concerning Meinong, Husserl, and Brentano.[4] I must concentrate on Meinong's criticism of some aspects of Husserl's philosophy, and on the presuppositions for this criticism in Meinong's own philosophy. When two giants are disagreeing with each other, in theoretical matters, we may safely suppose that neither of them really tries to understand the other in his own terminology. And we can say with Brentano: if one theory would be translated into the language of the other differences would dwindle. As Meinong's criticism hinges on his conception of consciousness and his differentiation between content and pseudo-object some very general remarks must be made first on some aspects of Meinong's theory of presentations (or presentational experiences) and of their objects.[5] Except self-presentation, all presentation have objects other than themselves, and, in most cases, the objects are ontologically independent of the presentations. (Pseudo-objects are not ontologically independent of their presentations although different from them.) The objects either exist or subsist or have merely *aussersein*. The presentational events consist of act and content and exist when they occur. There are two main classes of presentations, emotional presentation and intellectual presentation. (Emotional presentation must here be left aside.) Intellectual presentation is either judgments or ideas. Judgments present objectives, ideas objecta, i.e. individuals, properties, classes, etc. Objecta exist, subsist or have merely *aussersein*, as e.g. the oval triangle. (Emotional presentations are of values and obligations.) Act and content, the constituents of presentations, cannot be exactly described. Contents correspond to the objects which are presented by them and do, as part of the experience, exist. The correspondent objects do not always exist, and objects of judgments never exist, but subsist or have, in some exceptional cases, *aussersein*. The act of an idea or judgment is that part of the experience which remains constant when the contents vary.[6] As part of a presenting event it also exists.

INTERNAL PERCEPTION AND PSEUDO-OBJECTS

We must now go directly to internal perception and pseudo-objects, which are most important in Meinong's criticism of Husserl, and we must deal in a summary manner. What internal perception is cannot be exactly described. Meinong indicates it by examples. It consists of two classes 1) self-presentation, i.e. immediate, simultaneous awareness of one's own experiences or psychic states such as ideas, judgments, feelings, desires, pains or pleasures. In those awarenesses no other presentation is involved but the self-presented experience itself. Examples are toothaches, headaches, judgments. In self-presentation it is primarily the experience itself which is presented, whereby the act is more accentuated than the content — not so much *of* what the experience is.[7] It is not the job of self-presentation but of the other internal perceptions to present the object of the experience. 2) It is the active taking account of what we are judging (perceiving), having ideas of, feeling or desiring.[8] Example: Take the experience 'I am perceiving a church tower.' We take account of the object of our perception or of our presenting experience and its object. The church tower part in the experience 'I am perceiving a church tower' is an idea which corresponds to an object. But what is that object? In external perception it is a church tower.[9] In internal perception it cannot be the church tower because it is outside of and not inside us. It cannot be the content of the experience presenting the church tower; for I am thinking of the church tower and not of the content which presents it, which is a psychic event and is not beige and angular. The object with which this internal perception is concerned is the old 'immanent object', the church tower in my ideas.[10] It is now called by Meinong 'pseudo-object'; it quasi 'exists' in or for our ideas but, of course, does not really exist. The idea and its content exist. The object of external perception may exist. The object of the internal perception which corresponds to the object of the external perception merely 'pseudo-exists' for ideas. There are, then, in the subject, the presenting experiences, intellectual and emotional ones, and the pseudo-existing objecta, objectives, values, and obligations which correspond directly to the content of the internal presenting experiences.[11] It seems that each conscious presenting experience, each awareness of such an experience, is an instance of internal perception. When I am comparing two numbers, when I am making the perceptual judgment of a ticking clock, am dreaming of the Gobi desert, contemplating a circular square, I am internally perceiving.[12] Pseudo-objects are internal to and completely dependent upon the experiencing subject, although essentially different from his experiences. All other objects, existing, subsisting and those of merely *aussersein* are independent of the experiencing subject. (In the last analysis it might turn out to be that all objects of merely *aussersein* are only pseudo-objects.) The presentation or internal perception of pseudo-objects certainly involves difficulties which I cannot discuss here. At times, Meinong did not feel comfortable with his pseudo-objects, but he did not succeed in eliminating them, and they prove to be a useful theoretical tool in keeping separate experiences, their contents, and what the experiences are about.[13]

MEINONG'S CONCEPT OF CONSCIOUSNESS

When Meinong speaks of Husserl's conception of consciousness he superimposes his own conception of it.[14] Meinong himself does not use the term 'consciousness' technically but instead uses 'internal perception'.[15] The concept of consciousness in any other form than his own 'internal perception' — and that includes Husserl's — and even more so the concept of pure consciousness — seems to have been neither useful nor meaningful to Meinong, as it could not be empirically limited to a certain group of mental activities. But when he used it — and he used it rarely and, then, in discussing other philosophies[16] — he equated consciousness with his own internal perception, sometimes with and sometimes without self-presentation. Another alternative given by Meinong is consciousness as the forum on which all psychic life takes place. But this alternative is not further considered by him.[17] So, consciousness is a class of experiences which exist.[18] For Meinong, the difference between consciousness and pure consciousness will amount to the following:[19] Pure consciousness is the *apriori* awareness of something which cannot be traced to or is not based on empirical data.[20] (Pure consciousness can, thus, be characterized by its special kind of objects.) Any internal perception which is not pure consciousness is consciousness *simpliciter*. And this, in short, is the manner in which Meinong understands Husserl's consciousness. Husserl's term 'reflection' is also understood by Meinong to mean internal perception without self-presentation which is immediate, non-reflective and experiential.[21] For Husserl, pure consciousness is known *apriori* or eidetically. The phenomenology of pure consciousness is criticized by Meinong.[22] For the better understanding of his criticism we must turn to Meinong's empiricism and conception of the *apriori*.

EMPIRICISM AND *A PRIORI*

We can understand Meinong's criticism of Husserl when we realize that Meinong was a strict empiricist — in epistemology. In the face of his extreme realism this may sound peculiar. But his ontological results derive from analyses of mental states and from his basic assumption that all presentation (except self-presentation) is of objects which are something other than itself or, in their being, independent of it.

All his epistemological statements are based on psychological observations. In fact, he kept a psychological laboratory at the University of Graz. Of course, we know that, even for Meinong, the theoretical analysis of presenting experiences cannot be empirical in the strictest sense because they cannot be fixated for empirical inspection. But the analysis is entirely based on experience and is testable.[23] And as experiences exist when they occur, some judgments concerning them must be empirical (e.g. self-presentation). Meinong is so sensitive to Husserl's *a priori* treatment of consciousness because consciousness is for him a matter of experimental verification.[24] For example, he states that the question whether there are unconscious sensations (*unbewusst*) is an empirical one and not one which is answered by deduction from the definition of sensation or of consciousness.[25] Likewise, 'there is memory' and 'there is judgment' etc. are statements of existence and, thus, empirical. We see that his basic position is quite opposite to Husserl's. As I first said, however, the reflection upon presenting experience is certainly *a priori*, even for Meinong, but he is very critical of Husserl's standpoint concerning the *a priori* or the eidetic in these matters, as we shall see.

Now, we must turn, at least briefly, to Meinong's conception of the *a priori* before we concern ourselves with his criticism of Husserl's *a priori* proceedings. Meinong equates Husserl's term 'eidetic' with 'a priori'.[27] Roughly speaking, *a priori* (and thus eidetic) are, for Meinong, presentations of objectives about objects which do not exist, or about certain properties of or relationships between objects which may exist or do not exist (as, e.g. founded objects of higher order such as some complexes like melodies.) *A priori* is the opposite of empirical.[28] All objects which subsist and also those which have merely *aussersein* are existence-free. *A priori* is a charateristic of the presentations of certain objectives. The *a priori*, for Meinong, is either based on the empirical or is purely *a priori*.[29] The *a priori* reflection on experiences which become pseudo-objects in or for that reflection is based on the empirical judgments that there are those experiences. Pegasus is non-existing and an object of *a priori* judgments (except in philological accounts), but the conception of Pegasus is based on external perception. Melody, the subsisting object of higher order is based on existing sounds.[30] The recognition of a melody is *a priori*. Judgments of similarity or dissimilarity of existing objects are *a priori*, in the same way. The same holds of esthetic and ethical values. *A priori* considerations of numbers or logical principles are purely *a priori*. Those concepts are not based on experience, or, numbers and logical principles are not ontologically based on existing objects. (They are the objects of pure consciousness.)

Meinong uses the *a priori*, which is based on experience, in some of his criticisms of Husserl, especially of his phenomenology of pure consciousness.[31] It has been mentioned already that consciousness itself (not its objects) cannot be entirely treated in an *a priori* manner as it is subject matter of experiential and experimental psychology. Meinong does not mean reflection on one's own experiences, which is an empirical *a priori*, but laboratory investigations. In respect to the characterization of consciousness itself, any *a priori* which is not relevant to actually existing psychic experience is pointless. So the empirical basis is important, as e.g. the above mentioned existential judgments. If any given objectives and their corresponding judgments are studied (as pseudo-objects) experience is involved or pre-supposed.

Husserl claims, says Meinong, that the phenomenology of consciousness is *a priori*. We must keep in mind Meinong's understanding of consciousness which he superimposes over Husserl's. Now, Meinong's objections against a purely *a priori* treatment of consciousness, or rather pure consciousness, are more practical than philosophical. The criterion is relevance. The objections run as follows: experiences which are presented in reflection, i.e. internal perception, are apprehended as pseudo-objects.[32] Pseudo-objects are existence-free.[33] For example, if I internally perceive a certain house (no matter if it exists or not)[34] then all judgments concerning the internally perceived house are *a priori*. For it is a pseudo-object. The same also holds of experiences, justice, triangles, Pegasus, and the circular square when they are internally perceived. In internal perception, all these things pseudo-exist. Pseudo-existing objects may correspond to objects of all kinds of being: in our case, 1) justice, triangles, Pegasus subsist, 2) experiences and houses exist, 3) circular squares (and certain future judgements) have merely *aussersein.*[35] The difference between the three groups of objects, is, for Meinong, that the objects of groups 1) and 2) are worth investigating but circular squares are not.[36] Thinking about the objects of 1) and 2) serves the cognition of reality. Thought about circular squares is idle. The objects in 1) and 2) follow logical principles or are based on external perception or self-presentation. None of that holds for circular square.

If phenomenology is to be taken to be a theory of knowledge, the foregoing is important. For Meinong, the reflection upon experiences is *a priori.*[37] But the underlying empirical judgments that such experiences exist is most essential.[38] They are the empirical basis which make the otherwise *a priori* theory of knowledge relevant. But for Husserl, and by definition, empirical judgments do not belong to pure consciousness and have no connection with it. By its utter disconnection with reality the phenomenology of pure consciousness defeats itself,[39] according to Meinong.

ON HUSSERL'S IDEALISM

Husserl's idealism has already drawn much criticism, as early as Meinong's notes on his 1st vol. of *Ideas...* and does not require a long discussion.[40] According to Meinong, Husserl's philosophy is not only idealistic but even solipsistic. Existence is dependent upon the possibility of being perceived.[41] From the standpoint of one's own consciousness there is only one constituting consciousness.[42] Meinong himself could not quite escape idealism in respect to existing objects, which becomes evident in his theory of pseudo-objects and then also in his own remarks about the evidence of the existence and characteristics of the external world.[43] But these remarks were meant by Meinong to be an admission of our mental limitations only. Empiricism remains for him the backbone and basis of philosophy. In respect to the investigation of presentational experiences he maintains a strictly empirical approach which applies to the alter and the ego alike.

THE SUBJECT MATTER OF PHENOMENOLOGY

More interesting than the idealism reproach is Meinong's probing into the general subject matter of Husserl's phenomenology.[44] After reading Husserl, Meinong decided that Husserl's claim of having found a new philosophy amounted merely to his doing what traditionally had been done.[45] It is not easy to get a general picture of Meinong's criticism of Husserl as we have only the short commenting notes to the first volume of *Ideas*... Meinong, of course, interprets Husserl in terms of his own vocabulary. It is very clear that the two men did not properly communicate with each other during the period of their mutual hostile criticism. Meinong's almost aristotelian shorthand-kind of notes must be interpreted on the grounds of what we know about his philosophy.

Meinong believes that it is never quite clear what precisely constitutes the subject-matter of Husserl's philosophy, especially in the face of alleged incompatible standpoints assumed by Husserl.[46] It could be a theory of objects, a theory of knowledge, or both, empirical and/or a priori. (p. 17f, 53f) (The theory of objects, for Meinong, is *a priori*, even though not entirely 'purely *a priori*'.) Either possibility seems to have implications for Meinong which show it to be self-contradictory.[47] At any rate, Meinong claims that Husserl's statements are wide open for interpretation, and he seized the opportunity.

We remember that Meinong does not consistently make a distinction between consciousness and pure consciousness, as the separation meant as little to him as did consciousness itself. Furthermore, anything which is consciousness, pure or simple, is an experience consisting of act and content which exist while they occur. Anything about which consciousness is, is something other than it (except in self-presentation) lying outside it, and is either an object independent of it or a pseudo-object. Let us take an example, Husserl's essence.[48] (I realize that 'essence' is one of the most complicated concepts in Husserl's phenomenology and Meinong treats it accordingly. Meinong's discussions of it deserve a special paper. But it belongs to his discussion of the subject matter of phenomenology and, in a simplified form, it can serve well as an example.) Essence, then, belongs to consciousness (p. 18). For Meinong it either is an existing part of an experience or an object outside experience. Since for Husserl essences do not exist (p. 12f) and are cognized a priori they must, according to Meinong, lie outside consciousness and are not what Husserl intends them to be. For Meinong, then, they are immanent objects, i.e. pseudo-objects which, as we know, are the objects of internal perception or consciousness, in Meinong's sense; and Husserl missed that point.[49] If phenomenology is at least partially concerned with pseudo-objects the question must be raised as to which kinds – if any– of independent objects (and to which modes of presentation) the pseudo-objects correspond. Thus, Meinong leads Husserl straight to the theory of objects, which includes everything thinkable, and is too wide a field; it does not seem to him to be Husserl's subject matter.

If phenomenology is not a theory of objects, Meinong asks, what, then, is it? If it is not the objects of consciousness it must be consciousness itself, pure or plain.[50] This is internal perception with or without self-presentation. Meinong knows, of course, that, in the case of pure consciousness, Husserl is not concerned with experiences which can be experimentally tested.[51] But as experiences they do exist, for Meinong, and should, in principle, be accessible to experimental investigation. And any thought about them is at least rooted in experience. This is Husserl's dilemma. Meinong explains the dilemma with reference to Husserl's failing to distinguish properly between content and object.[52] Objects of consciousness lie outside it, even though they may depend on it as do pseudo-objects. They naturally may correspond to any of the three classes of being. Thus they do not belong to phenomenology, in Husserl's sense. But Husserl, says Meinong, does deal with such objects, even with objects of experience which are 'expressly included in Phenomenology',[53] and he thus contradicts himself.

GENERAL THESIS AND EPOCHE

Meinong devotes only little space to his criticism of Husserl's epoche.[54] He points out that, supposedly, for any epoche to occur at all, the general thesis must be presupposed. According to Meinong, the general thesis can be expressed as follows: 'the world as reality is always there'. The thesis is a *'Setzung'*, a basic general hypothesis which perceptions and other judgements have in common insofar as they are existential. (As we know, for Meinong, all perceptions are judgments of existence.)

Husserl's epoche, says Meinong, applies to the thesis.[55] For Meinong, Husserl's epoche is nothing but an ordinary leaving out of consideration, or leaving unjudged, or some such thing. (He repeatedly bemoans Husserl's unclear language.) That is, the epoche foregoes the general thesis and leaves out the existence of the objects to be considered. This is a preparation for an eidetic, i.e. *a priori* thought process.[56]

Meinong's attack, in general, proceeds as follows:[57] 1) In all eidetic, i.e. *a priori* deliberations 'facticity' disappears anyway. What is the use of the epoche? 2) Husserl expressly states that 'analysis of essences' in (*am*) consciousness takes place without epoche. If that is so, Meinong asks, what is the use of the epoche in phenomenology?[58]

Let us return to 1): Meinong states:[59] epoche can only be applied where eidetic considerations are concerned with the perceived or that which is believed to exist. If the judgment of existence is suspended so is necessarily the perceptive experience. I can reflect upon, that is, internally perceive, the object of my original perception. Then, the object becomes a pseudo-object which, of course, does not exist. Considerations of pseudo-objects are *a priori*. Moreover, the mere entertaining of the previous object of perception neglects its existence. This, then, is that in which Husserl's epoche or the elimination of the general thesis consists, as Meinong sees it.

Let us return to 2). On page 220 Meinong goes on to say: Why should the general thesis be eliminated in respect to objects in connection with which it has never been there, in the first place, as e.g. subsistences? The same holds for objects of merely *aussersein*. Subsisting objects are never externally perceived as they do not exist. The epoche as elimination of the general thesis does not apply to them. Usually, Meinong says,[60] the epoche is not necessary or even useful, as Husserl himself shows by 'eidetic considerations which expressly precede the epoche'.

DOUBT

Husserl compares his own thoughts with the Cartesian doubt. Meinong calls the Cartesian doubt 'an utterly artificial background for the epoche'.[61] Moreover, a comparison between the two does not hold up. Meinong's interpretation of Descartes' doubt goes as follows: it consists in the suspension of judgments or leads to the suspension of judgments (judgments, of course, are to be understood as psychic, presentational happenings). In most cases, the suspension takes place or can take place because there are reasons against the factuality of the objectives which are presented or because the judgment in question is judged to be false or unproven. Sometimes the suspension can occur at will. When a judgment is suspended, the objective can be presented by an assumption which differs from the judgment by its lack of emphasis. It is a mere entertaining of the objectives. Descartes' doubt, according to Meinong, is the attempt at a suspension of all those judgments which a certain person is actually able to suspend. It depends upon a particular person, and Husserl would not admit that concerning his own epoche.

According to Meinong, Husserl claims that there is a doubting process which leaves the judgment intact. However, that is nowhere found in experience, i.e. internal perception. For if the factuality of an objective is doubted it is automatically not judged by the doubting person. It is, then, only assumed, entertained.

HYLE AND NOEMA

About Husserl's Hyle, Meinong has the following to say:[62] 1) Husserl characterizes Hyle in the manner in which Meinong characterizes his own content. 2) Husserl identifies it with Brentano's physical phenomenon. Ad 1): as content it is part of an experience, it exists and is an object of (internal) perception, in self presentation. Ad 2): as Brentano's physical phenomenon Hyle would be a pseudo-object lying outside consciousness although dependent on it.[63] Both standpoints contradict each other. Meinong attributes this also to Husserl's failure to properly distinguish between object and experience, or, more specifically, between pseudo-object and content. The same holds of noema which is, according to my understanding of Husserl, closest to Meinong's pseudo-object. Meinong says that the noema concept deals with pure objects and not with consciousness itself.[64] Thus, it is not a content but a presented object (either one of higher order or a pseudo-object) and consequently belongs to the theory of objects. According to Meinong, Husserl treats it explicitly as part of experiences, but that implicitly he does not, because it does not belong to experiences.

In conclusion, we must keep in mind that, in contrast to Husserl, consciousness, for Meinong, i.e. internal perception, is an experience containing content, and its object is a pseudo-object. According to Meinong, Husserl's content must also take on the role of object. Hence the confusion. It is in this differentiation where Meinong' accusation originates that Husserl intentionally or unintentionally includes the theory of objects in his phenomenology. And the key lies in Meinong's separation of presenting experiences (act plus content) from presented objects, especially — for his Husserl critique — pseudo-objects which are ontologically and definitely different from content.

NOTES

0   M.-L. Schubert-Kalsi, *Alexius Meinong On Objects of Higher Order and Husserl's Phenomenology.*

1   Max Niemeyer, Halle, Germany 1913, 1922, 1928.

2   I thank Prof. R. Haller of Graz for his help in deciphering those portions.

3   For this, the following, and preceeding comp. *Philosophenbriefe* pp. 94-110.

4   J.N. Findlay, Meinong's theory of Objects, *Philosophenbriefe,* On Em. Pres., Kalsi's *A. Meinong On Objects of Higher Order and Husserl's Phenomenology.*

5   Em. Pres. XXXiii to LI.

6   Em. Pres. 50 ff.

7   Em. Pres. 8, Ges. Abh. 11 411ff, Ann. 11 138, 264.

8   Ges. Abg., 11 403ff.

9   Ges. Abh., 403ff.

10   Ges. Abh., 11 382, 403ff.

11   Comp. Ges. Abh., 11 407.

12   Ges. Abh., 1 313, Ges. Abh., 11 435.

13   Über die Erfahrungsgrundlagen unseres Wissens, Kalsi ms pseudo-objects.

14   Kalsi, *Alexius Meinong on Objects of Higher Order and Husserl's Phenomenology,* 230.

15   Comp. Kalsi, *Alexius Meinong* ... 229 and 24ff, 32ff.

16   Ann. 11 236f n. 4.

17   Ges. Abh. 11 180f., Kalsi 234. Ges. Abh. 1 135, 181.

18   Kalsi 230, 237, 212, comp. 224, 228ff, 233, 237.

19   Kalsi 211f, comp. 228ff.

20   Kalsi, p. 24-36, 212, 228, Ges. Abh. 11, 154ff. Numerous references in 'Üb. Moglkt. u. Wahrschlkt.' 233f, 237, 240, 238ff. etc.

21   Ges. Abh. 1 135, Kalsi 24, 228, 237f.

22   Kalsi, Introduction, 212, 214, 222f, 230ff.

23   Ges. Abh. 11 411f, Em. Pres.: Self-present., Ann. 11 138ff 264ff.

24   Kalsi 211, 228f, 231f, 237, 239, Ges. Abh. 11 414ff, Ges. Abh. 1 179.

25   Kalsi 234f, 237f, 239f.

26   Kalsi 211f.

27   Kalsi 214.

28   Kalsi 211, 230f, 238, Ges. Abh. 11 154-157. 520, Ann. 11 77, 193. Möglk. & Wahrsch. References.

29   Em. Pres. chp. 13, p. 149f, Ges. Abh. 11 399ff, Kalsi 216, 234f, 239.

30   Kalsi pp. 11-36, 235.

31   Kalsi 212, 234.

32   M. on H. 212, 237.

33   Kalsi 212, 24, 26.

34   Comp. Kalsi 212, 234f.

35   Kalsi 234f.

36   Kalsi 211f.

37   Kalsi 211f, 216f (but comp. 239, 234f.

38   Kalsi 234f, comp. 211f.

39   Kalsi 212f, 223f, (218) 228 (230f), 231f.

40   Kalsi 216f, 225f, 227, 232f.

41   Kalsi 225f, 229.

42   Kalsi 232f.

43   Em. Pres. 103, Erfahrungsgrundlagen, Ges. Aus., V 467, Kalsi 226: It is 'thinkable' that behind the intuitive (*anschaulich*) world there is no physical world. This may hold for 'logical possibility' but not for empirical possibility.

44   Kalsi 231f, 211f, 218f, 230f, 233f, 234f.

45 Kalsi 212, 226f, 230, 236, 241f.
46 Kalsi 211f, 223, 232f.
47 Kalsi 211, 232f.
48 Kalsi 214ff, 218f, 231.
49 Kalsi 211f, 216f, 29, 222f, 229 (for whole paragraph).
50 Kalsi 218f.
51 Kalsi 212, 225, 229 and above.
52 Kalsi 236f, 240f.
53 Kalsi 211.
54 Kalsi 218f, 220f, 236f.
55 Kalsi 218.
56 Kalsi 221.
57 Kalsi 219f, 222f.
58 Kalsi 220.
59 Kalsi 220.
60 Kalsi 220f.
61 Kalsi 219f, 247.
62 Kalsi 239-241.
63 Brentano (McAlister) 35, 61, 70, 77ff, 400ff.
64 Kalsi 240ff.

BIBLIOGRAPHY

HUSSERL :

1) Berger, Gaston: *The Cogito in Husserl's Philosophy*, translated by Kathleen MacLaughlin. With an Introduction by James M. Edie. Northwestern University Press 1972.

2) Brentano, Franz: *Psychology from an Empirical Standpoint*, edited by Linda McAlister, New York, Humanities Press '73.

3) Eley, Lothar: *Die Krise des Apriori in der transzendentalen Phänomenologie E. Husserls*. Martinus Nijhoff, Den Haag 1962.

4) Findlay, J.N.: 'Husserl's Analysis of the Inner Time Consciousness,' The Monist Vol. 59 No. 1 1975.

5) Husserl, Edmund: *Ideen zu einer reinen Phänomenologie*. Gesammelte Werke Vols. 3-5 Martinus Nijhoff, The Hague, 1950.

6) Kockelmans, Joseph J. ed.: *Phenomenology. The Philosophy of Edmund Husserl and its Interpretation*. Doubleday and Co. Garden City, New York 1967.

7) Levin, David Michael: *Reason and Evidence in Husserl's Phenomenology*. Northwestern University Press 1970.

8) Salomon, Robert C. ed.: *Phenomenology and Existentialism*. Harper and Row, New York 1972.

SELECTED BIBLIOGRAPHY

MEINONG

Meinong, Alexius, *Gesammelte Abhandlungen*, Leipzig 1929, volumes I and II. (Contained in vol's I and II of Gesamtausgabe.)
Gesamtausgabe, volumes I through VI, Akademische Druck und Verlageanstalt, Graz, Austria, 1972:
The following titles from *Gesamtausgabe* were used:

vol. I 'Hume-Studien I: Zur Geschichte und Kritik des modernen Nominalismus', 1877
'Zur Psychologie der Komplexienen und Relationen,' 1891
'Über Begriff und Eigenschaft der Empfindung,' 1888
'Beiträge zur Theorie der psychischen Analyse,' 1894
'Abstrahieren und Vergleichen,' 1900
'Über Urteilsgefühle, was sie sind und was sie nicht sind,' 1905

vol. II: 'Hume-Studien II: Zur Relationentheorie', 1882
'Über Gegenstände höherer Ordnung und ihr Verhältnis zur inneren Wahrnehmung,' 1899
'Über Gegenstandstheorie', 1904
'Zur erkenntnistheoretischen Würdigung des Gedächtnisses', 1886.

vol. III. 'Über emotionale Präsentation', 1917

vol. IV. *Über Annahmen* II (2nd. ed. 1910)

vol. V. 'Über die Stellung der Gegenstandstheorie im System der Wissenschaften', 1907
'Über die Erfahrungsgrundlagen unseres Wissens', 1906

vol. VI, *Über Möglichkeit und Wahrscheinlichkeit*, 1915

Meinong, Alexius: On Emotional Presentation, translated with an Introduction by Marie-Luise Schubert-Kalsi, Northwestern University Press 1972.
Chisholm, Roderick M.: *Realism and the Background of Phenomenology*, Glencoe, 111. 1961.
Chisholm, Roderick M. 'Meinong's Homeless Objects,' *Revue Internationale de Philosophie*, 1973
Eaton, H.O. *Austrian Philosophy of Values*, Univ. of Oklahoma Press 1930.

Findlay, J.N. *Meinong's Theory of Objects and Values*, 2nd ed. Oxford 1963.

Hicks, J. Dawes, 'The Philosophical Researches of Meinong,' *Mind*, 1922.

Kalsi, Marie-Luise Schubert, *Alexius Meinong: On Objects of Higher Order and Husserl's phenomenology*, Martinus Nijhoff, The Hague, 1978.

Kindinger, Rudolf ed. *Philosophenbriefe*, Graz, 1964.

Russell, Bertrand: 'Meinong's Theory of Complexes and Assumptions', *Mind*, vii, 1904.

MEINONG ON POSSIBILITIES AND IMPOSSIBILITIES *

RICHARD DYCHE

Most of the more interesting and influential criticisms of Meinong, beginning with Russell's, have assumed that Meinong's possible and impossible objects are individuals. They are like the trees, birds, people, and butterflies of the world in which we live, except that they are incomplete and are not in space and time. That they are incomplete, for Meinong, is easily and uncontroversially verifiable and this will not be discussed. The matter of individuality is a wholly different kettle of round-squares and needs serious attention. This is so because of Meinong's defenders, as well as his critics. Namely, recent as well as classic defenses of Meinong (see below) have assumed and stated what Russell (so far as I know) merely and crucially assumed. This is, namely, that Meinong's irrealia are individuals. This is nowhere shown by reference to Meinong texts. This is, also, curious, since Meinong is just the kind of philosopher who would typically be concerned with such a question. That is, Meinong is just the very paradigm of the philosopher who would – on his own initiative – ask for the ontological assay of these entities. Granted, he says such things as that the golden mountain is golden. It has, however, also to be granted that Meinong does not explicitly raise the question of the functional mode of copulation in such cases – at least not in the seminal 'The Theory of Objects' manifesto. But he did write other pieces, after all, and they are not so nearly polemical as is *Über die Stellung der Gegenstandstheorie im System der Wissenschaften*. They are, rather, constructive and analytical in nature. Among these is a book on possibility and probability, *Über Möglichkeit und Wahrscheinlichkeit*, in which he addresses the question of these very entities and in which he makes reference to all the earlier pieces relevant to 'Gegenstandstheorie' as though his position in the former is quite consistent with all of the latter. The task before us is straightforward. It is to raise the question of the putative individuality of irrealia, according to Meinong, by looking at some (to my mind) crucial passages of the book on possibility and probability.

The way into this chamber of Meinong's very beautiful edifice is to notice that entities such as the golden mountain and the round square are seen by him to be, respectively, possible and impossible objects. Noticing, further, that in the work on possibility and probability he holds that possibility and impossibility, in a sense, both reside with incomplete objects, it becomes clear that a reso-

See notes at the end of this chapter.

lution of our puzzlement over the character of the round square, Medusa, and such putative entities may be found in the discussions in *Über Möglichkeit und Wahrscheinlichkeit* of such incomplete objects. Irrealia fall within the class of objects described as being incomplete. It needs to be asked whether these incomplete objects are, in any sense, individuals. If it should turn out to be the case that they are not individuals, then it must be asked what kind of objects they are.

It is my view that for Meinong they are not individuals. They are *not* individuals of any sort at all, if by 'individual' one means, following Aristotle, 'individual substance', that is 'that of which predications may be made but which may not be predicated of anything else'. They are not individuals, whether complete or incomplete. Hence Meinong is not committed to the thesis that there are possible and impossible individuals, even though he is convinced that there are *de re* possibilities and impossibilities. Indeed, what he says is that there are possible and impossible *objects*. In his theory the class of objects is not coextensive with the class of individuals. The former includes the latter while the latter is not coextensive with the former. Further, the class of incomplete objects (which embraces all the irrealia of which Meinong speaks) not only is not coextensive with but also falls wholly outside the class of individuals. Once it is seen that Meinong views the class of individuals and the class of incomplete objects as two mutually exclusive subsets of the domain of objects, then it may be possible to find Meinong's theory to have spawned a less forbidding sort of Medusa than has commonly been thought to be the case, though his theory will still, no doubt, offend against the sensibilities of any philosopher of strong nominalistic proclivities.

The evidence that Meinong systematically distinguished between individuals and incomplete (that is, possible and impossible) objects is surprisingly straightforward. It begins in the *Erfahrungsgrundlagen unseres Wissens* and becomes most explicit in *Über Möglichkeit und Wahrscheinlichkeit*. Here it appears that Meinong tends to think of them as properties or complexes of (or complex) properties, that is, as that kind of universal. And in general my impression is that Meinong's whole metaphysics is a metaphysics of properties and states of affairs. That is, while individuals are not properties, they are functions of properties.[1] Thus, apart from individuals, there are only properties and states of affairs — all this being contingent, of course, on the possibility that it can be argued that incomplete objects are properties and complications of properties. So, it must be seen what evidence can be found for this.

First, what is the justification for my use of the term 'individual' in speaking of this metaphysics? My view is that if there is any room in Meinong's theory for individuals at all, then room for such entities is going to be found in the domain of what he calls objects of perception (*Wahrnehmungsobjekte*). In the discussion of these latter in *Über die Erfahrungsgrundlagen uñseres Wissens*,[2] the term 'Ding' is introduced for such objects. In all his discussions of irrealia with which I am familiar, he does not refer to irrealia as Dinge. Now, in common German usage, 'Objekt' and 'Ding' are loosely interchangeable terms. Nonetheless he does not refer to irrealia as Dinge but only as Objekte while he consistently uses the term Ding for objects of perceptions. Of course, he also calls the latter Objekte but, then, that term is simply a term for anything what-so-ever that can be a target of our mental activities. One can think of Meinong's use of the term as deriving from its use in the phrase 'objects of thought'. Meinong's theory of objects is the study of all the possible objects of our mental activities; and clearly both the activities and the targets of these activities may be of various differing sorts. So, what is interesting is not that he sometimes speaks of objects of perception as objects, but that he so regularly speaks of them as Dinge and so consistently fails to call irrealia by that same name. He seems to reserve the term Ding for a specific technical usage — that is, it seems to be reserved for what we have called individuals. So far, there is the claim that Meinong does not use the word Ding with reference to a possible or impossible object. Is there any more direct evidence that he has a concept of an individual which does not include or comprehend the class of irrealia?

In *Über Möglichkeit und Wahrscheinlichkeit* he explicitly uses the term individual (his term is Individuum) and does so in a manner consistent with my suggestion above. Furthermore, it becomes contextually clear that Individua and Dinge are the same entities. We will cite heavily from the text, since this is a controversial point.

Pages 168 through 169 of the text introduce the term Ding once again and oppose Dinge der Wirklichkeit to incomplete objects by way of the completeness of the former. In the next section, 'Seins- und Soseinsmeinen', p. 190 bottom, Meinong moves from speaking of Individuen to speaking of a Ding which one sees, in such a manner as to leave no doubt that Dinge, or objects of perception, fall into the class of individuals. His concern in this passage is the way in which assumptions of or explicit indications of complete determinateness enter our speech and our thoughts of complete objects (i.e. of individuals, which is to say, also, of Dinge der Wahrnehmung). Thus Dinge (objects of perception) are individuals and fall outside the class of incomplete objects. I should want to claim that it is difficult to read the sections of *Über Möglichkeit und Wahrscheinlichkeit* on incomplete objects, Seins- und Soseinsmeinen, and on analytic and synthetic judgements without sensing the association of and interchangeability of the terms Ding and Individuum. That much seems to me, at least, to be fairly clear. But might not objects of perception be only a subclass of individuals, leaving it open that incomplete objects could be individuals of a uniquely incomplete kind? That is, indeed, the usual reading of the theory under consideration. Nonetheless there seems to me to be some reasonably firm evidence to the contrary. I think there is evidence to the effect that either all individuals are actual (he sometimes says Dinge der Wirklichkeit) inhabitants of space and time and are actual and possible objects of perception, or at least, that if there are individuals which are not objects of perception, nonetheless incomplete objects (hence, irrealia) are not to be numbered among them. Where is such evidence to be found?

Properties or complex properties are not individuals. At least, as we have explicated 'individual' and, I think, in most nonnominalistic metaphysical theories, they are not thought of as being individuals. And, clearly, the discussion of the structure of individuals and their relation to properties as presented in the *Erfahrungsgrundlagen* makes clear that Meinong also did not think of them in that manner.[3] I wish to present some indications that Meinong either explicitly thought of the objects in question as being properties or that, at a bare minimum, he, consciously or not, tended to think of them in that manner.

There is, first, a systematic consideration having to do with the internal logic of this metaphysics. Meinong has an analysis of the constitution of the individuals collectively inhabiting the cross section of reality we are immediately confronted with in sensory perception. The result of that analysis is that it is just precisely through the instantiation of properties that individuals emerge in the world. Further, he comments that if, indeed, one were to think away the properties, there would be nothing left of the individual. Of course, he does hasten to add that this does not show that the individual is identical with its properties. This, however, is connected with his notion that instantiation is coinstantiation and coinstantiation is the emergence of a higher unity of properties (instances of properties) or of some kind of unanalysable unifying configuration of (instances of) properties. Obviously, if the properties are removed that higher unity likewise disappears. One could not remove all the properties of a thing only to come upon the propertyless unity or configuration begging for more properties like a derelict begging for coins. To remove the properties would also be to remove the unifying configuration or higher unity of those properties which had been the individual. It is in this sense that my earlier remark to the effect that this theory views individuals as functions of properties is to be understood. But now, we are driven to notice that in *Über Möglichkeit und Wahrscheinlichkeit* Meinong speaks of individuals as constituted by the 'implektieren' of incomplete objects in the former. Now I see no reason not to think that 'implektieren' comes to the same thing as 'substantializieren' except, perhaps, as it may emphasize some differential aspect of that *same* relation or nexus not brought out by the term 'substantializieren'. In this case it may not be mistaken to regard these as two names for what usually passes as instantiation. 'Implektiert' has been translated by Grossmann as 'embedded', but this will not do since one thing embedded in another is by virtue of the embedding a part of that in which it is embedded. Meinong denies that the incomplete object is itself a part of the complete object in which it is 'implektiert'[4]. Further, Meinong makes precisely the same point about the relation between properties and the substances they constitute through instantiation[5]. The instantiation of properties constitutes the individual (Erfahrungsgrundlagen) and hence it seems structurally correct to think that incomplete objects form complete objects (individuals) by being instantiated, in which case they need be thought of as property-like. Suppose incomplete objects are incomplete individual substances. Then it seems that they might in some sense indeed be parts of, or at least in, the concreta they constitute, which is just what is denied. It seems natural, in the context of Meinong's remarks, to make the assimilation of irrealia to properties, complex and simple. If this assimilation is not made, then at least two problems arise. First, if 'implektieren' and 'substantialieren' are not terms for (perhaps different aspects of) the same function, then what is the relation between the two different functions for which they individually stand? Second, and this is perhaps just the same as the first, if incomplete objects are not properties or complications of properties, then what is the relation between the claim that individuals are just functions of properties and the claim that individuals are constituted of implektiert incomplete objects? Lastly, through the relevant parts of the work on possibility, Meinong often refers to the *Erfahrungsgrundlagen unseres Wissens* in such a way as to imply that he has the details of that work very well held in memory and, also, in such a manner as to imply that he personally, at least, sees no conflict of any basic kind between the doctrines of the two works.

Of course, one might attempt to argue that Meinong, in fact, went through a change between the two works in question and that, willy nilly, he is mistaken about this matter. In this he is no more and no less fallible than any other author is about the meaning of what he has written.

This, however, may not do, by reason of a number of passages in the work on possibility, which seem to indicate that Meinong is perfectly correct in so viewing the relation between the doctrines in the two works. At this point it would be good to turn from the purely systematic considerations of the discussion above to the text of *Über Möglichkeit und Wahrscheinlichkeit.*

In the section Über Möglichkeit und Wahrscheinlichkeit in which he works out the notion of incomplete object, he says,

> ... there can be no object (Gegenstand) of which it would not be correct to say, regarding *any* specific individual with which we may be concerned, whether in the sense of that individual's what-being or in the sense of that individual's how-being, that it (Gegenstand) belongs to or does not belong to that individual. That is, quite simply, the meaning of the principle of the excluded middle. The same holds of attributes or conditions ...[6]

Meinong clearly is interested in a perfectly general characterization of incomplete objects and is saying something about the class of individuals on the one hand, and a relation they bear to all the other objects there are. Namely, for each and every individual it is the case that each and every nonindividual object either belongs to or does not belong to that individual in question. Now clearly, 'belong to' is used somewhat metaphorically and is to be understood somewhat loosely. He goes on to say that this is equally the case with properties and conditions. This appears to be an exhaustive division of all objects that are not individuals into the class of attributes on the one hand and the class of conditions on the other hand.

He has begun this argument saying that each and every non-individual object either does or does not belong to any given individual, and has proceeded to what is difficult to understand as anything other than a division of all objects which are not concrete individuals (later in the same passage he speaks of the Konkretum rather than of the Ding) into two classes, namely, attributes on the one hand and conditions on the other. Now it is true that 'The same holds of attributes or conditions' is susceptible, perhaps, to more than one reading. One might say that it could be asserting that what has been claimed true of a certain sort of entity also is true of attributes and conditions. For this reading to go through, however, there needs to be some appropriate contextual indication which I fail to find in the text at that point. Contextually viewed, the point seems to me to be that all objects other than Dinge are attributes or conditions and that the same holds for any attribute as well as for any condition, namely, that it (attribute or condition) belongs to or does not belong to any given individual with which one might be concerned. This seems to me to be almost conclusive. My suggestion is that 'belongs to' be taken to come to the same as 'is instantiated in' in the case of properties and 'obtains of' in the case of conditions or objectives. The class of incomplete objects is, it seems, coextensive with the class of properties, leaving an additional class of non-individuals, namely, the class of conditions, e.g. objectives.

It is, perhaps, of some relevance to notice that other things which Meinong says, in the same section, commit him in just this manner as well. This may be approached by way of some remarks made by Professor Findlay about Meinong and about the question of universals quite in general. In discussing Meinong's incomplete objects, Professor Findlay has argued that there is a fundamental ambiguity in the term 'universal'.

> Sometimes we mean by 'universal' objects such as 'man' or 'triangle', i.e. incompletely determined objects, and sometimes such entities as qualities and relations, e.g. humanity or triangularity ... Now it is clear that there is an unbridgeable gulf between an object such as 'man' in abstracto and the complex of properties called 'humanity' ... There are indeterminate characteristics, relations and objectives, and there are indeterminate objects which, if they were fully determined, would be concrete things ... The object 'man' is an indeterminate object belonging to the same category as do concrete things. If the phrase were not strange and apparently contradictory, we might call it an indeterminate concretum.[7]

Just prior to this set of fascinating remarks, Professor Findlay has connected such incomplete things with the genera and species of Aristotle. It is argued that Aristotle did not mean them to be classes, but thought of them 'in intension', e.g. as indeterminate individuals. These serve as a nucleus from which complete concrete entities are formed by the addition of accidents or determinations.

One hesitates to argue with Professor Findlay on matters of Meinong interpretation. With all due respect, I find it necessary to do precisely that. The points just mentioned are not made by Professor Findlay on the basis of Mei-

235

nong texts; he nowhere cites the text in this connection. Rather, these points seem to be Meinongean points advanced by Professor Findlay quite independently of Meinong himself. One has intimations of the influence of Russell's own undocumented view of Meinong at play in Findlay's discussion. Neither Russell nor Findlay provide textual exegetical evidence on this head. Although it is true that later in *Über Möglichkeit und Wahrscheinlichkeit* Meinong does mention genera and species, he does nothing to indicate that he views them as indeterminate concrete entities. Nor does he do anything to distinguish them from complications of properties. And it does not seem clear that one could not explicate genera and species in terms of properties. Beyond this, in the earlier section on the nature of incomplete objects, it seems to me that I find Meinong speaking in a manner that supports my interpretation. We can lead the way back to the relevant text, perhaps, by way of some systematic remarks on the passage from Professor Findlay.

Surely, if 'man' does not stand for a, perhaps complex, property while 'humanity' does, then 'something blue' does not stand for a, perhaps complex, property while 'blue' does. That is, if 'man' stands for an indeterminate concretum and 'humanity' for a complex property, then 'something blue' should stand for something like an indeterminate concretum while 'blue' stands for a property. Yet the way Meinong's first extended analysis of an example of an incomplete object proceeds, one gets the distinct impression that Meinong does not really distinguish carefully between something blue and the property blue. It is to be noted that Meinong himself, does not seem explicitly anxious to insist on the distinction between sorts of universals to which Professor Findlay alludes, which itself is interesting, given Meinong's penchant for explicating just such specific differences between members of the class of Objects generally. The first example of an incomplete entity with which he deals is that of something blue. This discussion follows immediately upon the argument we examined above, to the effect that all non-individuals, all objects that are not concreta, are either properties or conditions.

In what sense, Meinong asks, is the object of thought 'something blue' determined, when we think of 'something blue' in the abstract. What determinations make up this entity? Or, of what properties must we think when we consider to what this entity comes? His discussion of this question runs through *Über Möglichkeit und Wahrscheinlichkeit*, pages 170-171, and is taken up again in the second half of page 172. His discussion of the sense in which this object is incomplete does not concern us. For present purposes, it should be sufficient to point out that having said he was interested in 'something blue', he slips into asking whether 'blue' either is or has extension, and then raises the general question about the relation between color and extension. Following this, still on page 170, he speaks again of 'something blue'. On page 171 top, he asks whether, granted that 'etwas blaues' in the abstract does not have extension, it, nonetheless, may be unextended or possess the property not-being-extended. His answer is that just as we should say it does not have extension, so also we should deny that it has the property not-being-extended. We see this, he says, when we recognize that blue is neither extended nor unextended. Notably he has switched once again from 'something blue' or 'a blue object' to plain and simple blue. Clearly the last point he makes is one regarding the property blue. It seems to me that whether Meinong explicitly recognizes this or not, he in fact collapses 'something blue' into the property blue.

There is a systematic point that might be made as well. One might, though I do not press this too strongly, hold the following: If 'something blue' is not a property, but rather is a thing of some sort (and, perhaps, universal) which has the property blue in the sense of instantiating blue, then it is not incomplete with respect to extension, in so far as being a thing which is blue implies the property of having, though not, perhaps, any specific, extension. The property blue, though, whatever one chooses to say about 'etwas blaues', itself carries no implication of that sort whatsoever. It, by itself and in abstraction it totally indifferent to and non-committal regarding extension. The only sense in which it might be considered complete with respect to some other characteristic would be the sense in which its instantiation in an entity would have entailments regarding the instantiation of some other properties. Furthermore, if something blue is not a property or a complex property then it simply would be misguided or not clearly to the point for Meinong, in asking about its determinateness or lack of same vis à vis some other property, to raise, as I have shown he does in fact raise, the question of whether blue (in the abstract) is extended. If 'etwas blaues' is not a property, then to ask after its incompleteness ought to come to asking whether it, besides being qualified by the property blue, is also qualified by the property of having extension or of being of some heaviness or other, etc.

A very short return to the text may be in order, for if still additional support for this interpretation is demanded, the following should suffice: On page 172, Meinong briefly switches from discussion of something blue in the abstract to the triangle in the abstract. Having spent a few lines on its incompleteness, he says it would be good to return to the previous example, '... zu unserem Beispiele von Blau und Schwer zurück' ('... to our examples of blue and heaviness ...'). That is, the example is couched in terms of the incompleteness of the properties of being blue and having weight. In the very next sentence, in elucidating what the example of 'Blau' and 'Schwer' comes to, he switches immediately to talk about 'etwas Blaues'!

As to the universality of these entities, this has been noted by commentators already. Interestingly, in *Stellung*[8], pages 119-123. Meinong clearly associates these entities with the traditional problem of universals. This definitely, it seems to me, is a reference to the tradition beginning with Locke, Berkeley, and Hume, as discussed in Meinong's *Hume-Studien*, which means, then, a discussion of universals in terms of whether properties are universals or not. It is interesting that Grossmann says that it seems to him that Meinong's incomplete entities really are properties, except that, he says, he can see no obvious sense in which a property is incomplete. This, it seems obvious, is not critical exegesis, but rather Grossmann on Grossmann's view of properties. A cursory reading of the *Über Möglichkeit und Wahrscheinlichkeit* analysis of incomplete objects makes it clear that, even if irrealia (contra our interpretation) are not properties, nonetheless properties are, in Meinong's view, incomplete objects. Meinong might be wrong about the incompleteness of properties, but that would be another story entirely.

I take the force of these considerations to indicate that Meinong's irrealia are both universals and (sometimes complex) properties. If this is the case, then his theory turns out to be very different from what has been thought to be the case. This also will mean that virtually all the arguments thrown up against his theory have, indeed, been misguided.

NOTES

* This is a revised version of the material from my Ph.D. dissertation, *Meinong's Theory Of Objects: A Reinterpretation And Defense*, Rutgers University, 1976, presented at the Meinong workshop.

The research behind this was only possible through the facilities and encouragement offered by the publishers of the new Meinong *Gesamt Ausgabe*, the Akademische Druck-u. Verlagsanstalt, Graz-Austria, and also by the Lehrkanzel für Philosophische Grundlagenforschung, Universität Graz, under the direction of Professor Dr. Rudolf Haller, as well as by Fulbright-Austria, under the direction of Professor Dr. Anton Porhansl, which made a lengthy stay at the Universiteit of Graz possible.

1 Meinong, Alexius, *Über die Erfahrungsgrundlagen unseres Wissens, Gesamt Ausgabe*, Band V, (Akademische Druck-u. Verlagsanstalt, Graz–Austria, 1973), pp. 25, 26, 29.

2 Ibid., pp. 25-30.

3 Ibid., p. 27.

4 Meinong, Alexius, *Über Möglichkeit und Wahrscheinlichkeit, Gesamt Ausgabe*, Band VI, (Akademische Druck-u. Verlagsanstalt, Graz–Austria, 1972), pp. 211-212.

5 *Über die Erfahrungsgrundlagen unseres Wissens*, p. 27.

6 *Über Möglichkeit und Wahrscheinlichkeit*, p. 168.

7 Findlay, John, *Meinong's Theory Of Objects And Values*, Second Edition, Oxford, 1963, pp. 164-165.

8 Meinong, Alexius, *Über die Stellung der Gegenstandstheorie im System der Wissenschaften, Gesamt Ausgabe*, Band V, (Akademische Druck-u. Verlagsanstalt, Graz-Austria, 1973).

SECTION VI

PHENOMENOLOGY, SCIENCE, AND PERCEPTION

ON HEARING SHAPES, SURFACES AND INTERIORS *

DON IHDE

In 1793 a scientist-priest, Lazzaro Spallanzani, began a series of experiments upon the motive abilities of nocturnal animals, most notably the bat. After a series of variant experiments, Spallanzani actually blinded a bat and when he discovered that the bat could still navigate so as to avoid obstacles he reported:

> The blinded bat can be made to fly freely in a closed room either during the day or at night. During such flight we observe furthermore that before arriving at the opposite wall, the bat turns and flies back, dexterously avoiding obstacles such as walls, a pole set across his path, the ceiling, the people in the room and whatever bodies may have been placed about in an effort to embarrass him. In short, he shows himself just as clever and expert in his movements in the air as a bat possessing its eyes.[1]

Spallanzani was incredulous at this performance and concluded that the bat must have *some special sense* unknown to humans when he later wrote, 'I am inclined to believe, at least so far, that in the absence of sight there is substituted some new organ or sense which we do not have and of which, consequently, we can never have any idea.'[2]

A year later the surgeon, Louis Jurine, upon reading of the Spallanzani experiments performed an experiment in which he plugged the ears of bats with wax and found that such bats could *not* navigate as did the blind bats of Spallanzani. Jurine concluded, 'The organ of hearing appears to supply that of sight in the discovery of bodies and to furnish these animals with different sensations to direct their flight, and enable them to avoid those obstacles which may present themselves.'[3]

And although today this discovery might be taken as commonplace as only one instance of animal echo-location along with dolphins, whales, certain moths and the like, both the experiments and the conclusions were rejected as scientific heresy by the scientific community of the 18th century. Such noted persons as Georges Cuvier and George Montagu literally ridiculed the work of Spallanzani and Jurine, characterizing this work as requiring more faith than philosophic reasoning and leading to the cryptic remark by Montagu: 'Since bats see with their ears, do they hear with their eyes?'[4]

In the paper today I shall, in effect, say 'yes' to this cryptic question by taking an auditory turn into an often overlooked and sometimes denied dimen-

See notes at the end of this chapter.

sion of auditory experience through the tools of phenomenology. I shall examine some of the *spatial* significations to be found through listening by taking note of our hearing of shapes, surfaces and interiors.

To set the context for what might appear a first part of the Spallanzani-Jurine heresy, note that there has been a long tradition of the interpretation of experience which links listening to time and seeing to space. This tradition, often inexplicit but nevertheless taken for granted, has led some to conclude that hearing does not yield space at all. In fact, a philosopher as recent as Strawson echos the hoots of Cuvier and Montagu when he denies spatial significance to hearing at all:

> The fact is that where sense experience is not only auditory in character but also at least tactual and kinesthetic as well — we can sometimes assign spatial predicates on the strength of hearing alone. But from this fact it does not follow that where this experience is supposed to be exclusively auditory in character, there would be any place for spatial concepts at all. I think it is obvious that there would be no such place.[5]

I shall not here directly attack what I take to be not one, but a series of errors arising out of Strawson's position, among which lie the empirical error of not recognizing that the organ of hearing *is* the organ of balance thus making it physiologically impossible to divorce hearing from kinesthetic significances in the human case; the error of typical analytic disembodiment which disregards the role of the whole body in all perception; and the final error of mistaking the *conception* of sound for the experience of sound.

Instead, I shall turn more directly to a phenomenologically rooted examination of auditory experience and try to demonstrate in action the three following points which differentiate phenomenology from the more standard views: a) First, the entire analysis is one which shows that the so-called phenomenological reductions function hermeneutically, that is, they serve to loosen the sedimented traditions of belief *about* various dimensions of experience without reducing the possibilities *of* that experience. The reductions reduce or place out of play certain 'presuppositions', not experience itself. This is the Husserlian moment of phenomenology. b) But secondly, the focus of phenomenology upon 'the things themselves' serves to uncover forgotten, hidden or latent aspects of these things such that the sense of these significations stand out as both 'having been there all along' and yet are also something which is discovered. c) Third, in the redescription of the phenomena there arises *necessarily* a certain oddness of language precisely because the reconstruction obtained through the reductions is supplementary to what had previously been believed. These new expressions are the Heideggerian moment of phenomenology. All three of these themes will interact in the analysis to follow.

The secret for beginning lies in the utmost simplicity. Heidegger in both *Being and Time* and in *Poetry, Language and Thought*, observes:

What we 'first' hear is never noises or complexes of sound, but the creaking wagon, the motor-cycle. We hear the column on the march, the north wind, the woodpecker tapping, the fire crackling. It requires a very artificial and complicated frame of mind to 'hear' a 'pure noise'.[6]

and again:

Much closer to us than all sensations are the things themselves. We hear the door shut in the house and never hear acoustical sensations or even mere sounds. In order to hear a bare sound we have to listen away from things, divert our ear from them, i.e., listen abstractly.[7]

Sounds are first the sounds of things. But such things are both spatial and temporal. The question here is what spatial significances may be found to lurk in phenomenological listening?

SHAPES, SURFACES AND INTERIORS

At the experiential level where sounds are heard as the sounds of things, it is ordinarily possible to distinguish certain *shape-aspects* of those things. The following variations begin in what for human hearing is admittedly one of the weakest existential possibilities of listening. Nor is it claimed that every sound gives a shape-aspect (but neither does every sighting give a shape aspect in the ordinary sense). I begin with the least obvious and weakest significance and work towards the more obvious and stronger significance. At first such an observation seems outrageous: *we hear shapes.*

The shape-aspects which are heard, however, must be strictly located in terms of their auditorily proper presentation and not predetermined or pre-limited by an already 'visualist' notion of shape. The shape-aspects which are heard are 'weaker' in their spatial sense than the full outline-shape of a thing which is ordinarily given all-at-once to vision. But a 'weakness' is not necessarily a total absence for in this 'weakness' there remains an important, if primitive, spatiality for hearing.

Children sometimes play an auditory game. Someone puts an object in a box and then shakes and rolls the box, asking the child what is inside. If, more specifically, the question is directed toward shapes the observer soon finds that it takes little time to identify simple shapes and often the object by its sound. For example, if one of the objects is a marble and the other a die (of a pair of dice) and the box is rolled, the identification is virtually immediate. The difference of shape has been *heard* and the shape aspect auditorily discriminated.

What is amazing, is what appears spontaneously in the simple variation. The very first time I played this game with my son I had placed a ball-point pen in a box without his seeing it and rolled it back and forth. I asked him what shape it was. His answer was, 'It's like a fifty pence shape, you know, on its sides, only it's longer.' A fifty pence coin has seven sides, the ball-point pen had six, and it was, in his parlance, 'longer.'

Nor is the shape-aspect all that is given in the richness of simple auditory presentations. If the game is allowed to continue so that one learns to hear things in an analogue to the heightened hearing of the blind man's more precise listening to the world, a quickly growing sophistication occurs. A ball-point pen gives a quite different auditory presentation with its plastic click from that of a wooden rod. A rubber ball is as auditorily distinct from a billiard ball as it is visually distinct. The very texture and composition as well as the shape-aspect is presented in the complex richness of the event.

It is often this learning itself which offers itself for suspicion to the 'sensory atomist' whose notion of a build up or constructed knowledge also infects the understanding of learning. Phenomenologically there is a great distinction between *constructing* something and its *constitution*. In constitution the learning that occurs is a learning which becomes aware of what is there to be seen or heard. There is the usual inversion called for in *epoche* here, as Merleau-Ponty remarked, *'learning* is *In-der-Welt-Sein*, and not at all that *In-der-Welt-Sein* is *learning.'*[8] This difference may be illustrated by two vastly different ways in which perceptual experience is employed in the empirical sciences.

In some psychology many of the experiments are deliberately designed to first disrupt all previous 'learning' by radically altering the context. To view a white sheet of paper under blue lighting through a darkened tube which cuts off the normal context and field significance of the experience is to radically alter ordinary experience. But the learning which is tacit in ordinary experience is then further cut off by allowing the experience to continue only for an atom of time, thus preventing any adjustment. In this way the experiment is set up so that it often cannot help but circularly re-enforce the 'abstraction' of the 'sensory atomist's' view of perception which begins with the 'abstraction' of 'sense data' or similar 'stimuli'. The experiment constructs the condition for the pre-formed conclusion and interprets what it finds as a *primitive* of experience.

Phenomenological learning does not construct what is to be seen, it constitutes it in terms of its meaning. What is to be heard is *there* and anyone entering this region of knowledge may hear the distinctive marks which differentiate one entity from the other. Once having been learned, the previous lack of awareness and lack of discrimination is seen not as a fault of the 'object' but of the inadequacy of our own prior observation.

This problem is partially involved in our frequent failure to discern the space-aspects of auditory experience. We have not learned to listen for shapes. The whole of our interpretation in its traditional form runs from it, and only in the dire situation of being forced to listen for shapes do ordinary humans attend specifically to the shape-aspects of sound, such as in the tragedy of blindness.

But even here there is a complication which arises from the global or plenary quality of primary experience. For the blind or deaf person experiences his 'world' as a unity and his experience as a plenum. His sense of lack is conveyed by the transcendence of language and he even becomes quite adept at 'verbalisms', the ability to define things through words although he may not recognize them when presented to him. One blind person describes this sense as:

> Those who see are related to me through some unknown sense which completely envelops me from a distance, follows me, goes through me, and, from the time I get up to the time I go to bed, holds me in some way in subjection to it.[9]

It is here that the 'sensory atomist' finds so much 'evidence' for his constructionist view of the world. It is well known that many, indeed most persons who are blind cannot visually recognize certain objects presented to them until they feel these objects. But there is another possible interpretation to such 'evidence'. It is not that the object is built up, but that the learning which goes on in all experience must go on here, too. The radically new experience of seeing, when a blind person gains sight through a medical procedure, is revealing. His *first* sight, when reported, often turns out to be precisely 'like' those first impressions reported in the first turn to reflective *listening*. He is impressed by what we might call the *flux* and *flow*, the implicit temporality of the new dimension to his experience. J.M. Heaton reports that when the blind are given sight, 'at first colours are not localized in space and are seen in much the same way as we smell odours.'[10] Odors, sounds, tastes, upon *first* note, appear not as fixed, but as a flux and flow. The first look is a stage of experience, not something which belongs isolated within one 'sense'.

This learning is often painful. For the patient it is not a mere addition to their experience, but a transformation of the whole previous shape of the plenum of their experience.

> The chief difficulty experienced by these patients is due to the general reorganization of their existence that is required, for the whole structure of their world is altered and its centre is displaced from touch to vision; and not only perception but language and behavior also have to be reoriented.[11]

It is not, however, that upon being given sight, spatiality is first discovered. It is *re-constituted*. A subtle example of this was given to me by a student trained in phenomenology who had been blind, but who, through treatment, gained limited sight. She noted that one quite detectable difference in her lived spatial organization, when given sight, was a gradual displacement of a previously more omni-directional orientation and spatial awareness to a much more focused *forward* orientation. Although she noted that even when blind there was a slight 'preference' for a forward directed awareness, this became much more pronounced with the gaining of vision. Again, as will become more apparent as the spatial significations of the auditory dimension become more pronounced, the relative omni-directionality of awareness and orientation is 'closer' to the space-sense of sound than that of vision.

In a gradual clarification of the distinctive spatial sense of auditory experience the first discrimination of shape-aspects heard in such spontaneous experiences as that of the game described above, becomes more precise when attention is paid not only to the presence of the spatial-aspect, but to how it is given in perception. By utilizing a pairing of sight and sound, this factor becomes easier to locate.

I turn to my visual and auditory experiences. I note now that in both dimensions there is a multiplicity of phenomena, but I also note that these do not always overlap. I see before me the picture of the sailboat, the note concerning last night's sherry party, a postcard from Japan, etc. But I hear the mortar mixer, the bird song, and the traffic on the street.

Next, I note that it seems at first that every stable thing before me visually presents a spatial signification which is, moreover, given-all-at-once. Each object has at least an *outline shape*, and this shape in the objects mentioned is discerned immediately. But of the sounds I do not seem to get shapes, certainly not outline shapes, and certainly not all-at-once.

In comparing this non-overlapping of shape in sight and sound in terms of the question of how shape-aspects are given, I soon find that the question of time is involved as well. The all-at-onceness to the outline shape before me is a matter of *temporal instanteneity* or of *simultaneity*. But when I return to those experiences which give me shape-aspects I find that the shape-aspect given is not a matter of instantaneity, but of a *sequential* or *durational* presentation. If the ball is dropped and does not bounce I may not get more than a 'contact point' as a vague and extremely 'narrow' signification, as in two surfaces contacting each other. But if the ball is rolled for several instants, if the rolling endures through a time span even if quite short, I get a sense of its shape as an *edge-shape*. This shape is presented, not in terms of temporal instantaneity, but in terms of temporal duration. But in both cases there is a need for some 'time' as even visually the object presented in too small an atom of time remains equally spatially indiscernible. But there is a difference of need here in which the temporal duration for the discrimination of an edge-shape by sound must be relatively greater. Here again seems to emerge a clue to why the traditions have maintained the asymmetries of 'spatial poverty' for sound and 'temporal richness' for sound in comparison to the 'spatial richness' and 'temporal poverty' for sight.

But this comparative variation bespeaks only one, albeit important, variation in relation to spatial significations. Further variations, however, tend to diminish the asymmetries to a degree. If I return to the pairing of sight and sound and introduce the (rapidly) moving thing into visual experience a difference occurs. The arrow, the drop of water, the falling stone which appears before me falling or flying at speed does not show itself as a clear and distinct shape. It presents itself as a 'vague' shape which only when the motion stops — or, in some cases if the field is large enough and the speed slow enough for me to fix my eyes upon the object as it moves, does the thing reveal its shape.

Some form of fixing is required for the clarity and distinction of the outline shape.

Yet the 'weak' or 'vague' shape-aspect of the visually moving object is 'closer to' the many shape-aspects which auditory experience yields in its constant 'flux'. A duration is needed to discriminate shape in this constant 'motion'. Thus if 'extended' temporal duration which persists in the flux and motion of sound in time is what appears as the main presentational mode of heard shape-aspects, the much shorter and more 'instant' norm of visual stability allows duration to be either overlooked or forgotten and thus apparently less important in the visual discrimination of spatial significance.

An edge-shape is 'less' than the outline shape, but it is a shape-aspect nonetheless. It is as if the ear had to gradually gain this shape of the thing in its durational attention. It is from such temporal considerations that 'linear' time metaphors may arise. In this respect auditory shapes seem, on one side, to be closer to tactile shape discriminations. With listening for shape-aspects, it often takes repeated and prolonged listenings until the fullness of the shape appears. But in daily affairs this serves no useful purpose when a mere glance will do the same in less time. Thus we fail to hear what may be heard and an existential possibility of listening is passed over.

But a third variation shows that there is even less absolute difference between sight and sound when size is taken into account. The edge-shape is usually admittedly quite 'small'. The marble-rolling-in-contact with the box or the die-striking-the-box presents only a small aspect of itself. But visually there is a reversion to a sequential discrimination, too, if the thing is immense. If one stands below the skyscraper it is unlikely that the whole will be taken in at once. One allows one's gaze to follow the outline of the building and the gaze in relation to the vastness becomes a sequential following of the outline-shape. The all-at-onceness does again become possible if distance is increased, as for example, when I see the whole skyscraper from above while stuck in a traffic pattern in an airplane above Manhattan. But again the comparative reign of the now 'middle-sized' stable and mute object returns and the comparative 'weakness' and difficulty of auditory shape discrimination returns, but now it is understood as a matter of relative distancing in space-time. It remains the case that the shape-aspect which is discerned auditorily in its 'weakest' possibility is a spatial signification.

There is a further factor to the hearing of shapes which reveals itself in the 'weakness' of hearing the shape of the thing. That factor is one which raises the question of *how* the thing is *voiced*. The mute object does not reveal its own voice. It must be given a voice. In the examples listed, for the most part a voice is given to the object by some other object. One thing is struck by another, one surface contacts another and in the encounter a voice is given to the thing.

There is clearly a complication in this giving of voice for there is not one voice, but *two*, a '*duet*' of things. The billiard ball rolling on the hard surface of a marble table not only sounds its shape-aspect as round in the rolling, but I also hear the hardness of the table. The 'same' roundness is heard when I roll the billiard ball on its felt covered table, but now I also hear the different texture of the billiard table. True, just as in listening to an actually sung vocal duet, I can focus auditorily upon either the tenor or the baritone, but my focal capacity does not 'blot out' the second voice, it merely allows it to 'recede' into a relative background. Thus also in listening to the 'duet' of things which lend each other a voice, I must learn to hear what each offers in the presence of the other. The way in which mute things gain or are given voices in my traffic with the world is an essential factor in all spatial significations in sound.

Although only a massive shift in perspective and understanding will ultimately allow the fullness of auditory spatial significations to emerge, the movement from weaker to stronger possibilities of listening is one which increases our familiarity with such significations. Less strange than the notion of hearing shapes, *we also hear surfaces*. This autidory experience is involved with our ordinary experiences of things.

Who does not recognize the surface in the sound of chalk scratching? Or, I hear footsteps in the hallway, whoever is walking now on the tile whose surface produces the characteristic clacking sound of hard heels which, the moment the first step is made into the living room is changed for the dull thuding sound of the person on the rug.

Surfaces, auditorily more familiar to us than shapes, must also be heard in terms of a voice being given the things. Just as in the discernment of shape-aspects, and shape-aspects may grade off into surface significations, there is usually a 'duet' of voices in the auditory presentation. Furthermore, there is often more than a surface signification, a signification which grades off at the upper end into an anticipation of hearing interiors. I hear the textural and compositional character of the thing and distinguish easily between the sound of a bell and that of a stick hitting pavement.

Unaccustomed to the language of hearing shapes and surfaces, listening may remain unaware of its full possibilities. But the paradigm of acute listening in the auditory abilities of the blind man again provides clues for subtle possibilities of the ordinary sighted listener as well. The blind man through his cane embodies his experience through a feeling and a hearing of the world. As Merleau-Ponty has pointed out, he *feels* the walk at the end of his cane. The grass and the sidewalk reveal their surfaces and textures to him *at the end of the cane*. But at the same time his tapping which strikes those surfaces gives him an auditory *surface-aspect*. The concrete sidewalk sounds differently than the boardwalk and in his hearing he knows he has reached such and such a place on his familiar journey.

To be sure, the surfaces heard by the blind man or the ordinary listener are restricted surfaces. They lack the *expanse* which vision with its secret 'cartesian' prejudice for 'extension' presents because the auditory surface is the revelation of an often small region rather than the spreading forth of a vista. But within its 'narrowness' a surface is heard.

But striking a surface and thereby getting in a 'duet' the surface aspects of two things is not the only way in which the mute object is given voice nor is it the only way in which sound reveals surfaces. For the blind man's tapping also gives an often slight, but nevertheless detectable voice to things in an *echo. With the experience of echo, auditory space is opened up.* With echo the sense of distance as well as surface is present. And again surface significations anticipate the hearing of interiors. Nor, in the phenomenon of echo, is the lurking temporality of sound far away. The space of sound is 'in' its timefulness.

The depth of the well reveals its auditory distance to me as I call into its mouth. And the mountains and canyons reveal their distances to me auditorily as my voice re-sounds in the time which belongs so essentially to all auditory spatial significations. But these distances are still 'poorer' than those of sight, though distances nonetheless. This relativity of 'poverty' to 'wealth' is apparent in the occasional *syncopation* of the visual and auditory appearances of the thing. Such a common experience today may be located in the visual and auditory presentations of a high flying jet airplane. When I hear the jet I may locate its direction quite accurately by its sound, but when I look I find no jetplane. The sound of the jet 'trails behind' its visual appearance and, by now accustomed to this syncopation, I learn to follow the sound and then look ahead to find the visual presence of the jet.

But as I come to smaller distances the syncopation lessens and the sight and sounds converge so that ordinarily the sight and sound of the things seem to synthesize in the same place. Yet, with careful attention as I stand in the park and listen to the automobiles and trucks rush past I find that even here there is a slight 'trailing effect'. I close my eyes and follow the sound which, upon opening my eyes, I find only slightly 'trails' the source as seen. Soon I can detect this 'trailing' with my eyes open. Again in this distance the temporality of sound is implicated.

This often unpractices and unnoticed form of human echo-location which is spatially significant may also be heightened. For the echo in giving voice to things returns to us with vague shapes and surfaces. The ancient theory of vision which conceived of a 'ray' proceeding from the eye to the thing and back again is more literally true for the sounding echo's ability to give voice to shapes and surfaces. The blind man who has learned and listened more acutely than we, produces this auditory 'ray' with his clicking cane. Yet anyone who listens well may hear the same.

I repeat the experience of the blind man, carrying with me a clicking device. As I move from the bedroom to the hall a dramatic difference in sounding occurs and soon, as I navigate blindfolded I learn to hear the narrowing of the stairs and the approaching closeness of the wall. Like the blind man I learn to auditorily perceive the gross presence of things. But in the relative poverty of human auditory spatiality I miss the presence of the less gross things. I cannot hear the echo which returns from the open backed Windsor chair but I do discern the bulking wall as a vague presence. Yet in a distance not too far from human experience, I know that the porpoise can auditorily detect the difference of size between two balls through his directed echo abilities, a difference which often escapes even the casual look of a human.

I listen more intently still. The echo gives me an extremely vague surface presence. I strike it and its surface re-sounds more fully. Yet even in the 'weakness' of the echo I begin to hear the surface aspects of things. I walk between the Earth Sciences building with its concrete walls along the narrow pathway bounded on the other side by the tall plywood walls fencing off the construction of the new Physics building. In the winter the frozen ground echos the click of my heels and I soon know when I have enetered the narrowness of the pathway and once at the other end the sound 'opens up' into the more distant echoing of the frozen ground which stretches to the parking lot. But as the days go by and I listen, I soon learn that not only is there a surface presence, not only is there the 'opening' and the 'narrowing', but there is also a distinctly different echo from the concrete wall and the plywood fence. The surface-aspect only gradually becomes less vague in the sharpening of our listening abilities. In the echo and in the striking of the thing, I hear surfaces as existential possibilities of listening.

While there is no question here of exhausting even the relative and often vague 'poverty' of shape and surface aspects, the march towards the 'richness' within sound must continue. It is with a third spatial signification that this 'richness' begins to appear. For stronger than shapes and more distinct than surfaces, I *hear interiors*. Moreover, it is with the hearing of interiors that the possibilities of listening begin to open the way to those aspects which lie at the horizons of all 'visualist' thinking. For with the hearing of interiors the auditory capacity of making present the *invisible* begins to stand out dramatically. To vision in its ordinary contexts and particularly within the confines of the vicinity of mute and opaque objects, things present themselves with their interiors *hidden*. To see the interior I may have to break up the thing, do violence to it. Yet even these ordinary things often reveal something of their interior being through sound.

A series of painted balls is placed before me. The laquer shines, but it conceals the nature of the interior of the ball. I tap first this one, its dull and unresounding noise reveals it to be of lead or some similar heavy and soft metal. I strike that one and there is no mistaking the sound of its wooden interior. The third resounds almost like a bell for its interior is steel or brass. In each case the auditory texture is more than a surface presentation, it is also a threshold to the interior.

I am asked to hang a picture in the living room. Knowing that its weight requires a solid backing, I thump the wall until the hollowness sounding behind the lathed plaster gives way to the thud which marks the location of the stringer into which I may drive my nail. What remained hidden from my eyes is revealed to my ears. The melon reveals its ripeness; the ice its thinness; the cup its half-full contents; the water reservoir, though enclosed, reveals exactly the level of the water inside in the sounding of interiors. Hearing interiors is part of the ordinary signification of sound presence and is ordinarily employed when one wishes to penetrate the invisible. But one may not pay specific attention to this signification as the *hearing* of interiors unless one turns to a listening 'to the things themselves.'

In the movement from shape-aspects to surfaces to interiors there is a continuum of signification in which the 'weakest' existential possibilities of auditory spatial significations emerge.

In all of this listening there is a learning. But that learning is like that of the blind man first being given sight, he does not at first know what he sees. Neither do we know what we hear although in this case what is to be heard lies within the very familiarity with things in their present but often undiscovered richness. But once learning to hear spatial significations, the endless ways in which we hear interiors comes to mind. We hear hollows and solids as the interior spatiality of things. We hear the *penetration* of sound into the very depths of things and in the penetration into the very interior of things we hear again the wisdom of Heraclitus, 'The hidden harmony is better than the obvious.'[12]

I have here begun to open up some progressively more important spatial significations of auditory experience. These do not exhaust the spatiality of sound, but point to its ever greater richness which reaches towards the sublime in music.

NOTES

* This article is a revision of a chapter from *Listening and Voice: A Phenomenology of Sound* (Ohio University Press, 1976) which appeared simultaneously with the 1976 S.P.E.P. Conference.

1 S.S. Stevens and Fred Warshofsky, *Sound and Hearing* (Nederland, *Time-Life* International, 1966), p. 122.

2 *Ibid.*, p. 122.

3 *Ibid.*, p. 122.

4 *Ibid.*, p. 123.

5 P.F. Strawson, *Individuals* (London: Methuen, 1971), p. 65.

6 Martin Heidegger, *Being and Time*, trans. Edward Robinson and John Macquarrie (New York: Harper and Row, 1962), p. 207.

7 Martin Heidegger, *Poetry, Language, Thought*, trans. Albert Hofstadter (New York: Harper and Row, 1971), p. 26.

8 Maurice Merleau-Ponty, *The Visible and the Invisible*, trans. Alfonso Lingis (Evanston: Northwestern University Press, 1968), p. 212.

9 J.M. Heaton, *The Eye: Phenomenology and Psychology of Function and Disorder* (London: Tavistock Publications, 1968), p. 42.

10 *Ibid.*, p. 42.

11 *Ibid.*, p. 43.

12 Philip Wheelwright, *The Presocratics* (New York: Odyssey Press, 1966), p. 79.

DISTORTIONS IN HUMAN EMBODIMENT:
A STUDY OF SURGICALLY TREATED OBESITY *

DONALD McKENNA MOSS

INTRODUCTION

For the past two years I have been interviewing morbidly obese patients, who choose to undergo intestinal bypass surgery to induce weight loss. These patients weigh at least twice their ideal weights —usually 250-500 pounds. Briefly, this operation constructs a bypass or detour between the stomach and the large bowel; food passes through only 18 inches of small bowel, instead of the usual 21 feet. This bypass prevents the normal caloric absorption which takes place in the small bowel. Weight loss as well as numerous annoying and often hazardous somatic side-effects are the result.

The experiences of these patients offer an abundance of material for reflections on the taken for granted structure of normal embodiment. The 250-500 pound patient frequently experiences himself or herself as 'hardly human,' as 'like something from outer space,' or as 'the biggest person who ever lived.' The desires to 'rejoin the human race' and to cease to be a self-conscious freak are reasons frequently given for the decision to have an intestinal bypass operation. With weight loss, some patients experience themselves explicitly as 'normal again' and others report the return of 'natural' movement, i.e., spontaneous, taken for granted, and self-forgetful movement in which every motion no longer has to be planned, thought out, and deliberately, laboriously performed. Such self-conscious experiences of 'being abnormal' and 'being normal again' give us access to aspects of embodiment that never stand out in such prominence in the individual of normal weight.

Today, I would like to focus on one feature of normal and abnormal embodiment: that is, the extent to which the individual experiences the body as 'my own,' as 'my property.' I have divided my presentation into the following topics: I. Theoretical Background, II. Owning and Disowning the Obese Body, III. Property, IV. Diffusion of Body Ownership throughout the Family, and V. Medical Ethics and the Ownership of the Obese Body. I will close with some thoughts on the significance of these issues for the phenomenology of the body.

See notes at the end of this chapter.

254

I. THEORETICAL BACKGROUND:
THE BODY AS 'MY OWN' AND AS A FUNDAMENTAL PROPERTY

Merleau-Ponty has dealt extensively with the significance of the body, particularly in terms of the specular image and the child's appropriation of the mirror perspective on himself, the objective perspective from a distance (Merleau-Ponty, 1964 a, 1964 b, 1968). In his Sorbonne lectures (1964 b), Merleau-Ponty was particularly interested in the distinctly human quality of the child's fascination with the mirror image. 'It is necessary that the child understand that there are two points of view on himself, that his body which feels is equally of the visible not only for him but for others. There is thus an interdependence between the development of the specular image and the development of the relationship with others. The child must learn to see himself as *role*.' 'Consciousness of the body is interdependent with that of outside things.' What is at stake here is the development of the child's ability to *own* this objective and visible self as *myself*. Elsewhere in these same lectures, Merleau-Ponty reminds us of Hegel's thesis that the notion of property is connected with the 'consciousness of a fundamental property, that of the human body, of *our* body.'

Similarly, Erwin Straus has emphasized that the human, lived body is not experienced anonymously as the body, but rather as *mine*, as *my own* body, with a kind of intimacy far exceeding the mineness of the property that can be disposed of (Straus, 1967; Straus and Griffith, 1967). Straus asserts: 'The possessive relation expressed by the words 'my,' 'yours,' 'his' ... contains, in fact, one of the most difficult problems for our understanding. It indicates the transition from physiology to psychology' (1966, p. 150). In agreement with Merleau-Ponty, Straus also believes that: 'The experience of the body as mine is the origin of possessive experience. All other connotations of possessive relations are derived from it' (1966, p. 151). Elsewhere Straus clearly recognizes that the mineness of the body is not sharply demarcated against the realm of the Allon; the boundaries between self and non-self, I and It are not fixed. In pain or in illness our own body is alienated from us. We experience disease as a foreign power or entity within us, attacking us, seizing us, and overpowering us (1969, pp. 45-47).

Using a different terminology – that of body image – Paul Schilder (1923, 1935 wrote that our image of our own body is by no means static. It is an *Errungenheit*, not a *Gegebenheit*, an achievement, not a given. Body image cannot be taken for granted, it presupposes a highly affective and interpersonal process of appropriation.[1] 'There are forces of hatred scattering the picture of our own body and forces of love putting it together' (1935, p. 166). Finally, the body image remains fluid in response to the changing demands of the current situation. The individual acquires virtual images of his body, which recur with some consistency in similar situations, yet these virtual images undergo constant adaptation and transformation as the body engages in each new situation. In particular, the spatiality of the body image is inseparable from the spatiality of the current situation.

To summarize: Merleau-Ponty addresses the child's appropriation of his own body in its objectivity, as a fundamental property, through a process of reflection. Straus emphasizes the experience of the body as my own, and also the basic ambiguity of the human body, which is both I and It. Schilder describes the acquisition of the body image in the life history, as well as the pairing of body and world.

II. OWNING AND DISOWNING THE OBESE BODY

For the obese individual, the other's perspective on the visibly obese body is stigmatizing and deprecating. It reveals an irrefutably visible aspect of myself which is difficult to 'own' — to become aware of, to acknowledge, and to appropriate into my sense of who I am. Thus the fundamental property, the body, is not *my* property and not *my* body. For many obese persons the visibility of the body is suffered passively and shamefully in the eyes of others. This is an inability to live the display of my body in the eyes of others. For such individuals the world is filled with regions of shame within which one is conspiciously exposed; these regions are shunned and many forms of hiding and concealing become habitual. (For many of these patients their home ground, the region where they can forget the body entirely, relax in genuine comfort, and become absorbed in the situation of the moment, is remarkably narrow. Often it is limited to the home and immediate family and sometimes only to the patient's own room and company. Even the world of solitude contains innumerable reminders to call the patient back to an acute awareness of the obese body. Each situation and each encounter represents, so to speak, a potential mirror).

The obese individual faces difficulty in appropriating and mastering this body. The potential for a relapse into a passive, helpless suffering of shame seems always to be present. In shame, a body cannot stand up to the eyes of the other. The usual self-forgetfulness of the body, which loses itself in behavior directed toward the situation, the thing, or the other, is eradicated. There is a return of consciousness from its home in the world to the body — where it is not at home. The individual is not at home with himself in such a moment either. Such a moment constitutes shame. In shame, consciousness is inwardly directed — from the other's eyes back onto oneself. The urge is to shrink away, to hide, to escape the gaze, or to cease to exist as this body. As one patient put it, she wished she could go away and leave this fat, frozen, stuck body. In contrast to this, proud active display is outwardly directed. Even when the display is self-conscious, the movements are flamboyantly directed to the eye of the other. In pride one performs actively for the other; the body is an activity.

In shame one suffers passively the visibility for the other of this helpless body-mass.

There is a continuous dialectic between helpless, passive shame and active free display of the body. In my interviews with obese patients I am continually presented with an individual's efforts to master or take charge of the visibility of his body for me. This *presentation* may seem to be an obscure process, but it involves very specific, concrete verbal and bodily behaviors. We see them whenever we are with others, but in the obese they are more transparent and conspicuous. This presentation process involves efforts both to achieve and to avoid ownership of the body and its parts. What is most noticeable at first, is that these individuals utilize a multitude of tactics to avoid owning their visible appearance and integrating it into their identity. Self and body are divorced or disunited in a number of ways. Even the more passive obese individuals present their appearance to me in a way that selectively directs my attention toward or away from this or that aspect of their appearance. They decide, as it were, which aspects of their appearance they are or aren't going to inhabit under my gaze, and exhibit to my gaze. Notice here that exhibiting and inhabiting are closely linked, the bodily presentation to the other necessarily involves some nascent self-recognition and ownership.

The whole body may be disowned. It may be described in impersonal, it — or thing — language: as 'not-me,' as 'that thing I am encased in,' or as 'this stuff I am trucking around.' It may remain almost entirely unlanguaged — as a global, unarticulated, but painful and inescapable presence. The body may also be divided up along various lines — head/body, front/back, outside/inside, left/right — one part to be owned, emphasized, and focused on as 'me,' and the remainder of the body to be deemphasized, excluded from discussion and awareness, or explicitly thematized and disowned as 'not-me.' Note that there is an active *presentation process* even in the refusal to be identified with certain parts of the body.

The normal, taken for granted articulation of the human body into a front and a back, a head and a body, an inside and an outside, and a left and a right, is made more conspicuous in the case of the obese patient. Normally our sense of body ownership is rather ambiguous and fluid: the body is both me and not-me, I and It, and, according to the demands of the situation, 'I' may be more in my face, in my pen hand, in my legs, in my exposed back, etc. The obese individual frequently distorts the basic ambiguity and fluidity of the human body, to seize fluid lines and set them into a permanently fixed self-definition: I am always this attractive face, I am never this grossly obese body; this body that you see is never me, I am always this beautiful personality that resides invisibly inside this hulk. Each such fixed self-definition also constricts the range of situations whose invitation I am open to, and increases the range of situations whose call I cannot even allow myself to hear, lest I re-experience my inadequacy to respond. *Self constriction and world constriction are here equivalent.*

III. PROPERTY

The failure of many obese patients to feel that this body is *my* body is paralleled by the more general tendency of the obese, described by Hilde Bruch (1973), *not* to feel a sense of agency, control involvement, and initiative in their own lives and behavior. The phrases 'it just happened to me,' 'she did this to me,' and many equivalents keep coming up as the patients relate their histories, expressing, I believe, a pervasive feeling of helplessness, dependency, and passivity. Body-ownership and individuation are intimately related; an impairment in the sense of the body as fundamental property necessarily involves an impairment in individuality. My long term follow-up studies of intestinal bypass patients consistently show that when a patient re-appropriates the newly thin body, the patient also becomes more able to 'hold my own,' to 'live my own life,' to cease living for and through others, and 'to be a person myself.'

Let us pause briefly to reflect on what it means to *own property* in the everyday sense. Property, we know, entails both certain privileges and certain intrinsic responsibilities.

1) I can do something with it, I can use it, it has utility for me – as long as it functions or operates properly according to its nature – as my instrument,

2) I can show it off, display it, parade it, and its apparent value reflects upon my own prestige, the display of property is also self display,

3) As my property, I – more than anyone else – am concerned about its condition, I tend it and care for it,

4) I am *responsible* for what is done with my property, I accept fault or blame for consequences it has been involved in, I am liable for such effects legally, but I also *feel* liable (if someone is injured in my home, or by my car, I am likely to feel personally involved and implicated in the injury),

5) I have custody and control over my property, it is my duty to make and announce decisions concerning its well-being and disposition, others will question me prior to taking action affecting my property.

Each of these constituent characteristics of everyday property is even more intimately characteristic of the *own body*. My body is my own insofar as: 1) it is the instrument of my actions, 2) its display involves self-display, 3) I tend and care for it, 4) I am responsible for its action and inactions, and 5) I have custody over it. (The body is also mine in a way qualitatively surpassing any object: It is the means by which I have a world and hold sway in the world; it is as well the carrier of my life and mortality, the means by which I feel life flowing through me and the means by which I am bound to the realm of all material things with their governing laws of decline, decay, and transience. These last features will not be addressed here).

In my investigations I have come to understand increasingly diverse aspects of the behavior, mannerisms, expressions, and experience of obese patients as essentially interrelated in terms of impaired ownership of the body, and of desperate efforts to re-master, or re-appropriate an obese body. By viewing these scattered facts under the category of *ownership behavior*, we bring their inner coherence into a new prominence. For example, the obese body is stigmatizing when displayed and contributes to a self-conscious shame. At the same time the obese individual, after many failures at dieting, has an intense feeling of helplessness and futility, of inability to do anything about the obesity itself. The sense of being in control of this body-property is lacking. Dieting fails, and efforts to hide or disguise the weight cosmetically or by clothing style are felt to be equally pointless. Some patients continue to make perfunctory gestures in these directions, but no longer really inhabit the efforts. In retrospect they recognize the time when it became too painful to even try, i.e., the time when they gave up real efforts and hopes, and ceased, so to speak, to inhabit the body.[2] There are also gradations of body-disownership: many obese women speak of the point at which they gave up striving for attractiveness or desirability, and concluded they could at best maintain a neat and *acceptable* appearance.

Other patients will give up even these minimal gestures. We occasionally see a complete neglect of the body and appearance, a grossly unkempt, ragged, and dirty appearance. Yet we must be sensitive to nuances here: What looks like a disavowal of ownership may also be a desperate, distorted means of re-establishing ownership, e.g., the repulsive, grossly neglected body may be actively flaunted, as a way of owning the totally devalued body in the face of unsympathetic others. This stance is a defiant self-assertion, a spiteful curse flung in the faces of uncaring others, a repudiation and protest against the others' values which constitute a judgement on me. Frequently these patients will articulate the feeling accompanying such a self-assertion in terms of a curse: 'I've taken enough crap, shit on you,' or 'the hell with who's watching, I'm going to go anyway ...' This perverse, spiteful, defiant stance also contains a kernel of positive communication with others, an attempt to penetrate the hard crust of the other's indifference, to force an acknowledgement of one's own existence – to 'get to' the other, one way or the other. Thus the stigmatizing feature is no longer hidden; it is actively taken up and waved as a flag of contempt toward the repudiated others, and as a last effort at self-ownership. It is thus a form of liberation from bondage and powerlessness, and expresses an attitude of 'fat is beautiful' or 'fat liberation.' The move toward proud display of formerly stigmatizing features is a constituent shared by many liberation efforts.

In general we cannot assume that merely because the body is experienced or languaged as an *object*, it is being *disowned*. One woman was humiliated at her immense backside to the extent that she would lean into the mirror so as never to view more than her attractive front. Nevertheless, powerfully aware that this rear bulk was visible to others, she anticipated any attention or remarks, by an exaggerated jiggling of her rump as she entered a room, and by constant joking comments such as — 'here I am and here comes the caboose,' 'look at that shelf,' 'my disgusting ass,' etc. In these examples there is a peculiar appropriation going on. She directs our gaze to her deficits; she lifts them out of the background and displays them. 'Ass' and 'caboose' are used in such a way that they express disgust or ridicule on one level, yet at the same time deflect it. She has thereby shifted the locus of control back to herself. She remains helplessly *visible*, but has captured the others' eyes and now directs them. The rear of her body will be languaged as object, but as *her* object, and she will language it herself.

Some obese patients utilize a peculiar form of double negative in languaging their bodies, thereby executing a complicated deflection of ownership. Examples: 'I have never not been feminine,' 'I have never not had a shape,' I have never not been accepted.' In a subtler form of these remarks, a pejorative takes the place of the second negative: 'At least I am not grotesque,' 'I'm not your basic fat lady,' 'well, I'm not the biggest blimp in our church.' We must break up these statements if we are to understand the structure of the experience involved: 'not feminine,' 'not accepted,' 'no shape,' 'grotesque,' 'basic fat lady,' and 'biggest blimp in our church' are the primary constituents of this experience, which the individual must come to terms with. As pejoratives each of them is a *negation* of the individual's worth, whether or not the grammatical negation is present. These negations seem to impinge on the obese individual, like destructive vectors or missiles from over there — from the environment and those around one, and yet potentially they have to do with oneself. They are like so many reflections in a mirror. One can hate the mirror, shun it, shatter it, or notice someone else in it, yet the primary revelation of the mirror is never fully obliterated. For example, the world shows a woman that some obese women are unfeminine, shapeless, grotesque blobs: the woman may respond by owning her weight problem, but anticipating and deflecting this extreme negation. To express this concretely, the individual sees this reflected revelation coming, and sidesteps verbally, allowing it to pass by or apply to someone else. 'I am fat, but at least I'm not as big as her.'

One final word about this absorption with reflected negations or pejoratives: With weight loss the individual may still grapple with refuting these negations for months and years before genuine, spontaneous positive self-feelings emerge, if they ever do. 'I *don't not like* what I see in the mirror,' 'I don't look as bad as before,' and 'I'm not such an overgrown horse any more' are experiential phases which must often be traversed before one reaches the phase of: 'I enjoy looking in the mirror,' or 'I feel sexy.' While it lasts, this absorption with reflected negations also entails a pre-occupation with others' opinions and attention. Long after others have ceased to perceive an individual as corpulent, he will continue his monotonous vigilance for references to it. As Binswanger said of Ellen West, these obese individuals have alienated the center of gravity of their existence onto the *Mitwelt*, the world of fellow humans.

There are other equally common forms in which the obese endeavor to reappropriate their problematic bodies, including the striking instance of those obese who attempt to establish absolute, unrelenting body ownership and self containment. Absolute body ownership is no more normal or viable than total lack of ownership. The normal body is in a constant flux: as a whole and in its part it is alternately held in one's own custody and given over into the care of others. *The norm entails a flexible, fluid alternation between possession and surrender according to the demands of the situation.*

IV. DIFFUSION OF BODY OWNERSHIP THROUGHOUT THE FAMILY

The sense of body ownership may also be diffused, in some ways, throughout a family. Originally the acquisition of an awareness of my own body is mediated by another, and this mediation may be of such a nature that the sense of ownership is stifled, inhibited, or confused. It must be kept in mind always that the ownership and awareness of my own body are not given at birth. The human infant is born into the custody, the intimate care of one or more adult humans, who tend the infant's body, make decisions regarding its treatment and disposition, control its display, and accept responsibility for the infant's existence and its actions. The infant gradually develops and learns to take charge of each of these areas — to a greater or less extent. The immediate experience of ability, capacity, and potency inherent in effective autonomous activity plays a large role in the infant's taking charge. The child's early initiatives toward self-directed activity and self-ownership may be discouraged, stifled, and replaced by parent-directed activity. Parental love and affirmation, or parental rejection and negation, form the nucleus of self-love or self-negation, those powerful forces which, as Schilder pointed out, affect the unity or the disintegration of the body image. Love in this case has the significance of allowing to be (Binswanger). Some parents of obese children have been shown to stifle initiative, to treat the children as helpless, and to persist in doing basic caring tasks for the child. A primary deficit in individuation, self-awareness, and self-ownership is the result.

Hilde Bruch (1973) has described the parental attitudes and behavior which can inhibit the child's development of a healthy awareness of his own feelings, impulses, body, and self. Feeding is an example: The child may be fed overindulgently or deprived, but in either case the mother feeds the infant and child according to her inclinations and not according to the child's expression of hunger. The child's awareness of hunger is thereby inhibited. The child becomes more attuned to the mother's presence or to a rigid schedule or to a host of other situational and emotional variables as cues to eating. Many experiments have verified that obese individuals are rather insensitive to physiological hunger, i.e., to cues arising from gastric motility (Schachter, 1971). As a result they eat in response to almost everything under the sun except their own body's need for more nourishment.

Bruch gave many other examples of analogous parent-child interactions where the child's budding individuality, budding capacity for self-direction, and budding awareness of personal wants and aims are all stifled. She described, for example, the rigid, doll-like, early teen age children who enter her office led by the mother's hand, submit passively to being undressed and guided to a seat by the mother, and who seem to move only in response to the mother's instructions. The child's clothing is chosen by the mother and put on by the mother, and is thus not an expression of the child himself. The mother, by fussing over the child's physical care and hygiene, conveys to the child that this body is *not his own*, but rather *his mother's*.

As a psychoanalyst, Hilde Bruch regards this primary deficit in self-ownership — manifested in the kinds of child-parent interactions described here — as of aetilogic significance in the occurrence of obesity. I wish to suspend this question of aetiology entirely. I will focus rather on problems of ownership in the families of the obese, without regard to the factors disposing to obesity in the individual case.

When interviewing obese patients, one frequently finds more or less distinct evidence of such a diffusion of body ownership throughout the family. When we listen to the family discuss 'Debby's problem,' it becomes clear that the problem in fact is most intensely a problem for one or the other parent (or even sibling). One father repeatedly answered questions actually directed to his obese daughter and summed up 'her' attitude as: 'she should be a lot thinner, more like a normal girl ...' Usually it is a parent who first perceives the problem, labels it as a problem, conveys his or her dissatisfaction about the problem to the child, and prods the child toward physicians, pills, diets, shots, etc. Often the only initiative or freedom left to the child is a spiteful and defiant non-compliance with the dieting, and the faint smile of victory when the parent again tells a new doctor that: 'Debby is very special, nothing seems to work in her case.'

The same problem may be seen in anorexia nervosa: anorexics, usually young adolescents, can starve themselves — often to death — in a desperate power struggle with parents. Frequently such patients lack awareness that it is they who are being injured: they can say, e.g., 'My body was not my own. It was my parents' concern. By neglect I would get back at my mother' (Bruch, 1973, p. 370).

During contacts with obese patients, it is valuable to keep property questions consistently in mind: *Whose body is this, who has custody of this body, who tends this body, who controls the display of this body*, and *who is most obviously concerned about the condition of this body*?

We often find that the child is treated by a parent as an extension of the parent, and put on conspicuous display by the parent to enhance parental pride. Frequently the obesity is criticized only in terms of its tarnishing effect on parental prestige. Once again a constituent of property, the ability to display oneself proudly in one's own right, is usurped by the parent. Obesity is a potent weapon against this usurpation: Daddy's little beauty gains 90 pounds! In such a case the child correctly perceives *whose property the beautiful shape and face are – whose 'glory' they enhance.*

This diffusion of body ownership may be perpetuated in adulthood in the relation with a spouse. During a recent conference for the families of prospective intestinal bypass patients, one husband spoke consistently for his wife. He remarked: 'Since *we* had a hysterectomy, *we've* had this enormous weight gain.' Questioned privately about his feelings about the risky bypass operation, he emphasized his willingness to risk the operation to ensure the long term survival of the wife, and her health, now threatened by obesity:

'She is my possession. I have four kids – I can replace them. I can replace my car if it's gone. But I can't replace my wife, I've settled on her. She is mine.'

Asked about his feelings about her weight, he replied:

'She's mine, the weight is there, the weight is mine.'

This alienation of custody is not merely verbal, nor is it merely in the husband's mind. When the surgeon began to instruct this couple about the arrangements for the operation, the husband did all the talking. The wife wandered out of the room, and when a nurse asked her whether she wasn't concerned to learn the details of an operation she would undergo, she responded that the husband would take care of that. She is thus an active accomplice in her own disownership. *In whose custody is this body? And who talks for this body?*

In another case, both husband and wife presented themselves simultaneously for intestinal bypasses. They emphasized that it was a joint decision, and that they always do things together. When advised that it might be wise for them to undergo the operation successively, and not simultaneously (since the patient's demands during convalescence often put strains on the rest of the family), they responded that they wanted to be sick at the same time, so neither would feel isolated from or out of touch with the other. To illustrate further the deficit in individual body ownership, i.e., the extent to which the operation was 'for us' and not 'for me,' the wife remarked that if her husband developed serious complications necessitating reversal of the bypass,[4] she would have her intestinal bypass reversed too. She could not imagine losing weight while her husband remained fat. For this couple it is clear that the entity 'our bodies' was not produced by combining the two pre-existing and clearly demarcated entities 'my body'. Phenomenologically, 'our bodies' is a prior and more primitive phenomenon than 'my body.' Psychology sets out on the wrong foot when it assumes that the human being comes into the world as an individual, isolated psyche, because it is then forced to pose the pseudo-question: how does community come about˄ Further, the human being does not come into the world in full possession and custody of his body. Ownership and custody of the infant's body is originally a family affair. *The 'own body' is a late arrival in the human family.* Our poorly differentiated husband and wife team does not live at the level at which 'my own body' is a psychological reality.

V. MEDICAL ETHICS AND THE OWNERSHIP OF THE OBESE BODY

I wish to suggest that the *property questions* raised in the last section also have practical, ethical implications for patient care. The typical treatment approach to obesity only too often contributes further to the individual's alienation from his body. A powerful message has already been conveyed to the obese person in the family, particularly in childhood: that there is something fundamentally wrong with him, which is likely to be beyond his own power to alter. This message is reiterated by the typical medical approach.

The medical treatment of obesity founders on the fundamental ambiguity of the human body, which is always both I and it. The obese patient is shuttled back and forth between medicine and psychology, causality and morality, technical explanations and moral accusations, reenacting in this journey the centuries old split of body and mind. Medicine historically, has played a central role in the languaging of the body, and continues to do so today. The individual with an impaired body often reappropriates this body only through the intervention of the physician. Foundering in ambiguity, the patient and the family grasp eagerly for a verbal diagnostic judgement, which will articulate the general situation of ill-being into a more specific disease situation, with its own moral imperatives for all involved. But the degree and kind of this new languaging and new ownership are intrinsically limited by the structure of modern medical discourse and treatment.

Medical discourse is an it-, process-, or thing-language, which provides numerous means by which individuals may assign responsibility for a condition such as obesity to internal causes (e.g., my thyroid, pituitary, hypothalamus, sugar level, metabolism, a recessive gene, or congenital excess in adipose cells). These attributions are certainly in part accurate, but they are partial truths taken up repeatedly in a totalizing and absolute fashion.

Corresponding to the medical discourse is the medical treatment model, in which the patient passively submits to the doctor's active intervention. The example I cited above, of a husband making decisions concerning his wife's body is paralleled by the physician's relationship with the patient. The recurrence of anger and blame on the part of obese patients against their physicians, for the doctors' failure to cure the weight problem, is a good indication of the patients' perception that the weight problem is the doctor's problem. The effort to establish that the weight is due to the pituitary, hypothalamus, metabolism, etc., is also an effort to establish that the problem is the doctor's affair and not the patient's. These ritual words qualify one for full acceptance into the physician's care. For the dark interior of the body — hidden from me and beyond my direct control — is viewed as the physician's domain. Yet if, as Hilda Bruch asserts, the absence of a sense of owning my body contributes greatly to the emotional and eating disorders of the obese, then the physician's readiness to take over custody of the obese body reproduces the original pathogenic family constellation and runs contrary to the direction necessary for true recovery.

I do not have any easy formulae to resolve this dilemma. The simple demand that the patient assume custody over his body easily degenerates into moralizing — an only too common component in the treatment of obesity.[5] The patient will often insistently demand, and pay highly for, his own disownership. Nevertheless, I dosbelieve that there are countless situations of physician-patient contact, in which the way the patient is addressed and involved in the treatment can strongly facilitate or further stifle the unfolding of the patient's individuality. (When, for instance, the person doing the talking is not the same one who is to feel the scalpel, the questions can be redirected back to the patient concerned. Or when the husband and wife present themselves as 'one patient with two heads,' the physician can stubbornly insist on reaching each treatment decision independently — without regard to the parallel decision affecting the spouse.)

I also believe that the property questions I have outlined above can assist one in becoming aware of the communications about individuality implicit in such medical communications and interactions. Posing the proper questions is always the first step toward change and understanding:

> Who speaks for this body?
> Who makes decisions regarding this body?
> Who dresses and adorns this body?
> Who displays this body?
> Who cares about this body?

VI. AFTERWORD ON PROPERTY, ALIENATION AND BONDAGE

There is another context, encompassing these developments, which should be made explicit. The ever intensifying alienation in modern life pointed out by Marx, has been paralleled by an increasingly indirect relation of man to his own body. Marx wrote: 'Alienated labor alienates from man his own body, external nature, his mental life, and his human life' (Marx, 1844). It is thus perhaps not an accident that the words I use continually to place questions, property and ownership, are in political economic terms. Nor is it accidental that psychology begins to attend to the lack of self-awareness and self-ownership of children, women, psychotic persons, and obese persons, just at that time when the old assumptions — that the child and wife are the property of the husband and father, and that sick and crazy persons are the disenfranchised wards of the paternalistic state — are finally being rooted out. I have already hinted at this political connection earlier by my reference to the flaunting of the gross and neglected body as a form of liberation from bondage. Now I suggest that Marx suggested these issues in the manuscripts of his youth. In general, according to Marx, the historical form which we call private property, is a degenerate form of relationship to things and to other humans. It has made us 'so stupid and partial that an object is only ours when we *have* it.'

Marx by no means elucidated the full extent of the problem of property, ownership, and alienation. We now glimpse — beyond his historically and economically determined alienation — a universal and existential alienation. The modes of the body inevitably include both *being* and *having*, and there are forms of ownership corresponding to each. Throughout his development, the individual is confronted with the task of re-appropriating — coming to *have* as his own — a body experienced as limit, problem, and object.

The obese body, and all impaired bodies, threaten to become mere organism and thing. Sweaty and uncomfortable in the heat, too broad to pass through a narrow turnstyle, unable to assume the positions required for normal hygiene, suffering the strain of an overburdened heart, and too weak and short of breath to ascend a stairway, the obese individual struggles constantly to reappropriate this body-object as his own. In a striking fashion, the obese exemplify for us the universal human need to come to terms with one's own mortality and materiality.

NOTES

* The research for this paper was supported by the Staunton Clinic, Department of Psychiatry, University of Pittsburgh.

1 Throughout this paper I will use appropriation in the original sense of 'making one's own.' The German *Aneignung* carries the same meaning. Alienation and *Entfremdung* express the precise opposite.

2 By 'inhabiting the body,' I do not mean the mere presence of biological life, but rather the fullness of personal presence, of an expressive vitality, and of personal caring for the body. The alive but unhabited human body is as forlorn and perceptibly empty as the abandoned house. By 'inhabiting and action,' I mean to suffuse it with self, to really feel a part of it. To inhabit means to dwell in, and etymology (*in-habitere*) tells us that this is one variation of the basic human modality of *having*.

3 It is possible to distinguish theoretically, and to a certain extent empirically, between primary deficits in body ownership which stem from a childhood failure ever to appropriate the body, its impulses, and appearance as my own, and secondary deficits in body ownership, based on the later disowning of a once-owned body, when, with late weight gain, the body becomes impaired, devalued, and in general difficult to own.

4 In the event of serious problems, the continuity of the intestines is restored and the weight is regained.

5 There is a lot of moralizing in the treatment of obesity, although it is frequently disguised by medical and scientific language. The patient is accused and blamed for being weak, bad, a glutton, and a transgressor against the law that 'animal appetites' should be restrained. Cartoons of obese women as pigs and as hungry vultures accompany the diet drug ads in the obesity journals. The intensity of the condemning, punitive attitude which the obese so frequently evoke is itself worthy of a separate investigation: for example, what indigestible truth, what unacceptable revelation about ourselves does the obese individual confront us with? I submit that this intense punitive attitude is an effort to deflect or ward off his unacceptable truth about ourselves — above all the truth of our own organic and material being, our own animal- and thing-likeness. In spite of the 'moralistic' component in the treatment of obesity, the ethical or moral dimension of many treatment situations, which implicitly convey a message to the individual patient about his individuality and responsibility, is often overlooked.

REFERENCES

Bruch, H.: *Eating Disorders*, N.Y.: Basic Books, 1973.

Marx, K.: Economic and Philosophical Manuscripts. In *Marx's Concept of Man*. E. Fromm (ed.) N.Y.: Frederick Ungar Publishing, 1961.

Merleau-Ponty, M.: The Child's Relations with Others. In *Primacy of Perception*. Evanston: Northwestern University Press, 1964 a.

Merleau-Ponty, M.: *Maurice Merleau-Ponty à la Sorbonne. Bulletin de Psychologie*. 236: XVIII, 3-6, November 1964 b.

Merleau-Ponty, M.: *The Visible and the Invisible*. Evanston: Northwestern University Press, 1968.

Moss, D.: Brain, Body, and World: Perspectives on Body Image. In *Existential-Phenomenological Alternatives in Psychology*. N.Y.: Oxford University Press, 1978.

Schachter, S.: Some extraordinary Facts About Obese Humans and Rats. *American Psychologist*. 26: 129-144, 1971.

Schilder, P.: *Das Körperschema*, Berlin: Springer Verlag, 1923.

Schilder, P.: *The image and Appearance of the Human Body*. N.Y.: International Universities Press, 1935.

Straus, E.: *Phenomenological Psychology*. N.Y.: Basic Books, 1966.

Straus, E.: Phantoms and Phantasmata. Paper delivered at the 4th Lexington Conference. Lexington, Ky., 1967.

Straus, E.: Psychiatry and Philosophy, In *Psychiatry and Philosophy*, M. Natanson (ed.) N.Y.: Springer Verlag, 1969.

Straus, E.; Griffith, R. (eds.): *Phenomenology of Will and Action: the Second Lexington Conference*. Pittsburgh: Duquesne University Press, 1967.

PHENOMENOLOGICAL EVIDENCE AND THE 'IDEA' OF PHYSICS *

FRANCIS J. ZUCKER

1. *Phenomenology and Physics*

This essay is an exercise in applied phenomenology. Husserl mentions 'applications' of phenomenology explicitly in *Ideas III*[1] (p. 81), in connection with the clarification of the foundations of geometry. Implicitly he talks of them whenever he urges the phenomenological clarification of the sciences (for example in *Crisis*[2], § 8, § 9).

Applications of phenomenology are not phenomenology itself; Husserls makes this point emphatically in *Ideas III*[3]. The distinction in *Crisis*[4] between the reduction of the scientific entities to the lifeworld, and the phenomenological reduction of the lifeworld itself, parallels the difference between applied and pure phenomenology.

To do pure phenomenology, as Sokolowski says[5], is to think about being truthful. The material examined in pure phenomenology includes the 'empirical universals', which are the major forms of experiencing the lifeworld[6], and which serve as the starting points of the various scientific disciplines. As attention shifts from the lifeworld universals to the specialized terms introduced by science, phenomenology passes from pure to applied. Since this examination is to proceed in the full light of evidence, Husserl confirms that it merits the predicate 'phenomenological'.[7]

The scientific entities of the exact sciences refer to 'Nature as idea, as a regulative ideal norm' (*FTL*[8], pp. 292), a mathematized nature which is placed 'beneath the Nature dealt with in actual living.'[9] In this quotation, 'idea' is both the eidos of an entire 'category of objectivity' (i.e., of 'mathematized Nature'), and — in view of the noematic-noetic correlation pervading all of phenomenological thought (the '*category of objectivity and category of evidence are perfect correlates*'[10]) — at the same time also the eidos of the 'category of possible experiences' of mathematized nature, i.e., it is the 'regulative ideal norm'. Through these possible experiences, mathematized nature is re-embedded, as it were, in the lifeworld (rather than being placed 'beneath' it, as in the above quotation), and thus Husserl can say of the idea of physics that it is 'the logos, in a higher sense, belonging to actually experienced Nature.'[11]

See notes at the end of this chapter.

The term 'idea' in the title is intended in the sense of this lifeworld logos. It is the task of applied phenomenology — which I hope to sketch out in what follows — to clarify noematically and noetically the mathematized nature hypostasized by physics so that, as 'logos', it may again belong to the lifeworld, and enrich it. The further clarification of the logos would then be the task of pure phenomenology. The other term in the title, 'evidence', refers to the ways in which truthfulness is exhibited in the noematic-noetic analyses. Phenomenological criteria of evidence are stricter than those of the currently dominant analytic philosophy of science; this stringency fuels the motor for a wealth of applications in the philosophy of physics, some of which I will present.

Husserl started this work in his justly famous Galileo analysis,[12] and a number of contributions have since been made.[13] All in all, however, there have been few attempts to test the mettle of the phenomenological method in the arena in which analytic philosophy has been so successful: in the clarification of quite specific questions in the methodology and structure of physics itself. Nor has there been much of an effort to penetrate to the final logos of physics, i.e., to the noematic-noetic elaboration of its meaning at the deepest, most abstract level. Why this hesitation? Is it merely that few phenomenologists consider themselves proficient in the physical sciences, or that some of them perhaps actively dislike them? It seems to me that one might look for an additional reason in a self-misunderstanding of phenomenology, possibly due in part to Husserl himself.

Many of us, I suspect, visualize physics (or any of the other sciences) as a tree grown in the soil of the lifeworld, whose roots 'must be watered with the source of conceptual validity, the intellectual perception'[14], while the upper reaches of the tree are so remote from the sources of meaning, so derivative, as to merit scant attention from the phenomenologist. As Husserl put it: 'Philosophy ... by its very essence, is the science of true beginnings, of origins, the *rizómata panton* ... a science concerned with the roots of things.'[15] J. Klein points out (approvingly) that Husserl's employment of the Empedoclean *rizómata* rather than the more traditional *arché* suggests that 'roots' were more important to him than the 'perfect form'.[16] In our image, the perfect form is the tree, and it is thus perhaps not surprising, though unfortunate, that most phenomenologists feel they need not trouble themselves with the fully developed science.

But the image of the tree is all wrong, and Husserl himself knew it. Physics is not at all tree-like. Many special theoretical domains sprout forth from the level of the lifeworld, for example: planetary motion, terrestrial kinematics, hydrostatics; and magnetostatics, electric currents, geometric optics. These initial domains do not 'branch out' as physics develops, rather they *coalesce* into more inclusive and 'abstract' theories; in our example, into classical mechanics and electromagnetic theory. Physics, to be sure, keeps on discovering new facts and new theoretical domains, but the entire effort of theoretical physics, its telos, is bent on incorporating these into as few super-theories as possible, and indeed preferably into a single one. Husserl comments on this coalescence in *Crisis*: 'Isn't nature altogether mathematical,' he asks, 'must we not think of it as an integrated mathematical system, i.e. as actually representable by an integrated mathematics of nature ...?'[17] Admittedly, there is no follow-up; but if Husserl advises us, in *Ideas III*, to use the eidos of the ontological domain as a 'red thread' in marshalling evidence, and if we remind ourselves of the phenomenological core-maxim already quoted from *FTL* that the eidos of the objectivity and the eidos of the corresponding evidence are perfect correlates[10] – are we not being clearly told, then that evidence is forever inadequate so long as we do not have the final logos of a science? That in order to trace out the roots of our non-tree, in other words, one needs also to examine its top? If we do so, we will find (as I will try to indicate) that the noetic correlates of the higher-level noemata extend into areas of the lifeworld, and thus also of the subjectivity, that can *only in retrospect* be recognized as having been relevant already in the historically first steps into physics. However carefully the phenomenologist might distinguish clearly between historical (and cognitive-psychological) analyses on the one hand, and genetic-phenomenological ones on the other, he is still, I suggest, lightly caught in the historicism (and psychologism) Husserl so passionately fought, so long as he mistakes Husserl's historical focus in the Galileo analysis as an injunction against extending the search for roots beyond merely historical studies. Husserl does not ask us to thus confine ourselves in the quotations just cited; indeed it seems to me that pure phenomenology *requires* the full scope of the applied work for its own progressive completion. Scientific truth is part of truth and, in the end, truth is meant to be one and indivisible.

In lieu of the mistaken tree, then, we might be better off to picture applied phenomenological work in terms of the 'mixed' phenomenological-ontological' method which Husserl describes at the end of § 16 in *Ideas III*. While insisting, throughout that important paragraph, on the clean separation between noema and essence, and restricting the domain of pure phenomenology to the former, he does also refer repeatedly to the mere change in focus that turns noema into essence; and he grants at the end of that paragraph (and also in the equally important following § 17) that ontological considerations do play their part in phenomenological work, and that valid results can indeed be obtained by including them explicitly.[18] I know of no other way of assimilating the sedimented meanings of physics to our understanding than by repeated changes in focus between critical (phenomenological) and ontological attitude: thought, which starts by bracketing the scientific entities, moves not only 'from noematic sense to constitutive apriori and back in critical assessment of the original noema'; it must also, at the end of each swing, re-open the brackets so as to *bring in* the phenomenological harvest. That means, on the noematic side, turning the constitution of physical terms and theories into their logical reconstruction; and on the noetic side, formulating the eidos of the constitutive apriori so as to have it available as a foil in clarifying the sedimented meanings studied in history and genetic epistemology, both of them ontologically-oriented scientific disciplines.

We continue this process in a series of expanding pendulum swings, by bracketing successively higher-order (more abstract) physical terms and theories, and turning up the correlative, successively deeper genetic strata on the noetic side.[19]

If the work is conducted in this spirit, the scope and significance of the phenomenological contribution to the philosophy of physics quickly reveal themselves. In Section 2 ('Quantity and Physical Object'), I try to take up the discussion roughly where Husserl left off in *Crisis*. In conformity with Husserl's claim that 'every originary intuition 'comprises' the essence of the region corresponding to it,'[20] I show that the measurement of length already implies a major feature of the eidos 'physical object'. The corollary, that the originary intuition prescribes the principles of method,[21] leads to a first demonstration of the normative value of the strict evidential criteria in phenomenology which, it turns out, force the choice of a scale for temperature that differs from the one in current use. While this scale modification does affect the meaning of some of the basic terms in the theory of heat, it leaves the theoretical formalism untouched. In Section 3 ('Constitution of Theory'), the phenomenological criteria entering in the constitution of two physical theories actually affect their formal structure, i.e., they force their logical reconstruction. (Sections 2 and 3 unfortunately require the writing of a few equations; the reader who has to skip them and the immediately adjoining discussions can, I think, still follow the drift of the argument.) Section 4 ('Noematic Analyses of the Objects of Physics') outlines the classical phenomenological task of tracing 'modes of givenness.' The meaning of 'object' in physics is found to undergo important modifications as one progresses from the material thing in the lifeworld to the objects of quantum mechanics. At its deepest level, physics seems not to describe irreducible building blocks of matter but the set of conditions for resolving the universe into isolable objects – the 'compossibility', that is, of all there is in our one world.[22] The correlative noetic conception is briefly stated in Section 5 ('Toward the Logos of Physics'): it is that physics expresses the formal preconditions of the possibility of objectifying experience. Though Kantian-sounding, this formulation owes much more to C.F. von Weizsacker;[23] its justification can, unfortunately, only be hinted at in the present context. Because of the mathematical nature of physical theory, noetic clarification must deal with the roots of mathematical meaning as well. These roots can be studied historically, and they are equally the subject matter of a scientific discipline that did not exist in Husserl's time, but which he called for under the title 'phenomenological psychology' (today's 'cognitive psychology' or 'genetic espitemology'). I will try to show that the physical entities cannot, therefore, be analyzed noetically without constant reference to material that can only be made available through the *noematic* analysis of the 'objects' (i.e., the mathematical performances) studied in that new discipline. This yoking of the logoi of physics, mathematics, and psychology prefigures the essential connectedness of all the sciences in the phenomenological reduction.

2. Quantity and Physical Object

In a first step beyond the scope of Husserl's Galileo analysis, let us briefly consider the arithmetization of the measurement process (i.e., the establishment of quantitative scales), a topic that has been carefully analyzed in ordinary (analytic) philosophy of science. If Husserl is right in saying that 'method is determined by the eidos of the objectivity in a particular domain'[21], it must conversely be possible to bring that eidos before us in a reflection on the essence of quantification, and indeed to begin 'constituting' it. This step is not one that has explicitly been taken in ordinary philosophy of science, but it could perhaps be justified within that context. In a further step, I use the 'originary intuition' of quantification normatively, as promised, to force the choice of a temparature scale which ordinary philosophy of science would insist on regarding as merely defined by convention.

All of us know that two lengths L_1 and L_2 measured along a straight line combine additively to form a total length L_t:

$$L_t = L_1 + L_2.$$

To separate the operational and the arithmetic elements more clearly, let us call the laying of two lengths end to end a 'combining operation' (denoted by '&'), and write

$$L(l_1 \ \& \ l_2) = L(l_1) + L(l_2), \tag{1}$$

where the l's stand for the extended physical things (yardsticks), and the L's are the numerical values. This relation is obvious if we start out with ruled yardsticks; it can be proven conversely that (1) is a necessary — though not sufficient — condition for the existence of a quantative scale in the first place.[24] Nature provides us with combining operations that lead to such a scale only in special cases. A property such as the hardness of materials, for example, though physical, cannot be characterized by a combining operation '&' that splits up additively as in (1); thus 'hardness' is not a quantity.[25]

One further example of a quantitative scale, which we will need in the following Section, is the 'intensity' I of light, as measured by a photometer. If we superpose the light spot $I(s_1)$ produced on a screen by light source s_1 with the light spot $I(s_2)$ from an independently-lit source s_2 (for example, two ordinary light bulbs), the total intensity as measured by the photometer satisfies the addition rule (1):

$$I(s_1 \ \& \ s_2) = I(s_1) + I(s_2). \tag{2}$$

This superposition of light spots is called 'incoherent', to distinguish it from the 'coherent' superposition in Section 3. Because (2) is satisfied (and several other conditions, not mentioned here, as well), the photometer scale is not merely ordinal[25] but quantitative.

The physical quantities do not have to be real numbers, as in (1) and (2). If they are, they are called 'scalars'. 'Force' and 'velocity' are quantities called 'vectors': they possess a scalar magnitude and also a direction in space, and satisfy an addition law that looks like (1) but must be understood vectorially. In the next Section we will encounter a quantity that is 'complex' (i.e., characterized by a real and an imaginary number), and there are several other, higher types of quantity: 'quaternions,' the various sorts of 'tensors,' 'spinors,' and, in quantum mechanics, the 'operators.' In each case, one can specify in precise operational terms and additive combination relation of the *form* (1).

Using lengths and weights (which also obey relation (1) when placed side by side on the pan of a balance) as his paradigms, the Fifteenth-Century neo-Platonist Nicolas Cusanus enjoined philosophers to search out quantity in all appearances, and thus opened the door to Galilean physics. The concern of physics, however, is not with quantitative scales for their own sake, but with physical *objects*. How is the idea of a physical object connected with (1)?

An object is something we can point to as distinct from its environment, from the rest of the world. A *totally* isolated object would be invisible, its presence would not be discoverable — in short, it could not be said to exist. At the very least, an object has to act on a probe, though the effect of the probe on the object may still be taken as negligible. To be able to establish a quantitative scale, we have to be able to fabricate unit elements which can be combined in the manner of (1) — in the manner of peas in two pots whose contents are merged. Interaction between the unit elements would immediately destroy the additivity, as would be the case with peas, say, if you mash them while they are being merged. The condition (1) therefore says that a physical object remains 'itself' with respect to some property in the presence of other objects; the two light spots upon being superposed retain the number of units each contained separately, they neither clot into less than their sum nor spawn more of their own, and thus satisfy (2). The additivity relation, then, is constitutive for there being identifiable, separate physical objects; to the extent that a perhaps quite complex 'phenomenon' (an appearance or event) can be characterized in terms of quantities, it may be regarded as resolvable into individual and isolable objects.

Quantitative scales can often be established for properties that do not seem to belong to physical objects. Consider the well-tempered musical scale, for example. Like a scale for length, it too consists in multiples of a unit (the halftone interval, for example), and we can count the number of these units in any interval, or sum of intervals; thus relation (1) is satisfied. Can we nevertheless find an immanent scale characteristic that would allow us to distinguish between a physical property such as length, and a psychological one such as the pitch interval? A unit of length can be moved about in space, and can thus measure unit distance anywhere along a body of arbitrary length. A kilogram weight placed together with other kilogram weights on a pan that balances an unknown weight can count equally well as the 'first', 'second', or 'last' kilogram of that weight. Units of length and weight, in other words, can be 'translated' up and down their scales. The half-tone interval can not: while a musical tone that changes in loudness is still perceived as 'the same' tone, a change in pitch means that one tone fades out and is *replaced* by another; thus the interval C – C-sharp, though 'equal to' the interval D – D-sharp as a half-tone step, nevertheless cannot be 'shifted' into it. The so-called 'translation invariance,' which here appears as a characteristic constitutive of physical properties will be mentioned again in Section 4.

Having shown that certain aspects of the idea of physics are already contained in the 'originary intuition' of quantitative measurement, we will now flex our phenomenological muscle by employing evidence normatively. Our example is the temperature scale. No combination law exists for temperature, but a quantitative scale can be defined indirectly by tying the degrees of temperature to the increase in length under heating of a column of mercury.[26] The expansion of the column immediately established an ordinal scale, i.e., it enables us to tell which one of two given temperatures is the higher one (corresponds to the longer column). Assume now a column length L_1 at temperature T_1 which expands to L_2 upon heating the column to T_2. Experiments with heated materials tell us that the increase in length is a certain fraction f of the length at T_1. Thus

$$L_2 = L_1 + fL_1 = (1 + f)L_1. \tag{3}$$

If the length at T_1 had been $L_1' = (1 + f)L_1$ to begin with, the length at T_2 would have been

$$L_2' = L_1' + fL_1' = (1 + f)L_1 + f(1 + f)L_1. \tag{4}$$

The increases in length corresponding to the same temperature difference $T_2 - T_1$ are not the same in these two instances, since $L_2 - L_1 = fL_1$, whereas $L_2' - L_1' = fL_1' = f(1 + f)L_1$. If we tie temperature increase to column expansion, we must therefore, for the sake of consistency, stipulate that the increase from T_1 to T_2 (which we might as well decide to call the 'unit' increase, i.e. 'one degree' above T_1) is correlated with a *fractional* increase in length, as in (3) and (4); it would not do to arbitrarily declare the length increase corresponding to some particular starting length as defining the one degree increase for *all* starting lengths.

Assume now that we again start with L_1 at T_1, heat by one degree to L_2 (at T_2), and now continue heating. At what length L_3 will the temperature have gone up by another degree (to T_3)? In the spirit of the foregoing we would say quite simply that

$$L_3 = L_2 + fL_2. \tag{5}$$

This is not, however, how the temperature scale has actually been defined. The stipulation used for a one-degree increase beyond the first degree is

$$L_3' = L_2 + fL_1, \qquad (6)$$

i.e., the length increase correlated with the one-degree temperature increase from T_1 to T_2 is used to define a one-degree increase from T_2 to T_3, or in fact anywhere else up and down the scale. Gone is the tie-in with the *fractional* length increase. It turns out that no formal inconsistency is introduced by this choice; thus in the eyes of ordinary philosophy of science, either definition is indeed possible, the decision in other words is purely conventional.

Not so from the point of view of phenomenology. Since the temperature scale is to be defined in terms of column expansion, the 'eidos' of the natural phenomenon 'expasion due to heating' must be allowed to determine method fully. The eidos is the structure, the law of heat expansion; i.e., it is the fractional length increase relation (3), and an eidos-determined method therefore constitutes the unit temperature increase in accordance with (5) not (6). If we are being told by nature that a one-degree increase in temperature (starting at *any* temperature T) corresponds to a length increase that is simply proportional to the column length itself, then the choice of the unit size at different temperatures would have to invoke some new evidence to depart from the proportionality relation — and such evidence does not exist.

The temperature scale used by physicists, defined on the basis of (6), has a peculiar property: it has an 'absolute zero', i.e. a coldness limit below which the temperature cannot fall. This limit, however, has no clear physical significance: according to 'Nernst's Theorem', an infinite amount of energy would be required to reach it — which means, in effect, that it cannot be reached. (It is thus confusing to the layman to read that one has achieved a temperature in the laboratory of 'almost absolute zero' — at say, one-thousandth of a degree above it — since this sounds as if, some day soon, absolute zero itzelf might be reached, whereas in fact it still requires an infinite amount of energy to bridge the remaining gap.) If, on the other hand, the definition were based on (5), one would obtain a temperature scale that is logarithmically related to the one officially adopted, and which would therefore extend from minus to plus infinity. 'Infinite cold' would then look as unreachable on that scale as 'infinite heat', as in fact both are. Such a scale has been proposed, and laboratory workers near 'absolute zero' have used it.[27] Its true importance, however, is conceptual not practical; because the temperature enters in the definition of the terms 'entropy' and 'quantity of heat', the meaning of these terms, which are basic in the theory of heat, is affected. In fact, entropy becomes synonymous with quantity of heat in this modified theory (taking some of the mystery out of 'entropy'), and the quantity of heat of the standard theory becomes a heat-energy function similar to the 'potential' in mechanics or electrodynamics.[28] These conceptual shifts do not, however, affect the formal content of the theory of heat.

It is beginning to look as if the insistence on phenomenological criteria of evidence can in some cases lead to the constitution of a physical theory modified, in some sense, with respect to the generally accepted theory. The following Section will discuss two examples in which even the formal structure of the theory is affected.

3. Constitution of Theory

In the conceptual laundering prescribed by Husserl,[14] Occam's razor is wielded with a resolve reminiscent of radical empiricism: *'only within the limits in which something is given to it'* Husserl says (his italics) in his 'Principle of Principles'[29], does the originary intuition justify a cognition; and in *Ideas III* he demands[30] that to each elemental term pertaining to an entity, an explicit element in its mode of givenness should correspond. Have we not learned long since in the philosophy of science, though, that the radical empiricist program cannot be carried through, that theories cannot be formulated without terms that have no direct phenomenal reference? But Husserl never thought otherwise: he did not wield the razor to downgrade the theoretical entities, but on the contrary, to throw their ontic status into bolder relief; as the conceptual laundering proceeds, the theoretical prejudices with which we necessarily start are not to be elemininated but purified, until their essence stands out. In fact, as both examples will show, the strictness of evidence *forces* the precise delineation of the essence.

Consider two narrow slits in a screen which serve as the two sources $I(s_1)$ and $I(s_2)$ in an experiment on the 'interference properties' of light. The two slits are in turn illuminated by a single, monochromatic light bulb placed to the left of the screen. Because of its common origin, the light from the slits is 'coherent'; a second screen, that is, placed to the right of the first, will not be illuminated uniformly, as it would be by two separate, 'incoherent' sources, but will instead show a pattern of fringes, i.e., of alternating light and dark strips. Thus equation (2) for the superposition of incoherent light (which served to define the photometer scale) is no longer obeyed; instead, we must add another term on its right-hand side to account for the periodic intensity variation across the second screen:

$$I(s_1 \ \& \ s_2) = I(s_1) + I(s_2) + 2\sqrt{I(s_1)I(s_2)} \cos a, \qquad (7)$$

where the symbol & stands for the coherent superposition of light (to distinguish if from the symbol & in (2) for the incoherent superposition), and a for the angle-dependent factor that generates the fringing.

The fringes had early reminded physicists of water ripples, and the equation they wrote was that governing water waves or waves along a stretched rope, i.e., periodic motion in space and time of a quantity called the wave amplitude, E (for 'electric field', which it later turned out to be). This quantity is the excursion of the wave from the median position, and it is measured in units of length, i.e., by a real number. But in two ways the analogy with mechanical waves does not seem to stand up to evidence: light waves are static when we look at the fringes, there are no visible parts and in fact we *measure* no variations in time;

if there is an underlying movement, it is too fast to be noticed not only by the human eye but also by our instrument, the photometer. And secondly, the photometer does not measure the wave amplitude E directly, but the quantity I, obtained by computing the time average of the square of E. This indirect relation gives no assurance that E is a real-number quantity, since a complex number, too (and a 'quaternion' as well, and other sorts of numbers) produces a real-number I as the square of its magnitude. Thus both from the point of view of radical empiricism and of phenomenology, the theory is flawed by the presence of two gratuitous elements to which no mode of givenness corresponds: the time variable, and the real-number nature of the amplitude field E.

How do we proceed if the requirements of evidence knock the familiar wave equation out of our hands? Let us remind ourselves of the idea of physics to the extent that we have already become acquainted with it. The two slits, according to (7), do not act like independent physical objects with respect to the property measured by I, since the I's are not simply additive. Yet the slits are, after all, two separately radiating objects in space, even if they in turn are illuminated by a single light source; could we perhaps find some property *other* than I which *will* be additive as in (1)? In other words, let us now use (1) normatively, because it is part of the idea of a physical object.

The combination rule (7) is known in trigonometry as the 'cosine superposition law', which can also be written in terms of the complex numbers E^c:

$$I(s_1 \ \&' \ s_2) \ = \ \left| E^c(s_1) \ + \ E^c(s_2) \right|^2 \ = \ \left| E^c(s_1 \ \&' \ s_2) \right|^2. \tag{8}$$

On comparing the second and third expression, we see that E^c is the sought-for property. More rigorously, we can use Frobensius's theorem to prove that if the combined light in (7) is to be a function of the *sum* of two terms, then these terms *must* be complex numbers, or else quaternions — these would in fact be needed if we wished to accomodate polarization effects — but cannot possibly be real numbers (nor the higher order 'Cayley numbers'). A rather simple argument then allows us to conclude that the equation governing the distribution in space of E^c is the so-called 'reduced wave equation', in which the time variable does not appear and which otherwise differs from the ordinary wave equation only in the complex nature of the field amplitude.

With the help of the 'idea' of physics, then, we have reconstructed a piece of the science itself, and in this particular instance (chosen for this reason) the reconstruction differs somewhat from the original theory, which was based on the analogy with mechanical waves. Can we decide which is 'correct'? Since the predictions are, in photometer optics, identical, we shall have to look outside this field for a decision. Clearly, it is time-dependent optical phenomena that will adjudicate the issue. In lieu of photometers, we must now use photon counters to be able to follow, at least in certain circumstances, the time variations. The result is clear-cut: in the case of visible light, only that produced by a laser oscillates in time in the manner predicted by the ordinary wave equation; sunlight, or the light from an electric bulb, does not, it is not at all wave-like in time but radiates in short irregular pulses that cannot be resolved into periodic time variations. The reduced wave equation, by contrast, in modestly restricting itself to the domain of photometer measurements for which it was designed, remains correct for laser as well as sunlight.

The question of correctness can also be raised with respect to the theoretical context: which equation is the appropriate special case of the deeper-level quantum statistical theory of radiation? To begin with, the field amplitude from this point of view must certainly be complex, since it is so in quantum statistics. It can further be shown that, for laser radiation, the ordinary wave equation comes out of the quantum formalism (with complex field amplitude, though), whereas for natural light the reduced wave equation is retrieved.[31] It was for the sake of the latter, of course, that the mechanical wave model was originally set up.

The assertion in all elementary and intermediate physics texts that wave optical phenomena are governed by a real-amplitude wave equation is thus not justifiable within the field itself (using phenomenological criteria of justification), and false within the larger experimental as well as theoretical context. Our logical reconstruction, by contrast, has produced a specialized theory perfectly tailored to the domain of photometer optics, and immune to making false predictions outside it.

The second example is from statistical thermodynamics (or 'statistical mechanics'), which in the textbooks comes in two principal variants, classical and (on a deeper level) quantum mechanical. In the former, atoms and molecules are treated as classical particles; this theory yields numerical values for the large number of material constants which ordinary thermodynamics (the elementary theory of heat mentioned in Section 2) knows only as empirically determined values. While it is remarkable that classical statistical mechanics can compute the material constants at all, the results are frequently far off the mark. Since quantum statistical mechanics predicts correct values for these same constants and for additional ones as well, it is taken by the physicist to be the true theory, which relegates the function of the classical variant to a merely historical and pedagogical one.

Physicists have known for some time, however, that the classical theory can be freed of its flaw by treating the atoms and molecules 'semi-classically', i.e., by assuming that they are totally indistinguishable from each other, which of course lifeworld particles never are. The ensuing semi-classical statistical mechanics predicts the same numerical values for the material constants as quantum statistical mechanics, although the scope of these predictions is, of course, not as wide.

The indistinguishability of microparticles is therefore considered to be an *ad hoc* medley of classical and quantum features. From the phenomenological point of view, this is not so: the semi-classical theory turns out to be the only possible theory on the non-quantum level; it is the theory, in other words, that ought to *replace* the classical one. Two ways of arguing this point suggest themselves. As mentioned in the following Section, the concept of an idealized physical model already implies, even in elementary classical mechanics, that two bodies of the same theoretical sort are, in terms of the theory governing their motion, indistinguishable from one another; this of course would also apply to molecules. In the case of ordinary classical mechanics, the theory is indifferent to a shift from lifeworld distinguishability to physical-model non-distinguishability; in statistical mechanics, by contrast, this shift affects the statistical distribution of the physical properties of the molecules, and thus turns the predictions from incorrect into correct ones.

The second way employs the eidos 'quantity' normatively, as in our coherent optics example. In thermodynamics, entropy is additive, in the sense of (1), with respect to spatial composition. (Doubling the volume of a material doubles the entropy.) The fundamental concepts of thermodynamics, including the notion of a temperature scale (*any* temperature scale) and of 'equilibrium', turn out to depend on this quantitative nature of entropy. It was early noticed, however, that the classical statistics of molecules violates the additivity of entropy ('Gibb's Paradox'). In constituting statistical mechanics, which is to lie on a deeper level than thermodynamics, we demand that in the more restricted domain within which thermodynamics is valid its principal structures should be retrievable from the theory being constituted. That means enforcing the additivity property of the entropy and this in turn, as can rather easily be shown, brings the non-distinguishability of the molecules, and hence the correct statistical properties, directly in its wake.[32]

4. *Noematic Analyses of the Objects of Physics*

The following is a mere sketch of some of the noematic tasks ahead for the phenomenologist investigating the Logos of Physics. Even as a rudimentary sketch, it is inadequate, its worst gap being the total omission of the topic of time, surely the most fundamental constitutive element in physics (or in almost anything else, for that matter).[33] What I will discuss is the meaning of equations in physics, the notion of the 'physical model' as a link between lifeworld things and objects on the abstract level, and the modes of givenness of some of the deeper physical entities.

We found an essential connection in Section 2 between the concept of a quantified observable as defined (in part) by the additive combination rule (1), and the idea of a physical object as isolable, with respect to that observable, from other objects in the world (including objects of the same sort). Quantity, then, is constitutive of the object as a physical one. Thus, although the light intensity I and the complex field amplitude E^c in Section 3 both refer to light, they stand for two different physical objects, for two different ways of quantifying and thus objectivating light, depending on the manner in which the light has been 'prepared': incoherently or coherently, corresponding to quantifications (2) and (3), respectively.

Physics relates different quantities to each other through equations. If we know the value of E^c at the two slits, we can, with the help of the reduced wave equation, which governs interference optics, find the field amplitudes everywhere in the region beyond the slits. An entirely different equation governs incoherent fields; this theory is known as 'geometric' or 'ray' optics.[34] In this case, if we know the values of I in one region of space (called the 'object plane'), we can calculate its values everywhere else (in the 'image planes'). The function of equations, then, is the gathering into a single form of all possible value distributions of quantities like E^c or I throughout space. Put in another way, the quantity E^c (or I) does not, by itself, constitute the physical object 'coherent light' (or 'light in terms of rays'); the position in space, i.e., the quantity 'length' as measured from some coordinate origin, is equally needed in both cases. It is thus always a *lawfully-connected cluster of quantities* that constitutes what we mean by 'physical object.'

To consider one further example: in planetary motion, the change of position along the orbit in time is determined by the velocity, and the change of velocity by the position. If one knows the position and velocity of the planet at one time, one can calculate their values for all other times. A physical object is therefore defined, somewhat more generally than above, as a cluster of quantities such that, given their values at one time, the values are fixed throughout space for all future and past times (if the equations are 'reversible'), or at least for all future times (if 'irreversible'); thus the equations of physics make *predictions* concerning quantitative values in appearances and events.

The equations which connect quantities to a cluster are gained by 'induction' from experiments, i.e., by 'educated guessing'. As physics becomes more sophisticated, the qualification 'educated' assumes a growing importance: the deeper the theory, the more decisive the role of theoretical arguments in its construction. These arguments have to do with the 'symmetries' and 'invariances' of space and time, for example with the notion that the form of an equation should not, in a physically isotropic situation, pick out one direction in space as physically different from another; or with the notion that, given a particular initial value for a quantity, the value at a later time should depend only on the time difference that has elapsed, not on the absolute time. To cite one instance: in the abstract formulation of classical electromagnetic theory, the quantities that appear in the simpler, more specialized theories which that theory subsumes can be stacked into two higher-order quantities called 'tensors'; the equation that relates these two can then be written down purely on the basis of abstract reasoning, thus eliminating the role of induction on that level. Induction remains relevant, however, in the construction of the tensors themselves, i.e., in the determination as to what sort of quantities are relevant in electromagnetism in the first place. This circumstance seems to have been largely overlooked in the usual methodologies of science. It is as if the deductive features of physics become more prominent in the degree in which the eidos of its deeper entities reveals itself. To this point we will return after having taken a look at some further features of physical objects which seem to change as we enter the deeper levels of physics.

Husserl emphasized the process of idealization which precedes the constitution of the physical entities.[35] In this process, perceptual forms becomes *Limesgebilde*, 'limiting forms' which are mathematical in nature. One can link the lifeworld things to the idealized forms with the help of 'physical models.' A small, geometrically perfect sphere rotating around a larger one, for example, still 'look like' the moon and earth for which they stand. However, they differ in one important respect from the lifeworld moon and earth. The description of a real thing never exhausts the possible information about it – further details concerning its structure and looks can always be added. The physical model, on the other hand, is completely specified as soon as the quantitative values are listed which it is supposed to exemplify. One can of course add that the small sphere is, say, painted silver and the large one blue, but this information is irrelevant to the spheres *qua* physical model. Of the pattern of light fringes on a screen one could also still say that it is 'thing-like'; one would have to imagine the screen moved all around in space, though, to visualize the total E^c-field as such a 'thing'. And if we pass from visible radiation (light) to the diverse invisible sorts (infra-red, microwaves, X-rays), we are left with mere meter readings everywhere in space. The E^c-field is then still an idealization from these readings, but we would be hard put to point at anything at all like an ordinary thing of which it is the idealization;[36] the physical object has become the Cheshire cat's grin. Or rather, grins. On the level of abstraction on which electromagnetic theory lies, a tremendous range of phenomenally very diverse physical events is subsumed under this one formalism; they fall under many special disciplines, such as electrostatics, electric currents, radio waves, and the radiations just mentioned. The physical model links lifeworld appearances uniquely to physical theory only on these lifeworld-near disciplines. Beyond a certain level of abstraction and generalization, the linkage is no longer unique: many different physical models, as we have just seen, now correspond to one very general theory. On the level of quantum mechanics, two such models may even be contradictory in lifeworld terms: it is well known, for example, that an electron can in that theory appear to be wave-like or particle-like, depending on the way in which it has been 'prepared.' The electron is wave-like if made to pass through a double-slit arrangement, particle-like when it travels from the cathode to the anode in a vacuum tube, and anything in-between when the set-up is not clearly one of these two limiting arrangements – as it is not, for example, for an electron bound in orbit around the nucleus of an atom.[37] The quantum equation governing the electron covers all these cases; there is no logical inconsistency whatever in the eidos 'electron'.

Phenomenological method is a sound guide into the world of the deeper physical entities. While its basically realist stance, so rightly emphasized by P. Heelan,[38] rejects a merely instrumentalist interpretation (electrons as a 'convenience' of thought for the integration of otherwise unconnected data), its focus on the modes of givenness of the scientific entities keeps one elastic with respect to their precise ontological status. The following two examples will underline the necessity of the latter by showing how much more subtle the modes of reality turn out to be than any preconceived lifeworld or metaphysical notion of it could possibly anticipate.

In the statistical theory of thermodynamics mentioned at the end of Section 3, an immense number of possible 'microstates' (an ensemble of molecules whose exact positions and velocities are clearly defined at all times) is known to correspond to a single 'macrostate' (an ordinary physical object as treated in the classical theory of heat, without reference to molecules). The entropy of the macrostate can be shown to be a measure of the spread of possible microstates corresponding to it; this, we are told, means that entropy measures our 'ignorance' concerning the 'actual' microstate. I will now suggest, however, that the mode of givenness of microstates is necessarily merely *potential*; we should rather say, therefore, that entropy measures the indefiniteness of the molecular configuration, and not a merely subjective ignorance.

A molecule that can be either in the left or in the right half of a container is a 'message source' worth one 'bit' of information. If the molecules is discovered, say through a scattering experiment, in the left half, and a wall is quickly inserted to keep it there, then this *possible* bit of information has become *actual*. The entropy of the one-molecule system turns out at the same time to have been halved due to the molecule's now occupying only one half of its previous space. Thus entropy corresponds to potential information concerning the detailed structure of a physical system, and as this information is actualized, as the microstructure is made 'manifest', so to speak, the entropy drops (and finally becomes zero). There is a clear sense, then, in which the microsystem 'gives itself' as *complementary* to the macro-system, and Bohr knew as much when in his 'Faraday Lecture'[39] he said that *'the very concept of temperature stands in an exclusive relation to a detailed description of the behaviour of the atoms'* (Bohr's italics).

It may be worth while to indicate a formal aspect of this queer mode of givenness. Let S be the proposition 'the macrosystem has the entropy S and certain additional thermodynamic properties', and M_i the proposition 'the microsystem is actually in the state M_i'. The conjunction

$$S \wedge (M_1 \vee M_2 \vee \ldots)$$

is then certainly true, in fact it represents the basic idea of statistical mechanics. If now we regroup these terms on the basis of the distribution law of ordinary logic in the form

$$(S \wedge M_1) \vee (S \wedge M_2) \quad \ldots,$$

we notice that each expression in parantheses, and therefore the disjunction as a whole, is false: a physical object, we had just seen, cannot simultaneously be a macrosystem with entropy S and any particular microsystem — no matter which. Not mere human ignorance, but the concept of potentiality is the noematic key to the ontological status of the term 'microstate.'

The role of potentiality is still further enhanced in the modes in which the objects of quantum mechanics give themselves. Non-distributivity here becomes part and parcel of the theory itself (hence the expression: quantum 'logic'[40]), not merely of the relation between the properties of objects on two different theoretical levels, as above. Quantum mechanics is the deepest physical theory we have at the moment; if, as physicists must hope, it turns out some day to be only an approximation to a yet more comprehensive theory, perhaps to *the* unified theory that encompasses all the still unconnected areas of physics in one 'coherent mathematics of nature' (Husserl[17]), the objects of that deepest theory are unlikely to seem less odd to us. To illustrate the role of potentiality in quantum mechanics, consider two billiard balls which, after a collision, of course remain the same two billiard balls they had been before (except for tiny dents, perhaps). The quantum mechanical formalism, by contrast, makes it impossible to conceive of two high energy microphysical particles in this manner after collision. Not only are the two particles, if of the same sort, as indistinguishable from each other as the molecules at the end of Section 4, so that one couldn't possibly tell 'which one' of the two scattered particles is 'identical' with one of the incident ones. One cannot even, in most cases, speak of them as two separate scattered particles, they form a single global system until a specific experimental setup peels them out of their mutual entwinement. One cannot, therefore, predict *what sort* of physical entities will emerge from the interaction until the setup has been prepared which determines what particular quantities are to be measured: several sorts of particles may be *possible*, each defined by a different quantity (or quantity cluster).[41] We are thus forced to say that matter does not, in the end, consist of uniquely defined entities, it is not a sum of finished building blocks: the potential parts have to be teased out of bulk matter before we can speak of their actual existence as spatially and temporally definite entities, and it is the environment — artificial, as in an experiment, or natural — which codetermines the exact sort of entity that does show itself.

The concept of a reality that exists independently of the type of question we (or nature) address to it, independently of our being capable of knowing it, at least in principle — this common-sense reality concept which modern physics, prior to quantum mechanics, had accepted as a matter of course, is false. It was false already on the level of the lifeworld, as phenomenologists well know; natural science, in a manner far more subtle than could have been foreseen, has now corrected the error on the microlevel as well.

5. *Toward the Logos of Physics*

To what eidos of physics do the foregoing noematic sketches point? Quantity, as we saw in Section 2, represents a property with respect to which an appearance or event can be resolved into isolated objects. By clustering several quantities into a lawfully connected whole and thus constituting a fully defined 'physical object', one has identified the additive elements into which an entire domain of appearances or events can be resolved. As we have just seen, the additivity of these entities signifies no more than that they can, on demand, be exhibited separately; the possibility of resolving all there is in the world into such entities does not imply that the world 'consists' of them as of actual existents. What of the equations that govern the fundamental entities? We can say this much: since the equations relate quantities to each other, they specify the network of conditions under which these quantities must co-exist. Put in another way, physics appears to state the set of conditions under which objects can be lifted out of their context of interwovenness with the rest of the world; physics is the formal theory of the *compossibility* of all there is, as we said before,[22] when the world has been objectivated as far as objectivation will go.

Noematic analyses do not exhaust the phenomenological inquiry into the meaning of physics: 'any straightforwardly constituted objectivity (for example: an Object belonging to Nature) points back, according to its *essential sort* (for example: physical thing *in specie*), to a correlative *essential form* of ... intentionality, which is constitutive for the objectivity.'[42]

Let us then ask what contributions this noetic correlative van make to our understanding of physics.

If physics, on the noematic side, is the formal expression of the possibility of resolving the world into objects, then the noetic side, correlatively, must be the subjective possibility of thus objectivating our experience of the world. We are immediately reminded of Kant's analogous claim that the preconditions of the possibility of experience are the preconditions of the *objects* of that experience. In his *Metaphysical Foundations of Natural Science*, Kant tried, but failed, to develop the preconditions of the possibility of (objectivating) experience into a set of principles from which to *derive* the physics of his day. This is a possibility that ought also to be considered by phenomenologists, because Husserl, after referring to the 'coherent mathematics of nature' asks: 'Why is it that we have no prospect of discovering nature's own axiomatic [Husserl means the axioms of the basic physical laws] as one whose axioms are apodictically self-evident?'[17] Inspired by (but arguing independently of) Kant rather than Husserl, C.F. von Weizsäcker has been at work on the 'integrated mathematics of nature' over a period of many years, approaching this topic both ontically, i.e., within the normal context of research in theoretical physics, and noetically, i.e., in terms of a theory of the preconditions of experience which is to furnish the axioms for the most general laws of physics. For it is only for the final, all-encompassing physics, Weizsäcker feels, that we can expect a correlative general theory of experience; Kant was bound to fail with the limited physics then available.[43] To the extent that this program succeeds — to date, Weizsäcker has been able to state some axioms that do appear to be 'apodictically evident' in any theory of objectivation, and to construct certain features of quantum mechanics from them — we will gain a *new type* of understanding of the fundamental equations of physics: whereas previously (in Section 4) we merely observed that the form of the equations governing theories tends to become more intelligible on apriori grounds the deeper the theory, we would now, at the deepest level, understand also why they have precisely that mathematical form which in fact they have. A more radical turn than this in the function of transcendental philosophy from the merely passive analysis of existing science to an active collaboration in its *construction* would be hard to conceive.[44]

All instances of quantification in the lifeworld can now be recognized as initial steps in the development of a mode of experiencing that pushes objectivation to its furthest limits;[45] thus the logos of physics becomes visible, in retrospect at any rate, at the gateway of the subjective performances (measurement!) that lead to its full development. The true significance of the intuition of Nicolas Cusanus (and Galileo) concerning quantification can only be appreciated, it seems to me, with this further development in mind.

Assuming that we do succeed in formulating the axioms for the 'coherent mathematics of nature', we still require a vast range of noetic analyses before the logos of physics on all its levels and in all of its ramifications can be said to have truly become embedded in experience. It is worth while to pick at least one topic as an example, merely so as to discover what would be involved in such a study. Consider the notion of 'velocity'. In Newtonian mechanics and, at least apparently, in the lifeworld of our time (we should not venture an untutored guess concerning the lifeworld in, say, the stone age), velocity is derived from the notions of space and time. In the special theory of relativity it looks conversely, as if space (some also say: time) might be a construct based on velocity, which would be the more elementary notion. If we try to constitute these two notions of 'velocity' by starting from Husserl's analyses of inner time consciousness, in which 'time' and 'flow' both play essential roles, it is at any rate conceivable that the relativistic velocity might turn out to be more fundamental, in the order of constitution, than the Newtonian notion; we must not, at any rate, misguided perhaps by the metaphor of the tree-like growth of science out of the lifeworld, legislate in advance on this question.

Anyone familiar with cognitive psychology (or 'genetic epistemology', as Piaget likes to call it) will immediately recognize the relevance of that discipline to the noetic study of 'velocity'. Piaget in fact reports on studies which suggest that velocity is an experience not derived, on the one hand, from quantitatively conceived notions of space or time, but dependent, on the other hand, on their ordinal comprehension (i.e., on the understanding of spatial and temporal order, not of length or duration).[46] From the available material it seems that a topological (i.e., not quantiative) form of the relativistic law for the addition of velocities precedes the nonrelativistic addition law genetically, but the matter requires careful investigation.

Does the relevance of genetic epistemology to questions such as these mean, as Piaget believes it does, that genetic epistemology renders phenomenology obsolete? Certainly not. Noetic analyses are carried out within brackets, unlike psychological studies. Gurwitsch agrees that genetic epistemology is an 'unacknowledged phenomenological psychology'[47] — but the latter, too, was to be a scientific discipline, and not a study within the epoché. In the instance just cited, one would have to bracket the 'velocity' examined in cognitive psychology in order then to constitute its essence. The noematic deposit of this constitution, i.e., the sedimented meanings (in parallel with the sedimented meanings that emerge from historical studies), can then be expected to link up directly with the noetic study of 'velocity' as meant in physics. Only in this way can we see just where, in the sedimented layers of the intersubjectivity (lifeworld) and of the subjectivity itself the physical concept 'velocity' is rooted. On the basis of our example, and of a few more, I would be prepared to argue that the genetically more *primitive* layers (such as the perception of movement in a merely ordinal, rather than metric, space) enter in the constitution of the more *advanced*, and supposedly more 'abstract' concepts of physics — in direct violation of the tree metaphor.

One merely needs to recall the contributions of cognitive psychology to our understanding of the performance of mathematical operations to realize the scope of that discipline's relevance to our concern. Because of this concatenation, the noetic clarification of the logos of physics requires a great deal of as yet unaccomplished work. It remains true from the phenomenological point of view, on the other hand, that the *outcome* of these noetic investigations, the eidos of the subjective performances required for the fullest possible objectivation of experience, must be strictly correlative to the eidos of the noematic investigation of the physical entities. This correlational apriori implies what has already been mentioned: that the 'apodictically evident' axioms, as the formal expression of the 'essential form' of the objectivating intentionality, must entail, and be entailed by, the final formalism of physics, by the 'coherent mathematics of nature', which governs the 'essential sort' of 'Object belonging to Nature.'[17, 42]

Phenomenology, to sum up, strikes me as having to guard against claiming too little and, at the same time, too much for its method: too much, in thinking that firm foundations for a science can be laid once and for all by clarifying the genesis of its starting concepts in the lifeworld, without taking into account the more sophisticated concepts and specific theories that characterize its more advanced stages; too little, in consequence of this neglect, in not realizing the scope and significance of the contributions it can in fact make if applied at all levels of a scientific discipline.

288

NOTES

* The financial support of the *Deutsche Forschungsgemeinschaft* is gratefully acknowledged.
1 Husserl, E. *Ideen zu einer reinen Phänomenologie und phänomenologischen Philosophie.* Drittes Buch. The Hague: Nijhoff, 1952.
2 Husserl, E. *The Crisis of the European Sciences and Transcendental Phenomenology.* Translated by D. Carr. Evanston: Northwestern University Press, 1970.
3 p. 81, lines 11-24.
4 §§ 35, 36.
5 Sokolowski, R. *Husserlian Meditations.* Evanston: Northwestern University Press, 1974.
6 *Ibid,* p. 76. I recommend §§ 22-27 in this superbly clear book as background material.
7 *Ideas III,* p. 81, lines 24-34.
8 Husserl, E. *Formal and Transcendental Logic.* Translated by D. Cairns. The Hague: Nijhoff, 1969.
9 *Ibid,* p. 292.
10 *Ibid,* p. 161.
11 *Ibid,* p. 293.
12 *Crisis,* § 9.
13 See the following articles and books, and the references cited therein:
  Gurwitsch, A. 'Galilean Physics in the Light of Husserl's Phenomenology'. In: *Galileo, Man of Science.* Edited by E. McMullin. New York: Basic Books, 1967.
  Gurwitsch, A. 'On the Systematic Unity of the Sciences'. In: *Phänomenologie Heute.* Festschrift für Ludwig Landgrebe. Edited by W. Biemel. The Hague: Nijhoff, 1971.
  Kockelmans, J.J. *Phenomenology and Physical Science.* Pittsburgh: Duquesne University Press, 1966.
  Kockelmans, J.J. *The World in Science and Philosophy.* Milwaukee: Bruce Publishing Co., 1967.
  Kockelmans, J.J. and Kisiel, T.J. *Phenomenology and the Natural Sciences.* Evanston: Northwestern University Press, 1970.
14 *Ideas III,* p. 102.
15 Husserl, E. 'Philosophie als strenge Wissenschaft'. *Logos,* vol. 1, p. 340, 1910/11. See also *Crisis,* p. 55.
16 Klein, J. 'Phenomenology and the History of Science'. In: *Philosophical Essays in Memory of Edmund Husserl.* Edited by M. Farber. Cambridge: Harvard University Press, 1940.
17 *Crisis,* p. 55.
18 *Ideas III,* p. 89, lines 9-10.
19 One can argue the need for re-opening the brackets already in pure phenomenology, on more fundamental grounds than I cite here. See, for example, J.N. Findlay, 'Phenomenology and the Meaning of Realism', in: *Phenomenology and Philosophical Understanding,* edited by E. Pivcević, Cambridge: Cambridge University Press, 1975, p. 155f. In his Yale University Ph.D. thesis, 1973, 'Husserl's Phenomenological Program: A Study of Evidence and Analysis,' D. Hemmendinger argues forcefully that the repeated changes in focus between critical and ontological attitude are implicit in phenomenological methodology at its deepest level.
20 *Ideas III,* p. 91.
21 *Ibid,* p. 22, lines 5-9.
22 Prof. A. Gurwitsch suggested the Leibnizian term 'compossibility' to me in a conversation a few weeks before his death.
23 Weizsäcker, C.F. von, *Die Einheit der Natur,* Part II. Munich: Hanser Verlag, 1971. (*The Unity of Nature.* Translated by F.J. Zucker. New York: Farrar, Strauss & Giroux, 1978.)

24   Carnap, R. *Philosophical Foundations of Physics*, Part II. New York: Basic Books, Inc., 1966.

25   We are free, on the other hand, to establish an ordinal scale, since we know how to decide, in terms of 'scratch tests', whether one material is harder than another.

26   The expansion of any other material would do as well, to begin with. As the theory of heat is further developed, the mercury is replaced by an 'ideal gas', and finally, at the deepest level of classical thermodynamics, by the output efficiency of a 'Carnot engine' (an idealized heat machine). The argument below for a logarithmic temperature scale could be carried through more elegantly in terms of these Carnot engines.

27   See the contribution by E. Hedelmann, 'Thermodynamik' in: Baravalle, H. von, *Wärme und Kälte, Magnetismus and Elektrizität*. Bern: Troxler-Verlag, 1955, pp. 101-162.

28   This conceptual shift in turn affects our account of the historical development of the theory of heat during the past century. Carnot, one can show, thought in terms of our logarithmic temperature scale, and was, roughly speaking, on that account misunderstood by Clausius and Lord Kelvin, who formulated modern thermodynamics.

29   Husserl, E. *Ideen zu einer reinen Phänomenologie und phänomenologischen Philosophie, Erstes Buch*. The Hague: Nijhoff, 1950. (§ 24.)

30   *Ideas III*, p. 101.

31   Zucker, F.J. 'Partial Coherence Theory: the Non-Statistical Approach'. In: *IEEE Transactions on Antennas and Propagation*, Jan. 1967, pp. 7-15.

32   Zucker, F.J. 'Information, Entropie, Komplementarität und Zeit'. In: *Offene Systeme*. Edited by E. von Weizsäcker. Stuttgart: Klett Verlag, 1974. (Section 4.)

33   See, for example, Čapek, M., ed. *The Concepts of Space and Time*. Dordrecht and Boston: D. Reidel Publishing Company, 1976. Note especially the Introduction. Also, ref. 23 (Part II) and ref. 32 (Section 5).

34   The two theories turn out to be connected: geometric optics is a certain limiting case of interference optics. In many applications, for example in lens design, it is sufficient to use the ray constructions of geometric optics; the deeper interference optics merely adds an occasional refinement in the calculations, for example to account for the fringing effects in the focal region of a lens.

35   *Crisis*, § 9. See also ref. 13.

36   Drieschner, M. 'Objekte der Naturwissenschaft'. In: *Neue Hefte für Philosophie*, No. 6/7. Göttingen: Vandenhoeck & Ruprecht, 1974.

37   Even when particle-like, an electron is not like a *classical* particle. It does not have a precise track; if one tries to locate its successive positions with increasing accuracy, it spreads out more and more like a wave.

38   Heelan, P.A. 'Horizon, Objectivity and Reality in the Physical Sciences'. *Intern. Philos. Quart.* 7 (1967): pp. 375-412.

39   Bohr, N. 'Faraday Lecture'. *J. Chem. Soc.* (1932): p. 349.

40   Heelan, P.A. 'Complementarity, Context Dependence, and Quantum Logic.' *Foundations of Physics* 1, No. 2 (1970): pp. 95-110.

41   Two sorts of 'operators' appear in quantum mechanics: one, the 'Casimir operators', refer to properties that may be said to define the existence of objects, such as the number of particles in an interaction, or their electric charge; the other sort of operator refers to contingent properties, such as the energy or the spin components. It is only the quantity cluster corresponding to the latter which is malleable by the experimental setup.

42   *FTL*, p. 246. (Italics of entire quote omitted.)

43   The zig-zag implicit in von Weizsäcker's work program, between actual theory construction and the formulation of justifiable axioms for that theory, is the climax of the 'pendulum swings' mentioned in Section 1 and reference 19.

44   In his attempt at constructing the final physics, von Weizsäcker does not start from quantity, but from the more elementary notion of a simple yes-no question. As a result, 'physics' to him encompasses *all* cognitive experience, not merely quantifying experience. The implications of this distinction cannot, unfortunately, be discussed here.

45 Piaget, J. 'Les données génétiques de l'épistémologie physique', In: *Logique et connaissance scientifique*. Edited by J. Piaget. Paris: Editions Gallimard, 1967. p. 604ff.

46 Oral quote. Gurwitsch refers to Piaget in the Landgrebe Festschrift article cited in reference 13.

COMMENTS ON PROFESSOR ZUCKER'S PAPER

DAVID HEMMENDINGER

Toward the end of his paper, Professor Zucker says that Husserl's analysis of natural science is both too modest and too demanding. It is too modest in that the 'stringency of phenomenological evidence' permits not only the description of the objects of science and the critical reinterpretation of theories, but also their critical reconstruction. It is too ambitious because Husserl seemed to think that the foundations of the science could be clarified once and for all by tracing them back to their origins in the life-world. Professor Zucker outlines how we can use the stringency of evidence to make such reinterpretations of concepts and theories, and he also argues that we only find out what the *logos* of physics is as the science develops, and this means that as we learn, we must go back and re-evaluate the relation between the objects of physics and the life-world. I wish to discuss some implications of his position.

First, I think that he is right in arguing that the phenomenological concept of evidence can be fruitful for science. Recent discussions of the philosophy of science have been full of talk about the problem of the growth and change of theories. Most of the participants in these discussions agree that the simple inductive or hypothetico-deductive accounts of scientific explanation are inadequate because they don't do justice to the activity of doing science. They disagree, however, about the extent to which scientific change is or can be rational; I am referring to such people as Thomas Kuhn, Karl Popper, Paul Feyerabend, and Imre Lakatos. Feyerabend, in particular, presents an extreme view; according to him, science has no proper methods and 'anything goes', including inconsistency, as long as it gets results. Others, like Lakatos, are more moderate and claim that while the history of science shows that we have to abandon any simple notion of scientific development it is still possible to isolate promising, or as Lakatos calls them, 'progressive research programs'. However, when it comes time to say what constitutes a progressive program, Lakatos simply says that 'the direction of science is determined primarily by human creative imagination and not by the universe of facts which surrounds us,'[1] and thereby gives up the game to sociology. I submit that the alternatives which he offers are incomplete. We are not given mere facts; as Professor Zucker remarked, Husserl pointed out some while ago that facts are theory-laden. Still, if we are not surrounded by a universe of facts, we *are* surrounded by a universe, and Lakatos omits a third possibility, that the direction of physical science be determined by the *idea* or *logos* of physics. This idea, the 'true meaning' of physics, is not laid out before us in advance, and Professor Zucker has emphasized that we only recognize it in retrospect, as the inner logic of the science. Through the combination of noematic analyses on the side of the object of physics, and noetic analyses on the side of the subject who does physics, though, we can have some knowledge of that logos, and as we have it, we also have some knowledge of the direction of growth of the science.

The stringency of phenomenological evidence is the key to the discovery of this logos. In doing physics we may not always pay attention to it. Having done something, though, having achieved some result in the form of an apparently successful physical theory, we can then go back and ask, what is the evidence on which the result is founded? In particular, we can seek to recast the theory in terms of this evidence; that is, strictly within the limits of the *given*. As Professor Zucker indicates, this requirement means both rejecting theoretical concepts that specify physical events beyond what is in principle testable in that theory, and also being guided by the *idea* of physics in developing our concepts. Since that idea is not clear in advance, it seems that much of our science is necessarily done without adequate attention to evidence at first, because part of what is meant by 'adequate attention' becomes clear only after some physical theory makes its appearance. The first appearance will not be the best one, usually, unless we are lucky, or unless we have come to know something about the logos of physics.

My second point is about Professor Zucker's characterization of the object of physics. He argues that the idealization process which initiates physics makes measurement of extensive magnitudes the central feature of the science. If objects are to be studied in any way, they must be identifiable; as Husserl says, I must be able to return to them as 'the same.' In physics, the object must be isolated, partially but not entirely. It must interact in *definite* ways with those parts of its environment which are the scientific instruments, the extensions of the observer's body. If it doesn't interact, it isn't detectable in *definite* ways to which I can return, then it isn't an object for a science. To say that definite interactions are characterized by some extensive magnitude like length, weight, or mass, rather than by intensive magnitudes like temperature, is to say a complex can be resolved into parts. If I analyze some complex things, studying only extensive magnitudes, then I can 'sum up' the measurements of the parts to get the measurement of the whole. In other words, parts which are characterized by extensive magnitudes retain their identity whether isolated or combined. The appropriate operation of addition may not be simple; if I build a three-dimensional structure out of rods, then I cannot merely add the lengths of the pieces to arrive at the dimensions of the whole; I must use the laws of trigonometry. Professor Zucker has suggested some other examples where apparent non-additivity conceals another sort of additivity and hence shows that there may be extensive magnitudes behind the surface of things.

If we consider some typical extensive magnitudes and contrast them with some which are not extensive, then on the one hand, we have things like length, weight, energy, motion; and on the other, temperature, texture, and, let us say, tickling. I have chosen the latter list with Galileo in mind, for these are some of his examples from the passage of *Il Saggiatore* where he makes what is called the distinction between primary and secondary qualities. Is Professor Zucker then suggesting that we not only return to this distinction, but accept only primary qualities as real, because they alone are what physics is about? I think not, just as I think that Galileo did not say that. Galileo's distinction is not a Cartesian rejection of sense experience, rather, as he himself says, he is distinguishing between those qualities without which he cannot conceive the object and those on which that conception does not depend. Thus, he is defining the object of physics as Professor Zucker does, in terms of extensive magnitudes. The object of physics, then, is not the same as the perceptual object, for the latter is characterized by many qualities which cannot be given an extensive scale of measurement. However, this is not a return to a 'two-worlds' view; I am not suggesting that there are separate worlds of perception and of physics.

The question we must ask is, which qualities are truly given? People sometimes talk about the life-world as the realm of immediate experience, arguing that it is the entire foundation for all experience. In this view, modern science has committed the fault of becoming detached from its origins in the life-world. If we insist that all evidence is immediate evidence, contrary to what Husserl said in the *Logical Investigations* and in other works, then it will appear as if the evidence of physics is not real evidence but only abstraction. I have argued elsewhere that evidence is as much a process of clarification as it is of direct insight, and that in clarifying, we come to understand the object and our own intending acts anew.[2] Searching for evidence within physics, then, is in part a matter of clarifying our experience of the life world; we do it to find out what measurable magnitudes lie behind those experiences. We do not thereby deny the reality of the immediate experience, but we do claim to be able to explicate it in terms of other evidences, with their own kind of validity.

The phenomenological approach to physics thus accepts neither the view that only immediate experience is admissible, nor the view that truth lies in mathematical abstraction. Rather, this approach stresses learning how to interpret experience; how to discover evidence which is not on the surface. The search for extensive magnitudes is part of this process; we must seek those features of experience which can be measured. On the one side, we examine our experiences to seek underlying evidence. On the other side, we take the mathematical formalisms — the theories — which seem to work or be correct, and ask why; where is the evidence on which they are founded? The first form of a theory may not be the best one, which is why we need rational reconstruction, or in Husserl's terms, genetic phenomenology.

I have spoken about two features of Professor Zucker's account which I find valuable. I would like to indicate a way in which they can be combined.

Phenomenology offers another alternative to the accounts of science in terms of either creative imagination or a universe of facts, and also it offers an alternative to the split between immediate experience and mathematical abstraction. As to the former, we recognize that evidence has both subjective and objective sides; as to the latter, that not all evidence is immediate and not all mathematical abstraction which works is equally good as an account of nature. I think that we can put these together by returning to an approach to the philosophy of science which has been considered outmoded, though others have also been arguing recently for its value.[3] This is the study of scientific theories as *models* (by which I mean: mathematical models). A good model, as Mary Hesse has pointed out, like a good metaphor, says more than we had intended in creating it. Features of the model which had not appeared relevant at first turn out to be relevant and to lead to further discoveries. I think that Professor Zucker's distinction between theories which are founded on phenomenological evidence, and those which are not, is the parallel to the distinction between good and bad models. In insisting on this evidence, then, we are setting up standards for good models in science, and to the extent that we understand the idea of physics, we understand what kinds of models are good ones. We cannot set up criteria initially, because we do not recognize fully what is the idea of physics, but as we advance, we can specify these models increasingly well. The essence of a good model is that it make evident what the theory describes. A good model gives us a better understanding of that part of physics which is modeled, and in turn, that better understanding leads to a new and more illuminating model. Here, in short, is the dialectic between the object-side and the subject-side, or, more, precisely, a model is *between* the two, it is determined both by the noematic reconstruction of the object of physics and the noetic reconstructions of the activity of intending these objects. Each develops and changes, and models express the state of these reconstructions along the way.

I referred to Galileo before, and I do so again now, because this is what large parts of his dialogues are about. In these dialogues, his spokesman, Salviati, gives lessons in how to interpret experience and how to carry out experiments so that the physical theories become not merely plausible accounts, but actually evident. In the process of making them evident, of course, the object of the physics may change; for instance, the distinction between terrestrial and celestial bodies becomes abolished — because the reflection on sense-experience and on what the experiences *mean* seems to call for that change. We can also consider Newton and his crucial experiment in optics, in which he passes white light through a prism, and then passes the resulting rays through a second prism to show that depending on the orientation of the second prism, the rays either are bent more in the same direction, but without any further separation into colors, or are recombined into white light. Here is a demonstration that, in a sense not yet fully spelled out, the rays are *parts* of the white light; a physical object has been accounted for in terms of other physical objects, its parts, and we can now go on to look for the appropriate laws of combination. The experiment is crucial, not because everything in Newton's theory stands or falls according to its results, but because it makes evident the hypotheses, as well as the object-type implicit in these hypotheses; that is, it deduces the hypotheses from the phenomena, as Newton says. This, then, is the project of the application of phenomenology to physics: to learn what it is to obtain the hypotheses from the phenomena under the guidance of a leading idea.

NOTES

1   'Falsification and the methodology of scientific research programs', in Lakatos and Musgrave, eds., *Criticism and the Growth of Knowledge* (Cambridge: Cambridge University Press, 1970), p. 187.
2   'Husserl's concepts of evidence and science', *The Monist* 59:1 (January, 1975), pp. 81-97.
3   For instance, Mary Hesse, *Models and Analogies in Science* (Notre Dame: University of Notre Dame Press, 1966).

SECTION VII

PHENOMENOLOGY AND HERMENEUTICS

THE CONFLICT OF INTERPRETATIONS *

HANS-GEORG GADAMER
and
PAUL RICOEUR

GADAMER: My introductory remarks to our joint discussion will be brief. But I hope they will provide an initial theme. After my short conversation with Professor Ricoeur about what he would be saying, I feel quite sure our two contributions will complement one another.

My proposal for our topic, the conflict of interpretations, was by way of honoring Ricoeur, who in his book on this question formulated a problem I have been working on for a long time. I am not offering a solution to this conflict of interpretations. My aim is rather a better understanding of the methodological and philosophical involvements of the different directions of interpretation which stand in such striking conflict.

The first point I have to make is this. Interpretation is a word that has been as it were charged with an electricity at least since the days of the later Nietzsche, as expressed for example in the typically provocative fashion in the famous statement: I do not known moral phenomena: I know only moral interpretations of phenomena. Indeed in Nietzsche the philologist the philological skill reattained the position of predominance that had been taken for granted in the higher education of former days. For example, everybody knows that Bacon called his own enterprise the *interpretation* of nature, because in his time philology was *not* the secondary thing in the eyes of common opinion that it has become today. But our problem, of course, is to show how this new shift-in-meaning of interpretation fits in the context of today's philosophy.

It was not the professors of philosophy that achieved this change. They were preoccupied with epistemology, i.e., the justification of the positive sciences. It was mainly Nietzsche that brought about this new style of interpretation; though it was embodied as well in the works of the great novelists of the 19th century. Then of course both the critique of ideology and psychoanalysis call for the same new sense of interpretation. For it is clear that interpretation in Nietzsche's usage constitutes a new approach to the whole problem: It means unmasking *pretended* meaning and signification. It does not mean simply philological skill in clarifying or articulating the meaning of a text. And the whole question of course is: Is it possible for philosophy and critical reflection to

See notes at the end of this chapter.

accept two different and quite irreconcilable attitudes towards any given meaningful whole?

For the sake of simplicity, I shall speak of a meaningful total or whole as a *text*. I am choosing that way of putting the matter of course as an old philologist. But philosophical hermeneutics is not restricted to exercising philological skill in interpreting texts. As Galileo or perhaps Nicholas of Cusa first expressed it, I believe, the book of nature is a book written with the finger of God. And since Hegel a similar claim has been made, namely, that the book of history was written by the world spirit. Consequently, by text-interpretation is implied the totality of our orientation of ourselves in the world, together with the assumption that deciphering and understanding a text is very much like encountering reality.

This is why the Idealist theory of interpretation can no longer suffice. That was Heidegger's point, as well as crucial for what I learned from Heidegger. To be sure, hermeneutics is an old method in some of the fields of the humanities, especially in theology, where since the Reformation there has been a special commitment to the authentic access to the '*text*' as *kerygma*, in opposition to the dogmatic tradition of the Roman Church. Another and obviously permanent field of hermeneutics is law. In the case of legal interpretation, the ordering of civic life by codified or uncodified laws includes an immense distance between the prescriptions of the law and the ideal of justice in any particular case.

So these two fields of hermeneutical labor are well-known in the modern epoch. But the evolution of hermeneutics reached a climax in the Romantic era. At that time, the task of re-discovery and re-entry seemed to apply not just to the Bible in relation to the special dogmatic tradition of the Roman Church; and not just to the law in any given jurisdiction; but especially in modern states where, after the adoption of Roman law, the conflict between the scientifically elaborated Roman law and the traditional, uncodified legal customs of the people reached a high-water mark. The Romantic era came to realize that in the wake of the French Revolution, *the whole tradition* of Western civilization was at stake. From this moment onward the question was how to bridge the abyss between our post-revolutionary epoch and the almost indisputable self-evidence of the Christian humanistic tradition of previous centuries.

That is the background for modern-day hermeneutics. Schleiermacher was the first to introduce hermeneutics as a common human concern for mutual understanding and for gaining access to the very *ground* of what is at stake — especially, in Schleiermacher's case, the truth claim of Holy Scripture.

Well, given the radical questioning of Nietzsche, Idealist hermeneutics can no longer suffice. Nietzsche was less the inventor of some other particular philosophical doctrine than the symbolic expression of the crisis of modern life. We have here, I think, a unique case in world history, namely, that somebody said of himself: I am dynamite — *and he was*. Normally, people who say, I am dynamite, are insane!

The problem, therefore, is this: What is the meaning of hermeneutics if 'interpretation' can no longer be understood and defined as the explicit *fulfill-ment* of the intentionality of discourse actually created in a tradition – in other words, of the text, of what someone means and everyone accepts as discourse; so that the gap between the interpreter and the interpreted text could ultimately disappear. It seems to me no longer unproblematic to interpret the Christian humanistic heritage of our history in almost monolithic solidarity. This was the illusion of the Romantic era formulated in the Hegelian concept of the absolute spirit. Certainly, Hegel's saying that the absolute transparence of the other oc-curs in the experience of art and in the experience of religion has something convincing to it. I mean that in both these fields, nobody feels this unbridgeable gap between oneself and another, between oneself and the truth. The basic as-sumption in such experiences is that I and thou are no longer in our differences. The work of art and the message of religion collect and bring together a new community, since even historical distances disappear in the contemporaneity of art or the kerygma.

But how can we make this truth-claim of our tradition compatible with the new concept of interpretation introduced by Nietzsche and elaborated by the others mentioned? How can we hope to reconcile this radicalism of interpreta-tion as unmasking with an attitude of participation in a cultural heritage which forms and transforms itself in a process of mediation? I think Heidegger opened up the way to do this by raising a question even more radical than the radical-ism of Nietzsche.

Here let me recall briefly the now familiar entry of Heidegger into the phi-losophic scene of our century by way of his destructive criticism of modern sub-jectivism including that of his own teacher and admired master, Husserl. This criticism concerned the notion of consciousness. It did not of course claim that the labor of research done by phenomenological philosophy and especially by Husserl had not been valid at all. Heidegger did not deny the radicality and in-tensity of Husserl the thinker. But he saw an unsolvable problem behind his foundation of phenomenology as rigorous science; and he became aware at the same time of the challenge issuing from the heritage of Hegel.

In his first books he suggests that Hegel was the one who integrated histor-icity into the content of the investigation of truth in the most radical way. In Heidegger's eyes this integration was of course further mediated by Dilthey, in particular. It was in connection with Dilthey's work that the word, hermeneu-tics, came up in Heidegger: indeed in a very provocative expression that implies a revision of the hermeneutical foundation of Dilthey's historicism – 'hermeneu-tics of facticity.' 'Of facticity' – I want to emphasize the radicalism of this formulation, especially after listening yesterday to some of the discussion. I would stress that Heidegger was penetrating enough to realize that it is impos-sible, not to say ridiculous, for a philosopher today to write an ethics. How can any philosopher *invent* something that does not exist? We should recognize that Heidegger was consistent enough to ask: What real basis for solidarity is left for posing philosophical questions after the rise of the nihilism predicted by Nietzsche? *Facticity* — this emphatic word means something that is not capable of being chosen. So our 'existence' is not a matter of our free choice, but simply *is* a fact. We are given any moment of our life-time. Facticity in this emphatic sense means something that is absolutely opaque in relation to any form of interpretation. Hence, the claim of doing a hermeneutics of facticity was a real battle cry.

We have to realize that with this paradoxical demand Heidegger pointed to what may in our spiritual, cultural, and philosophical situation with its belief in science, be asked by anyone and to which science can never adequately respond: the problem of death. This ultimate point of solidarity is common to all human beings. While the answers to this question offered by religions may differ and be accepted or rejected, science cannot really give a proper answer at all, despite all the advances of modern medicine.

On this basis, Heidegger developed his hermeneutics of facticity. He interpreted the temporal structure of '*Dasein*' as the movement of interpretation such that interpretation doesn't *occur* as an activity in the course of life, but *is* the *form* of human life. Thus, we are interpreting by the very energy of our life, which means 'projecting' in and through our desires, wishes, hopes, expectations, as well as in all our life-experience; and this process culminates in its expression of an orientation by means of speech. The interpretation of another speaker and his speech, of a writer and his text, is just a special aspect of the process of human life as a whole.

Heidegger had a good reason for eventually dropping the word, 'hermeneutics.' I have learned myself that it is dangerous to use this word, because it always invites the expectation that here is a new wonder-weapon: that one can learn how to interpret more reliably, more surely, and with a deeper meaning than was ever done before. Hermeneutics is a new skill of mastering something — that is not what we learned and have to learn from Heidegger. I think Heidegger demonstrated that behind the whole activity of human life, seeking its points of orientation as *In-der-Welt-Sein*, is this mysterious openness to being which is inseparably connected with our finitude; an openness to questioning, an openness which lays the constant charge upon our human living to break through the illusions of our self-sufficiency.

My aim here is not to interpret Heidegger and his raising of the question of being. It is simply to place the question of hermeneutics, of interpretation, in the center of philosophy, and to go behind the conflict of interpretations that may preoccupy our scientific and methodological interests. From the viewpoint of 'interpretation,' we should not just focus on the idea of the finite structure of human life, or on the idea that there is death. To be sure, that represents a radical break with the Idealist claim of absolute knowledge and self-realization of the spirit. Our facticity is not only represented by the anticipation of the end. It is the same with the beginning. That we are thrown into the world and not invited is just the symbol for the constitutive fact that we are always on the way; and that is true for interpretation, too. Perhaps the key insight in my own work is that we are never at the zero-point, we are never starting out new, we are always already en route, *wir haben immer schon angefangen.* A good way to put this point across is the familiar story about a child's first spoken word. It is made up of the illusion on the part of the parents. For it cannot be what it seems, since a first word cannot exist as such. It is not language. It is not a word, if there is just this one word. Consequently, the story illustrates why interpretation is the element in which we live, and not something into which we have to make entry.

The question, therefore, becomes, How can we expect that in interpreting (which means elaborating our experience in life as a legitimate way to develop self-understanding) we can escape the illusions of objective self-consciousness and the foundations of knowledge upon self-conscious method? In posing this question we are confronted by the two extremes mentioned above. On the one hand there is interpretation in the Nietzschean sense that refers to any form of interpretation as was practiced by Marx or by Freud. On the other hand there is the experience of life in communicative processes, the actual working out of daily life, where communication as the exchange of words in use structures the whole of social reality and encompasses the cultural features of this reality; sciences, the humanities, etc. What then is the place in social interaction for unmasking interpretation, this interpretation that goes behind the apparent meanings? An example from the social pathology of everyday life spoken about by Freud may serve to illustrate the question: I make a blunder in speaking. The other person stops to listen to what I say to him and starts to think: 'Oh, there is something behind it all. One should no longer take this man's explanations at face value. He is concealing something, or at least something within him is concealing itself subconsciously.' I think you see the conflict immediately. Is there a continuous process of understanding each other going on for the most part; or is the direct opposite what is usually taking place? Does the analyst — in this case, everyone — who sets out to reveal the sub- or unconscious background of the interlocutor attest to communication? Certainly not. This is not to deny the tremendous task and astonishing results being achieved by the investigation of the unconscious; or to question the therapeutic effort to heal obtrusive conflicts between the conscious and unconscious in order to re-introduce the patient into communication. But going behind, unmasking, showing forth hidden desires that are longing for their fulfillment as revealed by the inner tension in our souls — that is something besides communication. We have to assume as the basis of our social life that the other means what he is saying, and we have to accept his utterances without straightaway interpreting him against his own intentions — at least until there is sufficient evidence to suspect that the opposite obtains. Where a gap becomes actual, communication is broken down; then we begin to consider his utterances as a mask of the unconscious. At any rate there is no easy solution to these problems from a theoretical point of view. There is, however, a similar set of problems in the field of politics. The intrinsic analogy between psychoanalysis and the critique of ideologies has often been stressed.

Be that as it may, it might be helpful to think about these issues in the context of Heidegger's insight that interpretation is not a sovereign attitude over against a pre-established context of meaning, so that I can decipher it and possess it exhaustively and definitively. Interpretation is an ongoing process of life in which there is always something behind and something expressly intended. Both an opening of a horizon and a concealing of something takes place in all our experiences of interpretation.

That is true. Nor did Heidegger neglect to insist that thinking we can penetrate this deepest darkness of one's own mind was an illusion of Idealism. We can objectify ourselves; we can decipher the text of our own life, seeing it as a full series of symptoms of an illusion. And yet how can we make our way through this in a way that does justice to concrete life as an interpretive process? For me the preeminent model has been the *dialogue*. Plato was right in saying that thinking is at best a dialogue with oneself. But in a *real* dialogue, like the dialogues he wrote, the key point to be grasped is that there is no subject who states and fixes the objective content of an utterance, and then argues this fixed idea as the whole point. Instead there is an interplay between two persons, so that both expose themselves to one another with the expectation that each tries in his own way to find a common point between himself and the interlocutor. Whereas if we find no common point, *wir reden an einander vorbei*.

I could of course take up two hours speaking about this problem, but I think it is neither in your interest nor my duty as a human being! My point is that the dialogue is a good model for the process of overcoming the structure of two opposing postures. Finding a common language is not contributing to a new handbook of science or thought; it is sharing in a social act. This is a rather useful conclusion — to discover that the process of dialogue and all that is involved in its unfolding actually consists in an ongoing effort to bridge any form of alienation and to bring persons together so that nobody stays rigidly where he started, but rather integrates and appropriates what is other. Both partners to a genuine dialogue change and move and eventually find some small ground of solidarity.

In this sense I think even the conflict of interpretations could have a resolution. For the critique of ideologies, psychoanalysis, and every radical form of critique should be and needs to be reintegrated into this basic process of social life — a way which I call (in a manner I find satisfactory) *hermeneutical*.

RICOEUR: I want to address my remarks to the last part of the paper by Professor Gadamer, to his proposal regarding the reintegration of conflictual situations in hermeneutics within the encompassing framework of a dialogical relationship. I am quite aware that to start immediately with the most radical and most dramatic condition of conflict between a hermeneutic of suspicion and a hermeneutic of reenactment is to put oneself in the situation of the unhappy consciousness. But I don't think that it's the task of the philosopher merely to brood over this situation of conflict, but rather to try to bridge it. It is, I think, always the task of philosophical rationality to try to mediate, to work out a mediation, and to do so with passion. To that purpose, I think that the paradigmatic case which has to be taken up here is not one of the most extreme conflict, but on the contrary, one in which the conflict is more manageable. The way I shall proceed is to start with conflict *within* interpretation in order then to move step by step towards conflict of a more radical kind. My studies in these last years have followed this kind of progression through the following fields of inquiry: the theory of texts, the theory of action, the theory of history, and lastly, psychoanalysis. Among these different fields a certain homology of problematics may be discerned and at the same time a certain progression, if I may say so, in the conflictual structure of the problematic. This similarity and this progression suggests, therefore, the treatment case by case and step by step of the conflictual situation of hermeneutics.

My proposal here, then, is first, to reflect on the global situation of conflict and then to take a more analytical approach. My purpose is not to fill the gap between the two extreme modes of interpretation, namely, that of a recapitulation in a Hegelian sense and that of the archeology of a deconstruction in a Nietzschian sense. I have no answer myself for this situation but at least as a philosopher, I shall try to approach it by this procedure of the progressive construction of mediation. Accordingly, as we shall see, psychoanalysis may not allow a direct approach, but may stand as an extreme case, as a kind of borderline case, a marginal case, for this procedure, for this progressive procedure. Because as we shall see between the three first steps, there is not only an homology, an analogy of structure, but also a progressive complexity in the structure of the problematic itself, an increasing complexity.

I

The central problematic which appears to be common to the three fields just mentioned, is the conflict between comprehension and explanation. And this central problematic is not only homologous among the three fields but suggests the idea of an order of increasing complexity from one field to the other, in such a way that the further case of psychoanalysis may appear less appreciated and therefore, less manageable. I shall devote less time here to an exposition of the theory of texts for I discuss it in detail elsewhere. As a first point, I only want to insist on the strategic position of this theory in relation to the whole pattern of inquiry. By holding the question of texts as the paradigmatic case for the conflict of interpretation, I give to the concept of hermeneutics an orientation and a scope somewhat different from the one which was implied by an earlier emphasis on the conflict between suspicion and reenactment. In that previous orientation, the problem of symbol existence was predominant, and the emphasis on symbols implied that there are several ways of reading symbols and therefore that the discrepancy between these ways of reading was intolerable. But if we put the emphasis on the concept of texts, and if we give to hermeneutics the same rights as that of texts extended in the sense which I shall propose, the problem of the double meaning of symbols seems to be the crucial issue. We might emphasize here that a hermeneutical question arises wherever there is a move from misunderstanding to better understanding.

My next point now is the epistemological conflict — and a typical one for this field — between comprehension and explanation. This is not an intractable conflict, but one that can be mediated within the hermeneutical field itself. It is not a conflict *of* interpretation but a conflict *within* interpretation. This, I think, is the predominant contribution of the theory of the texts to hermeneutical theory in general, which to my mind has not been confined within the borders of linguistics as we shall see later. Let us, therefore, consider for awhile what is specific in the dialectic of explanation and comprehension.

First, dialectic is unavoidable because it belongs to the nature of the text to display a verbal autonomy with respect to the author's intention, the capacity of the understanding of its original audience, and the circumstances which constitute its transmission in written form. This autonomy of the verbal meaning of the text generates an objectification of a specific kind which, broadly speaking, is contemporaneous with the emergence of recent literature. Of course, it should be said against any type of thesis on writing, that the most primitive condition of any kind of inscription may be found in the very constitution of discourse, even oral, to the extent that that which is said in my discourse is already distant from the act of saying it and *endures*, as Hegel said in the first chapter of the *Phenomenology of the Spirit*. But literature exploits this interval, this gap in innumerable ways, and generates situations of communication quite different from those of dialogual intercourse. And one of the most remarkable aspects of this objectification of discourse into text is the reliance on specific codes which are to broad works of discourse what grammar is to the generation of meaningful sentences in natural languages. Such is the starting point for insisting that the objectification of discourse in texts is not the deplorable case of alienation that Plato suggested in the myth of the *Phaidos*, where writing is held to be lost remembrance against the pure interiority of knowledge and of wisdom. The inscription in external marks and the encoding of discourse according to the rules of specific literary genres constitutes rather the necessary distanciation thanks to which linguistic communication is raised to the level of the written traditions on which our cultural existence relies.

Hence a second consideration: if the objectification of discourse in text is a natural step in the development of our linguistic competence, explanatory devices applied to texts are not then as such doomed to pervert and eventually to destroy its objective comprehension. It is the very process of exteriorization which calls for the detour through explanatory devices; and among these devices, I should consider the structural treatment of such classes of texts as narrative, and maybe some others, as the most appropriate approach to those exteriorized forms of discourse. It is, therefore, perfectly legitimate to consider the texts as the manifestation at the level of surface structures of the deep structures which rule the encoding of, for example, the mythology of a given cultural space. The decoding, therefore, has to be homogenous to the encoding.

However, as this is the first dimension of the problem and the most polemical point, any non-mediated dichotomy between a structural and an existential approach to texts would bring us back to the dead-end of hermeneutics of the Dilthey type. It is not because explanatory procedures are no longer borrowed from natural sciences but rely on semiotic models that the gap between *Erklären* and *Verstehen* would be more easy to breach. A return to a dichotomy situation is always possible. On the one hand some structuralists would claim that the surface structures of a text are only the epiphenomenon of their deep structure, that messages are only instantiations of codes, that texts are semiotic machines in regards to which all questions about their meaning and their reference is irrelevant. On the other hand, some romantic and existential hermeneuts would claim that any structural analysis is already an alienation which does violence to the message of the text, and that the aim of study is to establish a soul to soul relationship between author and reader. My contention is that understanding without explanation is blind as much as explanation without understanding is empty.

I already said in what sense the necessity of the detour through explanation is grounded in the exteriorization of discourse in written signs. We must now say that reciprocally the finality of explanation is understanding. Why? Because the codes themselves, say, narrative codes, like grammatical codes have no other function than to generate the concrete texts at the level of which human communication is exerted. Considered in analysis simply as code a narrative is, as it were, made simply virtual, I mean deprived of its actuality as an event of discourse. Only the reverse move from code to message, from system to event, makes possible this ultimate stage of the hermeneutical process which Professor Gadamer calls *Anwendung* or *Enteignung*, application, appropriation. The analytic stage would then supply mere segments on the interpretative arc which proceeds from naive understanding to mature understanding through learned explanation. Such is the kind of conflict which I consider as paradigmatic. Once more it's not so much a conflict *between* interpretations, as a movement of *many* interpretations, a movement between phases of understanding and phases of explanation, between phases of objectification and phases of appropriation.

In accord with its paradigmatic status for our analysis here, I wish to emphasize that the theory of texts is both the topic of a specific discipline linked to the actualization of discourse in literary genres, and the first term of a series of analogous cases which can be put under the title of quasi-texts; and in the second part of my paper now, I shall try to show how the present status of the theory of action and the theory of history may be considered as analogous to the present status of the theory of texts.

II

Concerning the theory of action, we could find in the Anglo-American discussion a situation quite comparable to that of hermeneutics as discussed in Germany fifty years ago. The claim that the language-game of nature, events, and causation and the language game of action, intention, and motive have nothing in common and that the task of philosophy is merely to disentangle their confusion, that, I think, is a situation quite comparable to the situation in which Dilthey left the problem of the *Geisteswissenschaften*, namely, where understanding has to be disentangled from a confusion with explanation. But precisely I think that this mere disconnection between understanding of motives and explanation of causes is as untenable in the sphere of action as it is in the sphere of the texts. And here we should have to consider what is in fact a motive. If a motive is not merely a redescription of an intention, it must have some explanatory force, and here all the arguments of Davidson against Anscombe and others are very strong. For my part it seems that in order for a motive to have explanatory force, it must be given in the form of a kind of small autobiography. By that I mean that I must put my motive under the rules of story telling; and it is quite possible that this process of story telling might accompany the generation of intentions themselves, as if retrospection were always suffocating the prospective mood of action. There is therefore always a subtle discrepancy between the intentional movement of decision and this retrospection through which I tell the story of my motive. It is in this process of story telling that explanatory procedures may be introduced comparable in the theory of action to the explanatory procedures that we found in the theory of the text. The intersection between the theory of texts and the theory of action becomes more obvious when the point of view of the onlooker is added to that of the agent, because the onlooker will not only consider action in terms of its motive, but also in terms of its consequences, perhaps of its unintended consequences. A different way of making sense with actions occurs then, and also a different way of reading it as a quasi-text. Detached from its agent, a course of action acquires an autonomy similar to the semantic autonomy of a text. It leaves its mark on the course of events and eventually it becomes sedimented into social institutions. Human action has become archive and document. Thus it acquires potential meaning beyond its relevance to its initial situation.

This way of reading action has been pursued theoretically by Clifford

Geertz. According to his interpretation of culture we see that it is the writing of symbolic systems in ethnography which transforms the quasi-text of action into the text of ethnography. It is not surprising that the theory of action gives rise to the same dialectic of comprehension and explanation as the theory of the text. To construe the motivational basis of the string of action is an attempt similar to the construing of the meaning of the text. And this construing encompasses explanatory phases to the extent that motives must be causes in order to have an explanatory force. These explanatory phases may lead to inquiries of different kinds according to the principal of description which governs them. It is in that sense that the theory of action tends to increase the gap between explanation and understanding. But as wide as this gap is, no explanation can remain an explanation of human action which does not return to the initial connection between a motive and an intention. Even if the motive is not the real description of the intention it is related to action in a way which is irreducible to the logical exteriority between the cause and effect. Understanding is the milieu within which all explanation extends up to the breaking point in the motivational link.

This reciprocal relation between the theory of texts and theory of action receives not only support but amplification in the third field where the same dialectic of explanation and understanding may be described, the theory of history. And by that I mean, of course, historical inquiry. History generates the same problems and debates as the theory of texts (the theory, namely, of narrative texts) and as the theory of action. This does not happen by chance. On the one hand historiography is a kind of narrative, and therefore, a kind of text. On the other hand, since history is about human action, it's not extraordinary that we find the same structure of interpretation and explanation. This twofold allegiance justifies our putting the theory of action in this third place. But also, the fact that the dialectic here is more distended, right to the point of breaking, justifies that we take it as an introduction to the problem of psychoanalysis. Here too we could find in the history of the problem the two opposite sides, the same non-dialectical confrontation between the school of understanding comprising French and German historians (and Collingwood) and the school of explanation that adopts the Hempelian model of historical explanation.

I don't intend to go very deeply into this aspect here, but I do want to emphasize that here too the mere dichotomous approach to the problem cannot get us very far. Starting from the claim that explanation as historical has to be substituted for mere understanding, my point would be that the model proposed here by Hempel and his school cannot be applied since in fact the practice of history is the permanent denial of what is claimed by the model. Hempel himself has to recognize that at best we find in history explanatory sketches, not full-fledged explanations. But more than that, the kind of accounts that the historian gives have no predictive value. They speak of important conditions and not causes, and conditions that are important according to certain kinds of interest. History has to speak in ordinary language, and counter examples abound that do not function in historical inquiry the same way as in the physical sciences. It is only to narrow down their scope to try to specify precise places, times, and circumstances where the adduced explanation is to apply. Anomolies like these suggest that the model has to be recast into the form of a dialectic of understanding and explanation. And together with some authors like W.B. Gallie my suggestion is that historical understanding at its first stage has to be grafted onto a more primative competence, namely, that of following a story. To follow a story is to understand something as a succession of actions, faults, and feelings that present coherent direction as well as surprises. The conclusion of a story is accordingly not something deducible, or predictable, but it does have to be both consistent and acceptable. Without this basis there is no story and no history. The interest of the hearer, of the reader, is not in the underlying laws but in following the plot as unfolded in a story.

This starting point is, I think, more appropriate than the romanticist's starting point, for example, the idea of a transfer over to an alien other person; because here we have a specific structure, a narrative structure, which makes possible a transition from mere understanding to developed explanation. It is interesting perhaps to see how the procedures of explanation are called for and required as much as the functioning of understanding itself, exactly as in the theory of the text where the surface structure calls for explanation in terms of the deep structure. Consider a situation viewed as at the level of simply following a story. In historical inquiry, the problem is not that of following, because we know what happens, but that of writing down what has been followed. The problems of the organization of the pattern of the story is more important than the surprise in the outcome of the story. A silent conflict therefore is generated here between the pattern which we try to recognize and the sequence of the story, the sequence which is intrinsic to all narrative. The trend of historical explanation is to subordinate the sequential to the pattern, to subordinate the aspect of sequence to the structural planes of a pattern. The process of explanation tends then to be more and more separated from that of understanding. The next step here would be to say that history is not a description of what past agents did in terms of their own motivation, but a prescription in terms of some consequences unknown to them. Then too, through the narrative, sentences about past events in history enter the description of consequences which only the historian knows. Configurations of events emerge therefore which are ruled by connections quite different from those that link motives and intentions for the agents themselves. This does not mean that the historian knows better, but that he knows otherwise, in another way. And it is here that all the explanatory procedures described by Hempel and others must be introduced because now the historians will bring in categories, principles, and rules which are unknown to the agents themselves. For example, if we speak of class struggle in the Roman Empire, we are using categories which were unknown to the Romans. For them there were no classes as let us say, for a medieval painter there were no rules of perspective. As to how far we can go towards explanations *without* understanding, my view is that the substitution, the complete substitution, of explanation for understanding would simply destroy history. What we want here is reflection upon the *function* of explanation and not just a study of its structure. It is quite possible that Hempel describes the structure of explanation quite well when he analyzes it as not very different from that of physical explanation; but in the end its function is to follow the story better. Consequently what has to be done is not posit a substitute for the story but rather inquire into its sequential order.

III

It is after those preparatory conditions now that we could return to the case of psychoanalysis. The point of the exercise of the mediations practiced so far is that it is the task of the philosopher to learn how to master mediation before being confronted with *un*mediated conflict. To do that in the case of psychoanalysis, however, may well imply some important changes in the way the problem is approached, and may even require the deemphasis of the theory. For my part, I see now that I paid too much attention to the theory as such, whereas it is quite possible that the theory is only the metalanguage of the experience, of the psychoanalytic experience, and that we should therefore start with what constitutes this experience. This experience taken in itself *is* a hermeneutical experience, since the patient has to live with his own feelings and impulses in terms of what can be said of them, and said of them to somebody else — within the framework of a kind of narrative of his own experience. An explanation in psychoanalysis, eccentric as it can be in regard to all the kinds of explanation of which we spoke in the theory of the texts, of action, and of history, nevertheless preserves a link with these other explanations by virtue of being inquiry as sequential understanding. What is new with the psychoanalytic experience cannot be denied, namely, the fact that we have to do with distorted symbolic actions and symbolic systems, that it is the principle of distortion which makes for the problem and not simply the content as such of symptoms and dreams. It is the fact that to give an account of this distortion we must introduce new theoretical terms which do not belong to the experience itself, terms such as libido, repression, cathexis, and so on. It is perfectly legitimate, therefore, that the explanation be not written in the terms native to the experience itself. But it seems to me that this explanation becomes a myth if it cannot be reappropriated within the experience itself in the following way. First, we have to understand that as distorted as symbolic systems may be, they remain symbolic systems. As far as we have to go in the direction of quasi-material processes, compensation, displacement, investment and so on, repressed symbols remain symbols and thus retain the meaningfulness of symbolic systems. Therefore, we have to forge the concept of the processes of desymbolization, that is, of what happens when symbolic structure are not only objectified (objectification being, as I said, always a natural and wholesome process) but reified, petrified. Some German interpreters, Freud, Lorenson, and others, speak of delinguisticized logic in privatized language. Here we may have a situation comparable to that of banishment or political ostracism; in other words, what occurs here is a state, let us say, of excommunication. We therefore have to preserve the concept of excommunication in order to make sense within hermeneutical theory of the process of re-symbolization which is the whole process of psychoanalysis. It is quite possible, then, that reified symbols *imitate* natural processes. It is quite possible that man functions like a thing; but psychoanalysis is a procedure of investigation, and the method of treatment proves that this symbolization can only be understood as the negative side of the process of re-symbolization.

To conclude, my position is that the whole process of the objectification of language, of human action, and of symbolic systems makes procedures of explanation possible, but that the problem of self-alienation has always to be grafted onto the process of objectification in order to be understood. Self-alienation, left unconnected with the process of objectification, appears absolutely cryptic and impenetrable, and the conflict with hermeneutics then seems intractable. It is in this way that I think dialogical rationality may, from a position on the border between elements in opposition, mediate unmediated conflicts, which perhaps are the core of our cultural situation.

Thank you.

DISCUSSION:

Q: Prof. Gadamer, you were talking about the discovery of the necessary opacity involved in a hermeneutic of facticity. I think before, as with Hegel and people like Dilthey, the idea of interpretation was to overcome opacity. Now, for you is it the task of hermeneutics to make things as transparent as possible regarding this necessary opacity as a negative thing, or is your idea that this opacity isn't necessarily a bad thing, and that hermeneutics should *not* overcome it but take a positive attitude towards it?

GADAMER: I spoke about opacity in opposition to the idealistic optimism concerning the possibility of overcoming every trace of the opaque. In that way I take it certainly as a restriction upon the possibility of insight or spirituality; but I would say that exactly this limitation upon our understanding has, how shall I say, a moment of reality. So that the limitations in our understanding of something are a part of our own real being. To show what I mean, take this illustration. One of my standard examples (I hope nobody is acquainted with it) is Mommsen's *History of Rome*. Opening one page of this work I know immediately that it can only be written by an historian who was a democrat in the so-called *Vormärz*. That means a democratic historian who had a special preference for the Republic and therefore never wrote the fourth volume about the era of Augustus, because that was not his job. But in seeing that he was in a way narrow and limited in his own interests, in his own insights, I gain a profile of his own spiritual character. This example is, of course, taken from a very intellectual academic field, but I think you can shift it to any form of life experience.

Q: I would like to ask Prof. Gadamer what is perhaps a naive question concerning the ongoing dialogue between unmasking and reenactiong interpretation. Would Prof. Gadamer agree or would he deny that the idea of unmasking the text implies that there is some real meaning or some true interpretation which does lie behind it, even if we in our constant efforts fail to reach it? If our efforts to interpret a text might be compared, say, to the continuous removal of the skin of an onion, so that ultimately we arrive at nothing, does that not mean that the whole conception of hermeneutic or interpretation is simply meaningless to us?

GADAMER: I am not of course the infinite spirit that knows the kernel of the onion. But I find it very important to say that this assumption, this anticipation of meaning or of significance, is a precondition for our effort to understand. In this I would agree with you that as an *intentional* factor, this assumption that there is meaning *in*, breeds our whole effort. But I think that is exactly so as a universal condition of our finite structure. I would claim it as belonging to our hermeneutical approach to the world, that we can never reach the position which would allow us to demonstrate what the kernel of the onion is.

Q: I find that response reassuring, but would Prof. Gadamer not have something more to say for Plato, and perhaps even Hegel, regarding this claim that while the dialogue is a continuous ongoing process, in our finite condition we never reach the kernel. Despite this, what we are aiming at, what we do intend — if you can put it that way — is the idea that there is an ultimate truth, as the Hegelians put it.

GADAMER: But you know that Hegal at least is on my side. He says it is dialectic. God may *know* but human beings *seek* truth. No God philosophizes. He does not need this ongoing approach of articulation; but this is a subject with so many sides, and there is not time enough here now to take it up. As to Plato, his insight was not the conception of the totality of what we could call, in a philosophical experiment, the entire system of possible relations, like the central monad of Leibniz, encompassing the whole relationship of all the monads, so that the full coincidence of the entire system of monads is a universe. That is not Plato. Plato saw, I think, that to reenact a relation, to see something under an aspect 'shadows' by necessity other aspects. About Hegel, I have my reservations, but in my contribution here I tried to find a way of overcoming the Hegelian end-point, and of assuming so far as I can, the whole content of his dialectical description, insofar as I can reenact it in this way. This movement of dialectically furthering our insight, that of course is common in Plato and Hegel; but when you give me the choice, I am for Plato.

Q: I would like to ask both Prof. Ricoeur and Prof. Gadamer about this shift from opacity to the idea of the *continuation* of opacity. This was touched upon in the final comments of both papers, first, in Prof. Gadamer's notion of the reintegration of critique as a definition or at least another account of what hermeneutics may be, and then in Prof. Ricoeur's notion of unmediated conflict. This notion of mediation seems to me to be central to the discussion here, and what I would like to ask is whether hermeneutics is to include a form of mediation, whether there is something which passes between two poles, and thus is mediated — so that there is interpretation of texts or of history, or of the other forms which Prof. Ricoeur discussed — or whether the vision or mode of understanding involved in interpreting these forms is *un*mediated. Perhaps each of you might take up that question.

RICOEUR: My contribution was not fundamentally different from that of Prof. Gadamer, because what he called dialogue is in fact a position of mediation. In dialogue I have to encounter the other as he is, I have to presume that he *means* something, that he *intends* something, and I have to bring myself into that which is meant and intended. And so the exchange of positions, what Prof. Gadamer called the fusion of horizons, is a fundamental presupposition of the philosophical overcoming of unmediated conflicts. What I tried to do was to focus on certain epistemological situations in which we may proceed accurately in this task of mediation, instead of starting from, let us say, the cultural situation of our time, this desperate situation in which there is no bridge to build between the ongoing process of what Nietzsche called the devaluation of the highest values, and our desperate attempt to make sense of our whole heritage. We are surely the children of these two processes, we belong to both. There is a part of our self which participates in this ongoing process of suspicion using not only the sciences but also this specific kind of hermeneutics which was invented by Nietzsche. (We can find it as well, retrospectively, already in Marx, in his deconstruction of what he called the world of representation in relation to the world of praxis.) We belong to this current. But we have a *double* allegiance as modern man: on the one hand, to continue this task of suspicion and yet, an opposite obligation, to recover the past because there would be no sense in doing archeology, or being interested in foreign cultures or in the deep past. It makes no sense for *suspicion*, but it surely does for *recollection*. So, I tried to say that if we stay in this state of affairs, then there is a kind of repetition of the situation of the unhappy consciousness; and in that situation there is nothing for philosophy to do except to hope that somewhere, someday, some mediation will appear between these opposites. My hope is that if we could narrow down somewhat the scope and then proceed analytically, then a certain aspect of the philosophical task could be fulfilled, which is to solve the problems one by one. We find Plato in all this. He says somewhere that there are those who reach the one too quickly, and others who remain in the many; but the philosopher proceeds through progressive mediations. That is what I tried to do by giving an ordered place to a number of problems which occur in the region between the explanatory sciences and hermeneutical disciplines; and it was this area of intersection which interested me as the place where we can do some positive work of mediation. I do not claim that this solves the huge and global problem of the contradiction of modern culture; but if we do this modest philological work in the interval between the one and the many, maybe thereafter we may be able to say something less incoherent about the one itself.

GADAMER: Following Prof. Ricoeur's response I should like to add a question of my own, on a point which has never been quite clear to me. I agree with him completely in the observation that this gap or conflict of interpretations is in a way abstraction, with the result that we have a serious problem about mediating links. How can we describe them convincingly? Again, how much might there remain of the extreme positions one is attempting to mediate? It is possible that they cannot be brought together on a new level and in a new form of approach. What I mean may be helped by an example. When we take an historical problem, say, the beginning of a war which changes the world, and our analytical research convinces us the man who was responsible for the beginning of this war was a special kind of man. My example is not fictitious. Something like this was said about Frederick II. Well I think it is obvious that there are two absolutely different topics: one to explain the individual behaviour and psychology of a political man in this situation, and another to have an historical interest in the beginning of the Silesian wars. I cannot see what you mean in this case by a connection, or a mediation, insofar as it is not mediation to say: Well, of course, there is a layer of individual, personal biographies, but history is certainly not the *sum* of that.

Here we reach my last point in alluding to another of your fine papers from recent years, from which I learned a lot, because you know we Germans were much more isolated than you in the last decades and so we had much to pick up. Well, you described the hermeneutic and the structuralist approaches, and then applied a hermeneutic also to that contrast. I could not see that it had the same level. I have no doubt that one can elaborate and use many forms of explanation. There is not just structuralism, there are many other ways to interpret a text. I certainly need a great deal of knowledge about language and historical conditions and cultural habits and so on, that is one thing. But to *concretize* all that in this unique statement or text that must recollect all these externalized and objectifiable aspects, to live through the meaning in concrete fullness, that is quite another thing. It seems to me, as well as I can describe it following your explanation, that we have here the attempt at a reintegration of a disintegrating system of special approaches. I have real difficulty here about how you will get things to combine. It is to aim for combining to say hermeneutic has the right and the goal to reconcretize any form of general description. And it remains the ultimate goal of any understanding. I would be satisfied if you could say yes to this, but I think you cannot; and I would like to know your reasons.

RICOEUR: Let us take a concrete example of a structural analysis to show how it redirects us towards understanding. Let me take the most extreme case, that of the structural analysis of the Oedipus myth by Levi-Strauss in *Structural Anthropology*. His claim is that we have to forget the chronology of the story, take all the sentences and distribute them into classes, and then look for patterns of relationships. But at bottom what results do we obtain? We finally reach the recognition of what Jaspers has called the boundary situations of birth, death, love, hatred, and so on. What we get from a structural analysis, as I put it, is a kind of depth semantics of the narrative, of what is at issue in the narrative, of what makes the narrative structure a place of conflict, and of what mediates its conflict. It would be a deadend if we were to say that these structures merely comprise codes, or perform a merely logical mediation, if they do not help us to read the narrative, not at the anecdotal level, but at the level of its plotting, as Northrop Frye would say. It shows us, therefore, the way in which the narrative moves from crisis to denouement. I may thereafter reincorporate the structural analysis into an understanding which will be no longer a kind of naive reading, but a learned reading. This is what I think we all do when we read a poem, first at the surface of the work, and then in a final reading, when we understand the underlying structure. In this final reading we forget all the analytical approaches; it is a kind of second life taken up in the reading itself. Isn't this what we do when we study, for example, the sonata structure of the first movement of a symphony of Beethoven? It's not lost time to see how the first phrase and the second theme work out in the composition, and finally in the coda — that does not spoil our pleasure. On the contrary, the understanding of the underlying structure comes also to underlie our pleasure. I think that we can give good examples of this reintegration of an explanation within an understanding. If on the other hand it were impossible, then I should ask the reverse question: what can we do with a philosophy of dialogue if it is not able to be reconnected with the discipline of the human sciences, if it is merely a face-to-face relationship, and if it cannot provide us with, if it cannot structure, an epistemology? The risk would otherwise be that we would oppose truth to method, instead of rethinking the method itself according to the requirements of truth.

GADAMER: Well, I thank you for your full agreement! That was exactly what I had in mind, that structural analysis as an analysis of the structure of some elements schematized in a generalizing approach must be reintegrated in the second, learned reading. But, now, how do you reintegrate the Freudian interpretation of individuals? You did it — you *felt* that you did it — in your book, you insist that these two should be brought together. You gave excellent description of what, for my own orientation, King Oedipus *means*, of why we *are* lost and terrified. But this works *not* by what we learned in our quite special interest in incest and shock and the Oedipus complex and so on. We are to link those things together in such a way that we see this tragedy of self-cognition which occurs in the story as at the same time the reenactment of archeology of our own soul, of our own childhood! I cannot bring it together like that. And I cannot say that that is the bankruptcy of philosophy. I think it is the opposite. It demonstrates, for example, in a concrete form that psychoanalytic interest involves a special social commitment to avoid the edges.

RICOEUR: I shall never defend the psychoanalytic explanation of a literary text because a psychoanalytic explanation has its function only in the psychoanalytic situation with the patient. Sophocles is not on the couch. Psychoanalytic explanation is only analytical because something happens in a myth which has some analogy in dreams. That is what is interesting. But a second remark is needed here: I should not say that the tragedy of Oedipus Rex is a psychoanalytic tragedy. On the contrary, it is overcome, because it is a tragedy of truth about sex. But nevertheless what we learn from that is that *good* symbols, symbols which have a cultural impact, have two dimensions. On the one hand, they are deeply rooted in conflicts, in arche-conflicts. On the other hand they are the process of overcoming these conflicts. Consequently, what is needed is the recognition of the dialectic of symbols which embraces both, so that these symbols emerge from all regressive trends and the regression is overcome. I think that Krips or Goldstein said something like that when they speak of regression for the sake of progression. We recognize the multidimensionality of *good* symbols to reenact some primitive conflicts by overcoming them. So it is the movement of overcoming the regression of conflicts that I discover in the tragedy of Sophocles, in this story of marrying one's mother and killing one's father. Just to say that is what the story is about is trivial; it is to enact the tragedy of truth, because the problem is to recognize the resistance to recognition which is the tragedy of Sophocles. But if we have not identified the depths of the conflictual situation, perhaps we fail somewhat to overcome the situation.

We therefore enrich our understanding of the tragedy by understanding how the tragedy of truth is overcome when it supersedes the tragedy of sex (which is not a tragedy, but comedy!).

Q: Prof. Ricoeur, do you distinguish between modes of comprehension which *can* take an explanatory character into themselves, and modes of comprehension which are such that they won't admit this reintegration of explanation into their structure?

RICOEUR: It is quite evident that when we raise different questions we get the answers which we deserve on the basis of our question. If you are raising a question about Frederick II concerning his libidinal structure, what do we expect here? A better understanding of what he did, or a better understanding of psychoanalysis and its types? It depends on the question that we are raising. But my claim is that it is always possible to return to the fundamental question: How do we enlarge the sphere of communication? This, finally, is the hermeneutical question. The aim here, if possible, to integrate the most erratic human behavior into the broader field of communication with our contemporaries and our predecessors. Finally, it is the structure of historicity which is thereby enriched. However, it is quite possible to raise questions which do not allow of being thus reincorporated. Such may be scientific inquiries which have their own aim apart from all this. On the other hand, there are scientific questions that return to the enlargement of self-understanding by the detour of the understanding of what made man, mankind, what it is. I think as the horizon of all questions we find the expansion of communication. The dialogue model is therefore all encompassing. It is a paradigmatic structure not only for I-thou relationship but also for the totality of our relationships.

GADAMER: That means that one cannot say for any single point of view that the reintegration of an explanation and a comprehension is altogether impossible. That is not a question concerning principles. It is an empirical question. And I would say that the last point is a question even of social responsibility, because I think that this disintegration of a society is in the end suicidal.

Q: I think there is an aspect to the comprehension of the conflict of interpretations that tends to come out as a result of some of the answers that Prof. Ricoeur is offering. His reference to Beethoven does more to explain how the reintegration of explanation into an interpretative procedure is possible. Now I think everyone knows that, say, Georg Solti and Von Karajan or any of a dozen other conductors all know how to analyze the first movement of Beethoven's *Eroica*. And yet every one of them conducts it in a different way, which means that we have a dozen interpretations, a dozen integrations. What is the connection of the theoretical component in this interpretation? And what, on the other hand, is the significance of the interpretative aspects? The conflict of interpretations comes not between the explanatory and the interpretative in this case, but between one interpretation and another. For instance, there is a conflict between a Marxist interpretation of an historical event and an Hegelian interpretation of an historical event. And despite the fact that Hegel has now been dead since 1831, one can still entertain the possibility of that kind of conflict. Despite the fact that Prof. Gadamer no longer finds Hegelian optimism possible, one can still understand the possibility of an Hegelian interpretation. So there's a conflict between Marxist and liberal historical interpretations of the Second World War or the First World War. Should one even try to do something about those conflicts, or rather should one attempt, instead of mediating them, to multiply them, and do something about holding all the multiplicities together?

GADAMER: Thank you very much for your question. You described these two fields as showing a conflict of interpretation. I would prefer to speak about a *competition* of interpretations; so that in the end there is a possible discrimination in terms of adequacy and inadequacy. In the ten reproductions of Beethoven we have a doubled doubling of the whole problem of ambiguity because we have the text, the notes, and the different possibilities of performance in a situation that is a little more complicated than in the other examples. Nevertheless, different facets occur in these different interpretations. An *interpreter* of these interpretations would claim: Well, I see some points which are covered better in this, better in that interpretation. And so, in the end, my inner ear feels superior to any given performance. I think you would agree to the way I have put it here. Thank you.

Q: Prof. Ricoeur, by discussing the conflict of interpretation as dialectical, do you do so on the Hegelian ground of recognizing these all as object, as product of the spirit, or what? On the other hand, Prof. Gadamer's pessimism about the reconciliation of conflicting interpretations, and his distinction between surface meaning and deeper text, seem to me to imply a kind of return to a Kantian *Ding an sich*, with all the paradoxes that go with that for Hegel. Would you be so kind as to comment on *that*, Prof. Gadamer?

RICOEUR: I am entirely on the side of Prof. Gadamer when he says that we have to do without a philosophy of absolute knowledge. This is in fact the lament of modern philosophy, that we have to raise Hegelian problems without the Hegelian solution. Each time we speak of negation, of dialectics, we are in fact the heirs of the system in ruins. In a sense, I perceive phenomenology, existential philosophy, and hermeneutics as an attempt to do the promised rational job in this situation of the impossibility of the system, and with the limiting idea not of there being something *an sich*, but simply *agreement*. But this was also the rhythm of the Socratic discourse, discussion, *homologia*; but with *homologia* as an horizon, we have only the history of interpretations. I think that we must live with that, but having as well the dialogual recognition that the other makes sense. Perhaps I cannot incorporate the other's interpretation into my own view, but I can, by a kind of imaginary sympathy, make room for it. I think that it is a part of intellectual integrity to be able to do that, to recognize the limit of my own comprehension and the plausibility of the comprehension of the other. It is in that way that I preserve *homologia* as the limiting idea of us all. But just as one recognizes there is no absolute performance of a symphony, so there is this recognition at least of difference, the capacity to situate differences with respect to or within my own interpretation. I would say the same with all-encompassing theories of history. I have a great deal of reluctance to do that because, in keeping with what I have said about narratives, I don't think the narration of history allows all-encompassing theories like those of Marx's and others. I may however understand these as a kind of working hypothesis, as the proposing of global images. Maybe we cannot have passionate history without a certain expectation of what *could be* the global meaning of history, but that must remain at the level, I think, of hypothesis; that must remain a kind of working hypothesis.

NOTE

* We should like to thank Professor Sol Winer for making available a copy of his recording of this symposium. Because it was of better quality than another we had made, it served at the main basis for our transcription. The present text represents a revision of the actual presentations and discussion as originally transcribed. The aim of the editing was to remove the accidental deficiencies of the oral presentation (repetitiveness, inaccuracy in phrasing, incomplete asides, etc.) or to overcome gaps or obscurities in the recording. Final approval of the text rested with Professors Gadamer and Ricoeur. Lastly, acknowledgement should be made of the assistance Fred Lawrence gave to Professor Gadamer in his reworking of the text. [*Eds.*]

TWO PHENOMENOLOGISTS DO NOT DISAGREE

E.T. GENDLIN

Heidegger wrote: '... that which is to become phenomenon, can be hidden. And just therefore, because the phenomena are immediately and mostly *not* given, phenomenology is needed.' (SZ 36) Phenomenology is partly '-logy,' logos. 'The logos lets something be seen,' and logos is or includes speech: 'Speech lets something be seen.' (SZ 32)

It is clear from these quotations, and from Heidegger's whole work, that phenomena are directly there for us, but only after they are uncovered by phenomenological assertions.

'What is it, which in an outstanding sense must be called 'phenomena?' ... Obviously just such, as immediately and mostly does *not* show itself.' (SZ 35)

The italics are both times Heidegger's, for the word 'not' in the above. Phenomena do not at first show themselves, at least not the phenomena we are concerned with in phenomenology. It is 'the function of logos' to enable a 'simple letting be seen.' (SZ 34)

But if the self-showing of phenomena thus depend on our linguistic formulations, two questions arise: 1) Are our formulations constitutive of phenomena, are phenomena totally dependent upon formulations? Or do they have some kind of independence? 2) Is there still a difference between phenomenology as Heidegger does it, and any other serious philosophy — since any philosophy bases itself in *some* way on experience. In other words, is there really such a thing as phenomenology?

I will answer both questions affirmatively. But the answer is not simple. We can be sure that Heidegger did not make a simple mistake either in his insistence in italics that phenomena do not show themselves without our assertions, or in his insistence that what he did was phenomenology.

Rather than imposing assumptions for a convenient account of 'experience,' phenomenologists begin with experience as we actually have it, and articulate that. Whether a sentence does or does not articulate experience is not entirely up to the sentence and its own meaning. Heidegger writes: 'Each originally drawn phenomenological conception and sentence, as a communicated assertion, stands in the possibility of degeneracy. It is passed on in an empty understanding, loses it groundedness, and becomes free-floating thesis.' (SZ 36)

For a sentence to be phenomenological, something more is involved, since

See notes at the end of this chapter.

the same sentence and its conceptual meaning can lack its phenomenological ground if it is understood only conceptually. To say that such 'empty understanding' is possible shows this additional role of the phenomenon. The phenomenon shows itself as a result of the sentence. But this means that once the sentence is grasped, the phenomenon *itself* must still appear. *It* must come and be seen. The sentence and its conceptual meaning are not simply constitutive of the phenomenon; the sentence and its meaning can be used without looking, so to speak, or can fail to lead us to something we then see directly.

The experiential aspects which phenomenological philosophers point to are held to be universal: any person should be able to corroborate any phenomenological assertion directly. What any phenomenological sentence points to, should appear directly, as an experiential aspect so distinct and separate from the mere sentence and its meaning, that it could be there or not be there, a totally distinct addition to the sentence and its meaning.

If this claim of phenomenology were simple and obvious, then phenomenologists would never differ. A phenomenon would always corroborate every phenomenological sentence that was used phenomenologically, and no phenomenologist *could* differ with it.

On the other hand, if this claim is denied, if it is merely that some assertions fit experience but other assertions contradict them and fit as well, then there is no such special thing as phenomenology.

But phenomenologists do differ, and nevertheless the claim to some type of independence of phenomena is not nothing.

It follows that we must investigate much more exactly the relationship or relationships between phenomenological *formulations* (words, symbols, sentences, conceptual models) and phenomena. (The use of this very word can only become clear if these relationships become clear.)

But did not Heidegger and also Husserl do exactly this? Were not Chapter V of *Being and Time*, and the *Logical Investigations* and *Ideas* exactly about the relationship between experience on the one hand, and words and various kinds of attention on the other? And yet these two phenomenological philosphers differ from each other, and from others, even in their account of this basic relationship, as well as on other topics.

What is worse, they do not apply their account of the relations between formulation and experience at each step of their discourse. They choose and use formulational models such as actuality-possibility, form-matter, knowing-feeling-willing, particular-universal, without stopping to look at just what the choice of formulation does to experience, and exactly what some alternative choice would have done.

Therefore we are not in a very good position to know what to think when, for example, Heidegger phenomenologically speaks of the 'what for' as basically constituting the object, while Husserl speaks of the willing or value aspect as it were obviously and experientially different from the start, and added on to givenness, while Sartre uses Hegel's categories (in-itself vs. for-itself) to 'describe' phenomenologically.

None of them turn to look at just how their own steps are, each time, grounded (and, in what respects not grounded) nor do they tell us how one would check each step against a phenomenon, except for the general indifferent assertion that there always is one, being lifted out. Clearly not every aspect of their sentences is corroborated thereby. These thinkers do not tell us how their formulational terms interact with experience. Clearly, this 'grounding' doesn't mean that the phenomena are simply identical with everything the formulation is. Perhaps there are different kinds of formulational effects. Perhaps some formulations intend to point, only, and would then enable further reformulation; perhaps others intend to represent or render, or create new aspects. Perhaps, too, the effect of a formulation or a further reformulation is not a simple either/or: merely, to show or fail to show the same phenomenon. Perhaps a 'same' phenomenon can still give rise to further and different aspects. It is not all so simple. For phenomenological philosophers there *are* specific ways in which universal experience *is* involved in how they reach each conclusion. There are several specific ways in which direct experience *can* function as a ground in each step of formulating. To say exactly how opens up a whole new field of inquiry.

Heidegger poses this problem, but only on the side of formulations. He says that any statement always already involves a metaphysics, a certain 'approach' to phenomena. Once we recognize this, we do not wish to fall back into just some one approach, a metaphysics if we attribute our approach to phenomena. But, he asks, what would be an approach which is not just another approach? Heidegger says that he does not answer that question. A whole future generation shall answer it.

In posing this problem in this way he is still looking only at the old problem of relativism: how can we proceed at all since any way in which we do will still only be one of a variety?

So formulated, however, the puzzle assumes exactly that which it tries to overcome, namely that the answer must be an approach, a type of formulation, and that reality is somehow fundamentally like some approach, so that as soon as we can have more than one we are in difficulty.

If, instead, we study the formulating process itself, and the roles of experience in it, we may find how experience can ground different formulations differently, so that we might then be glad (and also specific, and knowing) about different formulations.

It is far too general to say simply that formulations are constitutive of phenomena, but also too general to say that phenomena lie there, nicely sorted into essence-piles, waiting for formulations to pick them up. Both statements lift out something but they are poor statements, nevertheless. Instead of these generalities let us study exactly how, in specific respects, phenomena are affected by a given formulation, and differently affected by another. Let us also see exactly in what respects they have some independence during the steps of formulating. In this way we may discover more exact aspects of what Heidegger and Husserl pointed to. We may also develop the phenomenological terms in which to say what we phenomenologists do, when we take a step of formulating. And there may be different kinds of such steps.

Elsewhere I have formulated three bodies of such observations. There can be a long list of noticeable *signposts*,[1] which mark when one is phenomenologically proceeding, as against when not. For example, phenomenological statements have many logical implications which the philosopher does not intend. Something other than the statement is always involved: Something the reader must see, find, discover, experience. The next step of phenomenological procedure does not necessarily follow especially from the statement here. One will not be able to follow how the procedure gets to its *next* step, unless this more-than-statement, this experience, has been gotten, as *this* step. The next step may logically disturb the literal meaning of this statement, or it may seem to jump rather than follow. Logic is no longer the only guide from step to step.

None of these signposts would be willingly accepted by anyone whose procedure is more orthodox. They are quite uniquely the marks of those who ground their steps experientially. (The above was only a little from a much longer list of signposts.)

Another set of findings concerns different *types of experience-formulation pairs*. Formulations do not always attempt to say what an experience is. Sometimes they point ('Do you know *what* I mean?' 'I will say *this* another way.') Sometimes they metaphorically generate some quite new likeness between different things, rather than formulating either thing. Formulations and experiences can be found in rather different kinds of parts. And one *can* always move from one pair to another! (For example one can always move from having rendered to pointing again, and from pointing to a new rendering.)

Still another set I must abbreviate here consists of the peculiar *characteristics which experience exhibits when one moves from one formulation-experience pair to another*. It seems then that experience has not given units, and can respond to different schemes rather than having just one of its own. New aspects can always be created from any experience to relate to any other. And yet, also, an experience is always just this, and responds not at all as we might wish, to our formulations, but just as it will. I am going to say more about this.

I hope I have sketched out this new field, the study of experientially grounded steps of formulating, sufficiently, so that I can now engage in a fresh and much more limited discussion: Two phenomenologists do not disagree.

At first this seems very simple. Some phenomenon — some aspect capable of being experienced — is lifted out, or related to, at every point. Two phenomenologists, let us say you and I, disagree: There are two possibilities:

Either you and I are really describing two different phenomena, or we are describing the same one with two different formulations. If it is two different phenomena, we will soon agree. You will show me the phenomenon you are describing, and since it is a universal human experience your description can lead me to it. My description will show you the one I have been describing. We may have to improve our descriptions a little in response to each other's misunderstandings, but soon we will realize that we are talking of two different phenomena, each will see what the other points to. We are each grateful to the other for having been shown a new phenomenon, and we walk out arm in arm.

Or, if we are describing the same phenomenon, but our difference lies in the vocabulary, concepts, logical model, with which we approach it, then there are again two possibilities:

Either we soon realize that our differing formulations refer to the same thing, and now we can proceed together from here on. Although you may not like my formulation as much as you like you own (and I might prefer mine, although I could now like yours better, either way) we find that what we are lifting out is the same. So we can go on together. After all, it is via the phenomenon that we get to a next step, and so it does not matter that we spoke of it differently. We proceed on from this point arm in arm.

Or, we find that our two different formulations lead to two different further steps, even though in some sense the phenomenon we described was 'the same.' Formulated as you did it, the phenomenon turns out to have an aspect which does not appear when I say it. This aspect leads you to something further, to which I don't follow you. And, my formulation, too, may show something yours hides. The two formulations reveal two different aspects of the 'same' phenomenon. Their difference was not 'only' logical or verbal. Now again, you can show me the experiencable aspect your formulation lifts out from our phenomenon, and I can show you mine. So this is simply another instance of two different phenomena, this time two aspects of the 'same' phenomenon. Different aspects, if experiencable, are again two phenomena. Again we agree.

It cannot all be so simple, but there are some great advantages even in this simple version. If we were to consider at each step of our procedure, just what experiencable aspect makes us want to hold on to our formulation, then (even though every phenomenon is always formulated or attention-held in *some* way) we could always find just what experiencable difference either formulation makes. The exact aspects of the difference made, which we care about, might again have to be formulated variously. Again we could see what if any difference might be lost or gained. If we disagreed again it would not be the same issue. I assume, here, that we would not each be privately committed to some logical model which we would reapply stubbornly to each sub-aspect. Rather, as phenomenologists, we would be committed only to the phenomena or experiencable aspects, not to any model. The sub-aspects would not themselves be mere instances of our issue, because experience is not a scheme of particulars under one set of generalities. Therefore, even if we do again differ on how to formulate the sub-aspect which is our difference, and even if the further difference matters to us, it will not be the same issue.

It is in exactly this sense, that Heidegger and other phenomenological philosophers must be understood. It is in exactly this sense that they intended to be understood. There are always many spots in these philosophers where they tell us not to take the model aspects of one of their formulations too literally. How then do they want us to take these formulations? In terms of the experiencable aspects which the formulations reveal — and not at all as implying the loss of any other experiencable aspects which other formulations might reveal.

But doesn't this do away with formulation altogether, as if logical inconsistencies are all right, and the whole point of thinking clearly might be lost? Not at all! Formulations, and concepts and logic have their use precisely in the power to be precise, to make logical differences, and by differences to point at something experiential that is being missed.

In emphasizing the difference between logical formulations and experiential aspects I am emphasizing the need for both, and the irreplacable role which each plays in regard to the other.

Only after we have specified the experiencable aspect, different formulations which don't affect it can be considered equivalent for the time being. Or, if the different formulations make differences in 'it,' the discovered further aspects will again need specifying. This does not only resolve the difference so that we can proceed, rather it gives us the experiential aspects which our assertions really aim at. Only after that, is there the systematic possibility of considering different formulations equivalent, rather than endlessly pursuing them and losing what we were really concerned about.

That we can set two different formulations at an equivalence in respect to some *directly referred to* aspect is a principle of importance. I call it *functional equality*. It applies only at some given point in a discussion or line of thought, and continues to apply only as long as no experiencable differences made by the two formulations matter. We may think now, that they don't matter, but they may later on in a discussion or line of thought, and then must be dealt with. Or that may never happen. For a given point or line of thought the two formulations may function in the same way, in respect of some 'same' phenomenon, or aspect.

I also point to the basic phenomenological willingness to forgo implications that are *only* logical or conceptual. I assume two thinkers who will always be willing to drop 'merely formulational differences or implications' in favor of what the experiencable aspect itself implies. Is such a distinction really possible, and clear?

At any point in any line of thought it is possible to proceed in two different ways: For example, if you have just said something I think is nonsense, there are two ways I can respond: I can point out to you at length why what you said offends various truths or logical relations. Or, I can ask you to say differently the sense you thought you were making, since obviously you did not experience yourself talking nonsense. In the second case you will come up with a different formulation than the first one which failed to work for me; it will be a fresh alternative formulation of the sense you were trying to make. If this succeeds and a new aspect of experience is now given me, we can leave it for another time to determine if your first formulation did offend truth or logic, or if it was a matter of my limitation that the first version did not work for me.

Similarly, I myself may find that some formulation keeps a hold of some important experiencable aspect for me, even though I already see that the formulation otherwise offends various other concerns, which I also retain. Shall I discard the experiential aspect which this untenable formulation holds on to, for me? No, I will not think the experiencable aspect lost, just because this formulation cannot long stand. I will limit the formulation just to pointing, and if I can really not devise a better one (which should always be possible) I will apologize for it and warn others away from its erroneous logical implications which I don't intend.

But if I were following the logical, rather than the experiential next step, I would be led away, to that which I don't intend.

Every formulation has conceptual implications which one does not intend, and if seen, would warn others away from. (This does not mean that *all* its logical power is unused, as I shall show in a moment.)

Public discourse is much given to the rule that logic *alone* entitles one to further steps. When someone is shown that a set of statements offends logic, it must be withdrawn. Of course, privately the person may retain the original sense, and especially from a phenomenological viewpoint, the person can know that the form has been scuttled, not the point. But the usual rules do not permit answering: you have sunk my statement but not my point.

For example, my own initial conceptual approach here was in terms of two distinctions: 'formulation vs. experiencable aspect' and 'same vs. different.' But now, in discussing what was implied in my simple version and in 'functional equality' and in proceeding from an experiencable aspect, what has become of my same vs. different model?

Is a given experiencable aspect really either 'same' or 'different?' It can be *same* for some time and then turn out to have importantly *different* aspects lifted out in it. It is both the same and different. If I were doing dialectic, this would be the occasion to move to a new *conceptual* distinction. But I rather point to the *more specific sub-aspects* we each have. These make our phenomenon neither the same nor different. Once we see them we will not disagree, because: there they are. We will then also see how each affects our discourse, or is irrelevant. Sameness and difference do not univocally apply to experience in the process of being formulated.

Are two different *formulations* the same, or not? It depends whether there is an exaperiencable aspect to which they both refer, and which leads to the same next step. If so, they are 'the same,' although different.

Clearly, I have not let my logical categories determine my own steps, rather my steps have changed the logical categories 'same' and 'different.' I have given several different experiencable cases to which they can differently refer.

Thus we can always let the experiencable aspect lead us, and if different formulations let us have the same aspect leading in the same way, we can leave it to more traditional philosophers, or to another time, to examine further the formulational differences for their own sake.

But formulations and logical implications must not be taken *too* lightly. If different verbal and conceptual formulations really came down to totally the same thing, if they did not each have their own type of meaning-power, then they could not effect or lift out phenomena. It is only because of their peculiar conceptual precision that a given formulation can do something, others not or differently. In regard to this aspect of 'different' formulations, we need their differences sharp. The activity of clarifying them for their own sake is important also for experiential thought. But that doesn't mean that we cannot use their very sharpness to let us see, by the experiencable aspects they lift out, which of their differences needs to be pursued, and which (always many) others we can ignore, to let you and me get to each of our experiential points.

Thus my own first set of logical categories, 'same' and 'different' have now received the kind of reference to specific experiencable aspects, which should let us see at least some respects in which we do and don't need to assert that different formulations and phenomena are different, or can be the same.

My other conceptual distinction was 'formulation' vs. 'experiencable aspect.' These never were clearly distinct in my discussion, since I began by asking what the degree of their independence might be. So we need not be surprised if these two, also have come to refer variously to more specific experiencable aspects, rather than being two conceptual meaning. Nevertheless I spoke of 'them' and organized my discussion of the problem with 'them.'

These were of course never simply independent, rather I asked what the degree of their independence might be. I began by saying that if there are disagreements among phenomenologists at all, then phenomena are not simply independent, just to be looked at and reported on. But, if they are totally dependent on formulations, then there cannot be such a thing as phenomenology. But these two categories did not determine my discussion, rather my discussion can now aid us in defining these two better.

What we are seeking are the experienced respects in which they are dependent and independent upon each other.

If one can have an experiencable aspect even with an untenable formulation which mostly points, and some of whose logical implications must be disregarded, does this mean that one has the experiencable aspect quite alone and independently? It certainly seems to be most convenient for my argument, if that is so. However, we point by means of this otherwise inadequate formulation. Pointing, too, is a function which words serve in regard to experiencable aspects, if only the word 'this.' It is a kind of formulating.[2]

The independence of the experiencable aspect is at any rate possible only after it has been lifted out by some formulation. (I want to argue that events too, not only words, can 'lift out' an experiencable aspect, and such events perform a formulating *function* (or symbolizing function). To pursue this would lead us to think about formulations as instances of a larger class. (I cannot deal with this direction here.) *Once a formulation has lifted out or specified or pointed to an aspect, then we can devise other formulations to do so as well, and we can see if different sub-aspects of importance are made thereby.* In both regards *the aspect demonstrates its independence* to this degree, from its initial formulation which gave birth to it: *it can function in other formulations, and it can also give rise to sub-aspects which the initial formulation could not have led to.* Such aspects could arise from a different formulation, or even from the aspect itself as soon as it is found. We might be grateful to the formulation which first led us to the aspect, but the formulation cannot limit what the aspect can further lead to. I have done just that many times in this discussion already.

It is in the power of the *movement of steps* from one experience-formulation pair to another, that the independence respect of an aspect lies. We need not assume, therefore, that experience comes packaged in aspects. Formulations, events, attention, affect what will be found as aspects and sub-aspects. Nevertheless experienced aspects have exactly this kind of independence: *they* can lead to steps, to sub-aspects, which *their own first formulations* cannot lead to, and they can lead to other formulations than the initial one could lead to.

So long as one only moves one step, supposedly from experience to formulation, as is so often claimed in phenomenology, any independent grounding by phenomena must seem simple-minded, as a claim. Only if we examine kinds of *steps*, can we see the experiencable phenomenon exerting independent grounding functions, determining what a formulation just now means (meaning by 'means' how it functions in relation to experiencable aspects one moves to, and from), what formulations are equivalent, and if different, what the differences are, which result, as steps further.

II

I must now give some examples and convey much more directly what an experiencable aspect is, and how it is always capable of leading to many more and different aspects.

Also, I spoke of the possibility, which always obtains, of formulating whatever one of us is saying, in some different way. Another person can always say: 'Yes, I've got what you mean, but I don't like the way you're putting it!', thus showing the difference between experiencable aspect and formulation. And we can always reformulate 'it' and then also see what different aspects that further makes, or loses.

The inherent capacity of anything experienced to lead to further and different aspects, is grossly underestimated in most discussions.

Especially today in an urban society, the usual routines of personal interaction and language are usually insufficient to deal with most of our situations, so that almost anything we experience far exceeds the existingly formed actions and phrases.

Let me ask you for a moment, in a personal way, to recall one of your own situations in which you are not sure what to do. Whatever you have said to yourself about it, it has also more. What you have said may be quite accurate, but it leaves – does it not? – some felt sense of unresolvedness or confusion which is of some importance. Your actions when you take them, or some next thing you say or think *may* resolve this felt sense of 'more,' or it may not. You would know the difference quite clearly.

Heidegger discusses such a thing under the heading of 'Befindlichkeit,' and Sartre calls it 'nausea' meaning not what that ironic term implies, but our constant sense of ourselves in our world. These authors bring this up quite late in their treatment. (Sartre not till page 338 of *Being and Nothingness*.) But isn't it quite basic to how every simple step is taken in phenomenology? Is it not present whenver we make any point? *No formulation captures all of what we mean, why we say it, why we say it just now, in this regard, etc.* Even if it did, a little further discussion or further occurrences would reveal further aspects of it.

Compare now the potential complexity of this 'more,' which we experience, with the thinness of our usual discussions! Someone for example has introduced into ethics the distinction between 'causes and reasons.' It is argued that human conduct has reasons, not causes. We wish immediately to know exactly what aspects are intended to be different under these two words, isn't that so? Suppose now, it is said that causes follow by physical necessity, while reasons are ethical justifications. This difference can now lead us further. The intention probably was to mark out the field of ethics, leaving causes out. We might agree, depending upon where the argument leads. Even so, (say we agree that ethics concerns 'reasons' or justifications) we can also attempt to find further experiencable aspects within what is assigned to ethics as reasons: For example, it happens that at first we are unaware of why we want to do something, we feel 'caused.' We can still do it or not, so *in that sense* our doing it still has 'reasons,' not 'causes.' Yet, when we do it, and then later discover why we did, these reasons will feel different to us, than had we known and chosen on that basis. So now we have another differentiated experiencable aspect, which 'causes vs. reasons' helped us find. It isn't the same as the one intended by the first formulator. We can rename it to keep ourselves clear.

But there are times, perhaps often, when there are not one or two reasons, but a whole texture of facets, more than can be sorted out. Then there are not even 'reasons,' but a 'texture': (I mean, when we are inclined to pursue a whole chain, such as: '... and if I didn't do that, then I'd have to do this other which I don't want to because it never works for me, which I know is my own weakness, well not exactly, but part of it is I can't fake such and so, which has to do with this way that I get when I do, which is because ...' and so on!)

Is it not clear how poor mostly are the concepts and formulations with which we try to substitute for experiencings?

And if formulations are 'thin,' and yet they partly determine what we find, then would we not want to return to and hold on, at each step, to the experiencable aspect? Only so can we determine whether we agree or not, at a given point, and just what is being said at a given point, and just what use will be made of what is being said at a given point. But an aspect *must come* as *it* will.

Also, in our present age of mass literacy, it is becoming possible for us to articulate our own unique experience. 'Til now, for most people, their own experience could be articulated and reacted to, only by means of routine expressions, or even literary expressions made by poets and novelists, which did not at all describe the specificity of their own experience. That was always left as a felt darkness that had to remain an unknown 'more.' And yet, just therein are we the persons we are. One needs, and today can, not only take a step from experience to language, but also back again, to see the difference made, the aspect found, which then is more specific than the bit of language, and whose further aspects can be further found.

III

I must now answer a number of possible objections, and in the course of doing so a number of further aspects of formulating experience will arise,

1) Does what I have said imply that experience as such has no order of its own, this formulation lifts out this, and another formulation something else?

No, experience has *more order* than all our schemes put together, but it is an order of its own, different in kind, an 'organic' order. If we wish, we can think of experience as already having the structure of the living body's life process, and of evolution's further elaboration of that life process, and culture's elaborations of that, to which must be added our own elaborations in our personal ways of living. So *it* gives us the aspect that *comes* in response to a formulation.

Thus there need not be a mystery why experience, even before we formulate in words, is not just any old putty but is more organized than any of our formulational systems.

2) Did I say that this organization awaits us there, finished and packaged?

No, what we lift out is a product of the great order that is there, and our further lifting.

3) Do formulations just drop on us, somehow as a primitive other 'pole?' Don't different formulational models themselves arise from experience in some way? Did I assume a basic two-pole model?

No, language and theoretical patterns of thinking, conceptual models, are also cultural products and develop as further elaboration of experience.

When we formulate experience, that is by no means the first time experience and language have met! Experience is the living process in the cultural world.

Although experiential organization is much broader than that of language, linguistic sequences are part of — and the means of — many distinctions of inter-human situations and interactions. Therefore, they are also part of our bodily feelings, and can re-emerge from them.

4) Did we destroy the universality philosophy is concerned with? Are we not grounding ourselves always in just this person's unique experience of this unique moment in the discussion?

The very meaning of 'universality' changes, is it not lost altogether? If a formulation, conceptual statement, i.e. something universal, can give rise to many different experiencable aspects, and 'means' them, is anything ever universal?

And, if this is lost, do not 'formulations' cease to have any use or character altogether, since 'formulating' after all, implies for anyone hearing or reading it?

No — universality is not lost, but its nature does change:

The old meaning of 'universality' was the notion of 'classes' which include under themselves the 'particulars,' which are instances of the universal. The particulars are supposed to have no nature of their own other than the universal's nature, except that the particulars are concrete existents, embodiments, instances.

Husserl uses that model (early in *Ideas*) when he says that any experience can be considered as universal. One need only consider it as an instance of its kind.

I would retain Husserl's statement, but I would also go another step to another experiencable aspect: that one can take any experience as an instance of *many* kinds — all of them 'it's kinds.' Always many can be quite new. Once a kind has been formulated, it can lead to other instances each of which can further instance many other kinds. (ECM-V.)[2]

The difference is, of course, that I am considering an aspect as a partly creative product (of an experience that has its own character and a formulation that also has its own).

This comes from not assuming that nature or experience are an already divided set of unique particular entities, units, univocal bits, a static set. And this assertion is not only a refusal to accept an assumption, it also points to an experiencable aspect for anyone who directly formulates experience, in steps (not just in one step), and moves from one to a further and still further aspect formulation of 'the same' experience which is thereby kept as 'that' experience and also allows further aspects to arise from it.

Communication between people, it now seems, is not really a simple locating or reminding someone of some universal they already have. Rather, it is a process in which an aspect of experience comes to be, which was not before differentiated as such.

You create an aspect in me, and I in you, which we did not have before, as such. In fact, if communication always had to be only of what we already have – it would not be of much interest!

In this way universality is not lost, but it alters. Instead of being a static structure shared by everyone always already, it is *the capacity to become shared*. And it becomes shared by a creating in the other.

It now follows, startingly: *the more unique* to you (private, swampy, autistic-seeming) the experience is, which you formulate, *the more universally significant* it will be to all of us, because your formulation will create the more new aspects in us, and any other person.

5) Are not 'experiential aspects' and 'formulation' now interchangeable terms? An aspect is always formulated, even pointing is a kind of formulating. And formulations are to be taken in terms of the aspects they lift out.

No, when we shift from a formulation to a pointing, and thence to a further formulation, then the aspect shows its difference from formulation. (Or, also when we reformulate or go further.)

6) Does this not always push any decision out to an indefinite future? What the aspect is depends on the further aspects to be found, and so also the formulation depends on that? Could one argue that any decision is always only in the future?

No, just the opposite: a formulation can be used definitively, if one has the aspect to which it refers, or which it formulates, for the time being, for this juncture in this discussion. The method is one of stopping the endlessness, which non-experiential methods do not stop, but only ignore. (I mean that the thinness of the usual arguments does not deal at all with the further creative potential of experience, it simply substitutes thin patterns that come to their own end.)

7) But, now, is not everything dependent on what will be said to 'matter,' or be 'relevant' to the present juncture of the discussion? What if we disagree on that, or are in doubt?

Whether an aspect is relevant, or not, just at this point, is again a question of experiencable aspects. If I can be shown what aspect of our topic this affects, and then you say it is relevant and I don't agree, we are working on different aspects of our topic. We can show each other the two topics. Or, you will have shown me how what I now care about *is affected*, since I did not at first see the relevance. I will have been shown a new aspect of *my* topic. Relevance works as phenomena do.

Truth and relevance are not only up to formulation, but also to the fact that in response not just anything but exactly this aspect is revealed; comes. This is *not* arbitrary, *nor* mere logic alone.

8) But isn't it still true that different 'models' or approaches or methods in philosophy or theory will give different results?

Yes – but if we keep a hold not only of these formulations, but also the directly sensed experience of what we are investigating, then we can each time see just exactly what aspects each model reveals.

If we wish, we can *then* formulate those aspects further in our own preferred type of model. And, if that makes further differences, we can examine the relevance of these, as well.

I am radically asserting that formulations are *not* constitutive of phenomena in the simple sense that has been assumed in a relativistic viewpoint. What model first shows me something, need *not* be used to further formulate it. Both that aspect and the further aspects I find, can be formulated in any type of formulation (and the difference which may matter, can also again be formulated in any type.) It has been falsely assumed that aspects of experience become the property of the type of formulations that show them to us, but they do not.

Once that is realized, one may work with many theories, many models, many types of philosophy, and expect always to discover some aspects one will be glad to have discovered. One can then formulate them in whatever single model one likes, or actually employ several, as one wishes.

I am aware what much more would need to be said, and explored, before this method would recommend itself. I am looking foreward to our Circle discussion both to clarify some points, and to teaching me some others.4

9) Did I emphasize the experiential at the expense of thought, logic, formulation communication and conversation?

No! I have wanted equally to emphasize the independent power of both, else experience could not thereby be discriminated. I have wanted to restore to thinking the immense world-building power that it has whenever it grips into what it is about, so that this is revealed in its concreteness.

It is not my intention that thought and formulation be downgraded, but just the opposite, that their effects should be attended to. Many people, seeing the thinness of most of our theories, choose to accept thin thought as the only kind. It was my intention to point out noticeable, experiencable marks of thought that overcomes this thinness.

An example of this is my looking forward to our Circle discussion. I know that the process of discussion, alone, can show me both how far I have really formulated what I think I have, and can show me aspects I would not want to miss. I want to improve thought and develop another self-conscious step of this human power. Throughout, I emphasize a process of steps, not just one step.

10) Even if others disagree with me, will they not do so in the way I said? Therefore, did I not 'lock' us into *my* formulation, now? Naturally I will answer that it is only a first brief formulation and can be discarded while we retain what it pointed to — but doing this discarding and retaining will be in accord with *my* model, will it not?

You can further formulate what you retain and do it differently and with different further aspects. But isn't that now also part of *my* model? For example, you can formulate differently than my assertions about experience being organismic, and still deal with the same or different aspects of how experience and its environmental context are related, and yet transcend each other. But however differently you do it, won't it be just an instance of my saying that you can indeed do it differently?

But the point is not that we must find a model that isn't a model, or that we must be able to deny anything we ever said. Because of the difference between formulations and experiences, any *phenomenological* assertion is never going to turn out just plain false, but neither does that mean that further steps are then *nothing but* instances of such not-plain-false-statements. In phenomenology no model is ultimate in that way, nor totally non-ultimate, and that is fine. Of course, even that statement can and should be gone on from, and much further.

NOTES

1   Gendlin, E.T., 'What are the grounds of explication statements? A problem in linguistic analysis and phenomenology.' *The Monist*, Vol. 49, No. 1, 1965.

2   Gendlin, E.T., *Experiencing and the creation of meaning*. New York: Free Press, 1962 (Rev. ed., 1970), Chapter IV.

3   Gendlin, E.T., 'Experiential Phenomenology.' In M. Natanson (Ed.). *Phenomenology and the social sciences*. Evanston, Ill.: Northwestern University Press, 1973.

4   'Two Phenomenologists Do Not Disagree' was presented at the Heidegger Circle meeting in Chicago, 1976. In the present revision I have indeed profited from that discussion!

SECTION VIII

PHENOMENOLOGY AND THEATRE

APPEARANCE AND REALITY:
AN ESSAY ON THE PHILOSOPHY OF THE THEATRE

JAMES N. EDIE

The purpose of this presentation is to recapitulate a number of theses I have already argued on the problem of enactment and to provide a prospectus of a monograph on *The Problem of Enactment* on which I am presently working. I am interested primarily in those major playwrights who in their plays and other writings teach a theory of acting.

In his work on *The Unity of Philosophical Experience* Etienne Gilson suggested that the history of philosophy was to the philosopher what the laboratory is to the scientist. Namely, by working through the history of philosophy we find that all philosophical doctrines necessarily and ideally work themselves out to their ultimate conclusions. By studying the history of ideas we get an insight into what philosophy truly is.

> A philosophical doctrine is not defined merely by its general spirit, its fundamental principles and the consequences to which they *actually* lead its author. It is made up of many other elements which enter its structure and share in determining its concrete individual nature. What a philosopher has not seen in his own principles, even though it may flow from them with absolute necessity, does not belong to *his* philosophy. The possible consequences which the philosopher has seen, but which he has tried to evade, and has finally disavowed, should not be ascribed to *him*, even though he *should have* held them on the strength of his own principles ...

> ... in each instance of philosophical thinking, both the philosopher and his particular doctrine *are ruled from above by an impersonal necessity*. In the first place, philosophers are free to lay down their own sets of principles, but once this is done, *they no longer think as they wish – they think as they can*. In the second place it seems to result from the facts under discussion, that any attempt on the part of a philosopher to shun the consequences of his own position is doomed to failure. What he himself is trying to say will be said by his disciples, if he has any; if he has none, it will remain eternally unsaid, but it is there, and anybody going back to the same principles, be it several centuries later, will have to face the same conclusion. It seems, therefore, that though philosophical views can never be found separate from philosophers and their philosophies, they are, to some extent, independent of philosophers as well of their philosophies. Philosophy consists in the

See notes at the end of this chapter.

concepts of philosophers, taken in the naked, impersonal necessity of both their contents and their relations. The history of these concepts and of their relationships is the history of philosophy itself.[1]

I am proposing that within the broad area of contemporary philosophical concern which is called the 'Theory of Action' the philosopher can use the artificial presentation of acting in the theater as a laboratory for his deeper philosophical concerns. By studying 'plays' we will discover the deeper insights which will enable us to understand human 'action' in general.

There is an important distinction in the philosophy of language – which we will see later on also applies to the philosophy of action – between what are called 'autographic' and 'allographic' works of art. An autographic work of art is one like a piece of sculpture, a temple, or a painting, which has one continuous historical existence from the moment of its creation to the moment of its ultimate destruction or disappearance. With the Venus de Milo or the Victory of Samothrace, or the Mona Lisa you either have the authentic 'autograph' or you do not. Allographic works of art on the other hand are those, like symphonies or plays or works of literature, which depend for their existence on a notational system which is characterized by all of the properties of the ideality of language.[2] Namely, allographic works of art, thanks to their linguistic structure, share the characteristics of *ideality, repeatability*, and *sameness of content* each time they are performed. This is above all true of works of art which are primarily meant to be performed in the present and therefore to *repeat* at various moments in historical time the *same* meaning. This possibility of indefinite repetition gives us the very notion of a literary 'text'. The ontological status of the meaning of such a text is very different from that of an 'autograph'. We will be returning to this distinction and its implications later on. For now we are concerned with the theory of action, keeping in mind that we intend to use it in an examination of the writings of playwrights, who, like Pirandello, Sartre, Brecht, Anouilh, and Genet, not only exemplify in their plays but theoretically develop and hold theories of acting.

THEORY OF ACTION

In philosophy the generalized theory of action begins with the ancient distinction made by Aristotle between immanent and transitive actions, the former being mental and volitional acts which emanate from the subject and remain in the subject as perfections of the subject, whereas the latter are activities which any being can exercise on another: in the manner in which billard balls strike one another or men build houses and train horses. This ancient distinction culminated in Thomas Aquinas' theory of 'the human act', a theory which distinguishes specifically human acts from all others. Man can perform many actions which are not distinctively 'human,' such as belching, twitching, copulating, etc.

For an act to be distinctively 'human' it must involve deliberate intention and at least some fore-knowledge of the consequences of the act. It is on this distinction that the later Lutheran, Kantian, Jamesian, and contemporary theories of 'the free act' are based. A specifically human free-act involves moral and legal responsibility for the consequences of the action, and is one that is done deliberately, and for which one is held accountable. Such a theory of human action would seem at first glance to have nothing to do with the theater.

It is precisely *this* which would seem to distinguish acting in the real world from the kind of acting that is presented to us in the theater. For example, the world of Sartre, as it has been given to us in his major novels and plays, has a special ontological status different from our mundane world of perception, which we can never leave even while reading his works and living in his imaginary world. But as we become acquainted with that world and begin to live in it vicariously, we gradually enter a different time, a different place, a different moral, social and spiritual atmosphere from that of our own personal existence. In *The Devil and the Good Lord* we may live through the development of a whole generation of Protestant revolutionaries in the Sixteenth Century in a few hours of our own time. A work of art of this kind enables us, once we have entered it, to grasp in a special way its distinctive style, its own inner logic, its own necessary laws of development, its own ontological consistency, thanks to which we never *can* confuse this world with that of our own mundane existence. We can, it would seem, never strictly speaking, *enter* a world such as this (at least in the way we live our own lives). We can interrupt it, leave it at will, ignore it, but it is there to be imaginatively re-created and re-discovered *just as we left it* and without our being able to alter it, whenever we deliberately choose to put ourselves once again into aesthetic communion with it. It has an ontological consistency wholly independent of our own mundane existence.

This is, moreover, the basis for Aristotle's ancient doctrine that poetry — more precisely tragic theater — is a matter of much higher and graver import than history. History is just 'one damn thing after another;' history is our daily lives. But, when we enter the poetic realm, we all have the realization, when we have discovered a great work of fiction or theater, that it is precisely because of its distinctness from our own mundane existence that it is sometimes *more true* than the real world of our own experience. It is *more true* because it can give us at a glance, so to speak, an essential insight into some aspect of human experience which we, ourselves, will never experience, never *could* experience, except in imagination. Without being the 'real' experiences of *any* man they *could* be the experiences of *every* man — hence the 'typicality,' 'ideality,' and paradigmatic nature of works of art. But it would seem wrong to say that such worlds are *more real* than the world of our immediate perception, precisely because these are derived worlds and ones which could not have been invented except through a free, fictive use of the experiences of this ordinary, non-dramatic, mundane, perceptual world from which neither we nor the artist can ever escape and from which the artist necessarily draws his material, however he may vary, manipulate and aesthetically 'condense' it.

To turn to the special case of plays written by playwrights we have an even more specific situation. Like a musical score, a play is normally not written only to be read but to be *performed*. And we have here, clearly, a special kind of artistic imagination and a special kind of aesthetic experience. The world of Shakespeare's *Hamlet* exists in the same sense that Dostoevsky's Karamazovs exist, and has the same qualities of temporal, spatial, social and spiritual independence from our mundane world. But the world of a theatrical play requires an *enactment* which must take place within our mundane world in a special way. Whether Gordon Craig, Laurence Olivier, John Gielgud, Maurice Evans, Albert Finney, or Richard Burton plays Hamlet, we may well say that Hamlet *as a character* is unaffected in his essential existence *as* Hamlet. Here we have the special case of the actor in which the actor as actor *himself* (as Richard Burton or Laurence Olivier) never leaves the real world of perceptual reality though *as the character Hamlet* he must leave it. He thus participates in two modes of existence at the same time and, thanks to this, whenever he is successful so does his audience with him.

This dual mode of existence illustrates what in the philosophy of language is called the distinction between *la langue* and *la parole* (performance). *La langue* is language taken under its aspect as a formal system of phonological, morphological, and syntactical rules which set the ideal parameters which enable speech to take place — because without observing the rules of a language it would be impossible to make sense. *La parole*, on the other hand, is the act of speaking or performance itself, the historical moment at which all of the rules of *la langue* comes into play in the real world as unrepeatable, temporal events. A play like *Hamlet* taken in its ideal reality as an unchanging text is subject to numerous performative interpretations. For example the classical Elizabethan interpretation, which owes a good deal to ancient Stoic and Roman notions about tragedy, is very different from the Freudian interpretation given to the play by an actor like Laurence Olivier, and still more different from the flippant, deliberately anti-Freudian interpretation given by Richard Burton in 1964. We can also turn to Brecht who, with his fine sensitivity for the way in which the theater has to speak up decisively for the interests of its own time gave us his own, never performed, stage directions:

> Let us take as an example of such exposition the old play *Hamlet*. Given the dark and bloody period in which I am writing — the criminal ruling classes, the widespread doubt in the power of reason, continually being misused — I think that I can read the story thus: It is an age of warriors. Hamlet's father, king of Denmark, slew the king of Norway in a successful war of spoliation. While the latter's son Fortinbras is arming for a fresh war the Danish king is likewise slain: by his own brother. The slain king's brothers, now themselves kings, avert war by arranging that the Norwegian troops shall cross Danish soil to launch a predatory war against Poland. But at this point the young Hamlet is summoned by his warrior father's ghost to avenge the crime committed against him.

After at first being reluctant to answer one bloody deed by another, and even preparing to go into exile, he meets young Fortinbras at the coast as he is marching with his troops to Poland. Overcome by this warrior-like example, he turns back and in a piece of barbaric butchery slaughters his uncle, his mother and himself, leaving Denmark to the Norwegian. These events show the young man, already somewhat stout, making the most ineffective use of the new approach to Reason which he has picked up at the university of Wittenberg. In the feudal business to which he returns it simply hampers him. Faced with irrational practices, his reason is utterly unpractical. He falls a tragic victim to the discrepancy between such reasoning and such action. This way of reading the play, *which can be read in more than one way*, might in my view interest our audience.[3]

We thus see that *performance* brings about a coherent change in the sense of the original text each time it occurs. It is the text which *appears*; it is the performance which is *real*.

But these distinctions seem to me to be already pretty well known. We can easily forgive and even applaud the excitement of young minds rediscovering these distinctions between *appearance* and *reality*. There truly does seem to be an essential distinction between Burton as a really existing person and the character he enacts according to a script. What we in everyday life *lack* and what the actor in a stage-play *has*, is an *author*. Whereas the existence of a play has a completeness, an inevitability, a wholeness which permits and justifies its paradigmatic character and its poetic superiority to real history, our own existence lacks these qualities altogether. We have no script according to which we can live our lives; we are both author and actor at once and it is precisely the freedom and openness, the unfinished character of our life-action and the unforeseeability of the consequences of our own actions that distinguishes our experienced world of lived-time from that of aesthetic imagined time. It is also this which makes our lives *mundane* in the sense of prosaic and undramatic; the intensity, the typicality of the situation which the dramatist is free to create in order to illustrate and *condense* life can be discovered in our own lives, when they can be discovered at all, only *after the fact* and *little by little*. If to act is to attempt *to say 'myself'* then there is an essential distinction between my acting as a person in this world and my acting as a character in a fictive world. It is for this reason that Maurice Natanson described the theater as 'the hermeneutics of the soul'.

In order to illustrate this point let me call attention to the remarkable little play by Luigi Pirandello, entitled 'Six Characters in Search of an Author.' We will be using this play throughout much of the rest of this paper and I want to warn you that the point I am going to make with it now is going to be modified considerably later on. But let us begin with this first obvious observation. In this play six characters *enter the real world of stage production to request the producer to let them be enacted by real, live, actors. The only* trouble is that the *characters* are incomplete; their author had lost interest in them and had not finished their drama. They cannot go on to the completion of the drama themselves, though they feel that the drama is *within them*, precisely because they are only *characters*. Only an author can complete them. In his preface to this play Pirandello explains the situation:

> Why not (I said to myself) present this highly strange fact of an author who refuses to let some of his characters live though they have been born in his fancy, and the fact that these characters, having by now life in their veins, do not resign themselves to remaining excluded from the world of art? They are detached from me; live on their own; have acquired voice and movement; have by themselves — in this struggle for existence that they have to wage with me — become dramatic characters, characters that can move and talk on their own initiative; already see themselves as such; have learned to defend themselves against me; will even know how to defend themselves against others. And so let them go where dramatic characters do go to have life: on the stage. And let us see what will happen.[4]

What happens is that these *characters* discover that, without an author, they can never be completed, and without real actors they can never become embodied, can never be *enacted*. In short, the 'subjunctivity' of the characters is not the same as the 'subjunctivity' of the real person or the real actor. To the extent that Burton is successful as actor, we do not see Burton but Hamlet; he realizes for a time the 'essential character' of Hamlet. But in his real life his essential self is not to be a character but a person. If in play-acting he 'uncovers the soul' of the character of Hamlet, because that is what he is for *as actor*, in real life his actions are as frequently directed to *concealing* as to *revealing* his soul and, while he may have 'mastered' the soul of Hamlet completely, his *own* is still in process of creation, an unfinished and unpredictable task.

The conclusion would seem to be that the world of imagination, though sometimes *more true* than the real world of perceptual existence, can never be *more real* — or *as real*. It seems it must always remain a derived world, freely created in order to mirror, to illustrate, perhaps reveal the essential 'soul' of a mundane existence. But it is the world of perception which remains primary, the world which can never be left behind, which can be occasionally 'nihilated' by aesthetic and other forms of imagination, but which always retains the primary quality of 'reality'. This is why I cannot, strictly speaking, enter a play even by forcing my way onto the stage.[5]

THE THEORY OF THE THREE CLOWNS

But this distinction between stylized acting according to a script in the theater and action in the real world is really nothing more than a superficial introduction to the manner in which a study of the theater can illuminate the philosophy of action. Let me refer briefly to the 'Theory of the Three Clowns' as it was developed by that very great commentator of the theater, Augusto Centeno y Rilova. Everything that we have said up to now would fall under what he calls the work of *The White Clown*. The White Clown is the one who plays by the rules, who is exhibited in classical dramatic theater, who presents an 'objective' and 'ordered' play of the classical psychological emotions and social conflicts. The theater of the White Clown intends primarily to *entertain* and to exhibit the normal aesthetic values of poetic language, settings, character, and plot. The White Clown is a clown of 'objective action'.

But there are other clowns. *The Red Clown*, unlike the White Clown, possesses a political and social (perhaps even religious) theory or at least some disconcerting, revolutionary and unusually upsetting beliefs to get across to his audience. He is sometimes 'diabolical', 'heroic', or even 'epic', interested in the psychological vagaries of human subjectivity, in abnormalities, deviations, the dark side of human nature. He is frequently 'orgiastic', often 'naked', and makes 'systematic use of ugliness to flaunt convention.' He is not out merely to entertain but 'to be revolutionary, to destroy a bad order and make way for a better, to break eggs in view of magnificient omelets'. Many 'happenings,' many elements of 'living theater,' and the like are the work of the 'Red Clown' — as is obviously the symbolic and ritual theater of Brecht, Sartre, and the 'young playwrights of France.' Sartre, who is the theoretical leader and spokesman of the 'young playwrights of France' provides us with a theater which is truly phenomenological (in Hegel's sense): namely it searches for and brings to full articulation the concepts which will enable us to think our experience.

The world of our experience in the second half of the twentieth century is that of a world from which God is absent. Merleau Ponty in *The Visible and the Invisible* twice stated that the only properly philosophical questions now are: Where are we? and, What time is it? Wherever we may be in this post-Copernican universe we are pretty certain that *we are not at the center*, and that all of creation does not revolve around the human race. We are in a period in which existence is uncertain and experience is difficult to think through. Sartre's theory of the theater requires the creation of certain myths which will enable 20th century man to understand his freedom in this situation. It is for this reason that the new struggle (*agon*) in an existential play is never a purely psychological matter, even though psychological oppositions and psychological struggles may be very important. A Trotskyite like Hoederer is not opposed to a Stalinist like Hugo in *Dirty Hands* simply because of their incompatible personal psychologies and their psychological duel over Jessica. They are opposed, on the more fundamental level, on the basis of the moral and historical question of who is ultimately right. For that reason the kind of theater which wallows in the bathetic psychological destruction of its principal characters (think only of *Who's Afraid of Virginia Wolf?*, *The Boys in the Band*, or almost any play by Arthur Miller, Tennessee Williams, or the other psychological playwrights of our time) falls short of the goals of existential theater. Sartre's theater, like that of the ancient Greeks, must provide us with an *agon* which, through typifying certain common human situations, will enable us to understand and thus dominate our lives. This is done by forging myths which go beyond personal, idiosyncratic psychological experiences to the moral and historical meaning of human existence in its finitude.

The final clown, *The Blue Clown* is somewhat more enigmatic. He has not often had the leading role in the past, though he has usually been present to some extent; in our time – insofar as the theater of playwrights like Sartre, Genet, Anouilh, and others, are returning to the ancient Greek sense of theater which will present men of the present time with myths according to which they can make sense of their experience – he is coming into his own. *The Blue Clown*, according to Centeno, wants to establish 'a theater of existence'. This theater will not be merely 'social' like the work of the White Clown, nor merely 'heroic' like the works of the Red Clown, but 'cosmic'. The long-delayed work of the Blue Clown, whose symbol is the clear, blue, dark night, is existential in the true sense of the word. The theater of the Blue Clown is a theater of characters which are 'unconditional subjectivites' – i.e. 'their subjective existence witnessing whatever there is or whatever is done.' Now I do not mean to endorse – and cannot further expound here – Centeno's theory of the three clowns. I use it mainly to show that there is more to be said and that what we have said up to now involves only the work of the *White Clown.*[6]

PIRANDELLO

Let us then now return to that remarkable little play already mentioned by Pirandello. This play does not *mention* a theory of acting but it *expresses* an idea of such a theory. It is a theory of reality and appearance which distinguishes real appearances from apparent appearances and shows us that the merely apparent appearance may frequently be more real than the real appearance.

In Pirandello's *Six Characters in Search of an Author* there are basically four reversals which lead the audience to believe that deliberately fictional characters are real. First of all there is the level which dupes them into taking the 'characters' as real persons who are coming to persuade 'actors' – real persons – to enact their drama.

Secondly there are the actors – who act as 'actors,' and therefore not as themselves – when they begin to enter the play.

Then there is the unexpected entry of Signora Pace – the *real* Signora Pace – who owes her reality to the fact that she is listed neither among the characters nor the actors and *appears very suddenly* on the stage.

Finally, there is the final shocking revelation of murder on the stage at the end of the plot in which the actors, so to speak, putting themselves in the place of the audience, suddenly begin to shriek and scream at this murder as if it were a real event.

When the producer tries to calm them down by saying it's all pretense the 'father' comes forward to insist: 'not pretense sir! reality!'

These reversals are so forcibly made that the audience at each time is duped into siding with one group or other of those on stage, recognizing one as being more real than the other, and that was Pirandello's aim: namely to show that the levels of reality are arbitrary, conventional, and relative.

The 'actors' are those who exist in real time and real space who, as men, have unfinished lives to lead — lives that must be led without a script and without foreknowledge of the manner in which they will end. But, insofar as they take on the role of a 'character,' this role exists in a different realm, in a different time and space — the realm of the fixity of the imagination which is ideal, repeatable, and can be grasped prior to any particular action *in the unity of one idea*.

The 'characters' are the embodiment of just this drama and just these ideal roles. However they are characters who have lost their authors, whose author has become disinterested in their fate, and who, therefore, are incomplete. But a 'character' ought not to be incomplete. A 'character' ought to be an ideal entity, fixed for all time, whose drama is completely known. The drama of this piece is that the characters do not completely strive for reality. *On the one hand* they claim to vindicate their independence of reality as *characters. On the other hand*, since their fate is incomplete, the script has not determined their end, and they therefore have some of the characteristics of real human beings who know that there is a drama within them and are trying to work it out but are fated to failure because they are not really real after all and can only be real though the hand of an author who writes their 'book'.

SARTRE'S THEORY OF THE FREE ACT

To turn now briefly from the theater to philosophy, particularly from the theater of Pirandello, one cannot help but remark that Sartre's theory of consciousness and freedom is a sound vehicle with which to connect play-acting in the imaginary world with acting in the real world. Consciousness experiences itself as being radically independent of its 'objects' and of all 'things'. This experience of noetic distance, this experience of *not* being inserted in the causal structure of the determinate and the determined things which consciousness 'knows' provides the basic phenomenological foundation of moral as well as noetic freedom.

I think that the theory of the transcendence of consciousness with respect to its roles, its emotions, its innermost psychological acts, which Sartre has elaborated in his philosophical works and illustrated in his plays gives us a basis for a theory of enactment which will justify the essential analogy between acting on the stage and acting in real life. From Aristotle to Sartre there has been, in theories of action, a unified and rectilinear movement away from the externalized mask of behavior, the emotions which we read on the surface of the ego, on the *persona*, to the ego itself as the source of its many guises and disguises.

Aristotle proposed a theory of emotional empathy centered in the vicarious experience on the part of the spectators in the emotions portrayed by the actors. Stanislavski proposed a theory of emotional empathy which went beyond the *persona* to the real emotions of the characters as they are fixed by the idea of the play. Brecht attempted to 'alienate' real life from the roles of the characters and the idea of the play. Sartre takes the final step of showing that in real life, no less than in theatrical experience, persons are alienated from themselves, i.e., from their roles, their essences, their very emotions, and all learned behaviors. The law of the egological distance which consciousness is able and constrained to insert between itself and its own acts places a man according to Sartre, in the same relation to his own emotions and emotional behaviors as the audience is to the play, according to Brecht.

In his theory of consciousness and in his writings on the phenomenology of the imagination, Sartre has argued that all human action takes place before the gaze of objectifying consciousness. This is a necessary structure of all conscious experience and it is in being looked at by others that we discover ourselves as ethical subjects, as guilty, blamable, praiseworthy, as the subjects of rights and obligations, as situated in a human and finite world in which we are never alone. In his analysis of 'the look' he implies in one place that the idea of God is necessary to man precisely because his mode of being requires that there be an objectifying consciousness which sees him at all times and in all places, and provides him with his necessary audience. Without a spectator, without a witness, without being 'watched,' consciousness would lose its being, its essence, its past, and would be reduced to its momentary, fleeting spontaneity – to what it just now *is*, namely, its nothingness.

But the idea of an external observer, a God, or even an audience of spectators (which we can call *society*) is a creation of consciousness. The essential law of consciousness is that it can reflect on its own acts, objectify itself, and take itself as an object. And what appears to reflection in such a case are just those actions, states, and dispositions which give to consciousness its appearance as being. A man *is* not his emotions, his roles, or his acts because he is a consciousness of *acting* emotions, roles, and states. My egological acts, according to Sartre, are objects for transcendental, reflecting consciousness, more intimate perhaps, but no different in kind from any other objects.

> Phenomenology has taught us that *states* are objects, that an emotion as such (a love or a hatred) is a transcendent object and cannot shrink into the interior unity of a 'consciousness.' Consequently, if Paul and Peter both speak of Peter's love, for example, it is no longer true that the one speaks blindly and by analogy of what the other apprehends in full. They speak of the same thing. Doubtless they apprehend it by different procedures, but these procedures are equally intuitional. And Peter's emotion is no more certain for Peter than for Paul.

> Doubts, remorse, the so-called 'mental crises of consciousness,' etc. – in short, all the content of intimate diaries – becomes sheer *performance*.

Sartre provides theoretical justification for sociological facts: that no performance of any role in everyday life is ever wholly sincere, that in numerous instances we need to *pretend* to be 'ourselves,' that there is only a difference of degree between the real, 'sincere,' unselfconscious performances in which we act ourselves, and the 'dishonest,' calculating, fully conscious staging of a scene for a public, in short, that it is impossible ever fully to *be* onself. Sartre provides us with a rich fauna of actors in the instances of 'bad faith' which provide his typology of the enactment of roles: there is the waiter in the cafe whose movements are 'quick and forward, a little too precise, a little too rapid ... a little too solicitous.' His behavior is a game, he is playing at *being* a waiter in a cafe. There is the flirt, the grocer, the tailor, the auctioneer, the good speaker, the good student, the gambler — all of whom must play at being what they are because, by the law of consciousness, they are condemned always to be beyond, other than, and much more than what they are (or what they are defined by themselves or others to be). The enactment of roles is essential to society.

> A grocer who dreams is offensive to the buyer, because such a grocer is not wholly a grocer ... There are indeed many precautions to imprison a man in what he is, as if we lived in perpetual fear that he might escape from it, that he might break away and suddenly elude his condition.

To act is to play a game and all playing requires following the 'rules of the game.' We enact our roles in life like we speak our native tongue, i.e., according to those strict rules which determine the grammaticality and the validity of our performance — rules which seem, on reflection, to be fully fixed and completely rigorous, but which have never yet been fully codified or brought to the level of fully explicit awareness in ourselves. Sartre's theory of enactment provides us with a commentary on the line of development which leads from Stanislavski through Brecht to the contemporary experimental theater because it shows the unity of structure which relates consciousness to all its roles. It shows that between the dramatic roles of the theater and the real roles of everyday life there is only a difference in the exercise of an imaginative intention which is essentially one in its noetic and ontological structure. When we move from the *persona*, the mask, to the roles, the emotions, the *real* acts of the ego behind the mask, we find that the distance which separates the actor from his acts can never be completely traversed, that what we can grasp in reflection is always and only the action, and the result of the action, and never the actor himself, who always and eternally escapes our grasp. Behind the roles there is only consciousness, i.e., nothing.

But here we reach the essential paradox in Sartre's theory of action and enactment: it is precisely because there is no essential difference between the structure of acting in real life and enacting an ideal (imaginary) character on the stage that art and nature cannot and should not be identified. The aesthetic imagination and real imagination share an identical noetic (or real) structure;

but they are distinct in their noematic correlates as the objective poles of two qualitatively distinct intentions. Just because every consciousness must appear to itself in order to *be*, theater has an aesthetic advantage over real life; its masks can be more deliberately constructed, more formal, and of universal, mythical import – like those of ancient tragedy.

It would be interesting here to develop another dimension of performance in the history of the philosophical theory of western theater, namely the theory of empathy briefly alluded to above. Aristotle gave us the first sense of theatrical empathy when he defined the purpose of theater to be that of duping the audience into such intense psychological identification with what was happening on the stage in the lives of the principal protagonists that the audience would itself feel the strong emotions of pity, fear, remorse, and other base sentiments enacted before them in order thereby to 'purify' their souls of these dark and dangerous emotions. The audience was then to *live into* the lives of the characters on stage. Much later, Stanislavski gave us another dimension of empathy when he ruled that the true actor must empathize with the character presented to us. He requires that the actor should 'become' this character and live his life for days on end, making no distinction between his real self and the character he is enacting. Brecht gave us still another theory of empathy – the negative theory of 'alienation' according to which the empathy that the audience might naturally feel towards the character as portrayed on the stage is *impeded* precisely so that the audience will *not* share these emotions but rather see them as portraying an imperfect human nature which can and ought to be changed. The Brechtian audience, far from empathizing with what is taking place on the stage, ought to stand up at the end of the play and feel the revolutionary emotion: This should not happen! Things must change! This is not necessary and not natural! Finally, Sartre introduces the fourth stage in the evolution of the theory of empathy when he shows that even in the everyday life of the ordinary person there is a difference between consciousness and the acting self, a distance between being and doing which cannot be traversed. There is no being without acting and action is the essential substance of a person's being without, however, that person's ever *being* his act.

Action and enactment share a unity of analogy based on the fact that the eidetic structure of ordinary and aesthetic imagination is really the same, but this is a unity of analogy rather than a strict identity because of the difference in their intentional objectives. Sartre repeats what all philosophers of the 'free act' from Aristotle to Alexander Herzen have known: namely, that to act is to be directed toward what is-not, toward the possible, the ideal, the imaginary. There is an ordinary exercise of the imagination which is inseparable from perception; it is involved in every perception of possibility, of absence, in every realization that the given situation does not contain its own meaning but must be understood on the background of what could be but is not yet actual. Imagination is the power to experience the present as absent and the absent as present. Without imagination action would be arbitrary and haphazard, pure trial and error. But human actions proceed according to rules and achieve purposes. To this extent there is no difference of kind in the exercise of ordinary and aesthetic imagination, between action and enactment.

But the meanings or purposes at which ordinary life-action is aimed are only dimly protended; the meaning of our life is something which we find out only after the fact, by reflection, when it has already been done. Before the accomplishment of a free act, its meaning is unfixed and, to reflective consciousness, largely unknown. It is action without a script and without fixed rules. It is action which creates its essence rather than action which follows from its essence. A life is for one time only.

Enactment on the contrary, is always a repetition, something sacred and liturgical, a rite. It is the repetition of a meaning whose rules have already been ideally fixed. It is, of course, precisely because all the rules of any game are never completely fixed and univocally explicit prior to the playing of the game itself that life and art resemble and analogize one another. But the meaning of a play is essentially one which has been thought of before, which is the point of convergence of a multiplicity of intentionalities, past and present, which can be indefinitely re-enacted according to the emotional and obsessional needs and requirements of the collective consciousness which supports it and which it illustrates. The meaning of a life, on the other hand, lies in those individually characterizing choices which are unique and never shared by the collectivity, that particular concatenation of historical events in irreversible series which cannot be grasped as a whole, in the unity of an idea, except after the life is dead and gone, which always remains beneath the level of the ideal because it is real. Sartre says in his study of Genet that for Genet there is no 'profane' time, only 'sacred' time. This is as much as to say that Genet is not of this world, a saint, an actor by essence, whose whole life is the obsessional repetition of a liturgical drama lived in its imaginary ideality outside the laws which govern mundane events. In Genet's case, as in that of Kean, we suspect the madness of poetic possession. But the point is clearly made. Though it is the same imagination which functions in this-worldly political and social action and in the enactment of the ideal which we call the *aesthetic*, the imaginative intentions are distinct. The ideal world of the aesthetic imagination is in some sense more true and even more real than this world of mundane experience within which it must be enacted. It is more true and more real in the sense that it can give us at a glance, in the unity of one idea, an essential insight into some aspect of human experience which we, ourselves, will never experience, never could experience, except through this distinctive use of imagination. And it is precisely in its idealizing function that it is of use within the real world, and thus provides us with a laboratory within which to study the reality *and* the theory of human action.[7]

NOTES

1   Etienne Gilson, *The Unity of Philosophical Experience*, New York, 1950, pp. 300-302, italics mine.

2   Cf. James Edie, *Speaking and Meaning: The Phenomenology of Language*, Indiana University Press, 1976, Chp. 1.

3   *A Short Organum for the Theater*, par. 68.

4   *Naked Masks, Five Plays by Luigi Pirandello*, ed. Eric Bentley, New York, 1952, p. 366.

5   See my comments on 'Man as an Actor' in *Phenomenology of Will and Action*, edd. Straus and Griffith, Duquesne University Press, 1967, pp. 221 ff.

6   Centeno y Rilova, Augusto, and D. Sutherland, *The Blue Clown, Dialogues*, University of Nebraska Press, 1971, *passim*.

7   These final paragraphs have been taken in part, from my article 'The Problem of Enactment,' *The Journal of Aesthetics and Art Criticism*, XXIX, 1971, pp. 312 ff.

THEATRE AS PHENOMENOLOGY:
THE DISCLOSURE OF HISTORICAL LIFE

BRUCE WILSHIRE

Theatre is a fine art. As such it is fictional — in an appropriately broad sense of that term. It is presented *as* presented-for-contemplation-and-not-for-everyday-use. The presentation may involve a representation: something not present, or not actual at all, is nevertheless represented for our contemplation. But even in the case of 'found art,' in which an actual object, a sink say, is presented to us, we are aware that it is presented-for-contemplation-and-not-for-everyday-use, thus aware of an irreducible element of fictionality. All fine art requires detachment: the curtailment of our everyday awareness and intentions.

Yet in detaching ourselves from the actuality we better reveal the meaning of it. In severing our everyday involvement with the thing we step back from it and allow it to reveal the vast network of involvements which gives it the meaning it has for us. In not being able to use this sink in the construction of my house, for example, I see it not just as satisfying my immediate need to build a structure, but as satisfying the whole network of human needs which gives it the meaning it has for all of us: e.g., the procurement, containment and disbursement of useable quantities of life-sustaining and cleansing liquids within an abode — a network that is easily disrupted. Instead of being absorbed in that small fraction of the thing's meaning essential for whatever involvement absorbs me as an individual at the moment, we are presented with the universal and world-historical network of involvement which gives us both its meaning and ours. For we *are* the beings who use instruments, e.g., sinks.

Theatre as fine art is a detachment which reveals the peculiarly acute and special involvements of persons with persons. These range from ephemeral involvements of empathy and sympathy to involvements of imitation and identification — in the family, say — in which we are formed permanently as the beings we are. We are formed by all our involvements, with sinks for example, but not in the strong sense in which we begin to look much like sinks, or in which we are authorized as being what we are — and become what we are — because we conform to them as to exemplar models of life, and receive their acknowledgement for having done so. With humans we are involved in this way.

Theatre is a fine art, so a fiction, in which we experiment deliberately with modes of mimetic involvement in the attempt to discover the meaning and reality of our largely non-deliberate modes of mimetic involvement in everyday

See notes at the end of this chapter.

life. The actor as artist stands-in for another, the character; he is proxy for the character. We are aware that Richard Burton, say, is not Hamlet, but only like Hamlet in certain ways. We are aware of neither Burton alone, nor Hamlet alone, but of the artistic fact Burton-as-Hamlet. We stand-in through the actor's standing-in, and we can experience the similarities between our relationships and Hamlet's. Detached from our involvements, we can begin to experience them for what they are. We do not believe that any actual Prince is on the stage and in the building with us, nor more obviously do we believe that a ghost of his father is there too, but in this fiction the mimetic hold of fathers upon sons is revealed just because we are not absorbed in the practical politics of our own family or our own nation-state. Enactment is physiognomic metaphor. We experience how Prince Hamlet must take King Hamlet's place, perform his functions, take revenge for him, etc. The weird, numinous presence of mimetic involvement is released in the room as the ghost of the father stands in our midst, and we discover how even *our* dead brood over us all and pull us into their orbit.

Let us present another example of how theatre as a fiction discovers relationships of mimetic involvement in which we are authorized and made what we are by our models. This time we take not a mimetic relationship in the family or in the state which molds persons permanently, but a passing mimetic relationship in which a strange but deep moment of empathy and sympathy, otherwise undetectable, is given presence. It is the play 'The Elephant Man.' The title refers to a monstrously misshapen man who was exhibited as a freak. On stage-left is a screen upon which are projected actual photographs of him. Bony and fleshy protuberances disfigure in a ghastly way his large head and crippled body. Little or no expression is possible on his face. On stage-right stands a well proportioned young actor who progressively contorts his limbs, countenance and posture as the photographs are projected. This is theatre which experiments on its own capacities as it experiments on the limits of our powers of involvement and identification. If we can identify revealingly with a monster then we can identify with nearly anyone.

Scene changes are made before our eyes as a cellist plays on stage-left, and we must imagine the time which has elapsed in the play's 'world.' In one early scene we see the misshapen man, John Merrick, displayed at the freak show. People pay to gawk at him simply because of the novelty of seeing a human being who is so unlike themselves, and with whom they have no involvement or identification — or so it would seem.

A London physician chances to see him, and prompted mainly by scientific curiosity pays a fee and removes him to his hospital. After failing to procure assistants who will relate to the monster as a fellow human being, the doctor seeks out the well-known actress, Mrs. Kendal, on the supposition that as an actor she can control or conceal the feelings of horror and revulsion that had prevented all the others from relating to him. He hopes that she will be able to seem at least to relate to Merrick as one human being to another.

Upon meeting Merrick, the actress is able to control her revulsion. He responds to her acceptance of him and blooms as a person before our eyes. He expresses a kinship with her. He notes that they both make spectacles of themselves for the entertainment of others. And yet the true self is just the very same body in its potentialities and in its actuality as it sits before her now: Merrick motions to his body with his one good hand. The actress motions in a hesitant way to her own body, as if to say, in a dawning consciousness, This too is just me right here. She begins to be pulled by the possibility of a strange kinship with him.

We find her standing-in for him with her friends, presenting his case, introducing him to highly placed associates and acquaintances: artists, socialites, the wife of the Prince of Wales. But most fundamentally, Mrs. Kendal — and perhaps each of the others as well — takes Merrick's place in the sense that she becomes able to see the world and herself through his eyes, and by way of his sensibilities. She is able to recognize his recognition of her because she recognizes him to be a human being. Her recognition of herself can be mediated through his recognition of her. And his recognition is one which is sensitive to aspects of herself that she has more or less successfully repressed. It is a recognition that is sensitive to the socially unacceptable and self-unacceptable in *her*: her moments — or more than moments — of not fitting-in; the monstrous aspects of *her* life.

In a climactic scene she disrobes to the waist and asks him to turn and look at her. There is nothing disfigured about her body; indeed by this act she acts for the normal and the well-formed and welcomes Merrick into their company. But the hushed resistance within herself which she has overcome in so uncovering her body to him discloses to us that through him she accepts her own painful inhibitions and vulnerability, her own previously unacknowledged particularity and privacy. She is fully natural, fully herself, only with the monster. He authorizes her in *her* particularity and uniqueness. She accepts herself and makes herself more fully her own through *him*.

Now we in the audience are made aware that we also feel a kinship to Merrick. We are reaching out also in a discovering empathy and identification. Assuredly, it is only actors before us, and the artist enacting Merrick is not actually misshapen but only enacts it in his posture and gait. But with this aesthetic distance from actuality our own potentialities for mimetic involvement and identification with Merrick begin to emerge in an acknowledgeable way. Usually, when confronting an actual monster, these capacities are realized for an instant and then are eclipsed and repressed by other feelings such as fear.

Merrick tells Mrs. Kendal that before he met her he had no thoughts because he had no one to think them for. He finds himself because he finds himself in this other person. This grotesquely individuated man needs Mrs. Kendal to accept him as a human being, for this will include him in humanity; it will confirm his possession of those universal traits essential to his being fully *human*. He will be authorized.

But Mrs. Kendal — and we in the audience — need him as well; we find it releasing and discovering to display ourselves for him. Because we regard him as human we can see ourselves in him. Each of us is released to be more fully *a* human being, a single one. Through accepting him as human we gain access to his recognition and acceptance of each of us in our unique humanity. We objectify and accept elements in ourselves of which we had previously been only blindly ashamed or self-deceptively unaware. These he authorizes.

We stand in through the actors as they stand in for those who find themselves through each other's presence.   So stretched by the art are we that at least for these moments we accept our kinship with monsters. The result of the experiment of theatre is discovery, and we come home to ourselves as we are: beings of inexhaustible particularity as well as indefinitely extendable horizons of human concern and identification.

We must learn to see theatre's fictive variations on mimetic themes of everyday life as a kind of phenomenology. Edmund Husserl, the founder of phenomenology, developed a method of fictive variations for probing the boundaries of the invariable meanings or 'essences' of things. For example, in our mind's eye we vary a table along its various parameters, size, shape, form. How much can we tilt, detach, remove a top − or not provide for it − and still have a table? How small can it become and still be a table *tout court* (and not a doll's house table)? Can it lack solidity and still perform a table's function? Through variations like these we discover invariable, even if vague, boundaries of meaning.

We can now see that *The Elephant Man* was theatre producing a variation upon itself which revealed its own structure. It was theatre as phenomenology unveiling itself. In disclosing that we can identify even with a monster − and indeed sympathetically − it afforded us a glimpse of the full range of our powers of identification and standing-in. Another variation upon this parameter of involvement is supplied by the theatre of Bertolt Brecht. His famous *Verfremdungs-effekt* − estrangement effect − derives from an attempt to so increase the element of aesthetic detachment that one's emotions of empathy can achieve no climax and release within the theatre; one retains them when one walks into the street, and they can become behaviorally effective there. But the effectiveness of his theatre requires that our identification with others is not simply eliminated. Hence even when theatre varies itself until no emotional release is possible within the theatre, still identification-with and standing-in remains.

Husserl's phenomenology is limited by the dominant role of vision in his conceptual model for mind (vision is the discriminating and isolating sense *par excellence*), and by his belief that the isolated philosopher, alone in his room, can imagine all that happens between people. But it is in rehearsal and performance in the theatre that we can best discover those tendencies of interaction between persons in each others' physical presence which can be discovered only when they are in fact in each others' physical presence. These are one's tendencies, e.g., of attraction, fusion, or repulsion, which must be experienced muscularly and viscerally to be known at all. They are too fleeting, too disturbing, or too habitual to be apprehended by the isolated phenomenologist imaginatively varying human behavior in his mind's eye. They may not occur to him at all in his isolation, for there are no others to provoke the tendencies and to 'reflect' them back. For the philosopher to assume that he can on his own and immediately step to the Archimedean point from which the sense of all things is constituted and objectified, there to trace through fictive variations the structures of sense generated, is for him just to assume that he is *not* engulfed bodily and mimetically with others. In begging the questions of this paper he begs the question of his own identity. Alone in his room he varies possibilities in his imagination, but within limits of variation some of which are hidden from him. He cannot imagine the limits of his ability to imagine. His aloneness as a *body* falsely persuades him of his absolute autonomy as a *self*, and eclipses his mimetic involvement with others so totally that this eclipsing eclipses itself.

It is momentous that Husserl tended to think of imagination on the model of vision. Consciousness 'looks' at essences or meaning (*Wessenserschauung*). But in a rehearsal there is nothing seen as an object of an act of imagination. Imagining is a kinesthetic involvement with others, luring us all together, which is already determining the performance imagined. The characters and their relationships are discovered by the actors *ambulando*. If the bodily self is to become imaginatively aware of its own absorption in others, its mimetic involvement with them, then its attempt to detach itself from itself in a calm and detached 'visual' imagining is apt to freeze, distort or impede the very involvement one is attempting to imagine.

So, theatre as phenomenology is a fictive variation of human relationships and of human acts *in act*. Theatre should not be regarded as contemplation set over against action and creation, but as contemplation through action and creation.[1] An aesthetic funneling and restricting — an aesthetic 'distance' — regulates the intercourse of the play's 'world' and the world in which the theatre building stands. It is just because of this protection that the audience can uncover itself at its most vulnerable levels: its archaic mimetic fusions with others, and its odder and deeper sympathies, about which it has never learned to speak in words. And it is just because of its own protection that the cast of actors can reveal themselves as likewise vulnerable and mimetically involved.

Moreover, in this pact, in this complicity if you will, the actors can do for the audience what the audience cannot do for themselves, and the audience can do for the actors what the actors cannot do for themselves. That is, the audience participates in the 'world' from the side of the world and in its relative passivity its mimetic involvements and engulfments in the world can be called forth through recognition of, and participation in, similar involvements in the play's 'world.'

The actors, on the other hand, participate in the world from the side of the fictional 'world,' and just because of the fictionality of their setting can initiate activity more daring, volatile and free than the constraints and dangers of the world ordinarily allow. Even in those productions in which the artists strive for pure fantasy, not just any absence or non-existence is pulled into the presence of the play's 'world,' but only that which can give us an experience of our power over possibility here and now in the theatre house; hence 'world' and world augment and feed each other in this instance only when the internal coherence of the fantasized 'world' most 'obviously' sunders it from all relevance to the world. We beings — we actual beings — discover our capacities for imagining and our power over possibility. Together the audience and the actors engage in incarnated imaginative variation on the meaning of human being and doing. Together they experiment on the nature and extent of mimetic involvement, identification, and sympathy, and also on our capacities for individuation and transcendence.

Already incorporating others' mode of being, because one stood mimetically in their authoritative presence, one cannot simply step back and pinpoint and objectify this mode of being. Since it is one, one takes it with him as he steps back. The actor can discover this reality which lies between people only between people, only with and through the others; and the members of the audience can discover it only with and through the person who stands at the focus — but it is only the focus — of the experiment, the actor. The actor's challenge is to disclose the other incorporated in him *as* other, as character, but he can do so only in the presence of others for whom he is another who mimetically enacts their common life.

Usually unsuspected by the audience (during rehearsals the director and others in the rehearsal space are the audience), the actor is listening to the sounds *they* make. He hears the sounds that slip from them. He hears them in the encompassing margins of his consciousness. The actor's mimetic tendencies are such only relative to other persons, but the actor cannot see his own body and face when he is actively with and for others, and he must rely upon the audience to signal him when he is on to something telling and essential. Nor can he hear his voice as it really is — a voice mimetically with and for others — unless others let him know what they hear. Not realizing that they are being heard and followed, and thinking that it is only a fiction to which they are responding, they in the audience are not on their guard, and so reveal themselves deeply as beings who are mimetically with others. The goal of all involved is that hush of silence which discloses the habitually unspoken, or perhaps the unspeakable. It is that common life shared undeliberately and mimetically. The centrifugal force of the enacted other, the fictional character, breaks down our delusive centeredness — our habitual engulfment in others, and others in us. Thrown into the periphery through the force of the fiction, one senses as in a dream a likeness into which one fits. One becomes aware of what one's body already is: an other which is with and for others mimetically. One also becomes aware of his possibilities as an individual. In theatre the community gives birth to its own thematized meaning: it is a mimetic *community* of *individuals*.

We can invariably tell the great classics of the theatre: they involve us the most as artistic participants because they engage us with what involves us the most existentially — the problem of our individual identity as persons. How are we to be authentic individual selves when at the same time we are engulfed with other beings in a common life? What could intrigue us more than this? Theatre is the art which employs mimetic involvement as its means or form, and the content of the classics is a revealing variation on this form; the form generates the content, the content the form. The problem of standing-in as an art is to reveal the problem of standing-in as life. We stand-in through Burton's standing-in for Hamlet, and test to see how we are all Hamlet-like. The Prince must stand-in for his father, and at the same time assert his individual interests. He is torn between the two, and since in way or another we all are, this conflict is at the heart of great drama.

Let us gather three classics from three different epochs – *Oedipus Rex, Hamlet, Waiting for Godot*. We note between them a startling similarity. The content of each is a variation on the theme of standing-in. The actors stand-in for characters who stand-in. Oedipus stands-in illicitly for his father the king, and with destructive effect. Hamlet stands-in licitly for his father the king, and yet with destructive effect also. The two tramps in *Waiting for Godot* seem not to have been able to stand-in for the authority at all, and there is a destructive effect here too, a strange insubstantialness in their lives.

As long as we see the characters in these plays as perfectly individuated entities we will be unable to see how their identity involves a mimetic engulfedness in each other which is like a morass in which they struggle to individuate themselves. One must be authorized and empowered by one's own mimetic source. But how can one be and at the same time establish oneself as an individual being with his own interests? This is the problematic that lies at the bottom of all these plays and gives them their perennial attraction. We sense that it is our problem as well and that the characters are set before us to solve it vicariously. What reparation must we pay to the other as the cost of our becoming an individual being along with him in the world? What reparation must he pay to us as the cost of fathering us? The question concerns the price of individual identity itself.

We can begin to grasp why the relation of individual to group is ambivalent, unstable and volatile, and why there can be no simple solutions. Put schematically: If to become at all, a person must be named and otherwise designated by the culture, and if exemplar individuals must be lifted up as stand-ins for the culture, then individuals, to become themselves, must identify with these exemplars by taking *their* attitudes toward *themselves*, e.g., by taking as their own the names given by them. In a kind of magical or alchemical equivalence, the other becomes identical with oneself. He fuses with oneself. Yet to be human one must also be an individual human. But if one's enchanted mimetic involvement has made him one – one experientially – with the king of Thebes, for example, then how can one be individual without displacing or killing the king, for there can be but one king? But if one does this one defiles one's own source.

Through its fictive variations theatre thematizes mimetic engulfment, and the drama of individuation, vulnerability and guilt. In articulating our struggles with historic authority, it authorizes each of us anew, as a new source in time.

When theatre is understood phenomenologically, as fictive variation through physiognomy, the role of the fantastic in it becomes comprehensible. At times we push out beyond the limits of the physically possible in order to encompass and thematize those limits, hence to etch-out the meaning of the physically possible — as well as the meaning of ourselves as communal, but also fantasizing, free and individual beings. Our meaning cannot be expressed in the theatre without this meaning being authorized by all of us in attendance.

Long ago, in the *Poetics*, Aristotle spoke of 'probable impossibilities.' Though physically impossible in themselves, they nevertheless communicate the probable, the general tendency of the class, the essence of the actual. In becoming fantastic we do not become 'non-representational' — if by the latter is meant losing touch with our actuality. In the play 'Strider' the actor Gerald Hiken enacts a strangely colored horse, a Piebald.[2] It is not merely that we learn what a horse in general, or this sort of horse in particular, means to *us*, thereby learning about ourselves indirectly. We learn about ourselves with a unique and unsettling directness. Take the crucial scene in which the horse as a young colt is being named by his owner. In perceiving fancifully and bodily how a horse might experience being given a name, and perceiving this through seeing a man enacting a horse being named, we re-present the event of *our* being named and explode the shell of stereotypical appearances that prevents this momentous englobing relationship from being experienced afresh, focally, and in wonder. The dramatic tension of the metaphoric parallel destroys the stereotyped associations so that the full network of associations can be revealed. We are delivered into the experiential context in such a way that its entanglements, engulfments, and moods can become thematic.[3]

Hiken, enacting the colt rolling on the ground and hearing the name he is being given, says softly, 'Piebald,' 'Piebald?,' 'Piebald!' in a groping, fascinated voice. The revelation breaks upon him and upon us with dawning mystery and veiled alarm. How can *I* be the one who is named by the *other*? The physiognomic metaphors disclose the profoundly metaphorical nature of our existence: ours is an actuality and particularity mediated by otherness, and we can come home to ourselves only by appropriating this otherness as our own. We discover the key questions, and new possibilities of search open before us.

In perceiving imaginatively how a horse would react to being regarded as a distinctive individual, to being named Piebald, we are forced to re-imagine how we ourselves experience our inclusion, our exclusion, and our novelty; how we have our identity at that precarious intersection of mimetic involvement and communal conformity, on the one hand, and of trembling uniqueness on the other. We confront ourselves afresh, and we confirm each other as questioners.

The physiognomic imagination of much recent theatre is so free that it is almost explicitly phenomenological. Ionesco, Beckett, Jerzy Grotowski, and Robert Wilson throw acute light on the perennial themes of engulfment and individuation, guilt and joy. We are essentially social and essentially individual.

In the decay of traditional authorities, how are we to be authorized *as* standing thus to the decaying authority? Grotowski, for example, stages a fictive variation in which we regain contact with our mythical and religious sources of authorization through violating them (*'Apocalypsis cum Figuris'*). Only this stings them into life and reconnects us to them, he claims. Any other way would be ahistorical, so escapist and bootless. The point is to authorize us afresh as beings seeking new sources of authorization.

Illuminated is the perennial human predicament: we both need others and are threatened by them, and we are threatened precisely because of our need. We need others to approve us and authorize us, and we are threatened by them either because they can withold this, or because they approve at the cost of engulfing and smothering us. Tragic theatre will never be outmoded, because there is no escape from this problem.

Theatre is joyous and essential because it authorizes us in our perennial struggle to authorize ourselves as authentic individuals. Not to sever ourselves from our sources in mimetic engulfment in the common life — for if this were somehow to be achieved we would cease to be human — but to articulate ourselves as essentially particular, essentially communal, and responsibly free: this is the task. Theatre washes out guilty attachment to source through opening us to our possibilities as individuals within community. It becomes a new source. Even as tragic it is joyous, for it restores us to ourselves.

NOTES

1   Cf., Janusz Kuczyński, 'Homo Creator vs. Homo Contemplator. The Dialectical and Phenomenological Concept of Man,' in *Christian-Marxist Dialogue in Poland*, Warsaw: Interpress, 1979.

2   The original Russian version of the play was conceived by Mark Rozovsky, a writer and director who created the piece out of a set of improvisations between actors at a drama school.

3   It is impossible for a man to be a horse. But this is a 'probable impossibility,' *Poetics* (XXV-17). That is, the impossibility enacted as a fiction illuminates the essence or form, and this has instances in the actual world.

*   This paper has appeared in *Dialectics and Humanism*, No. 2, 1981. Its appearance here coincides with the publication of my *Role Playing and Idendity: The Limits of Theatre as Metaphor*, Bloomington: Indiana University Press.